THE PAPERS OF ULYSSES S. GRANT

THE PAPERS OF

ULYSSES S. GRANT

Volume 3:
October 1, 1861–January 7, 1862

Edited by
John Y. Simon

SOUTHERN ILLINOIS UNIVERSITY PRESS

CARBONDALE AND EDWARDSVILLE

FEFFER & SIMONS, INC.

LONDON AND AMSTERDAM

To Robert S. Harper
(1899–1962)

Contents

Maps and Illustrations

Introduction

—————

For fourteen weeks, from October 1, 1861 through January 7, 1862, Ulysses S. Grant maintained headquarters at Cairo, Illinois, his army remained fairly stable in size, and he made no permanent advance southward. Yet these were not weeks of inactivity and stalemate. Cairo and Columbus, Kentucky, some twenty miles downriver, represented the crucial Mississippi River bastions of Union and Confederate defense lines stretching across Missouri and Kentucky. Neither side had the strength to break the other line on the Mississippi, but both were subjected to such barrages of misinformation that the strength of the enemy had to be probed through continual reconnaissances, raids, and demonstrations. Both sides, furthermore, had to maintain pressure so that enemy troops could not be detached for action on a weaker part of the line. Early in November, Grant used orders for a series of demonstrations to justify his first battle of the Civil War; although Belmont did not alter the basic military situation along the Mississippi, it prepared Grant and his army for more aggressive action.

Other factors were altering the war along the river. Late in December the seven thousand or so troops at Paducah and Smithland, Kentucky, were placed under Grant's command, making it possible to plan a broader advance into Kentucky. Command of Paducah brought Grant an able subordinate, Brigadier General Charles F. Smith, an experienced professional soldier whose judgment and ability Grant could trust. Even more important was the enlargement of the gunboat force at Cairo from the three converted steamboats available at the beginning of October to a flotilla including nine ironclad gunboats and thirty-eight mortar boats by the end of the year. The ironclads were innovations in naval warfare, subject to innumerable mechanical problems, while the mortar boats were little more than rafts; yet the Union flotilla was so far superior to anything the Confederates could construct that it played a decisive role in campaigns on southern rivers.

Equally important to Grant in preparing for advance was the change of commanding officers. On November 2, after one hundred days in Missouri, Major General John C. Frémont was removed by President Lincoln and eventually replaced by Major General Henry W. Halleck. At first it appeared that Halleck's insistence on caution and army routine would be as unproductive as Frémont's impetuosity and dazzling disregard of army regulations; but Halleck soon found Grant to be a reliable subordinate, whose knowledge of army procedures matched his own, and an aggressive commander who calculated his risks. Nor could Halleck have overlooked the fact that somehow Grant managed to keep his power-hungry subordinate, Brigadier General John A. McClernand, under control. On January 8, 1862, Grant received orders from Halleck for demonstrations in Kentucky. Uneventful in themselves, these demonstrations paved the way for the advance on Forts Henry and Donelson in the following month.

It should not be overlooked that Grant fought his first battle of the Civil War, his only battle of 1861, during the awkward period of change of command in the West when he was not really under the control of a superior officer. Belmont has always been the least understood of Grant's battles, not because he failed to explain why he had chosen that time and place to engage the enemy, but because, uncharacteristically, he said too much, providing a handful of motives to consider. "Belmont was severely criticised in the North as a wholly unnecessary battle, barren of results, or the possibility of them from the beginning," Grant later recalled. It was natural that the criticism should stand out in Grant's memory; yet the mixed results of Belmont brought far more praise than blame, especially when balanced against the failure of Union arms in other fields. Even mixed results established Grant as a fighting general, something much wanted in the North. Belmont, Grant said, gave his troops "a confidence in themselves . . . that did not desert them through the war." This probably applied to their commander as well.

Although Grant's major problems in late 1861 concerned the maintenance of pressure on the Confederate stronghold at Columbus while he prepared his forces for an advance, his correspondence reveals a host of concerns. Training volunteer soldiers as acceptable troops was no easy business, especially with ambitious politicians serving as officers, and with the added disadvantage of shortages of arms and equipment. The civilian population at his back in southern Illinois was not uniformly loyal, and across the Mississippi in Missouri Grant could not find "a sufficiency of Union sentiment . . . to save Sodom." Yet Union sentiment nearby could be equally troublesome: Union refugees of the upper South who fled to Grant's district needed relief; the fugitive slaves presented an extremely delicate legal problem. By the close of the year Grant began to discover the patterns of fraud and favoritism which had affected procurement of supplies at Cairo, and set about to correct the abuses. All of the major problems confronting Grant had political implications, and he handled them with surprising adroitness while maintaining a professional military attitude.

Since the editorial procedures followed in this volume are unchanged from earlier volumes, it should be unnecessary to repeat what has been stated in previous introductions. Perhaps a reminder is in order that texts derived of necessity from the earliest available clerical rendering may present Grant at a disadvantage not of his own making. Although Grant's own spelling was erratic, it never interfered with the clarity of his messages, and sometimes seems to have more psychological than orthographic significance. It is curious that in late 1861 Grant was consistently misspelling the names of the two men most important in advancing his career: his commanding officer, General Halleck ("Hallack"), and his political patron, Congressman Washburne ("Washburn").

We are indebted to C. Percy Powell and Karl L. Trever for searching the National Archives; to Barbara Long for maps; to Kathryn Overturf and Harriet Simon for typing; to Edgar F. Raines, Jr., and Marcia Swider, graduate students at Southern Illinois University, for research assistance; and to Roger D. Bridges, holder of a fellowship in advanced historical editing from the National Historical Publications Commission, for editorial assistance. Financial support for the Ulysses S. Grant Association for the period during which this volume was prepared came from Southern Illinois University and the National Historical Publications Commission.

January 19, 1970   JOHN Y. SIMON

Editorial Procedure

1. Editorial Insertions

A. Words or letters in roman type within brackets represent editorial reconstruction of parts of manuscripts torn, mutilated, or illegible.

B. [. . .] or [— — —] within brackets represent lost material which cannot be reconstructed. The number of dots represents the approximate number of lost letters; dashes represent lost words.

C. Words in *italic* type within brackets represent material such as dates which were not part of the original manuscript.

D. Numbered notes marking passages crossed out in letters from USG to Julia Dent Grant represent material deleted by Mrs. Grant in later years. It is the wish of her descendants that this material remain unprinted. Most deletions involve minor personal matters and are not extensive.

E. Other material crossed out is indicated by ~~cancelled type~~.

F. Material raised in manuscript, as "4th," has been brought in line, as "4th."

2. Symbols Used to Describe Manuscripts

AD	Autograph Document
ADS	Autograph Document Signed
ADf	Autograph Draft
ADfS	Autograph Draft Signed
AES	Autograph Endorsement Signed
AL	Autograph Letter
ALS	Autograph Letter Signed

D	Document
DS	Document Signed
Df	Draft
DfS	Draft Signed
ES	Endorsement Signed
LS	Letter Signed

3. Military Terms and Abbreviations

Act.	Acting
Adjt.	Adjutant
AG	Adjutant General
AGO	Adjutant General's Office
Art.	Artillery
Asst.	Assistant
Bvt.	Brevet
Brig.	Brigadier
Capt.	Captain
Cav.	Cavalry
Col.	Colonel
Co.	Company
C.S.A.	Confederate States of America
Dept.	Department
Gen.	General
Hd. Qrs.	Headquarters
Inf.	Infantry
Lt.	Lieutenant
Maj.	Major
Q. M.	Quartermaster
Regt.	Regiment or regimental
Sgt.	Sergeant
USMA	United States Military Academy, West Point, N.Y.
Vols.	Volunteers

4. Short Titles and Abbreviations

ABPC	*American Book-Prices Current* (New York, 1895–)
CG	*Congressional Globe* Numbers following represent the Congress, session, and page.

J. G. Cramer	Jesse Grant Cramer, ed., *Letters of Ulysses S. Grant to his Father and his Youngest Sister, 1857–78* (New York and London, 1912)
DAB	*Dictionary of American Biography* (New York, 1928–36)
Garland	Hamlin Garland, *Ulysses S. Grant: His Life and Character* (New York, 1898)
HED	*House Executive Documents*
HMD	*House Miscellaneous Documents*
HRC	*House Reports of Committees* Numbers following *HED, HMD,* or *HRC* represent the number of the Congress, the session, and the document.
Ill. AG Report	J. N. Reece, ed., *Report of the Adjutant General of the State of Illinois* (Springfield, 1900)
Lewis	Lloyd Lewis, *Captain Sam Grant* (Boston, 1950)
Lincoln, Works	Roy P. Basler, Marion Dolores Pratt, and Lloyd A. Dunlap, eds., *The Collected Works of Abraham Lincoln* (New Brunswick, 1953–55)
Memoirs	*Personal Memoirs of U. S. Grant* (New York, 1885–86)
O.R.	*The War of the Rebellion: A Compilation of the Official Records of the Union and Confederate Armies* (Washington, 1880–1901)
O.R. (Navy)	*Official Records of the Union and Confederate Navies in the War of the Rebellion* (Washington, 1894–1927) Roman numerals following *O.R.* or *O.R.* (Navy) represent the series and the volume.
PUSG	John Y. Simon, ed., *The Papers of Ulysses S. Grant* (Carbondale and Edwardsville, 1967—)
Richardson	Albert D. Richardson, *A Personal History of Ulysses S. Grant* (Hartford, Conn., 1868)
SED	*Senate Executive Documents*
SMD	*Senate Miscellaneous Documents*
SRC	*Senate Reports of Committees* Numbers following *SED, SMD,* or *SRC* represent the number of the Congress, the session, and the document.
USGA Newsletter	*Ulysses S. Grant Association Newsletter*
Young	John Russell Young, *Around the World with General Grant* (New York, 1879)

5. *Location Symbols*

CSmH	Henry E. Huntington Library, San Marino, Calif.
CU-B	Bancroft Library, University of California, Berkeley, Calif.
DLC	Library of Congress, Washington, D.C. Numbers following DLC-USG represent the series and volume of military records in the USG papers.
DNA	National Archives, Washington, D.C. Additional numbers identify record groups.
IaHA	Iowa State Department of History and Archives, Des Moines, Iowa.
I-ar	Illinois State Archives, Springfield, Ill.
IC	Chicago Public Library, Chicago, Ill.
ICarbS	Southern Illinois University, Carbondale, Ill.
ICHi	Chicago Historical Society, Chicago, Ill.
ICN	Newberry Library, Chicago, Ill.
IHi	Illinois State Historical Library, Springfield, Ill.
InU	Indiana University, Bloomington, Ind.
KHi	Kansas State Historical Society, Topeka, Kan.
MH	Harvard University, Cambridge, Mass.
MHi	Massachusetts Historical Society, Boston, Mass.
MiD	Detroit Public Library, Detroit, Mich.
MiU-C	William L. Clements Library, University of Michigan, Ann Arbor, Mich.
MoSHi	Missouri Historical Society, St. Louis, Mo.
NHi	New-York Historical Society, New York, N.Y.
NjP	Princeton University, Princeton, N.J.
NjR	Rutgers University, New Brunswick, N.J.
NN	New York Public Library, New York, N.Y.
OClWHi	Western Reserve Historical Society, Cleveland, Ohio.
OFH	Rutherford B. Hayes Library, Fremont, Ohio.
OHi	Ohio Historical Society, Columbus, Ohio.
OrHi	Oregon Historical Society, Portland, Ore.
PHi	Historical Society of Pennsylvania, Philadelphia, Pa.
PPRF	Rosenbach Foundation, Philadelphia, Pa.
RPB	Brown University, Providence, R.I.

USG 3	Maj. Gen. Ulysses S. Grant 3rd, Clinton, N.Y.
USMA	United States Military Academy Library, West Point, N.Y.
WHi	State Historical Society of Wisconsin, Madison, Wis.

Chronology

1861

OCT. 1.   USG withdrew troops from Norfolk, Mo., to Bird's Point, Mo., opposite Cairo, in order to strengthen his defensive position.

OCT. 2.   USG sent troops to Charleston, Mo., to intercept Brig. Gen. M. Jeff Thompson, Mo. State Guard, who, however, was still at New Madrid, Mo.

OCT. 7.   USG again sent troops to Charleston, again without encountering Thompson.

OCT. 7.   USG ordered the gunboats *Tyler* and *Lexington* on reconnaissance down the Mississippi River. The gunboats exchanged fire with C.S.A. batteries a few miles above Columbus, Ky.

OCT. 8.   USG reviewed troops at Cape Girardeau, Mo.

OCT. 14.   USG rebuffed an offer by C.S.A. Maj. Gen. Leonidas Polk to exchange prisoners.

OCT. 14.   U.S. and C.S.A. cav. skirmished about nine miles south of Bird's Point in Mo.

OCT. 14.   USG organized his troops into five brigades, commanded by Brig. Gen. John A. McClernand (Cairo), Col. Richard J. Oglesby (Bird's Point), Col. William H. L. Wallace (Bird's Point), Col. John Cook (Fort Holt, Ky.), and Col. Joseph B. Plummer (Cape Girardeau).

xxi

OCT. 16. USG sent troops from Cape Girardeau toward Farmington, Mo., to cut off Thompson's army, which was threatening Ironton, Mo.

OCT. 18. USG ordered a reconnaissance by the gunboat *Tyler* toward Columbus.

OCT. 21. The detachment of USG's troops from Cape Girardeau, under Plummer, defeated Thompson at Fredericktown, Mo.

OCT. 21. U.S. troops defeated at Ball's Bluff or Leesburg, Va.

OCT. 21. USG left Cairo for St. Louis.

OCT. 23. USG arrived in Springfield, Ill., to see Governor Richard Yates about obtaining arms and art. for his command.

OCT. 24. USG returned to Cairo, considering his visit to Springfield "only partially successful."

OCT. 24. In Washington, D.C., orders were prepared for the removal of Maj. Gen. John C. Frémont from command of the Western Dept. These orders were not delivered for nine days.

OCT. 31. USG appeared before a U.S. House of Representatives investigating committee at Cairo to discuss arms of his troops.

NOV. 1. Maj. Gen. George B. McClellan replaced Bvt. Lt. Gen. Winfield Scott as general-in-chief.

NOV. 1. USG was ordered to demonstrate southward along both banks of the Mississippi River.

NOV. 2. USG was ordered to send an expedition to the St. Francis River in Mo. to intercept Thompson.

NOV. 2. Frémont relieved by Maj. Gen. David Hunter, who took command of the Western Dept. on the following day.

NOV. 4. USG ordered one regt. from Cape Girardeau to Bloomfield, Mo.

Nov. 5. USG planned demonstrations against Columbus and Belmont, Mo., using troops from Paducah, Ky., as well as his own.

Nov. 6. USG ordered one regt. to advance from Bird's Point to Charleston, and nearly two regts. to advance from Fort Holt toward Columbus.

Nov. 6. USG ordered his commander at Bloomfield to communicate with him at Belmont.

Nov. 6. USG embarked from Cairo with about 3,000 men and anchored about twelve miles above Belmont.

Nov. 7. USG landed near Belmont, encountered some 2,500 C.S.A. troops. After U.S. forces destroyed the enemy camp, reinforcements from Columbus drove them back to their transports in some disorder. The expedition then returned to Cairo.

Nov. 7. U.S. forces captured Port Royal, S. Car.

Nov. 8. USG congratulated his troops on their gallantry at Belmont.

Nov. 8. USG sent a flag of truce party to gather the dead and wounded on the battlefield of Belmont.

Nov. 8. USG recalled his Bloomfield expedition to Bird's Point.

Nov. 9. Maj. Gen. Henry W. Halleck assigned to command the Dept. of the Mo., a command embracing most of the former Western Dept.

Nov. 13. USG met Polk on board a flag of truce steamboat to discuss an exchange of prisoners.

Nov. 15. Brig. Gen. Don Carlos Buell assumed command of the Dept. of the Ohio, which included all of Ky. east of the Cumberland River.

Nov. 16. USG wrote to Thompson to initiate an exchange of prisoners.

Nov. 18. Thompson captured the steamboat *Platte Valley* at Price's Landing, Mo., possibly in an attempt to capture USG.

Nov. 19. USG went to Price's Landing in search of Thompson, but learned that he had left the previous evening.

Nov. 19. While USG was away, McClernand ordered a cav. reconnaissance in Ky. toward Columbus.

Nov. 19. Halleck, who had arrived at St. Louis the previous day, assumed command of the Dept. of the Mo.

Nov. 20. USG asked Halleck for permission to visit St. Louis to discuss the needs and condition of his command. Halleck denied permission on the following day.

Nov. 22. USG sent McClernand to Springfield to arrange to fill and equip regts. then at Cairo.

Nov. 22. USG directed a gunboat reconnaissance down the Mississippi River to Lucas Bend, Mo.

Nov. 23. USG left for Cape Girardeau, returning by Nov. 25.

Nov. 23. Julia Dent Grant left Cairo for a visit to St. Louis.

Nov. 28. The *St. Louis*, first of the ironclad gunboats, arrived at Cairo.

Dec. 1. C.S.A. gunboats on reconnaissance upriver fired a few shots at Fort Holt.

Dec. 5. USG visited Columbus on board a flag of truce steamboat. He returned the following day to receive Col. Henry Dougherty, 22nd Ill., wounded at Belmont.

Dec. 6. USG ordered a cav. expedition to Belmont to spike some art. reported there. The expedition found nothing.

Dec. 8. USG cancelled a proposed expedition to New Madrid, Mo., after learning that the gunboats would be unable to participate.

DEC. 9. Julia Dent Grant left Cairo to visit her father in St. Louis.

DEC. 11. U.S. and C.S.A. cav. skirmished at Bertrand, Mo.

DEC. 13. USG prepared his command for an anticipated attack on Bird's Point or Fort Holt. No attack was made.

DEC. 15. USG sent his aid-de-camp, Capt. William S. Hillyer, to Chicago to investigate charges of fraud in lumber contracts for Cairo. Hillyer returned a week later with corroboration of the charges.

DEC. 20. Through orders establishing the District of Cairo, Halleck enlarged USG's command to include Paducah.

DEC. 23. In orders announcing the District of Cairo, USG also assigned Brig. Gen. Eleazer A. Paine, transferred from Paducah, to command at Bird's Point.

DEC. 24. Polk decided to send troops from western Ky. to central Ky. This move, discovered by U.S. forces three days later, eventually brought orders from Washington to maintain U.S. pressure in western Ky.

DEC. 26. USG left for an inspection trip up the Ohio River at least as far as Shawneetown, Ill.

DEC. 28. USG ordered assessments on C.S.A. sympathizers to support Union refugees in his district.

DEC. 29. Thompson seized Commerce, Mo., and shelled the steamboat *City of Alton*.

1862

JAN. 2. In response to numerous reports of contract irregularities, USG placed a new q.m. on duty at Cairo.

JAN. 7. USG sent three gunboats and a squadron of cav. on reconnaissance toward Belmont.

The Papers of Ulysses S. Grant
October 1, 1861–January 7, 1862

To Brig. Gen. Alexander Asboth

Cairo, [*Oct.*] 1st 1861.

GEN ASBOTH,

Your despatch to send two companies Burton cavalry[1] to Georgetown[2] is rec'd, my cavalry force is now so small these two companies being full two thirds of it that it looks suicidal to remove them   I will beg therefore that they be not removed until others can replace them.

U. S. GRANT
Brig. Gen.

Telegram, copies, DNA, RG 393, Western Dept., Telegrams; DLC-USG, VIA, 1. On Sept. 30, 1861, Brig. Gen. Alexander Asboth, St. Louis, telegraphed to USG. "General Smith will send the Benton cavalry Major Nemett in command immediately to Georgetown Mo, via St Louis & Jefferson city to join their brigade under acting Major General Siegel" Copies, *ibid.*; DNA, RG 393, USG Hd. Qrs. Correspondence. Alexander Asboth, born in Hungary, served in the Austrian army before joining Lajos Kossuth in the Hungarian Revolution of 1848–49. On Sept. 21, Maj. Gen. John C. Frémont, who had already given Asboth an irregular appointment as brig. gen., named him act. maj. gen. *O.R.*, I, iii, 502.

1. Benton Hussars, later incorporated in the 5th Mo. Cav., Col. Joseph Nemett.
2. Georgetown, Mo., about sixty miles west of Jefferson City, Mo.

To Capt. Chauncey McKeever

Head Quarters, Dist. S. E. Mo.
Cairo, October 1st 1861

SIR:

I have to-day concentrated my command at this place, Birds Point and Fort Holt. The work of placing these points in a strong defensive condition will be prossecuted with all our force.

There is no enemy on the Missouri side of the river from Cape Girardeau to New Madrid except Jeff Thompons force at Belmont. I had troops in Charleston last evening. All quiet there.

The packets plying between St. Louis and Cairo constantly leave freight at points above here intended for the interior. This enables the enemy to supply himself with all his wants. Day before Yesterday I sent a force to Charleston to bring back goods that had been landed for that place. Accompanying is an inventory of the goods seized.[1]

I have my serious doubts whether there is any law authorizing this seizure but feel no doubt about the propriety of breaking up the trade now carried on. I respectfully refer this matter to the General Commanding Western Department for instructions.

There is evidently a large force moving from Columbus to the interior. Whether upon Paducah or not I do not know.

I received a despatch from General Asboth to send two companies of Cavalry from here to Georgetown Mo. via St. Louis. My force is so small, especially in Cavalry[,] that before sending them I asked to have them replaced with other troops.[2]

> Respectfully
> Your Obt. Svt.
> U. S. GRANT
> Brig. Gen Com

To Capt. Chauncey McKeever
A. A. Gen Western Dept.
St. Louis Mo

ALS, DNA, RG 393, Western Dept., Letters Received. *O.R.*, I, iii, 511.

1. See letter to Col. C. Carroll Marsh, Sept. 29, 1861. On Sept. 30, 1861, USG telegraphed to Capt. Chauncey McKeever. "I sent yesterday to Charleston & apprehended the goods reported as landed by Steamer Platte valley yesterday" Telegram received, DNA, RG 393, Dept. of the Mo., Telegrams Received. On Oct. 4, McKeever replied to USG. "I am instructed by the commanding General to inform you that the seizure of goods made by you at Charleston, Mo., is approved." LS, *ibid.*, District of Southeast Mo., Letters Received.
2. See preceding telegram.

To Capt. Andrew H. Foote

———

Cairo, Oct 1. 1861.

CAPT. A. H. FOOTE U S. A.

SIR,

The Conestoga is here I recommend sending her back up the river where her services are much needed.

U. S. GRANT,
Brig. Gen.

Telegram, copies, DNA, RG 393, Western Dept., Telegrams; DLC-USG, VIA, 1. On Sept. 30, 1861, Capt. Andrew H. Foote, St. Louis, telegraphed to USG. "Would it not be well to send the steamer 'Bee' up the river for the gun boat 'Bee' Conestoga, if she has not arrived as she may be aground." Copies, *ibid.* On Oct. 1, Foote telegraphed to USG. "The 'Conestoga' of course goes where the General wishes. Please inform me if I am wanted, my services are important here, but will go to Cairo if they are needed there. We hope to send a heavy gun boat very soon" Copy, DNA, RG 393, Western Dept., Telegrams. On the same day, USG telegraphed to Foote. "I think there will be no active service requiring your services at present I will telegraph you if ~~any~~ important movements are made" Telegram received, *ibid.*, RG 45, Area 5. *O.R.* (Navy), I, xxii, 355. On Oct. 2, Capt. William S. Hillyer wrote to Capt. S. Ledyard Phelps. "You will proceed without unnecessary delay with Gun Boat Conestoga to Paducah Kentucky and report yourself to Brig Gen C. F. Smith Comg that Post for service" Copies, DLC-USG, V, 1, 2, 3, 77; DNA, RG 393, USG Letters Sent. Also on Oct. 2, Brig. Gen. John A. McClernand wrote to USG. "I have just received a telegram from Genl. Fremont, dated at Jefferson City, Oct 2nd, inst. as follows—'Gun boat under Commodore Rogers will be sent to Cairo for service where most needed until others are repaired." Copy, McClernand Papers, IHi.

To Col. Richard J. Oglesby

———

Head Quarters Dist S. E. Mo
Cairo ~~Aug~~ Oct 1st 1861

COL

Despairing of being immediately reinforced I deem it the better part of valor to be prudent. You will therefore move your entire force back upon Birds Point and take position there.

Select your encampment with the view of leaving as clear a field for defense as possible.

You will assume command at Birds Point untill such time as I may be able to Brigade the command about this Point

U. S. GRANT
Brig Genl Com

To Col R. J. Oglesby
Comdg Norfolk, Mo

Copies, DLC-USG, V, 1, 2, 3, 77; DNA, RG 393, USG Letters Sent. *O.R.*, I, iii, 511.

To Col. Richard J. Oglesby

————

Head Quarters Dist S. E Mo
Cairo Oct 1st 1861

COL

From information recd. this evening, Thompson will probably march upon Charleston tomorrow on his way North.[1]

Move out with one thousand infantry and all the Cavelry you can spare, and intercept him

Yours &c
U S GRANT
Brigr Genl Comdg

To Col R. J. Oglesby
Birds Point Mo

Copies, DLC-USG, V, 1, 2, 3, 77; DNA, RG 393, USG Letters Sent. *O.R.*, I, iii, 510.

1. See letter to Capt. Chauncey McKeever, Oct. 2, 1861.

To Col. James M. Tuttle

———

Head Quarters Dist S. E. Mo
Cairo October 1st 1861

Col

Before leaving Ironton I ordered the purchase of Wagons &c among which was one two Horse Wagon bought from Tong & Carson. They now report to me that payment is disallowed no Quartermaster having receipted for the wagon I believe it went into the possession of your Regiment. If so please direct your Regl Q. M. to receipt for the same and forward through these Head Quarters to the Mess Tong & Carson

Yours &c
U. S. Grant
Brig Genl Com

To Col Tuttle
Comdg 2nd Iowa Regt
Birds, Point, Mo

Copies, DLC-USG, V, 1, 2, 3, 77; DNA, RG 393, USG Letters Sent. James M. Tuttle of Iowa was appointed lt. col. of the 2nd Iowa on May 31, and advanced to col. on Sept. 6, 1861.

To Maj. Joseph D. Webster

———

Head Quarters Dist S E. Mo
Cairo ~~Sept~~ Oct 1st 1861

Col

Having determined to make our defences here and at Birds Point & Fort Holt as efficient as possible I wish to have appointed to each of those places an officer of the Engineer Corps who will direct the work under your General Supervision

At Fort Holt Col Ross has already commenced some work it would be well therefore to send an Engineer there at once to see that the work is right

All the different command will be instructed to give all the details you may call for

Yours &c

U. S. GRANT

Brig Genl Com

To Col Webster
Chief of Engineers
Cairo Ills

Copies, DLC-USG, V, 1, 2, 3, 77; DNA, RG 393, USG Letters Sent. On Oct. 1, 1861, Capt. John A. Rawlins for USG issued special orders. "Our limited forces making it necessary to fortify and clear off grounds for defence, the Commandants at Cairo, Birds Point and Fort Holt, Ky will detail as many men as may be required by Colonel Webster, Chief of Engineers, or his assistants. At least one commissioned Officer will be detailed for every twenty five men, to superintend the working parties; all work to be done under the orders and directions of Colonel Webster, Chief of Engineers and his Assistants" Copies, DLC-USG, V, 15, 16, 77, 82; DNA, RG 393, USG Special Orders.

To Capt. Reuben B. Hatch

———

Hd. Qrs Dist. S. E. Mo.
Cairo Oct 1 1861

CAPT R B. HATCH, A Q M.
CAIRO ILLS

You will cause to be appraised the value of steamer "Champion No 2"; also the value of her services per day, and take her into ~~the~~ service of the Government.[1]

~~You will supply the "Conestoga" with coal this afternoon.~~
~~If there is not a supply on hand more must be provided at once~~

U. S. GRANT

Brigadier General comdg

Copies, DLC-USG, V, 1, 2, 3, 77; DNA, RG 393, USG Letters Sent. Originally drafted as one letter, the second paragraph was sent separately. Parke-Bernet Sale No. 2078, Jan. 16, 1962; *The Collector*, LXXVII, 7–9 (1964), 15.

1. On Sept. 29, 1861, Commander Roger N. Stembel wrote to USG. "I have the honor to state for your information that on my return in this Vessel from a recent expedition to Owensboro K. Y. I was informed by Mr A. A. Robinson U. S. surveyor at Evansville Ind whose written statement, together with the names of three witnesses I have placed in your hands: that a steamboat called the Champion No. 2, being the property of one D. A. Conn, owner and proprietor of the Curlew Coal mines in Kentucky, had been engaged in the contraband trade, as well as conveying troops up the Cumberland River to the Tennessee line, with the sanction and under the control of the said Conn, deeming this act of his a violation of the Law made and provided in such cases—I determined to capture the Boat, should I meet with her any where on my passage down: and fortunately yesterday, I met her about twenty miles above this place on the Ohio River returning, (as Conn himself who was on board informed me), from Cairo wither he had been to deliver a quantity of Coals for Government use. I took possession of her without opposition and with the crew: brought them to this place and delivered them into your hands." LS, DNA, RG 393, District of Southeast Mo., Letters Received. On Sept. 29, 1st Lt. Clark B. Lagow for USG wrote to Charles D. Arter. "You will take charge of Steamer Champion No 2 and hold subject to orders" Copies, DLC-USG, V, 1, 2, 3, 77; DNA, RG 393, USG Letters Sent. See following letter. On Nov. 23, D. O. Conn, Curlew Mines, Ky., wrote to USG "in reference to the capture of 'Champion No. 2' by the gunboat Lexington." DLC-USG, V, 10; DNA, RG 393, USG Register of Letters Received.

To Charles D. Arter

Head Quarters Dist S. E. Mo
Cairo October 1st 1861

SIR

More boats being required for the use of this command I have directed that the Champion No 2 be used for our service. This then is to relieve you from further responsibility.

Your &c

U. S. GRANT
Brig Genl Com

To C. Arter Esqr
Surveyor of Port
Cairo Ills

Copies, DLC-USG, V, 1, 2, 3, 77; DNA, RG 393, USG Letters Sent. See preceding letter.

To Julia Dent Grant

———

Cairo, October 1st 1861

DEAR JULIA:

I sent you $300 00 this evening $100 00 for yourself and $200 to be left at the store to pay old man Hughlett. My savings one month more will pay him up.—You cant accuse me of not at least answering your letters. I have not received but about three letters since I come to Cairo, except old ones. I have received half a dozen old letters written a month or more ago.

What do you say to Fred. making the campaign with me?— I have no news for you. What I am doing I do not believe in writing about, in fact it is prohibited. There is one thing how- ever I can tell you. Columbus twenty miles below here has been reinforced 10.000 men within the last few days.[1] Among the officers below here there are several of my old acquaintances. McCown,[2] who left his Ambulanch and mules with me you recollect, commands a Brigade. Bowen,[3] Mit Kennerlys husband commands a regiment. Then there is Gen. Johnson Gen. Hardee and one or two other old army officers to say nothing of the great Gen. Pillow.—Dr. Sharp hears from Nelly evry few days. Her and children are well. I have not heard from Emma[4] lately.—I think you certainly do not receive all my letters for there are some of them I think you would notice the receipt of specially.

Yesterday I went up to Paducah[.] It is a beautiful town but now nearly deserted. This end of Ky will soon be in the same fix Mo. is in, a waste. The amount of suffering the coming winter must be horrible.—I receive letters from Mary Grant evry week or two and write occationally to her. I receive so many letters that I do not pretend to answer half of them.

Give my love to all at home. Kiss the children for me. A thousand kisses for yourself dear Julia.

Your husband
ULYS.

ALS, DLC-USG.

1. On Sept. 22, 1861, Gen. Albert Sidney Johnston called upon Governor John J. Pettus of Miss. and Governor Henry M. Rector of Ark. for 10,000 troops each. *O.R.*, I, iv, 421–23. On Sept. 28, Pettus informed Johnston that he had issued a proclamation calling for 10,000 troops, and it was probably through the proclamation that USG learned of the proposed increase. *Ibid.*, pp. 431–32. During the month of Oct. the number of men commanded by Maj. Gen. Leonidas Polk increased from 24,897 to 25,208; those at Columbus from 13,708 to 17,230. *Ibid.*, I, iii, 712, 730. Thus while some troops came to Columbus as a result of the call upon Miss., the increase in C. S. A. strength did not alter the balance of strength.

2. C. S. A. Col. John P. McCown of Tenn., USMA 1840, served in the 4th Art. until May 17, 1861.

3. See letter to Maj. Gen. John C. Frémont, Sept. 11, 1861, note 2.

4. Emily (Emma) Dent Casey, sister-in-law of USG.

To Capt. Chauncey McKeever

Head Quarters, Dist. S. E. Mo.
Cairo, Oct. 2d 1861

SIR:

Last evening hearing through a deserter from the rebel encampment at Belmont that Jeff. Thompson was breaking up there, to start for points North,[1] I ordered out to Charleston twelve to fifteen hundred men, all arms, to intercept him.[2] The party has not returned yet. Should anything important grow out of the expedition I will report by telegraph. This same authority denies the arrival of Hardee at Columbus, but says that he is expected soon. Also reports the return to Columbus of the force under Pillow. They report among the troops that they had been as far as Paducah and had driven out our forces there.—It has so far proven impossible to get morning reports correctly made out, by the different commands, from which to consolidate. I have been returning ~~morning reports~~ them for correction until now I think they will come in correct and in form.

	Respectfully
To Capt. C. McKeever	Your Obt Svt.
A. A. Gen Western Dept.	U. S. GRANT
St. Louis Mo.	Brig. Gen.

ALS, DNA, RG 94, War Records Office, Dept. of the Mo. *O.R.*, I, iii, 515.

1. On Sept. 30, 1861, Brig. Gen. M. Jeff Thompson planned to leave Belmont for New Madrid, Mo., leave his heavy baggage there, then advance to Sikeston. *Ibid.*, p. 712. On Oct. 3, Thompson was still at New Madrid due to the delay of his baggage wagons. *Ibid.*, p. 713.

2. On Oct. 2, Col. Richard J. Oglesby wrote to USG. "In obedience to your order last night to move with a force upon Charleston, to intercept the rebel forces under Jeff. Thompson, I sent Eleventh Illinois Volunteers, 450, Twentieth Illinois, 350, and the Second Iowa Volunteers, 350; total Infantry, 1,150; one division of Captain Taylor's artillery and 100 Cavalry, under Captain Stewart; the whole force under command of Colonel Tuttle, of the Second Iowa Regiment. The force left here at 3.30 o'clock this morning; arrived at Charleston at 8 o'clock. Colonel Tuttle reports that no [e]nemy has been near Charleston in force. He immediately sent out detachments in every direction to reconnoiter. Learning that about 500 of the enemy's cavalry would be at Charleston at noon to-day or during the day, he sent forward on the Belmont road a company of cavalry 5 miles to report their approach. The enemy did not reveal itself. At 5 o'clock p. m. the forces were put in motion, and have returned to this camp to-night. From all the information learned through Colonel Tuttle I am satisfied the enemy have not been at Charleston, and will not move by there. Belmont has been evacuated. My impression is they have fallen back on New Madrid." Copies, DNA, RG 94, War Records Office, Union Battle Reports; *ibid.*, RG 393, Western Dept., Letters Received; DLC-USG, VIA, 2. *O.R.*, I, iii, 198–99.

To Brig. Gen. John A. McClernand

Head Quarters, Dist. S. E. Mo.
Cairo, October 2d 1861

Gen.

After the discharge of a Soldier is ordered by a Commander of Department the Post Commander must sign the discharge to make it complete.

It is only before the application goes to Department Head Quarters for action that I wish to pass upon it.

Respectfully &c
U. S. Grant
Brig. Gen. Com.

To Gen. J. A. McClernand
Comd.g Post
Cairo, Ills

ALS, McClernand Papers, IHi. On Oct. 2, 1861, Brig. Gen. John A. McClernand wrote to USG. "It would appear from the 159th Sec of Army Regulations of 1861 that the power to grant discharges for disability rest with you. Major Brayman on returning from an interview with you last week, advised me that you so considered it and would pass upon all such applications. Since then, I have sent all applicants for discharges to your Head Quarters. To-day a case come back for my consideration. Please advise me as to the proper mode &c." Copy, *ibid.*

To Col. Leonard F. Ross

———

Head Quarters Dist S. E. Mo
Cairo Oct 2d 1861

COL

You will hold your Regiment in readiness to take Steamer for Cape Girardeau at once You will take with you none of your land transportation and only such rations as have already been issued to your command

U. S. GRANT
Brig Gen Comdg

To Col L. F. Ross
Comdg 17th Regt Ill Vols
Fort Holt Ky

Copies, DLC-USG, V, 1, 2, 3, 77; DNA, RG 393, USG Letters Sent.

To Col. Joseph B. Plummer

———

Head Quarters Dist S E. Mo
Cairo Oct 3d 1861

COL.

On the arrival of Col Ross with the 17th Ills Volls[1] you will designate a regiment to take his place here. The regiment so designated will avail themselves of the same transportation that conveys Col Ross Regt.[2]

It is rumored here by way of St Louis that a force has crossed the river at Columbus and are marching upon Cape Girardeau I do not credit the rumor however for the reason that I have reconnisance made every day or two beyond Chaleston and on all the roads leading North & west from Belmont. It would be well however to keep a lookout for the approach of an enemy and should you satisfy yourself that either Jeff Thompson or Lowe[3] unsuported by any one else are near you you can easily drive them from your vicinity.

Send me your morning reports each Monday morning and should you have any information of the movements of the enemy at any time report to me as well as to St Louis. Should the importance of the information justify it you may send a messenger to Jonesborough, Ills and telegraph

Yours &c
U S GRANT
Brigr Genl Comdg

To Col J B Plumer
Comdg U. S. Forces
Cape Girardeau Mo

Copies, DLC-USG, V, 1, 2, 3, 77; DNA, RG 393, USG Letters Sent. *O.R.*, I, iii, 518–19. On Oct. 4, 1861, Col. Joseph B. Plummer wrote to USG. "I have the honor to report that the 17th Ills Vols under the Command of Col. Ross arrived last night on the steamer Aleck Scott, and that in compliance with your instructions I detailed the 7th Ills. Vols. (Col. Cook's Regiment) to proceed to Fort Holt Ky. and that it left here this evening on the same Steamer. I would remark that I had recd information of the crossing of the enemy at Columbus, from various sources and was disposed to believe the report. I have sent out several spies, and hope to communicate to you to-morrow more reliable information than I have at present. There arrived here yesterday the ~~the~~ 10th Iowa Regt of Vols under the Command of Col. N Perczel, which now constitutes a part of the Permanent Force of this City." ALS, DNA, RG 393, District of Southeast Mo., Letters Received. On Oct. 2, Plummer wrote to Capt. Chauncey McKeever that he was "disposed to believe" a report that 60,000 Confederates had assembled to move on Cape Girardeau. *O.R.*, I, iii, 515.

  1. See following letter.
  2. On Oct. 2, Capt. John A. Rawlins wrote to Plummer. "You will designate and hold in readiness a Regiment of your command at Cape Girardeau, to relieve Col Ross at Fort Holt Ky. to be moved to Fort Holt by the same Steamer or Steamers conveying Col Ross Regiment to Cape Girardeau immediately upon

the arrival of Col Ross command at that place Wagons and Teams not to be transported either way" Copies, DLC-USG, V, 1, 2, 3, 77; DNA, RG 393, USG Letters Sent.

3. Col. Aden Lowe, Mo. State Guard, with whom Brig. Gen. M. Jeff Thompson planned an attack on Cape Girardeau or Ironton. *O.R.*, I, iii, 712–13.

To Col. Leonard F. Ross

Head Quarters Dist S. E. Mo
Cairo Oct 3d 1861

Sir

You will proceed with the Regiment under your command to Cape Girardeau Mo and report to Col J. B. Plummer[1] Commander of the Post for duty.

You may designate a suitable Officer to remain behind to take charge of the sick of the Regiment and move them after you so soon as you may be ready to receive them

Yours &c

U. S. Grant

Brig Genl Com

To Col L. F. Ross
Comdg 17th Ill Vols

Copies, DLC-USG, V, 1, 2, 3, 77; DNA, RG 393, USG Letters Sent. On Oct. 3, 1861, Capt. John A. Rawlins for USG wrote to Capt. Reuben B. Hatch. "You will receipt to the Seventeenth Regt Ill Vols. Col Ross comdg for their Transportation Said Regiment being now under marching orders for Cape Girardeau and to take with them none of their Land transportation" Copies, *ibid*. See letter to Capt. Chauncey McKeever, Oct. 4, 1861.

1. See preceding letter.

To Capt. Reuben B. Hatch

Head Quarters Dist S. E. Mo
Cairo Oct 3d 1861

CAPT

You are directed to rent or obtain more storage room for the use of the Commissary department at this post. I undestand there is a Wharf Boat at the upper end of the City which may be obtained at reasonable rates if so you are authorized to rent it

U. S. GRANT
Brig Genl Com

To Capt R. B. Hatch
Post Q. M.
Cairo Ills

Copies, DLC-USG, V, 1, 2, 3, 77; DNA, RG 393, USG Letters Sent. See letter to Capt. Chauncey McKeever, Oct. 17, 1861.

To Capt. Chauncey McKeever

Head Quarters, Dist. S. E. Mo.
Cairo, October 4th 1861

SIR:

Owing to the loss of health of the 17th regiment Illinois volunteers, Col. Ross Commanding, I have ordered them to Cape Girardeau, directing Col. Plummer to designate a regiment from there to replace them.[1]

Six companies of the 2d Ill. Cavalry have arrived here.[2] After receiving their arms they will be a powerful auxiliary to our force. Cavalry is much required for the purpose of reconnoisance.

I have nothing reliable from the enemy further than that Jeff. Thompson has broken up his encampment at Belmont and gone to New Madrid. No doubt it is with the view of going North from there but whether any other force goes with him I have no positive information My impression is there is no concerted plan to attack this place, Cape Girardeau or Paducah for the present.—When I first learned that Thompson had broken up his Camp I ordered out a force to Charleston to cut him off in that direction. I enclose you the report of Col. Oglesby who made the detail for the expedition.[3]

Before I assumed command of this Military District a Steam Ferry had been seized on the Mississippi and taken into Government service at Cape Girardeau. I knew nothing of the circumstances until within the last few days. Finding that Government was using private property under these conditions I ordered the Commanding officer at Cape Girardeau to require the Quartermaster of the Post to enter into a contract for the use of the boat.[4] I have just received the report of the Quartermaster and the opinion of Col. Plummer thereon. The owner of the Ferry demands seventy-five dollars per day. The Quartermaster, Lieut. Shields 20th Ill. Vols. regards eight dollars per day as a fair compensation and Col. Plummer, on advising with old Steamboat men regards ~~regards~~ Lieuts. Shields estimate as a fair value of the services. I have ordered therefore that the services of the Ferry, the Luella, be retained until otherwise directed, by higher authority, and no contract be entered into.[5]

Yours &c.

U. S. GRANT

Brig. Gen. Com

To Capt. Chauncy McKeever
A. A. Gen Western Dept.
St. Louis Mo.

ALS, DNA, RG 393, Western Dept., Letters Received. *O.R.*, I, iii, 519–20.

1. See letters to Cols. Joseph B. Plummer and Leonard F. Ross, Oct. 3, 1861.
2. On Oct. 3, 1861, Capt. John A. Rawlins for USG wrote to Col. Silas Noble, 2nd Ill. Cav. "You will report with your command to Col Oglesby Comdg Birds Point Mo Transportation has been provided and now awaits you, to convey you and your command with your Horses Equipments &c from Cairo to Birds Point" Copies, DLC-USG, V, 1, 2, 3, 77; DNA, RG 393, USG Letters Sent.

3. See letter to Capt. Chauncey McKeever, Oct. 2, 1861, note 2.

4. See letter to Col. John Cook, Sept. 28, 1861.

5. On Oct. 1, 1st Lt. James E. Shields, 20th Ill., wrote to Col. Joseph B. Plummer. "In accordance with your instructions I have had an interview with Mr Vancil, owner of Steamer Luella, for the purpose of fixing upon a just and reasonable rent, to be paid him by the U. S. Govt. for use of said Steamer—He claims, as the lowest remuneration which he ought to receive, seventy five dollars per day, from the time said Steamer was placed in U. S. Service—In my opinion, and in the opinion of Captains Lightner, and Watson, Steamboat owners, with whom I have conversed, Eight dollars per day would be a fair and reasonable rent for said Steamer—which is allowing him 10% on the original cost of the Steamer, and an additional amount of One hundred and fifty six dollars per month, to cover ordinary wear and tear of Machinery and fixtures—Therefore, in view of the difference in our opinions, I have informed him that we cannot enter into any arrangement" On Oct. 4, USG endorsed Shields' letter. "Your rejection of Mr. Vancils rates meets with my hearty approval. The boat will be retained in Government service, if required, without conditions." AES, DLC-Miscellaneous Mss. Plummer's letter of Oct. 1 to USG is printed in *PUSG*, 2, *320n.*

To Capt. Chauncey McKeever

———

Cairo, Oct 6, 1861.

Capt C. McKeever
A. A. G. U. S. A.
Sir,

I have no news of the concentration of a large force at Belmont will send a large force to Charleston to night, & make a reconnoissance towards Belmont tomorrow.

U. S. Grant.

Telegram, copies, DNA, RG 393, Western Dept., Telegrams; DLC-USG, VIA, 1. On Oct. 6, 1861, Capt. Chauncey McKeever telegraphed to USG. "It is reported that the enemy are concentrating in large numbers upon the river opposite the town of Columbus Ky, under A. S. Johnson and intending to move to C. Girardeau. Have you any news about it?" Copies, *ibid.*

To Capt. Chauncey McKeever

———

Head Quarters Dist S. E. Mo
Cairo Oct 6, 1861

SIR—

For the last two days I have had no reliable intelligence of the movements of the enemy—The gun boats have been out of order so as to be unable to make reconnoisances, and one of my spies from whom I expected a full & accurate report has not returned —Our scouts report nothing of importance—I have ordered a force of twelve hundred men to Charleston[1] They will leave early in the morning—My own opinion is that the enemy have no present intention of moving on Cape Girardeau—I think Paducah is more likely the point they design to approach—I have ordered one Gun boat to cruise down as far as Norfolk to night, and will send the other gun boat (now at Mound City repairing) to reconoiter further down to morrow morning—We are very much in need of the new gun boat promised and I trust she will be here very soon[2]—I expect to go to Cape Girardeau to morrow night to inspect the troops there and the condition of the post—[3]

Col Cooks ~~regim~~ 7th Ills regiment arrived here last evening and are now stationed at Camp Holt—I had ordered the exchange of Col Ross's and Col Cooks regiments before I received your instructions[4] to that effect

Since writing the above I have received a report from Col Plummer commanding at Cape Girardeau, informing me that there is a force of one thousand or fifteen hundred of the enemy under command of Col Lowe at Bloomfield, and that preperations are making at Benton to receive the enemy[5]—I had heard of this force of Lowe's and instructed him to send out scouts & ascertain his whereabouts.

Respectfully &c.

To Capt. Chauncy McKeever
A. A. Gen. Western Dept.
St. Louis Mo.

U. S. GRANT
Brig. Gen. Com

LS, DNA, RG 393, Western Dept., Letters Received. *O.R.*, I, iii, 523.

1. On Oct. 8, 1861, Col. William H. L. Wallace, Charleston, Mo., wrote to USG. "Yesterday afternoon I made a personal reconnoisance of this position & the approaches to it for two or three miles in each direction—The town is situated in a prairie & surrounded by cornfields The country is very level & in my judgement as a milatary position is bad, especially as against a superior force—The approaches are numerous & covered to within a mile to two miles of the camp, with heavy timber—I am encamped on a level plain near the R. R. depot—& the cornfields approach very near the camp—The guard & picket duty is very heavy —requiring about 200 infantry & 30 cavalry on duty all the time—Yesterday afternoon I sent mounted scouts out 6 to 7 miles on five different roads & this morning I have sent Capts ~~Nolman~~ Noleman & Stewart with 50 cavalry on the road to Sykeston—They will probably report by noon—The rumors are concurrent & general that Thompson is at Sykeston with from 2500 to 3500 men— 600 of whom are mounted—& nine pieces of artillery—His pickets were at Bertrand yesterday, 25 strong. I can learn of no movement from Belmont An accident occurred last night on the camp guard—A man belonging to the 11th Regt. had got out & attempted to pass back & was fired on by the guard & wounded seriously but not fatally—He was intoxicated No blame can be attached to the guard—The firing called out the entire command & the men formed very promptly & orderly—The two days rations we were ordered to bring will be exhausted tomorrow morning, & under the orders recieved I shall return to Birds point unless I shall recieve orders to the contrary, or the state of facts then existing shall be such as to require some other course—" LS, DNA, RG 393, District of Southeast Mo., Letters Received.

Wallace added further details in a report dated Oct. 9. "I have the honor to report to you that in obedience to your order of the 6th inst, I proceeded to Charleston at six o'clock on the morning of the 7th with two sections of Capt. Taylor's light battery, numbering about 70 men with 4 pieces—detachments from Capts. Nolemans and Stewarts cavalry companies, numbering about 90 men —the 8th Regiment Illinois infantry numbering about 760 men & the 11th Illinois infantry numbering 440 men—making in all a force of about 1360 men and 4 field pieces—The artillery was under the immediate command of Capt. Taylor— Capts Noleman & Stewart had command of the detachments from their respective companies—The 8th Ill. Infantry was under the command of Lieut. Col. Rhoads & the 11th under the immediate command of Lieut. Col. Ransom—The artillery and cavalry moved with the ~~baggage~~ train of baggage wagons by the wagon road leading by Harrisons Mills—The infantry proceeded by the cars on the Cairo & Fulton R. R. under my direct command to Charleston—Arriving at Charleston about 9 o'clk A. M. I immediately posted pickets of infantry on all the roads leading from the place, and selected a site for encampment on a beautiful plain near the rail road depot. About an hour after my arrival there the cavalry and artillery came up having made the march of fourteen miles in about four hours with a train of thirty baggage wagons—I at once detailed parties of mounted scouts from the cavalry and sent them out on all the roads, with orders to proceed five to ten miles in every direction & thoroughly scout the country especially in the direction of Belmont & Sykeston; and I then proceeded in company with Lieut Cols Rhoads and Ransom, Capt. Taylor and Capt. Noleman to make a thorough reconnoisance of the position, examining carefully all the approaches to the place—I found the country very level and presenting few stratagetic points—the country immediately about the town being covered with cornfields & further out by heavy woods—Finding no evidence of any ~~appro~~ force approaching from the direction of Belmont, and learning that the enemys pickets were at Bertrand, six miles west of Charleston, I despatched Capts Noleman & Stewart with about 60 cavalry early on the morning of the 8th to find their location, and at the same time I sent another mounted party under Lieut. Whitlock of Capt. Nolemans cavalry on the Belmont road—The party under Capt. Nolemans command reached Bertrand and encountered ~~the~~ a body of some fifteen of the enemy ~~and~~ who fled at the first fire—The[y] found that the mill at Bertrand had been used by Thompsons force at Sykeston to grind meal for their supplies. I found the people of Charleston and vicinity professedly friendly and exhibiting much more feeling of that character than they have done for a long time past—I was consulted by one or two influential men as to what course would probably be pursued towards men who had acted with the secession forces and were now willing to return to their allegiance & their homes, they stating that many persons now in the rebel ranks would gladly lay down their arms if they could be assured they would not be harshly dealt with—I took the liberty of saying to these persons that in my judgement, if these men acted in good faith they would recieve the immunities promised in Gov. Gamble's proclamation—On the morning of the 9th, my rations being exhausted, & the time for which I was sent out having expired, in accordance with my instructions from you I marched the command to this point—The reconnoisance resulted in showing that no hostile force was moving from Belmont in that direction, and the demonstration I think had a good effect upon the people of that vicinity—I feel under obligation to Lieut. Col. Rhoads & Maj. Post of the 8th—Lieut. Col. Ransom & Maj. Nevins of the 11th—Capts Taylor, Noleman & Stewart and their subaltern officers for the promptness and cheerfulness with which they carried out my orders, and the good order & soldierly bearing evinced by the men—Lieut. Rumsey of Capt. Taylors artillery rendered me very efficient service by acting as my aid—I have to report but one casualty. Thomas Conley a private in Co. K. 11th Regt. on the evening of the 7th while partially intoxicated attempted to force his way through the guard, and was fired on by the sentinel and severly wounded in the shoulder—The wound though serious is not fatal—The officers & men, though disappointed at not meeting the enemy are improved in tone and feeling by the march—" LS, *ibid.*

2. On Oct. 4, Capt. Andrew H. Foote assigned Commander William D. Porter to command the gunboat *New Era*, which he brought to Cairo on Oct. 9. *O.R.* (Navy), I, xxii, 358–61. On Oct. 6, the *Tyler* was at Mound City, the *Lexington* on reconnaissance, and the *Conestoga* at Paducah.

3. On Oct. 4, Capt. William S. Hillyer wrote to Col. Joseph B. Plummer. "I am directed by Genl Grant Comdg to inform you that he will visit you some time next week (probably) Tuesday for the purpose of reviewing the troops under your command I will accompany him and muster into the service any troops you may have who have not been sworn in. You will please see that the muster rolls are made out" Copies, DLC-USG, V, 1, 2, 3, 77; DNA, RG 393, USG Letters Sent.

4. Not found.

5. On Oct. 6, Plummer wrote to USG. "I have the honor to inform you that my scout reports that there is a force of the enemy at Bloomfield of one thousand

or fifteen hundred men under the Command of Lowe. There are only marauding parties between this point and that. Preparations are being made at Benton, at town eighteen miles from here, for the reception of a force there of the enemy." ALS, *ibid.*, District of Southeast Mo., Letters Received. Plummer sent an identical letter to Capt. Chauncey McKeever. *O.R.*, I, iii, 523–24. On the previous day, Plummer had written to USG. "I have the honor to inform you that I have recd information from various sources within the last two days, of the concentration of the forces of the enemy in large numbers at or near a place called William's Mills on the White Water about eighteen miles distant, but have doubted its correctness. A report has been recd this morning, which tends to corroborate those previously made. I have no idea there is any danger of an *immediate* attack upon this post. I will report by every Steamer and if necessary by telegraph from Jonesboro. I have out four spies, two of whom should have reported to me last night or this morning—but not yet returned. There are here one hundred and eighty horses recd one week ago—for the use of a battery of Artillery, but no Harness for them. I have been expecting the latter every day—without it the field pieces are useless except within the entrenchments and the horses are in the way. Are there not more Heavy guns to be sent here from St Louis? We are ready to mount them in the Field works. P. S. 100 Felling Axes are very much needed ~~by~~ Please send them by 1st Boat, will send requisition by next Boat as the Empress is just leaving—" LS, DNA, RG 393, District of Southeast Mo., Letters Received.

To Commander Henry Walke

———

Head Quarters, Dist. S. E. Mo.
Cairo, October 6th 1861

C A P T.

The services of your Gun boat being much required, I will be much obliged if you will report with her for service in the morning.

Respectfully Yours
U. S. G R A N T
Brig. Gen. Com.

To Capt. Walke U. S. N.
Comd.g G. B. Tyler
Mound City Ill.

ALS, Dr. David S. Light, Miami Beach, Fla. *O.R.* (Navy), I, xxii, 362. See letter to Commander Henry Walke, Oct. 7, 1861.

To Julia Dent Grant

———

Head Quarters, Cairo Oct. 6th/61

Dear Julia;

Father has been here and gone home I think well satisfied with his visit. I wish I could send for you to make even as short a visit as his. A longer one would be more pleasant. When I can see evrything a little more settled here I will send for you and I want you to bring Miss[1] & Jess with you. Fred. also if you feel like leting him make the campaign with me. This week I shall be quite busy. Tomorrow I am going to Cape Girardeau to review my troops there and shall continue on the same service until I get through with all under my command. This will take up all my spare time for a week.

For several days evrything has been quiet here but it may portend active movement on the part of the enemy. I always try to keep myself posted as to his movements but I am at a loss for the last few days.

Rawlins has shown me a letter from Mr. W[as]hburn,[2] written from Washington City from which it appears that he has been urging me for the place of Major General. He says he was highly gratified to find that my course had attracted the attention of the President and met with his approval. I am not a place seeker but will try and sustain myself wherever the authorities that be may place me.—Mr. Washburn has certainly acted very generously towards me and I shall feel ever greatful towards him for it, and want you to lay aside the rule of society which would require Mrs. W. to pay you the first visit and call upon her and make known the many obligations I feel to her husband. Say that I shall endeavor not to disappoint him.

Kiss all the children for me. A thousand kisses for yourself— I will send you twenty-five dollars extra to pay your Dentist's bill. Have it done by all means. I can keep you liberally supplied with funds from this out. You got of course the $300 I sent?

Ulys.

ALS, DLC-USG.

1. Ellen Grant.
2. Not found.

To Capt. Chauncey McKeever

————

Head Quarters, Dist. S. E. Mo.
Cairo, October 7th 1861

SIR:

Information which I am disposed to look upon as reliable has reached me to-day that the Confederates have been reinforced at Columbus to about 45,000. In addition to this they have a large force collected at Union City and are being reinforced evry day. —They talk boldly of making an attack upon Paducah by the 15th of this month.[1] My own impression however is that they are fortifying strongly and preparing to resist a formidable attack and have but little idea of risking anything upon a forward movement.—Jeff. Thompson and Lowe are no doubt occupying positions at Sikeston and Benton.[2] If the Cavalry here were fully armed & equiped they could be easily driven out.[3] There is no use going after them with any other ~~force~~ arm. I had a reconnoisance made to-day to within a few miles of Columbus. I enclose herewith Capt. Walke's report of it.[4]—I also have at Charleston a force of some twelvehundred, all arms. No news of an enemy passing there or having passed. This force took with them two days rations and will return to-morrow after making a reconnoisance as far as practicable in all directions.

Respectfully &c.
U. S. GRANT
Brig. Gen. Com

To Capt. Chauncy McKeever, Asst. Adj.
Gen. Western Department, St. Louis, Mo.

ALS, DNA, RG 94, War Records Office, Union Battle Reports. *O.R.*, I, iii, 199. On the same day, USG telegraphed the substance of this letter to Capt. Chauncey McKeever. "Reliable information satisfies me that no immediate attack ~~will~~ is contemplated upon Cape Girardeau; an attack contemplated on Paducah by the fifteenth (15). Send me more troops if possible & arms & accoutrements for those now here." Telegram received (punctuation added), DNA, RG 393, Dept. of the Mo., Telegrams Received; copies, *ibid.*, Western Dept., Telegrams; DLC-USG, VIA, 1. On Oct. 8, 1861, McKeever telegraphed to USG. "We have no troops here to send, telegraph to Gov Yates of Illinois to send you troops from Springfield, I will send you orders for them as soon as you give me the number required. 2000 muskets were sent to Genl. McClernand on the 4th inst." Copies, *ibid.*, V, 4, 5, 7, 8, VIA, 1; DNA, RG 393, Western Dept., Telegrams; *ibid.*, USG Hd. Qrs. Correspondence.

1. On Oct. 6, Brig. Gen. Charles F. Smith wrote to USG. "The latest news from Columbus comes thro' the Roman Catholic priest here, tho' he does not wish it whispered. Columbus is in his division of duties. He was told that the attack on this place might be looked for on or by next Thu[rs]day, the 10th, getting this from offs. & soldiers. I give the information for what it is worth. The prevalent idea is to make a feint on the front & attack on the flanks—3 columns of 7,000 each. The trees ~~in~~ all round are fast falling before our axes, rendering an advance by the roads a necessity. ~~a necessity.~~ Th~~i~~se rise in the river (18 ft.) has put me back much in several ways. The bridge is in pieces, for re-construction. A Cincinatti paper of the 2d inst. says the river had fallen there 3 inches." ALS, ICarbS.

2. On Oct. 7, Col. Joseph B. Plummer wrote to USG. "I have the honor to report that I have received information, which I believe to be reliable, that forces of the enemy came up Tuesday last, (1st inst) from below and landed at Columbus. Their numbers I have not ascertained, but would remark that they are supposed to be a part, o~~f~~r the whole of Hardee's Command. On the same day Jeff—Thompson's troops left Belmont, opposite Columbus, on boats and landed at New Madrid. On Wednesday morning they moved for S~~y~~ikeston twenty five miles from here, and have thrown forward a detachment to Benton, eighteen miles from here, which corroborates what I wrote a few hours ago. Their force consisted of about two thousand men, and are called 'Thompson's Brigade.' They are armed with Muskets, Rifles and Shot Guns." ALS, DNA, RG 393, District of Southeast Mo., Letters Received. Plummer sent exactly the same report to McKeever. *O.R.*, I, iii, 527. By Oct. 4, Brig. Gen. M. Jeff Thompson was in Sikeston, Mo., and had decided that Cape Girardeau was too strongly held to attack. On Oct. 8, he moved westward with a force of about 800 inf. and 500 cav. *Ibid.*, p. 714; *ibid.*, I, liii, 748.

3. On Oct. 10, McKeever wrote to USG. "There are no Cavalry arms and equipments on hand, I will order them to be sent to you as soon as they can be obtained." LS, DNA, RG 393, District of Southeast Mo., Letters Received.

4. See letter to Commander Henry Walke, Oct. 7, 1861.

To Capt. Chauncey McKeever

———

Head Quarters, Dist. S. E. Mo.
Cairo, October 7th 1861

CAPT. CHAUNCY MCKEEVER
A. A. GEN. WESTERN DEPT.
ST. LOUIS MO.
SIR;

Enclosed I send you the proceedings of a Board appointed by me to appraise property in Cape Girardeau taken for military purposes.[1] Having a personal knowledge of the property appropriated I most decidedly disapprove of the exorbitant estimate set by the Board. Three thousand dollars would, in my opinion, be a fare valuation of damages, and twice that sum would pay for the property outright.

Respectfully &c.
U. S. GRANT
Brig. Gen Com

ALS, DNA, RG 393, Western Dept., Letters Received.

1. On Sept. 28, 1861, a board consisting of Col. David Bayles, 11th Mo., Lt. Col. Andrew J. Babcock, 7th Ill., and 1st Lt. James E. Shields, 20th Ill., reported to USG that the value of the land, building, and landscaping of the Dittlinger brothers' property in Cape Girardeau was $8,341.58. A map enclosed with the report showed that fortifications had been erected diagonally across the five-acre property, touching one side of the house. The board recommended that the government pay either the full value of the property or pay rent of $100 monthly under an agreement to return the property "as good as found." DS, *ibid.* See letter to Julia Dent Grant, Aug. 29, 1861, note 1.

To Commander Henry Walke

Head Quarters Dist. S. E. Mo.
Cairo, October 7th 1861

CAPT.

You will proceed down the river to day with ~~the~~ gunboats Taylor[1] & Lexington for the purpose of reconnoitering the position of the enemy so far as practicable.

It has been reported to me that the enemy have a masked battery some three miles above Columbus on the Kentucky shore. I do not credit the report but it would be desirable to advance cautiously.

Yours &c.
U S GRANT
Brig. Gen Comg.

Copy, DNA, RG 45, Correspondence of Henry Walke. *O.R.* (Navy), I, xxii, 362–63. On Oct. 7, 1861, Commander Henry Walke wrote to USG. "Agreeable to your orders of this morning I proceeded down the river with the U S G B Taylor, and the 'Lexington' under Commander Stembel 'for the purpose of reconnoitreing the position of the enemy so far as practicable['] When approaching the head of Iron Bluffs we saw the rebel steamer Jeff Davis but could not get near enough to of effective service. Proceeding on 'till we came in sight of their batteries about two miles above Columbus, we opened in them and succeeded in drawing the fires of five batteries some of which proved to be mounted with rifled cannon Four of their shots passed over us, one of them coming within fifty feet of the bow. Not feeling ourselves strong enough to contend with their rifled cannon, we rounded to and returned to Cairo. When near the foot of Lucas Bend, the Lexington and Ourselves fired several shell in to Camp Belmont, from which they returned fires from their batteries, and on our return, just ~~below~~ above Norfolk we brought away two flat boats which we deliver subject to your order" ALS, Aaron J. Cooke Collection, MiU-C. *O.R.*, I, iii, 200; *O.R.* (Navy), I, xxii, 363. On Oct. 10, Maj. Gen. Leonidas Polk wrote to C. S. A. Secretary of the Navy Stephen R. Mallory. "Two of the enemy's gunboats came down to this place two days ago and opened fire on the batteries I was putting into position, shelling and throwing round shot. Their fire was returned with vigor and with such success as to cripple them both. One of them, we are informed, sank about ten miles above this, and the other was so much injured as to be obliged to be relieved of her armament." *Ibid.*, p. 793.

1. The gunboat *Tyler* was often called *Taylor*. See letter to Brig. Gen. John A. McClernand, Sept. 13, 1861, note 2.

To Maj. Robert Allen

———

Head Quarters Dist S E Mo
Cairo Oct 7th 1861

MAJOR R. ALLEN
Q. M. GEN WESTERN DEPT
ST LOUIS MO
SIR

I would respectfully but urgently request that requisitions now in your office from this command receive your early attention.—We are deficient in Clothing Transportation and Camp Equippage also have been supporting the Quartermasters Department on credit, untill with citizens here, the Government has ceased to have any credit. I would therefore urge the speedy transmission of Funds for the use of this post.

Capt Hatch Asst Qr Master having performed the duties of his office at this Post from the time it was first occupied by troops, I would reccomend that he be retained

Respectfully Yours
U. S. GRANT
Brigr Genl Com

Copies, DLC-USG, V, 4, 5, 7, 8, 79; DNA, RG 393, USG Hd. Qrs. Correspondence. Maj. Robert Allen of Ohio, USMA 1836, was appointed chief q. m., Western Dept., on Oct. 1, 1861. As asst. q. m. in the Mexican War, he had characterized USG's q. m. services as "useful." *PUSG*, 1, 107n.

To Capt. Chauncey McKeever

———

Head Qrs. S. E. Dist. Mo.
Cairo, Oct. 9, 1861.

The horses and other animals have been ordered to be turned over to the Qr. Mrs. Dept. and can be restored to their proper owners at any time, if not lawful prizes. The burning of the Steam Ferry was a wanton piece of Vandalism on the part of soldiers of Col. Oglesby's command, stationed at Norfolk, and unless the perpitrators are exposed by their comrades, the whole command should be made to suffer by stoppage of pay to at least double the amount of damages done.

Respectfully submitted for the action of the Comdg. Genl. Western Dept.

U. S. GRANT,
Brig. Genl. Comdg.

Copy, DNA, RG 393, Western Dept., Endorsements. Described as "Endorsement on report of Commissioners ordered to investigate the circumstances attending the destruction of the Steam Ferry Boat at Norfolk, Mo." On Oct.11, 1861, Capt. Chauncey McKeever returned the report to USG with his own endorsement. "General Grant will see that the amount is stopped on the next pay rolls." Copy, *ibid.*

To Capt. Chauncey McKeever

Head Quarters Dist S. E. Mo
Cairo Oct 9th 1861

CAPT CHAUNCEY McKEEVER
A. A. GENL WESTERN DEPT
ST LOUIS MO
SIR

Yesterday I visited Cape Girardeau and found that Col Plummer was working every available man upon the Fortifications and had really accomplished more in one week than would have been done under an inefficient officer in two months. At the same rate Cape Girardeau will be very completely fortified by Saturday requiring however some more heavy ordnance. I am very much in favor as a general thing of 24 pound pieces on Seige carriages instead of ponderous guns that take so much to mount and are moved from one place to another with so much labor. I never would use them except in permanent positions.

Cape Girardeau wants four.—can use six pieces—Col Plummer reports the Home Guards as of no use and not to be found when called upon. I authorized the discontinuance of all recognition of them—Also recomended—rather authorized Capt Powell[1] an efficient officer of the 20th Ill Vols who has been acting as engineer, to raise a company to manage the seige Guns. He reports that the company can be raised in two days at Cape Girardeau. This authority was given subject to the approval of the Comdr of Department.

Information here would indicate that troops are assembling ready to attack Paducah. My beleif is that the attack will not be made for the present however but should it I will give Genl Smith all the aid prudent. The fact is when I sent troops to Paducah I selected the fullest Regiments and those best armed and equipped, leaving here the raw, unarmed and ragged.—I would recomend that authority be given the Quartermaster here to purchase Horses for the use of Capt Houghtalings[2] company of Light Artillery. They can be purchased here as cheaply as at St Louis and on certificate to be paid there?

I would renew my recomendation that Huts be put up for Winter Quarters for such Garrison as it may be contemplated will occupy this place.[3]

I would further recomend for the considiration of the Comdg General whether it would not be a good plan to purchase a number of Coal Barges such as have been used for the Paducah Bridge and fit them up for Winter Quarters. They could be used for transporting troops for a southern expedition with much saving of steam power and could be made comfortable Quarters wherever landed. A full detail of the plan I would submit would take more room than I propose here. In a small way a constant supply of the essentials are being furnished the Rebels by steamers plying between here and Saint Louis. I have thought of sending a steamer to Cape Girardeau with a Guard aboard to follow each of these steamers and make every landing they do and pick up all freight landed by them.—I would state again that my information to day confirms the beleif that Cape Girardeau is only threatened by ~~Jeff~~ Thompson and Lowe—My correspondence to day with state authority does not indicate immediate reinforcement from that quarter—It will be impossible for me to furnish Genl Smith with a company of Artillery[4]

> I am Sir Very Respectfully
> Your obt Servant
> U. S. GRANT
> Brig Genl Com

Copies, DLC-USG, V, 4, 5, 7, 8, 78; DNA, RG 393, USG Hd. Qrs. Correspondence. *O.R.*, I, iii, 528–29. Also on Oct. 9, 1861, USG telegraphed to Capt. Chauncey McKeever the substance of his information. "I have had a large force some eight 8 miles beyond Charleston I am fully satisfied there is no force at present that can attack Cape Girardeau except Thompson & Lowes Col Plummer is fully prepared for thribble the force. Fortifications at Cape Girardeau in a highly defensive state" Telegram received, DNA, RG 107, Telegrams Collected (Unbound); copies, *ibid.*, RG 393, Western Dept., Telegrams; DLC-USG, VIA, 1, 2.

1. John W. Powell of Hennepin, Ill., enlisted as a private on May 8, then was promoted to 2nd lt., 20th Ill. Vols., on June 13. First detached from his regt. for engineering work on the fortifications, Powell was then authorized by USG to organize an art. co. of Mo. Home Guards. His battery was mustered in on Dec. 11 as Battery F, 2nd Ill. Light Art. William Culp Darrah, *Powell of the Colorado* (Princeton, 1951), pp. 47–52. See letter to Capt. John C. Kelton, Dec. 2, 1861.
2. Capt. Charles Houghtaling, Battery C, 1st Ill. Light Art.
3. See letter to Capt. Chauncey McKeever, Sept. 29, 1861.
4. On Oct. 9, McKeever twice telegraphed to USG about art. "Brig. Gen. Smith asks for an additional company of light artillery at Paducah. Can you not send it to him. There is not one here in the city." "There is not a single company of light artillery here fully equipped. Will see Callender about the howitzers" Copies, DLC-USG, V, 4, 5, 7, 8; DNA, RG 393, USG Hd. Qrs. Correspondence; *ibid.*, Western Dept., Telegrams.

To Brig. Gen. John A. McClernand

> Head Quarters, Dist. S. E. Mo.
> Cairo, October 9th 1861

GENERAL;

I have determined to seize a large quantity of wood corded up on the Mo. shore below here, and have given the necessary orders for boats, (and gun boats to protect them) for the expedition.

You will please detail Col. Lawler,[1] with his entire regiment, to furnish the Escort, and working party, in loading the wood. They should go armed and with one days prepared rations. Detail on board the Scott at 7 a.m. to-morrow.

> Respectfully
> Your Obt. Svt.
> U. S. GRANT
> Brig. Gen. Com

To Brig. Gen. J. A. McClernand
Comd.g Post
Cairo Ill.

ALS, McClernand Papers, IHi. On Oct. 9, 1861, USG also wrote to Commander Henry Walke at Mound City. "I would be pleased to have the services of your gunboat to morrow. Can you come down to night" Copy, DNA, RG 45, Correspondence of Henry Walke. *O.R.* (Navy), I, xxii, 365. See letter to Capt. Chauncey McKeever, Oct. 11, 1861.

1. On Oct. 10, Maj. Mason Brayman wrote for Brig. Gen. John A. McClernand to USG. "Col Lawler, with the effective force of his Regiment, has Orders to report to you, On the Scott, at Seven O'clock tomorrow morning—armed; with 20 rounds—with one days rations." DfS, McClernand Papers, IHi.

To Col. *William H. L. Wallace*

> Head Quarters, Dist. S. E. Mo.
> Cairo, October 9th 1861

COL.

Dr. Phipps represents that a greatdeel of Beer is being sold at Birds Point, much to the injury of men in hospital. You are authorized, and it will meet with my approval, to drive off evry man trading with the soldiers or place them under such restrictions as you may deem fit.

Yours &c—

U. S. GRANT

Brig. Gen. Com.

To Col. W. H. L. Wallace
Comd.g U. S. Forces
Birds Point Mo.

ALS, W. F. Whipple, Utica, Ill. John M. Phipps of Charleston, Ill., had served as 1st asst. surgeon, 8th Ill., since April 25, 1861.

To Capt. Chauncey McKeever

———

Head Quarters, Dist. S. E. Mo.
Cairo, October 11th 1861

SIR:

Since my last report I have ascertained that Thompson, with his troops, has gone West to Bloomfield or further. There is no force therefore threatning Cape Girardeau.

I sent the Gunboats Taylor & Lexington down near Columbus, to-day, not so much for the purpose of reconnoitering as to protect a steamer sent after wood belonging to Hunter[1] who is with the Southern Army.[2] About 100 cords was brought ~~in~~ up.

Respectfully

Your Obt. Svt.

U. S. GRANT

Brig. Gen. Com

To Capt. Chauncy McKeever
A. A. Gen. Western Department
St. Louis Mo.

ALS, DNA, RG 393, Western Dept., Letters Received. *O.R.*, I, iii, 531. See Commander Henry Walke to Capt. Andrew H. Foote, Oct. 12, 1861, *O.R.* (Navy), I, xxii, 366.

On Oct. 12, 1861, Col. Joseph B. Plummer wrote to Col. Joseph H. Eaton, sending a copy to USG. "I have but little to report since my last communication. Thompson and Lowe have concentrated thier forces, numbering about Three-thousand men., at a place called Spring Hill Thirty-six from here and Twelve miles this side of Bloomfield. They are represented to be suffering for the want of Provissions and living principally on Beef without Salt. Hardee is in the neighborhood of New Madrid and Pillow at Columbus. The defensive works of this are advancing rapidly towards completion, for the last eight days I have had nearly a Thousand men at work in the trenches. I recieved yesterday four additional which will be mounted and in position on Monday" LS, DNA, RG 393, District of Southeast Mo., Letters Received. On Oct. 11, Brig. Gen. M. Jeff Thompson reported from Spring Hill, Mo., that he intended to send 500 dragoons to cut the Iron Mountain Railroad and to send his inf. to Fredericktown. *O.R.*, I, iii, 223–24.

1. This may be the same Hunter whose farm is mentioned in the letter to Capt. Chauncey McKeever, Sept. 26, 1861.
2. See letter to Brig. Gen. John A. McClernand, Oct. 9, 1861.

To Brig. Gen. Jefferson C. Davis

———

Oct 11 *1861*

To Brig Gen Davis
   Can you furnish any horses if so how many
                                      Brig Genl Grant

Telegram received, DNA, RG 393, Dept. of the Mo., Telegrams Received. The reply was copied on the reverse of USG's telegram. "All our horses are in use" Col. Jefferson C. Davis of Ind., who had relieved USG at Jefferson City in Aug., 1861, was named act. brig. gen. by Maj. Gen. John C. Frémont on Sept. 21. *O.R.*, I, iii, 502. Davis officially became brig. gen. as of Dec. 18.

To Capt. Wilbur F. Brinck

———

Head Quarters Dist S. E. Mo
Cairo Oct 11th 1861

Special Order
   Capt W. F. Brinck Act ordnance officer of District will proceed to Saint Louis Mo. and attend in person to receiving

ordnance & Quartermaster stores for the use of the Artillery at this place

He will transact his business and return to this post with as little delay as possible

U. S. GRANT
Brig Genl Com

Copies, DLC-USG, V, 15, 16, 77, 82; DNA, RG 393, USG Special Orders. On Oct. 13, 1861, Capt. Wilbur F. Brinck wrote to USG. "I have the honor to inform you that it is impossible to procure the Ordnance and stores I have come here to obtain And by the advice of Col Fialia of General Fremonts staff I go up to Tipton tomorrow morning to see the General and Col Waagner Twelve Batterys of field pieces are being constructed at Cincinnati for General Fremont by immediate application I hope to secure what we need at Cairo I intend returning Tuesday" ALS, *ibid.*, District of Southeast Mo., Letters Received.

On Oct. 20, Brinck wrote to USG. "I have the honor to inform you that after a trip to Headquarters Dept of the West, and an immense amount of hard work, I can obtain one complete Battery to wit 4. six pdr's and 2 Twelve pdr Howitzers with Horses &c. Capt Callender (who sends his regards) advises that I remain here untill the Battery is ready to ship, for fear some order should be received from headquarters that he would be compelled to obey unless I should be on hand to insist upon our Battery being shiped first. The man who is on hand and the most presistant is the one who secures all he requires. It is almost to obtain an interview much less to secure supplies &c as evry nerve is being strained to supply General Fremonts army. I have all the Uniforms and will get many of the little matters very necessiry for repairs &c I have Telegraphed you this morning to know if I should remain but as yet have not received any answer" ALS, *ibid.* On Oct. 21, Brinck telegraphed to USG. "I can get one Complete battery. Am ready to return. Capt. Collender thinks I had better remain to guard against any contingencies. Shall I remain?" Telegram received (punctuation added), *ibid.*, Dept. of the Mo., Telegrams Received.

To Capt. Reuben B. Hatch

Head Quarters Dist S. E. Mo
Cairo Oct 12th 1861

CAPT

Send a Steamer to Cape Girardeau to follow the first Packet after her arrival and make all landings and seize all goods landed on the Missouri side.

Goods seized will be brought here and reported to these Head Quarters

U. S. GRANT
Brig Genl Com

Copies, DLC-USG, V, 1, 2, 3, 77; DNA, RG 393, USG Letters Sent. See letter to Capt. Chauncey McKeever, Oct. 17, 1861, note 5.

To Capt. Reuben B. Hatch

————

Head Quarters Dist S. E. Mo
Cairo Oct 12 1861

CAPT

You will procure such storage room as may be necessary for the use of our Gun Boat Fleet and assign it to Capt Perry of the Navy who has been assigned to duty here as receiving officer[1]

U. S. GRANT
Brig Genl Com

To Capt R. B. Hatch
Brigade Q. M.
Cairo Ills

Copies, DLC-USG, V, 1, 2, 3, 77; DNA, RG 393, USG Letters Sent.

1. On Oct. 5, 1861, Capt. Andrew H. Foote wrote to Commander Roger Perry ordering him to Cairo to take charge of all supplies for the gunboat flotilla. *O.R.* (Navy), I, xxii, 359–60.

To Brig. Gen. Lorenzo Thomas

————

Head Quarters Dist S. E. Mo
Cairo Oct 13th 1861

SIR

Please inform me if both Certificates of disability (made in duplicate) are sent to the Adjt Generals office

I have the honor to be
Very Respectfully
Your obt Servt
U. S. GRANT

Brig Genl L. Thomas
Washington D. C.

Telegram, copies, DLC-USG, V, 4, 5, 7, 8, 79; DNA, RG 393, USG Hd. Qrs. Correspondence. See letter to Capt. Chauncey McKeever, Oct. 17, 1861.

To Col. Amory K. Johnson

————

Head Quarters Dist S. E. Mo
Cairo Oct 13th 1861

COL

Send Sergt D Branson "H" Co 28th Regt Ill Vols as guide to a party of 20 to take a negro belonging to Mrs Unsell and bring the negro to Fort Holt quistion him and get all the information you can and report it to me.

The man will then be permitted to return home.

You are to make the detail of men

U. S. GRANT
Brig Genl Com

Col Johnson Fort Holt

Copies, DLC-USG, V, 2, 77; DNA, RG 393, USG Letters Sent. Col. Amory K. Johnson, 28th Ill.

General Orders No. 11

Head Quarters Dist S. E. Mo
Cairo Oct 14th 1861

GENERAL ORDER No 11

For the better convenience of administering the duties of this Military District this command will be Brigaded as follows, subject to such changes as may be deemed necessary in the future.

First Brigade, as now organized and Commanded by Brig Genl John A. McClernand with the addition of the 10th and 18th Illinois Regiments, Schwartzs Battery of Light Artillery and Stewarts Cavalry.

Second Brigade will be composed of Eighth Regiment Illinois Volunteers Seventh Iowa and Twenty second Illinois, Capt Hougtalings Light Artillery and five companies of second Illinois Cavalry yet to be assigned and will be under command of Col R. J. Oglesby.

Third Brigade will be composed of the Eleventh and Twentieth Illinois Regiments Second Iowa Regiment, Capt Taylors Battery of Light Artillery and Langens, Pfaffs, Burrill's, and Noleman's Cavalry and will be under command of Col W. H. L. Wallace.

Fourth Brigade Col Jno Cook commanding will be composed of the Seventh and Twentyeith Illinois Regiments, McAllisters Company of Light Artillery Delano's Cavalry and one Company of Second Illinois Regt Cavalry.

Fifth Brigade, Col Plummer commanding will be composed of the Eleventh Missouri Seventeenth Illinois and Tenth Iowa Regts. Head Quarters at Cape Girardeau

The command of the Post of Cairo including Mound City will be retained by Genl McClernand.

Brigade Commanders will make their reports immediately to these Head Quarters

By order of Brig Genl U. S. Grant Commanding

JNO. A. RAWLINS

Asst Adjt Genl

Copies, DLC-USG, V, 12, 13, 14, 80; DNA, RG 393, USG General Orders. *O.R.*, I, iii, 533–34. On Oct. 16, 1861, Brig. Gen. John A. McClernand wrote to USG. "Brigadier General John A. McClernand commandant of this Post has the pleasing and grateful duty of acknowledging the compliment paid him by your general Order No 11, attaching to his previous command, the 10th and 18th Illinois Regiments, Schwartz's Battery of Light Artillery, and Stewarts Cavalry, and trusts that the future will justify the confidence reposed in him" Copy, DNA, RG 94, Generals' Papers and Books, John A. McClernand. On Oct. 29, a member of McClernand's staff wrote to USG requesting five or six copies of the order. Copy, McClernand Papers, IHi.

To Maj. Gen. Leonidas Polk

Head Quatres, Dist. S. E. Mo.

Cairo, Oct. 14th 1861

GEN.

Yours of this date is just received. In regard to the exchange of prisoners proposed I can, of my own accord, make none. I recognize no Southern Confederacy myself but will communicate with higher authority for their views. Should I not be sustained I will find means of communicating with you.

Respectfully

Your Obt. Svt.

To Maj. Gen. Polk   U. S. GRANT

Columbus Ky.   Brig. Gen. Com.

ALS, DNA, RG 109, Documents Printed in *O.R. O.R.*, II, i, 511. On Oct. 14, 1861, Maj. Gen. Leonidas Polk wrote to USG. "I have in my camp a number of prisoners of the Federal Army, and am informed there are prisoners belonging to the Missouri State Troops in yours. I propose an exchange of these prisoners, and for that purpose send Capt Polk of the Artillery and Lieut Smith of the Infantry, both of the Confederate States Army, with a Flag of Truce, to deliver to you this communication, and to know your pleasure in regard to my proposal. The principles recognized in the Exchange of Prisoners effected on the 3d Sep between Brig Genl Pillow of the Confederate Army and Col Wallace of the U. S. Army, are those I propose as the basis of that now contemplated." LS, DNA, RG 393, District of Southeast Mo., Letters Received. *O.R.*, II, i, 511. On Oct. 14, USG telegraphed to Capt. Chauncey McKeever. "A proposition has been made this afternoon for an exchange of prisoners. The following is my reply. . . ." Telegram received, DNA, RG 107, Telegrams Collected (Unbound); copies, *ibid.*, RG 393, Western Dept., Telegrams; DLC-USG, VIA, 2. Documents relating to the Pillow-Wallace agreement to exchange prisoners are in *O.R.*, II, i, 504–10.

To Col. William H. L. Wallace

————

Head Quarters Dist S. E. Mo
Cairo Oct 14th 1861

Col

You will have to use discretion Send any force you may deem necessary

Yours &c
U. S. Grant
Brig Genl Com

To Col W. H. L. Wallace
Comdg U. S. Forces
Birds Point Mo

Copies, DLC-USG, V, 2, 77; DNA, RG 393, USG Letters Sent. On Oct. 14, 1861, Col. William H. L. Wallace wrote to USG. "I sent a party of twenty five cavalry under Lieut. Tufts of Capt. Noleman's company down on the Rushes ridge road this forenoon to observe whether the enemy were making any movements in this direction—About two o'clock this afternoon they came in collision with some 100 of the enemys cavalry—After firing some eight rounds Lieut. Tuft observed that the enemy were making an effort to outflank him & cut off his retreat—He then fell back, the enemy pursuing him about a mile—One of his men, a private in Capt. Nolemans company was killed—Another severely wounded—one horse killed and several wounded—Lieut. Tufts horse was shot under him—I have sent out a party of 60 cavalry under capt. Stewart on the Rushes ridge road & Capt. Pfaff with 30 cavalry to Norfolk—I will send you a more detailed account as soon as I can collect all the particulars" ALS, *ibid.*, RG 94, War Records Office, Union Battle Reports. *O.R.*, I, iii, 243. Wallace's report of the next day added few details. "On yesterday morning I sent Lieut. Tuft of Capt. Noleman's cavalry with 25 men of that company, southward on the Rushes Ridge road to observe whether the enemy were making any movements in that direction—About 2 o'clk P. M, when about nine miles from this point they were attacked by a body of about 100 Mississippi mounted rifles or cavalry armed with Maynard carbines, and after a sharp contest, Lieut. Tuft withdrew his party in good order—I enclose herewith a ~~copy of~~ Lieut. Tufts report—He acted with great coolness, prudence & courage & both he & the men under him are entitled to ~~the~~ high commendation for their conduct—Lieut. Tuft had his horse shot & Corporal Fletcher who was severely wounded has since died of his wound" ALS, DNA, RG 94, War Records Office, Union Battle Reports. *O.R.*, I, iii, 243. Reports of the engagement by 1st Lt. Samuel P. Tufts, 1st Ill. Cav., and Capt. F. A. Montgomery, 1st Miss. Cav., show that they place the number of their own men at 27 and 36 respectively, those of their opponents at 100 and 50. *Ibid.*, pp. 244–45.

To Brig. Gen. John A. McClernand

Head Quarters Dist S. E. Mo
Cairo October 15th 1861

GENL

Information deemed reliable having been received at these Head Quarters that a large body of troops supposed to be the Rebel Forces are encamped on the Mississippi River immediately opposite Chester.[1] You will therefore order the Gun Boat Tyler and Steamer Alex Scott with a Regiment of Infantry with sufficient number of days rations to proceed up the Mississippi River as far as Chester Illinois for the purpose of making reconnaissance Should the information prove correct they will dislodge them from their position

By order of Brig Genl Grant
JNO A RAWLINS
A. A. Genl

To Brig Genl McClernand
Commanding Post
Cairo Ills

LS, McClernand Papers, IHi. *O.R.*, I, iii, 534. On Oct. 15, 1861, Brig. Gen. John A. McClernand wrote to USG. "I have the honor to report an answer to your ~~special~~ two orders ~~No. 1086 and 1087,~~ of this date that the 27th Ill. under command of Col. Buford, has embarked on the Steamer 'Aleck Scott,' for the vicinity of Chester in execution of one of said orders and that a company ~~of~~ under command of a Captain of the 30th ~~Re~~ Ill. is ready to embark for Cape Girardeau in execution of the other." Copy, McClernand Papers, IHi. For the second order, see letter to Capt. Chauncey McKeever, Oct. 17, 1861, note 6.

1. Chester, Ill., on the Mississippi River approximately midway between Cape Girardeau and St. Louis.

To Capt. Chauncey McKeever

————

Head Quarters, Dist. S. E. Mo.
Cairo, Oct. 16th 1861.

CAPT. CHAUNCEY MCKEEVER
A. A. GEN. WESTERN DEPT.
ST. LOUIS MO.
SIR:

Two despatches from Gen. Frémont were received to-day and promptly attended to.[1] I also received a despatch from Gen. Sherman[2] stating that Hardee had affected a junction with Buckner[3] and they were threatning Louisville;[4] requesting me at the same time, in connection with Gen. Smith, to make a demonstration on Columbus. Sending troops to Cape Girardeau as I have done to-day and having out another expedition of some ten hundred men it will be a day or or two before any move could be made. I will communicate with Gen. Smith[5] and coopperate in any demonstration that may seem to recommend its self.

I have no reliable information from the enemy not already communicated.

Respectfully
Your Obt. Svt.
U. S. GRANT
Brig. Gen. Com.

ALS, DNA, RG 393, Western Dept., Letters Received. *O.R.*, I, iii, 536.

1. On Oct. 16, 1861, Capt. Chauncey McKeever twice telegraphed to USG by order of Maj. Gen. John C. Frémont. "Jeff Thompson with between two & three thousand men is at Farmington twenty miles east of Ironton. Send as large a force as you can from Cape Girardeau in the direction of Ironton or Pilot Knob to cut off his retreat into Arkansas." "Send one or two squadrons of cavalry and one or two sections of light artillery to Cape Girardeau, to the support of the movement against Thompson." Copies, DLC-USG, V, 4, 5, 7, 8; DNA, RG 94, War Records Office, Union Battle Reports; *ibid.*, RG 393, USG Hd. Qrs. Cor-

respondence; *ibid.*, Western Dept., Telegrams. *O.R.*, I, iii, 203. Copies (misdated Oct. 18), DLC-USG, V, 4, 5, 7, 8; DNA, RG 393, USG Hd. Qrs. Correspondence. On the same day, USG telegraphed to McKeever. "Your first & Second dispatch received in my order in ~~obedle~~ obedience to your first ~~Despa~~ I ordered all you require in your ~~Second~~ first & Second" Telegram received, *ibid.*, Western Dept., Letters Received; copies, *ibid.*, Telegrams; DLC-USG, VIA, 1.

2. Brig. Gen. William T. Sherman of Ohio, USMA 1840, was then commanding the Dept. of the Cumberland. On Oct. 16, Sherman telegraphed to USG. "I am Satisfied that Hardee is now with Buckner in front of Louisville Cannot you Reinforce Smith and threaten Columbus" Telegram received, DNA, RG 393, Dept. of the Mo., Telegrams Received.

3. C. S. A. Brig. Gen. Simon B. Buckner of Ky., USMA 1844, then in command of the Central Div. of Ky., Dept. No. 2, with hd. qrs. at Bowling Green, Ky.

4. Brig. Gen. William J. Hardee arrived at Bowling Green on Oct. 11 in advance of his command. *O.R.*, I, iv, 444–45. On Oct. 17, Gen. Albert Sidney Johnston estimated his force at Bowling Green at 12,000 men. *Ibid.*, p. 454. Confederate correspondence indicates that Buckner and Hardee were concentrating in anticipation of a Union attack and had no plans to attack Louisville.

5. See following letter.

To Brig. Gen. Charles F. Smith

Head Quarters Dist S. E. Mo
Cairo Oct 16th 1861

GENL C. F. SMITH
COMDG U. S. FORCES
PADUCAH KY
DEAR SIR

I sent you to day a copy of a dispatch received from Genl Sherman. If you have any plan to propose I am ready to cooperate to the extent of my limited means. I had to send off quite an expedition to the neighborhood of Ironton to day, by orders from Hd. Qrs Western Department and have another expedition out at the same time. Five Thousand is the greatest number of men I could start out with.

Respectfully
Your obt Servt
U. S. GRANT
Brig Genl Com

Copies, DLC-USG, V, 1, 2, 3, 79; DNA, RG 393, USG Letters Sent. *O.R.*, I, iii, 536. See preceding letter.

To Col. Joseph B. Plummer

———

Head Quarters Dist S. E. Mo
Cairo Oct 16th 1861

Col

A dispatch just received from Department Head Quarters, informs me that Jeff Thompson with between 2 & 3000 men is at Farmington Mo and directs that I send such force as can be spared from Cape Girardeau to cut off his retreat.[1] I send you in addition to the force now under your command one Regiment of Infantry 1 squadron of Cavalry & one section of Artillery.[2] With this force and the able bodied men of two other Regiments it will give you a force sufficient to meet Thompson with, and leave sufficient force at the Cape.

The expedition should be moved with all dispatch taking as many days rations as you can find transportation for. Should it become necessary you are authorized to press into the service of the U. States such private teams as the good of the service may require.

~~By order of Brig Genl~~   U. S. Grant
                                     Brig Genl Com

To Col Plummer
Comdg Forces,
Cape Girardeau Mo

Copies, DLC-USG, V, 1, 2, 3, 77; DNA, RG 94, War Records Office, Union Battle Reports; *ibid.*, RG 393, USG Letters Sent. *O.R.*, I, iii, 204. On Oct. 16, 1861, Col. Joseph B. Plummer wrote to Capt. John A. Rawlins. "I have the honor to report that the Steamer Alex Scott arrived here this evening with the 27th Regt. Ills Vols (Col Buford) on board together with the Gun Boat New Era, and that I reinforced them with two Companies of the 17th Regt Ills Vols which I sent up upon the Steamer Luella. They all left here at 'Retreat.' I received this morning a letter dated yesterday from the Hon J. W. Noell M. C—written at Chester Ills in which he reports Sixteen hundred of the Enemy at Perryville and the Home Guards retreating towards the river, without ammunition. From another source it is reported that that Thompson and Lowe are both at Dallas with about two thousand men which I am inclined to believe correct" LS, DNA, District of Southeast Mo., Letters Received.

    1. See letter to Capt. Chauncey McKeever, Oct. 16, 1861, note 1.

    2. On Oct. 16, Capt. William S. Hillyer wrote to Col. C. Carroll Marsh. "You will proceed with your Regiment and the Artillery and Cavalry detailed from Birds Point to Cape Girardeau & report to Col Plummer comdg as on duty to aid the expedition being fitted out from that place.—When the purposes of the Expedition ~~is~~ are accomplished and the force returned to Cape Girardeau you will then return with your Regiment & the Artillery & Cavalry attached to Birds Point without unnecessary delay." Copies, DLC-USG, V, 1, 2, 3, 77; DNA, RG 393, USG Letters Sent. On Oct. 16, Hillyer also wrote to George W. Graham. "You will furnish as soon as possible Steamboat transportation for ~~one~~ a Section of Artillery two companies of Cavalry and a Regiment of Infantry and all the Teams belonging to them & report to these Head Quarters" Copies, *ibid.* On the same day, Hillyer wrote twice to Col. William H. L. Wallace. "You will detail a Section of Taylors Battery, two companies of cavalry and Marshs 20th Ill Regt Infantry to proceed without delay to Cape Girardeau together with all thir Camp and Garrison Equippage baggage and Teams. Transportation to Cape Girardeau will be furnished at Birds Point as soon as possible.—they will take with them all the rations issued to them." "You will send Capt Stewarts company as one of the two Cavalry companies to Cape Girardeau. Capt Stewart is well acquainted with the country about Cape Girardeau and therefore he is designated" Copies, *ibid.* Also on Oct. 16, Wallace wrote to his wife. "We had a grand review today—Genl. Grant was to have reviewed us & I had the whole force in line at 10½ o'clk & waited an hour for the Genl—He then sent word that the sevices would be postponed till further orders—But I determined that the review should go on & I reviewed them myself—It was a fine sight—Six regiments of infantry, five companies of Cavalry & a light battery of six guns—It was as fine a column as I ever saw—The line was near a mile long—All were highly pleased with the display—Just at the close of the review I received an order to send the 20th Regt. (Col. Marsh'es) a section of Taylors battery & two companies of Cavalry up the river to Cape Girardeau—They are now going on board the boats—So *my brigade* is badly broken up already—" ALS, Wallace-Dickey Papers, IHi. On Oct. 16, Rawlins wrote to Capt. Reuben B. Hatch. "You will furnish and deliver to the bearer for Col C. C. Marsh whose Regiment is under marching orders as forage for his Teams Seven Bales of Hay and one Thousand pounds of oats immediately." Copies, DLC-USG, V, 2, 77; DNA, RG 393, USG Letters Sent. On Oct. 16, Hatch wrote to USG. "It will be impossible for us to comply with your order for I have not hay enough to feed all the stock full rations that are located here. I am hourly expecting hay from St Louis and from up the Ohio but have very little now." ALS, *ibid.*, District of Southeast Mo., Letters Received.

To Capt. Chauncey McKeever

———

Head Quarters, Dist. S. E. Mo
Cairo, October 17th 1861

CAPT.

In pursuance of telegraphic instructions from the Comd.g Gen. I sent from here Col. Marsh's regiment of Ill. Vols. three companies of Cavalry, and a section of Artillery, to be reinforced by two regiments from Cape Girardeau to go in pursuit of Thompson, and such of the rebel army as have been committing depridations on the Iron Mountain railroad.[1]

There is great difficulty in procuring storage here for Com.y & Qr. Mr. stores particularly since the fleet of Gunboats have commenced making preparations for fitting out.[2] I have directed the employment of a very large Wharf boat, capable of storing 2500 tons, subject to the approval of the Department Commander. This accomodation, it now seems, the Gunboat Fleet want. I ordered it more particularly for the Com.y & Ordnance departments. A great proportion of the rations issued from here, going by water to the different posts, an immense labor is saved, in hawling, by storage upon the water. I would ask if storage for the Gunboat Fleet is to be furnished by the Quartermasters department, or is Capt. Perry, Navy Reciving Officer here to furnish this accomodation, out of a different appropriation.

It is highly necessary, in view of possible high water, to revette the outer embankments of Fort Prentiss to prevent them from washing away.[3] There is no money in the Engineer Dept. to make the purchase of material with which to do it. Shall I order the Quartermaster to purchase the necessary material? The labor can be furnished by detail.

In the matter of signing discharges on Surgeons certificates I examined the Regulations well and come fully to the conclution that now that Gen. Fremont was in the field, I might regard myself as commanding an Army in the field also, and therefore be entitled to sign such discharges. Then too many of the cases coming before me are of such a nature that the applicants should not be detained a single day.

I would ask as to my authority to grant sick leaves; also if I have the authority to send officers or men on recruiting service to fill up companies here.

For the last few days the reports I get from the enemy are so contridictory that I feel but little like reporting. I am satisfied however that Hardee with five regiments has joined Buckner:[4] Also that a large force have crossed to the Mo. shore. This latter chiefly I think to gather the large crop of corn now maturing.— There has been added lately to the works at Columbus a Casemate Battery.

Several days ago I ordered a Steamer to Cape Girardeau to follow the first St. Louis Steamer and make all her landings below that point and seize all goods landed.[5] My orders were exceeded by seizing the Steamer also but she was released promptly on being brought into port. A copy of the report of the officer Commanding, marked "A" is enclosed.[6] Are these goods to be retained? I would again suggest that trade with S. E. Mo. should be cut off. The enemy are enabled to get valuable supplies by that route, and all the information in possession of Citizens of St. Louis.

Paper marked "B" contains a list of articles seized in the same manner landed by the Steamer Arrago.[7]

I would suggest that if consistent with the views of the Commanding General I would like to visit St. Louis and Springfield, strictly on business for this Command. I have frequently reported our deficincy in many of the necessaries to a complete ~~outfitt~~ outfit, and want to give my best efforts to remedy the evil.

I am Sir, respectfully
Your Obt. Svt.
U. S. GRANT
Brig. Gen Com

To Capt. Chauncey McKeever
A. A. Gen. Western Department
St. Louis, Mo.

ALS, DNA, RG 393, Western Dept., Letters Received. *O.R.*, I, iii, 536–37. On Oct. 21, 1861, Capt. Chauncey McKeever replied to USG. "In reply to yours of the 17th inst. you are informed, that your employment of a Wharfboat for storage purposes is approved by the Commanding General; and that you are authorized to order the Quartermaster to furnish the necessary storage for the Gunboat Fleet. You will also order the Quartermaster to purchase the necessary materials for the outer embankments of Fort Prentiss. You are authorized to visit St Louis and Springfield, whenever in your opinion the state of affairs may permit your absence. The War Department has decided, that no charges are valid unless ordered by the Department Commander, & upon that decision Deputy Paymaster General Andrews has ordered the Paymasters not to pay soldiers discharged on Surgeons certificates of disability, unless endorsed by the General Commanding the Department, or by his order. The Major General Commanding has decided, that no officer under his command shall grant leaves of absence (sick leaves not excepted) to exceed seven days. With regard to recruiting, all orders detailing recruiting parties must be sent to these Headquarters for approval." LS, DNA, RG 393, District of Southeast Mo., Letters Received; copy, McClernand Papers, IHi.

1. See preceding letter.
2. On Oct. 17, USG also telegraphed to McKeever about this matter. "The demand created here for Storage Room by Having to receive the amount &c for the Gunboats now building make our present resources entirely inadequate under existing orders, I do not feel authorized to order store houses built without authority from Head Quarters, what is to be done." Copies, DNA, RG 393, Western Dept., Telegrams; DLC-USG, VIA, 2. On Oct. 17, McKeever replied to USG. "Have storehouses built at once." Copies, DNA, RG 393, USG Hd. Qrs. Correspondence; *ibid.*, Western Dept., Telegrams; DLC-USG, V, 4, 5, 7, 8. On Oct. 13, Capt. Andrew H. Foote wrote to Maj. Gen. John C. Frémont. "I am informed that the Wharf Boat 'Graham' lying at Cairo, which I had supposed would be appropriated as a receiving vessel for our Ordnance and other stores, has been assigned to the Commissary Dept by General Grant. As this may embarass us at Cairo, may I ask of you that some directions may be given, by which room sufficient in that Boat (Graham's Boat) may be reserved for our stores—which would occupy one half of the Boat itself." ALS, DNA, RG 393, Western Dept., Letters Received. On Oct. 16, Foote telegraphed to Commander Roger Perry. "Say to Gen Grant, that the 'Montgomery will not answer for our stores and that I hope he will let us have the wharfboat Graham as the Commissary can be accommodated on shore better than we can be. Have the articles and stores contracted for, well examined, and send me a list of articles received." Copy, *ibid.*, Telegrams. *O.R.* (Navy), I, xxii, 369. On Oct. 17, Perry telegraphed to Foote. "Genl Grant states that he has all available storage & store occupied give us the wharf boat would oblige him to place all Commissary store on the wharf ~~boat~~ unprotected from the weather are the ten rifled Cannons intended for us" Telegram received, DNA, RG 45, Area 5. *O.R.* (Navy), I, xxii, 370. On Oct. 18, Foote replied to Perry. "I have received your telegram of yesterday, stating that General Grant says that all available storage on shore is occupied, and that if he should give us the wharf boat the commissary stores must be turned out on the wharf unprotected. In reply I have to inform you that I have written to General Frémont, and referred the matter to his decision. We must have our stores afloat,

and the steamer *Montgomery*, chartered by General Grant, is considered unsafe as a depot for that purpose. We ought to have every facility rendered us to equip with dispatch our boats at Cairo, which can not be done unless we have the *Graham*, wharf boat, as originally intended. I make the statement, that you may show it to General Grant, and thus relieve myself from the responsibility of any detention in fitting out the gunboats at Cairo, so far as it may occur in consequence of being deprived of the boat originally intended for that purpose." *Ibid.*, p. 370. See letter to Capt. Reuben B. Hatch, Oct. 19, 1861, and telegram to Capt. Chauncey McKeever, Oct. 20, 1861.

3. Fort Prentiss was located at the south end of Cairo, at the confluence of the Ohio and Mississippi rivers. See letter to Maj. Joseph D. Webster, Nov. 2, 1861.

4. See letter to Capt. Chauncey McKeever, Oct. 16, 1861, note 4.

5. See letter to Capt. Reuben B. Hatch, Oct. 12, 1861. On Oct. 14, Capt. John A. Rawlins wrote to Brig. Gen. John A. McClernand. "You will please detail one officer and twenty men to go aboard the Scott by 12 o.clock to day. They will take one days rations with them. In the absence of Authority it is my determination to break up trade with S. E. Mo and the object is that the Scott shall follow St Louis Steamers from Cape Girardeau down, making all their landings and seizing all goods so landed. You will please instruct the officer conducting the expedition of his duties. This detail is intended to continue untill further orders taking one days rations with them each trip" Copies, DLC-USG, V, 1, 2, 3, 77; DNA, RG 393, USG Letters Sent. On Oct. 15, Rawlins again wrote to McClernand. "The Steamer Terry is in waiting for the detail of men in pursuance of Special Order of date the 14th October inst. You will please order them immediately, if not already done." LS, McClernand Papers, IHi.

6. On Oct. 17, McClernand wrote to USG. "I have the honor to transmit to you the Report of Capt Johnson 30th Ill. Reg. of the 2d Expedition to Cape Girardeau in pursuance of your orders—The goods taken by Capt. Johnson are turned over to Capt. Hatch Post Qr Master to await further orders—No Expedition went out last night to Cape Girardeau by reason of dispatches recd by Commodore Graham that no boats had left St. Louis—What disposition shall I make of the goods taken by Capt Johnson?" LS, DNA, RG 393, Western Dept., Letters Received; McClernand Papers, IHi. On Oct. 17, Rawlins replied to McClernand's letter. "I am instructed by the Brig. Gen. commdg. to say, Your communications of the 15th & 17th inst. accompanying which were the Reports of Capt's R. S. Moore, and A. H. Johnson of their respective expeditions to Cape Girardeau under orders issued by you, in pursuance of orders of date the 14th inst from these Head Quarters, were duly received. The goods taken by them will be turned over by you to the Quarter Master of the Post, for storage until instructions are received from the Department of the West, where the said Reports will be forwarded" ALS, *ibid.*

7. The list of articles was followed by a note written by McClernand. "Those of the above articles, purporting to have been landed at Santa Fe Illinois, I have ordered to be reshipped to that place, and there put off subject to the order of their owners. The balance I have ordered Capt R B Hatch to take and safely keep subject to further orders—Will you please direct what shall be done with them?" AES, DNA, RG 393, Western Dept., Letters Received.

To Capt. Chauncey McKeever

Head Quarters Dist S. E. Mo
Cairo Oct 17th 1861

SIR

In obedience of instructions received from Head Quarters Dept of the West of date October 2d 1861,[1] I herewith enclose you a list of Officers for the Military Commission Viz:

Col W. H. L. Wallace 11th Ills Vols, Col J. M. Tuttle 2d Iowa Vols, Lt Col Frank Rhoads 8th Ill Vols, Major Rice 7th Iowa Vols, Capt J. Wetzel 8th Ill Vols, Capt Wm. H. Harvey 8th Ill Vols and Capt C. T. Hotchkiss

I would designate Capt C. T. Hotchkiss as Judge Advocate. And would suggest Friday the 26th inst and Birds Point Mo as the time and place for said Commission to meet.

Very Respectfully
Your Obedient Servt
U. S. GRANT
Brig Genl Comdg

To Capt Chauncey McKeever
Asst Adjt General
Saint Louis, Mo

LS, DNA, RG 393, Western Dept., Letters Received. At the same time, Capt. John A. Rawlins prepared special orders appointing the military commission which was forwarded to Capt. Chauncey McKeever. Copy, DLC-USG, V, 77. On Oct. 21, McKeever issued special orders authorizing the commission USG requested. Copy, *ibid.*, 81.

1. See letter to Capt. Chauncey McKeever, Sept. 29, 1861, note 1. For the business of the commission, see letter to Brig. Gen. John A. McClernand, Sept. 23, 1861.

To Capt. Chauncey McKeever

Head Quarters Dist. S. E. Mo
Cairo Oct. 17th 1861

CAPT.

Your communication of date the 16th inst. enclosing, Certificate of Disability, of Wm Estelle & calling my attention to Paragraph 159 General Army Regulations,[1] was received today, and in answer thereto I would state, that in the absence of the Major General Commanding the Department from Head Quarters in Command of an Army in the field, I construe the Paragraph referred to as authorising me to grant discharges on Certificates of disability, respectfully deferring to your decision I shall in future however forward them to Department Head Quarters, unless otherwise instructed.

Enclosed you will find a number of Certificates,[2] endorsed and ordered to be discharged, also the discharges mentioned in Par. 165 revised Army Regulations[3] upon which is also made the same endorsement as upon the Certificates of disability in pursuance of requirement of General Order No. 83[4] issued from the Adjutants Generals Office, but which of course was not intended to be delivered to the soldier until they had been filled up and completed by the proper Officer.

None of said Certificates of disability or discharges had been sent from these Head Quarters when your communication was received, they are therefore respectfully forwarded to Department Head Quarters of the West.

Your Obedient Servant
U. S. GRANT
Brig. Gen. Comdg.

To. Capt. Chauncey McKeever
Asst. Adjt. General
Western Department
St. Louis Mo.

LS, DNA, RG 393, Western Dept., Letters Received. On Oct. 17, 1861, Capt. William McMichael wrote to USG. "The resignation of the 1st Lieut. of Company "G." 20th Illinois Volunteers, would have been accepted, but it was impossible to decipher his name; and upon examination of the monthly return for September, of that regiment, it appears there no Lieutenants in Company "G." Please furnish the information necessary to have his resignation accepted." Copy, *ibid.*, Letters Sent.

1. On Oct. 14, Capt. Chauncey McKeever wrote to USG. "The Certificates of Disability in the case of Private William Estelle, Co. D, 2nd. Ill. Vols. are herewith returned. Your attention is respectfully called to paragraph 159 General Regulations. The Major General Comdg. the Department is alone authorized to grant discharges on certificates of disability." LS, *ibid.*, District of Southeast Mo., Letters Received.

2. Not found.

3. "Blank discharges on parchment will be furnished from the Adjutant-General's office. No discharge shall be made in duplicate, nor any certificate given in lieu of a discharge."

4. "Hereafter, when certificates of disability, in the case of a volunteer, are forwarded to the Commander having authority to grant his discharge, they will be accompanied by the blank referred to in par. 165, Revised Regulations, on which the discharge from service is finally made. And the said Commander will endorse thereon the same orders that he gives upon the certificate of disability. By this means the discharge, when complete, will carry with it the evidence of its authenticity, and the necessity for investigation on the part of the Pay Department will be removed."

To Col. Friedrich Hecker

————

[*Oct. 17, 1861*]

Since I have been in service I have probably commanded as many different regiments as any other officer of my grade, in the service and I am free to say without flattery to you that but few have come under my control that I regarded as so efficient as the one commanded by yourself. I regard the efficiency of your regiment as due to your untiring exertions and that you was to some extent thwarted by the resistence and insubordination of some of your officers. That your desire to rid the regiment of these officers looked exclusively to the good of the service. I was really in hopes that you might be sustained and that other regimental commanders might profit by your example.

I have seen however that by a recent act of Congress means have been provided for getting rid of the class of officers discharged by order from your Regiment.

Quoted in a letter from Caspar Butz to Ill. AG Thomas S. Mather, Nov. 2, 1861. ALS, MoSHi. Caspar Butz, a German revolutionary who came to the U. S. in 1849, was a Chicagoan prominent in the early Republican Party, but best known for his poetry written in German. Butz's letter, dated from "Heckers Farm near Lebanon," was probably written with USG's letter before him.

To Capt. Reuben B. Hatch

Head Quarters Dist S. E. Mo
Cairo October 17th 1861

CAPT

In accordance with instructions received from Head Quarters Western Department you are directed to cause to be built such storehouses as may be required for the Quartermasters and Subsistence Department at this post.

Details of Labourers will be furnished from the command here.

Materials necessary you will procure by purchase or otherwise communicating to Maj Allen Cheif Quarter Master of the Department the substance of your order and asking for any further instructions he may have

U. S. GRANT
Brig Genl Com

To Capt R. B. Hatch A. Q. M.
Cairo

Copies, DLC-USG, V, 1, 2, 3, 77; DNA, RG 393, USG Letters Sent. See letter to Capt. Chauncey McKeever, Oct. 17, 1861, note 2.

To Capt. Chauncey McKeever

———

By Telegraph from Cairo Oct 18th *1861*
To Capt McKeever

I have reliable information that Thompson & Lowe have less than Three Thousand 3000 men[1] I have sent force Through to Drive them from their Haunt It would not be prudent to send more from here

U. S. Grant

Telegram received, DNA, RG 107, Telegrams Collected (Unbound); copies, *ibid.*, RG 393, Western Dept., Telegrams; DLC-USG, VIA, 2. *O.R.*, I, iii, 204. On Oct. 17, 1861, Capt. Chauncey McKeever twice telegraphed to USG. "Col. Carlin has been driven back towards Pilot Knob by Jeff Thompson, who is reported to have five thousand men and four pieces of artillery I have sent two regiments of infantry and a battery of light artillery from here to reenforce him. Send additional force from Cairo or Cape Girardeau, if it can be done with safety." "I have just received a dispatch from Pilot Knob stating that the enemy is entrenched at a point half a mile north of Fredericktown with four pieces of cannon." Copies, DLC-USG, V, 4, 5, 7, 8; DNA, RG 393, USG Hd. Qrs. Correspondence; *ibid.*, Western Dept., Telegrams. The first of the telegrams is misdated Oct. 18 in *O.R.*, I, iii, 203. On Oct. 17, Brig. Gen. M. Jeff Thompson brought his cav., which had destroyed a bridge on the Iron Mountain Railroad, together with his inf. at Fredericktown, planning to remain "until the enemy discovers my weakness." *Ibid.*, pp. 224–26.

1. On Oct. 23, Thompson estimated his force at 2,000 men. *Ibid.*, p. 230. See also Jay Monaghan, *Swamp Fox of the Confederacy: The Life and Military Services of M. Jeff Thompson* (Tuscaloosa, 1956), p. 41.

To Capt. Chauncey McKeever

———

Head Quarters, Dist. S. E. Mo.
Cairo, October 18th 1861

Captain,

By a secret Agt. sent by me to Columbus and New Madrid I have confirmation of the report that Hardee, with about 5000 men, has joined Buckner.[1] The same Agt. reports that Jeff.

Thompson went North to join his force with Lowe's and attack Ironton.—At Columbus a new Casemat Battery has been erected, a new 84 pound rifled gun brought to the upper end of the city, and a chain brought up to throw across the river to obstruct navigation. In view of these facts I ordered a reconnoisance with Gun boat to-day. Enclosed I send you report of the Commander.[2]

Whilst at New Madrid the same Agt. learned from Gen. Watkins,[3] and others, that the Steamers Arrago[4] & Lake City are regularly in the employ of the South. Passengers, packages, and evrything wanted South are sent aboard by St. Louis Agts. received without the authority of the Provost Marshall or Collector, shipped to Prices Landing,[5] and there meet Agts, to conduct them to their destination.

I would recommend that all boats other than those owned, or chartered, by Government be prohibited from ~~traveling~~ navigating below St. Louis. Let these be authorized to carry all legal freights, mails, passengers &c. and Government receive the benefit.

In my report of last evening I expressed the desire to be allowed to visit St. Louis & Springfield on business connected with this Command. I now withdraw the request. The journey could not be performed, leaving any time for the transaction of business, under four days. I do not deem it prudent to be absent for this length of time.

> I am Sir, very respectfully
> Your Obt. Svt.
> U. S. GRANT
> Brig. Gen. Com

To Capt. Chauncey McKeever
A. A. Gen. Western Department
St. Louis Mo.

ALS, DNA, RG 393, Western Dept., Letters Received. *O.R.*, I, iii, 248.

1. See letter to Capt. Chauncey McKeever, Oct. 16, 1861, note 4.
2. On Oct. 18, 1861, Commander Henry Walke wrote to USG. "Agreeable to your verbal instructions of this morning I proceeded down the Mississippi to

reconnoitre. When near the Iron Banks I threw a shell over the opposite point, rounded to, threw one shell each in Beckwiths and Hunters Cornfields. Could not discover any indication of the presence of the rebels, or any change of position on their part, since our last reconnoisance" LS, DNA, RG 393, Western Dept., Letters Received. *O.R.* (Navy), I, xxii, 373. On Oct. 19, Walke wrote to Capt. Andrew H. Foote. "Yesterday morning, at the request of Gen Grant I made a reconnoisance down the Mississippi as far as Beckwiths Farm, fired one shell over the point opposite the Iron Banks, rounded to, fired one shell each in Beckwiths and Hunters cornfields and returned. The Genl was apprehensive that the Rebels were moving up the river, but I saw no indications of a change of position, since my last reconnoisance. Commander Porter accompanied me and on my return to Cairo gave me a written order to proceed to New Caledonia, up the Ohio, and take the hull of a new steamer being built there and bring her to Cairo. I did so, but she was in a sinking condition by the time I landed her at the wharf boat, her hull not being sufficiently caulked, to prevent her taking in water. I turned her over to Gen Grant. We reached Cairo about 7½ o'clock. I would like to enlarge the two bow ports to give our guns a wider range, as they are, at present, it would be impossible to fire directly ahead I saw Gen Grant this morning, and he expressed himself well pleased with our reconnoisance yesterday." LS, DNA, RG 45, Area 5. *O.R.* (Navy), I, xxii, 372–73.

3. Brig. Gen. N. W. Watkins of Jackson, Mo., Mo. State Guard, preceded M. Jeff Thompson in command in southeast Mo. By the end of 1861, Watkins wanted to return quietly to his home. *O.R.*, II, i, 148–49, 154, 159–60, 163, 168–69.

4. On Oct. 20, Brig. Gen. John A. McClernand wrote to USG. "Captain J. A. Callicott of Company "C" 29th Regiment of Illinois Volunteers returned yesterday, with his expedition embarked on the previous day for Cape Girardeau. He reports that he followed the Steamer 'Arago' from that place to this, but that she put out no freight on the way. No other downward Steamers were seen by him. So soon as I shall have received Col. Buford's report as respect the expedition under his charge to the vicinity of Chester; I will communicate the result." Copy, McClernand Papers, IHi.

5. Price's Landing, Mo., on the Mississippi River about halfway between Cape Girardeau and Cairo.

To Col. Joseph B. Plummer

Cairo, Ill., October 18, 1861.

COL. J. B. PLUMMER,
COMMANDING EXPEDITION, U. S. FORCES, S. E. MISSOURI:
COLONEL:

Colonel Buford[1] has just returned from his expedition up the river, and reports that you had been informed that General Hardee was at Greenville, with a force of 5.000 men. Hardee has not been in Greenville for three or four weeks. He has been in Columbus, Ky., until quite lately, and is now with Buckner, General Sherman informs me,[2] threatening Louisville.

I am satisfied that you can have no force to contend against but Thompson's and Lowe's. I feel but little confidence in your even seeing them, but information just received from Saint Louis reports Thompson as fortifying Fredericktown.[3] You will, therefore, march upon that place, unless you should receive such information on your march as to indicate a different locality for the ubiquitous individual.

It is desirable to drive out all armed bodies now threatening the Iron Mountain Railroad, and destroy them if possible.

Having all confidence in your skill and discretion, I do not want to cripple you by instructions, but simply give you the objects of the expedition and leave you to execute them. It is desirable, however, that you should communicate with the commanding officer at Pilot Knob, and return as soon as you may feel that point secure. It is not necessary that you should march your force in for that purpose, but simply communicate by letter from Fredericktown or such point as you may make in the expedition.

Yours, truly,
U. S. GRANT,
Brigadier-General, Commanding.

Copies, DLC-USG, V, 1, 2, 3, 79; DNA, RG 94, War Records Office, Union Battle Reports; *ibid.*, RG 393, USG Letters Sent. *O.R.*, I, iii, 204–5. With this letter USG sent a letter to the officer commanding at Cape Girardeau. "You will cause to be furnished to the bearer a horse saddle, and bridle without delay The bearer is in my employ bearer of important dispatches to Col Plummer which you may require him to show as a proof of him being the right man" Copies, DLC-USG, V, 1, 2, 77; DNA, RG 393, USG Letters Sent.

1. Col. Napoleon B. Buford of Ill., USMA 1827, 27th Ill.
2. See letter to Capt. Chauncey McKeever, Oct. 16, 1861, note 2.
3. See telegram to Capt. Chauncey McKeever, Oct. 18, 1861.

To Capt. Chauncey McKeever

———

By Telegraph from Cairo [*Oct.*] 19 *1861*
To Capt. C. McKeever
AAG
    Wells Just from Columbus represents Hardee is returned &
Crossed to Belmont. Pillow left last night with Seven Thousand
7000 men for Paducah. Reinforcements arrived last night from
Memphis. I do not give full credit—
                                                U. S. Grant

Telegram received (punctuation added), DNA, RG 107, Telegrams Collected
(Unbound); copies, *ibid.*, RG 393, Western Dept., Telegrams; DLC-USG, VIA,
2. None of this information can be verified.

To Capt. Chauncey McKeever

———

                                    Head Quarters, Dist. S. E. Mo.
                                        Cairo, October 19th 1861
    Refered to Hd Qrs. Western Department. I would recom-
mend the plan proposed or els the establishment of an express
from Jonesboro Ill. to Cape Girardeau and sending the Mail by
that route.
                                                U. S. Grant
                                                Brig. Gen. Com.

AES, McClernand Papers, IHi. Written on a letter of Col. Joseph B. Plummer to
Capt. John A. Rawlins, Oct. 13, 1861. "I beg leave to suggest for the consideration of the Commanding General the propriety of improving our mail facilities
between this point and St Louis (Also Cairo). Their are at present put up at this
point but two mails per week, and transmitted by the regular Mail Boats. Letters
are forwarded by the Government transports and occasionaly by other boats. But
the latter mode I do not consider safe. By placing compotent persons, detailed
from this Command, and duly sworn, Upon the Transports and such other boats as
may be ~~suited~~ selected for the purpose, there might be established a Daily Mail

between the points named, provided the Post Masters at St Louis and Cairo would cooperate in the arrangment. The additional Expense to the Government would be about sixteen dollars pr week, and the advantage to the service would be very great" LS, *ibid.* On Oct. 21, McKeever endorsed the letter. "Brig. Genl. Grant will direct the Quartermaster to establish from Jonesboro Ills to Cape Girardeau a daily express" AES, *ibid.* A copy of Plummer's letter, addressed to USG, is in DNA, RG 393, Post of Cape Girardeau, Letters Sent.

To Capt. Reuben B. Hatch

———

Head Quarters Dist S. E. Mo
Cairo Oct 19th 1861

CAPT

Having received orders from Head Quarters Department of the West to turn over to the Navy the Graham Wharf Boat you are required to furnish storage for the Commissary Stores, and ordnance also should they require it.

Yours &c
U. S. GRANT
Brig Genl Com

To Capt R. B. Hatch
Brigade & Post Qr. M.
Cairo Ills

Copies, DLC-USG, V, 1, 2, 3, 77; DNA, RG 393, USG Letters Sent. On Oct. 18, 1861, Capt. Chauncey McKeever telegraphed to USG. "The General commanding directs that you turn over to Captain A. H. Foote, U. S. Navy the Wharf Boat 'Graham' lying at Cairo for such use as he may think proper to make of it" Copies, DLC-USG, V, 4, 5, 7, 8, 81, VIA, 2; DNA, RG 393, Dept. of the Mo., Letters Sent; *ibid.*, USG Hd. Qrs. Correspondence. See letter to Capt. Chauncey McKeever, Oct. 17, 1861.

To Brig. Gen. Lorenzo Thomas

Head Quarters, Dist. S. E. Mo.
Cairo, October 20th 1861

Gen. L. Thomas
Adj. Gen. U. S. A.
Washington D. C.
Sir;

I would respectfully represent to the Sec. of War, and President, that the duties of Commissary of Subsistence has been performed, at this post, from about its first occupancy by three months troops, to the present time, by Reuben C. Rutherford, who, until early in this month, was Reg.l Qr. Mr. of one of the Regiments stationed here. Since that time Mr. Rutherford has continued to perform the duties without a commission.

The duties of the position are arduous, and somewhat intricate, having to supply so many different posts, and they continuously changing.—Since I have been in command of this Military Dstrict I can answer for it that he has entirely supervised his whole business, without the intervention of a Head Clerk upon whom he has become dependent.

Should there be a vacancy in the Subsistence Department of the Army I think it would be to the interest of the Government to appoint Mr. Rutherford, and retain him at this Post. I do therefore most heartily recommend him for the appointment.

I Am Sir, very respectfully
Your Obt. Svt.
U. S. Grant
Brig. Gen. Com

ALS, DNA, RG 94, Letters Received. See letter to Col. Joseph P. Taylor, Nov. 10, 1861.

Reuben C. Rutherford enlisted as a private in the 10th Ill. for three months' service on April 20, 1861. On May 18, he was promoted to 1st lt. and two days later assigned as regt. q. m. At the expiration of three months, on July 29, the 10th Ill. was reorganized and Rutherford remained as 1st lt. and regt. q. m. He failed to receive a commission, however, and resigned on Oct. 9, though remaining at Cairo as post commissary with the nominal rank of capt. He was not appointed to the commissary service until Nov. 26, 1862.

On Oct. 17, 1861, Capt. William McMichael issued special orders assigning Capt John P. Hawkins of Ind., USMA 1852, to duty as chief commissary, District of Southeast Mo. Copies, DNA, RG 393, Western Dept., Special Orders; DLC-USG, V, 81. On Oct. 25, Capt. John A. Rawlins issued special orders. "Capt J. P. Hawkins Subsistence Department U. S. A. having reported for duty in this Military District, is hereby assigned as Chief Commissary and Quarter Master of the District. He will be obeyed and respected accordingly. Capt Hawkins will not assume the duties of either Department but will have a general supervision over both including Regimental Quarter Masters and Commissaries and will act as inspector of those Departments." Copies, McClernand Papers, IHi; DLC-USG, V, 15, 16, 77, 82; DNA, RG 393, USG Special Orders. On Nov. 14, Hawkins was ordered by Capt. Thomas J. Haines to report to St. Louis for duty. Copy, DLC-USG, V, 9. Hawkins was later listed officially as having served Oct. 17–Dec. 16 as inspecting commissary, Dept. of the Mo., and Rutherford continued as post commissary.

On Dec. 5, Rawlins wrote to Capt. Reuben B. Hatch. "You will assign Capt. W. W. Leland Commissary of Subsistence to duty at once, and relieve Capt. R. C. Rutherford, as per orders from Head Quarters Dept. of the Missouri" Copies, *ibid.*, V, 1, 2, 16, 77, 82; DNA, RG 393, USG Special Orders. On the same day, Rawlins issued special orders. "Capt. W. W. Leland Com. of Subsistence, will immediately enter upon the duties of Com. of Subsisten[ce] at this Post, and relieve Capt. R. C Rutherford, receipting to him for all Commissary Stores &c. that may be on hand, and turned over" Copies, DLC-USG, V, 15, 16, 77, 82; DNA, RG 393, USG Special Orders. On Dec. 7, Hawkins wrote to USG "in reference to the removal of Capt. Rutherford from the Commissary Department." DLC-USG, V, 10; DNA, RG 393, USG Register of Letters Received.

To Capt. Chauncey McKeever

———

By Telegraph from Cairo Oct. 20 *1861*

To Capt. McKeever

There is now seven hundred thousand (700,000) rations in the wharf boat & there is more arriving. No place for it. There is a smaller wharf that can be got for the gun boat.—

U. S. Grant.

Telegram received (punctuation added), DNA, RG 393, Dept. of the Mo., Telegrams Received; copies, *ibid.*, Western Dept., Telegrams; DLC-USG, VIA, 2. On Oct. 20, 1861, Capt. Chauncey McKeever telegraphed to USG. "Let Captain Foote have the smaller wharfboat for the present. Order the Quartermaster to erect immediately a storehouse for commissary supplies." Copies, *ibid.*, V, 4, 5, 7, 8; DNA, RG 393, USG Hd. Qrs. Correspondence; *ibid.*, Western Dept., Telegrams. On Oct. 24, McKeever telegraphed to USG. "The General Commanding directs that the 'Graham' wharf boat be turned over to Captain Foote." Copies, *ibid.* On Oct. 29, Capt. Andrew H. Foote wrote to USG. "I am sorry to inform you that I have tried in vain to pick up an Army Register for you & General McClernand. Mrs Fremont had but a single copy. I regret to learn that great inconvenience will arises to the Commissary from want of room in the Wharf Boat in consequence of our wanting the Graham Boat. I hope therefore that you will retain one half of that Boat, offices included, and we will endeavor to get on with the other half. I will direct Commr Perry to call & get your directives on this subject. It is my earnest desire to use no more storage & office room than our wants require, as well as to accommodate in all other respects while laboring to promote conjointly the highest interest of the government." ALS, *ibid.*, District of Southeast Mo., Letters Received. See letter to Capt. Chauncey McKeever, Oct. 17, 1861. On Oct. 31, Foote wrote to Maj. Gen. John C. Frémont that "so much feeling has been manifested . . . that I have relinquished our half of the boat." *O.R.* (Navy), I, xxii, 388. On Nov. 2, Foote wrote to Asst. Secretary of the Navy Gustavus V. Fox. "At Cairo, a week since the Brigadier Genl. said he would not give a place assigned by Genl. Fremont, to our store, had it not been a positive order from Genl. Fremont." Robert Means Thompson and Richard Wainwright, eds., *Confidential Correspondence of Gustavus Vasa Fox* (New York, 1918–19), II, 9–10.

To Capt. Chauncey McKeever

———

Head Quarters, Dist. S. E. Mo.
Cairo, October 20th 1861

Capt. Chauncey McKeever
A. A. Gen. Western Dept.
St. Louis, Mo.
Sir:

Since my telegraph of yesterday nothing new has been learned of the movements of the enemy. I have a force at Charleston sufficiently large to watch the movements of the enemy in that direction should any be made.

I find it necessary to mention again the destitute condition of the Quartermaster Dept. here. No money having been paid out here credit is exausted. It is now with difficulty that coffins for the dead can be procured.[1]

Our Hospitals require some work to make them comfortable for the sick which cannot be done without money. About $3.000 will be required for this purpose, which, if possible, should be supplied at once.

About forty stoves are also required at once.[2] Requisitions I believe have been made for them and I would urgently request that they be ordered as soon as possible.

> I am Sir, very respectfully
> Your Obt. Svt.
> U. S. GRANT
> Brig. Gen. Com

ALS, DNA, RG 393, Western Dept., Letters Received.

1. On Oct. 17, 1861, USG wrote to Capt. Reuben B. Hatch. "You are required to furnish coffins for all men of this command who die if called upon from the public work shop when practicable when not practicable by purchase." Copies, DLC-USG, V, 1, 2, 3, 77; DNA, RG 393, USG Letters Sent.

2. On Oct. 21, Maj. Robert Allen telegraphed to USG. "What kind of stoves do you want? Do you want cooking or heating stoves? Are any intended for Sibley tents?" Copies, DLC-USG, V, 4, 5, 7, 8; DNA, RG 393, USG Hd. Qrs. Correspondence.

To Julia Dent Grant

Cairo, Ill. Oct. 20th 1861

DEAR JULIA,

I was in hopes that I should have my Photograph[1] to send by this time but the frame is not yet made. I will also send you several copies, ~~by~~ not in frame, one of them for Lank.[2]—I sent you $50 00 to pay Dentist bill and your rent.

We are all quiet here though how long we shall remain so is hard to tell. There is a very large force at Columbus compared to ours.—I am very sorry that I have not got a force to go south with, at least to Columbus, but the fates seem to be against any such thing. My forces are scattered and occupy posts that must be held. I will not write however what I intended. It will not interest you only that it would be a defence for my not being in Columbus to-day instead of where I am but would be very improper for the public to know particularly at this time when a publication of it would show our weekness to the enemy. There is but very little doubt, ~~but that~~ no doubt, but that we can hold this place. What I want is to advance.—I received a letter from you; one from father and one from Mary.

I intended writing to Lank to-day but I have been writing all day and have grown tired. I am much obliged to him for his long letter and would like to have him write often even if I do not answer them.

Give my love to all our friends and remember me to all the neighbors. Capt. Hillyer has gone to St. Louis and will try to bring your father with him. He said a couple of weeks ago that if he could get out of St. Louis without signing his death warrant, as he termed it, that is his solemn pledge to loyalty, he would come down and see me. Hillyer will get him through without that if he can. If he comes he probably will be here in about ten days. Dr. Sharp comes in to see me evry day. He seems well pleased. Nelly writes to him often. She and children are well. Kiss the children all round for me. Tell Jess not to be afraid of *Big boy*, big boy is afraid to hurt him. Kisses for yourself dear Julia. Write often. Your *hateful* husband.

U<small>LYS</small>.

ALS, DLC-USG.

1. See letter to Mary Grant, Oct. 25, 1861.
2. M. T. Burke. See letter to Jesse Root Grant, April 21, 1861, note 5.

To Capt. Chauncey McKeever

By TELEGRAPH FROM Cairo [*Oct.*] 21 *1861*

To CAPT C MCKEEVER

AAG

Three 3 small regts Infantry three Companies of Cavalry & Section artillery sent from here to Girardeau left Girardeau Friday[1] morning—

U S GRANT

Telegram received, DNA, RG 107, Telegrams Collected (Unbound); copies, *ibid.*, RG 393, Western Dept., Telegrams; DLC-USG, VIA, 2. On Oct. 20, 1861, Capt. Chauncey McKeever telegraphed to USG. "When did the expedition leave Cape Girardeau for Fredericktown and what was its strenght. Have temporary buildings erected immediately for winter quarters for the troops at Cairo & Birds Point." Copies, *ibid.*, V, 4, 5, 7, 8; DNA, RG 393, USG Hd. Qrs. Correspondence; *ibid.*, Western Dept., Telegrams. On Oct. 20, Brig. Gen. Samuel R. Curtis, Benton Barracks, telegraphed to USG. "Genl. Thompson with Some four thousand troops has burned bridge over Big River & Threatening or taken the force at Iron Mountain. It Seems to me a force Should be sent across from St. Genevieve to Their Relief. It is out of my Power." Telegram received (punctuation added), *ibid.*, Dept. of the Mo., Telegrams Received.

In response to the second part of the telegram of McKeever, on Oct. 22, Capt. John A. Rawlins wrote to Capt. Reuben B. Hatch. "In accordance with instructions received from Head Quarters, Western Department, you are hereby ordered and directed to cause, to be built and erected immediately temporary buildings for barracks and winter quarters for the troops and army at Cairo, Illinois, and Birds Point Missouri. Details for laborers will be furnished from the respective commands at this place, and Birds Point, Missouri The necessary materials for the building of the said barracks and quarters you will procure and obtain by purchase or otherwise,—Communicating to Major Allen Chief Quarter Master of the Western Department, the substance of your order, and asking for any further instructions he may have." Copies, DLC-USG, V, 1, 2, 3, 77; DNA, RG 393, USG Letters Sent. On Oct. 25, Rawlins issued special orders. "The troops at Cairo Birds Point and Fort Holt will proceed immediately to the erection of Huts, such as will be suitable protection against the inclemency of the season. Each Company will erect their own Quarters and Quarters for Regimental Head Quarters. Quarter Master and Commissary Storehouses, Stables &c will be built by detail from the respective Regiments. The site for each set of quarters will be designated by Brigade Commanders under the supervision of Col Webster Chief Engineer, who will also furnish plan of buildings" Copies, DLC-USG, V, 15, 16, 77, 82; DNA, RG 393, USG Special Orders.

1. Oct. 18.

To Capt. Chauncey McKeever

———

By Telegraph from Cairo Oct. 21 *186*1

To Capt McKeever
A A G

I have some prisoners which I will release & send to Columbus with a flag unless otherwise directed today[1] Jeff Thompson returned to Belmont last night. he has but few men but many prisoners supposed to be Unionists from Missouri

U S Grant

Telegram received, DNA, RG 107, Telegrams Collected (Unbound); copies, *ibid.*, RG 393, Western Dept., Telegrams; DLC-USG, VIA, 2. Brig. Gen. M. Jeff Thompson was still at Fredericktown, where a battle was fought on Oct. 21, 1861.

1. No contrary orders have been found, and Brig. Gen. John A. McClernand released three prisoners on Oct. 23, receiving sixteen in return from Maj. Gen. Leonidas Polk. *O.R.*, II, i, 511–13.

To Capt. Chauncey McKeever

———

By Telegraph from Cairo Oct 21 *186*1

To C. McKeever
St Louis

I will be in St Louis in the morning

U S Grant

Telegram received, DNA, RG 107, Telegrams Collected (Unbound); *ibid.*, RG 393, Western Dept., Telegrams; (misdated 1866) DLC-USG, VIA, 2. On Oct. 21, 1861, Capt. Chauncey McKeever telegraphed to USG. "Can you come here tomorrow, it is very necessary that I should have a personal interview with you answer" Copies, *ibid.*, V, 4, 5, 7, 8; DNA, RG 393, USG Hd. Qrs. Correspondence; *ibid.*, Western Dept., Telegrams. On Oct. 21, Capt. John A. Rawlins wrote to Capt. Reuben B. Hatch. "You will provide Railroad transportation, by Special train for Brig Genl. U. S. Grant from Cairo to St Louis via Odin immediately. Orders received from Head Quarters Dept. of the West making it necessary for him to be in Saint Louis tomorrow morning" Copies, DLC-USG, V, 1, 2, 3, 77; DNA, RG 393, USG Letters Sent.

To Brig. Gen. John A. McClernand

———

Head Quarters, Dist. S. E. Mo.
Cairo, October 21st 1861

GEN.

I am suddenly called to St. Louis and shall leave this evening by special train.

In my absence the command of this District is in your hands. I am satisfied that it could not be in better.

I am Gen. very respectfully
Your Obt. Svt.
U. S. GRANT
Brig. Gen.

To Gen. J. A. McClernand
Comd.g Post
Cairo Ill.

ALS, McClernand Papers, IHi. On Oct. 21, 1861, Brig. Gen. John A. McClernand wrote to USG. "Your favor of this date is this moment received. I regret the necessity which calls you away so unexpectedly and suddenly. I acknowledge both the compliment and obligation attendant upon imposed by the confidence which you are pleased to repose in me. Believe me, Sir, that While I cannot expect to equal, or even approximate the merit of your military administration you may rest assured that I will do all in my power to justify your confidence expectations of me and to insure success." Df, *ibid*. See preceding telegram.

To Commander Henry Walke

———

Headquarters District Southeast Missouri,
Cairo, October [*21*], 1861.

CAPTAIN:

The steamer *Belle Memphis* will start soon for below. Will you please, when you see her start, convoy her?

Yours, etc.,
U. S. GRANT,
Brigadier-General, Commanding.

O.R. (Navy), I, xxii, 376. Although this source gives the date as Oct. 22, 1861, the proper date is Oct. 21. Information supplied by Gordon T. Banks, Goodspeed's Book Shop, Inc., Boston, Mass.

To Capt. Reuben C. Rutherford

Head Quarters Dist S. E. Mo
Cairo Oct 21st 1861

SPECIAL ORDER

The Post Commissary will turn over to the Regl commissaries of such Regts, as have not yet been paid off a small sum to each, on their receipts to be used exclusively in paying dues to the Hospital fund.

It is presumed that when Regts have been paid off the commissaries have funds arising from sale to officers

U. S. GRANT
Brig Genl Com

To Cap Rutherford A. C. S.
Cairo Ills

Copies, DLC-USG, V, 15, 16, 77, 82; DNA, RG 393, USG Special Orders.

To Brig. Gen. John A. McClernand

DATED, St Louis [*October*] 23 185 [*1861*]

TO GENL McCLERNAND

I will try & be back tomorrow night until that time give Capt Foote his own interpretation of orders affecting him Release the prisoners Thursday[1]

U S GRANT

Telegram received, McClernand Papers, IHi. On Oct. 22, 1861, Brig. Gen. John A. McClernand telegraphed to USG. "Is it intended that the orders to Commodore Foote should make all the gun boats & water craft at the point independent of the commander of this district & of this point, shall I release the prisoners & send them with a flag to morrow." Copy, DNA, RG 393, Western Dept., Telegrams.

1. Oct. 24. See telegram to Capt. Chauncey McKeever, Oct. 21, 1861.

To Capt. Chauncey McKeever

——————

BY TELEGRAPH FROM Cairo Oct 25 *1861*
To CAPT C MCKEEVER
A A G

I desire authority to send some four Thousand 4000 foreign manufactured muskets to ~~to~~ W Eagle Iron Works at Cincinnati for alteration to make them serviceable please answer immediately

U S GRANT
Brig Gen

Telegram received, DNA, RG 393, Western Dept., Letters Received; copy, DLC-USG, VIA, 2. On Oct. 27, 1861, Capt. Chauncey McKeever telegraphed to USG. "Your Dispatch about the muskets has been referred to Capt Callender I have no power to act in the matter Capt Callender will not pay the account unless he makes the contract" Telegram received, Yates Papers, IHi; copy, DNA, RG 393, Western Dept., Telegrams. On Nov. 1, McKeever wrote to USG. "It will be necessary to send the four thousand muskets to the Arsenal in this city. Captain Callender declines to make any contract for altering them, unless the muskets are sent to him at the arsenal." Copies, DLC-USG, V, 7, 8; DNA, RG 393, USG Hd. Qrs. Correspondence.

To Capt. Chauncey McKeever

Head Quarters, Dist. S. E. Mo.
Cairo, October 25th 1861

CAPT. CHAUNCEY MCKEEVER,
A. A. GEN. WESTERN DEPARTMENT,
ST. LOUIS, MO.
SIR:

I have the honor to report my return to this command last evening. You have no doubt received the report of Gen. Mc-Clernand as to the result of a *Flag* of *Truce* sent to Columbus during my absence.[1]—I have nothing new to add.

My mission to Springfield was only partially successful. The Governor has neither Artillery nor small arms at present at his disposal but if my command, or this command, is not supplied when he does receive them one company will be equipped with a battery of James' rifled cannon. This cannot be before the last of November.

I think I will send the 2d Iowa Regt. to St. Louis immediately after Muster[2] and hope you will replace them with all the troops disposable.

Respectfully Your Obt. Svt.
U. S. GRANT
Brig. Gen. Com

ALS, DNA, RG 393, Western Dept., Letters Received. *O.R.*, I, iii, 556.

1. Printed *ibid.*, II, i, 511–13.
2. See letter to Capt. Chauncey McKeever, Oct. 27, 1861, note 1.

To Brig. Gen. John A. McClernand

———

Head Qrs. Dist. S. E. Mo
Cairo, Oct. 25th 1861

Refered to Gen. ~~McLernand~~ McClernand. If the wheat mentioned was seized whilst on the way to St. Louis it should be placed so the owner can recover.

U. S. GRANT
Brig. Gen Com

AES, McClernand Papers, IHi. Written on a letter of Oct. 24, 1861, from Col. William H. L. Wallace to Capt. John A. Rawlins. "While I was at Charleston Mo. about the 8th inst. certain wagons loaded with wheat were brought in by the scouts, and after examining into the matter and satisfying myself that the wheat was being hauled to Price's landing for shipment to St. Louis, I permitted it to go, and remarked that I knew of no objection to the produce of the country taking that direction to market. I have just received the enclosed letter from Mr. J. C. Moore of Charleston from which it appears that wheat shipped upon the faith of what I said has been seized by some person at Prices landing—I enclose the letter to you that you may take such action in the matter as may be deemed proper by the General Commanding. Mr. Moore, the writer of the letter, is a citeizen and resident of Charleston, and whilst I think his sympathies are with the rebels, I am equally well satisfied that he has done nothing openly in aid of their cause. If I might be permitted to make a suggestion in regard to the policy to be pursued in such matters I would say that it seems to me that encouragment should be given to induce the produce of that region to seek a market within our lines." ALS, *ibid.*

To Brig. Gen. Charles F. Smith

———

Head Quarters Dist S. E. Mo
Cairo Oct 25th 1861

GENL C. F. SMITH
COMDG U. S. FORCES
PADUCAH KY
GEN

I am just informed by Mr Casey[1] of Caseyville Ky,[2] a strong unconditional Union man that a regiment of cavalry is organizing at Princeton Ky.[3] for the Southern Confederacy. At last accounts they had about 500 men well mounted but not yet armed further than they have succeeded in pressing arms from the community around.

Princeton is twelve miles East from Eddyville[4] on the Cumberland river. The two places are connected by a good Mac-Adamized road.

Mr Casey says that cavalry sent from Paducah by steamer leaving there at dark, would reach Eddyville by 12 o.clock at night and of course could make the balance of the march in from two to two and a half hours.

I report this to you so that you may if you deem it prudent, take steps to secure these fellows. It has been one week since Mr Casey has heard from these troops but he does not doubt but they are still there.

> I am Sir Very Respectfully
> Your obt Sevt
> U. S. GRANT
> Brig Genl Com

Copies, DLC-USG, V, 1, 2, 3, 79; DNA, RG 393, USG Letters Sent. *O.R.*, I, iii, 556. On Oct. 25, 1861, Brig. Gen. Charles F. Smith wrote to USG. "I regret I did not get yr letter of this date this morning. Having information of some days standing that a hundred well mounted & tolerably armed body of rebel Cavalry made their Hd. Qrs. at a church 4 miles from Eddyville on the road to Princeton I sent the Conestoga with 3 full Cos. of Inf.y at 4 o'c this afternoon to try and effect their capture or destruction. Had I known of the force at Princeton I would have made an effort at them. I telegraphed you to day to get all the latest and most reliable information you may have about the force at Columbus or in its vicinity and the distribution of the same also if you have any reliable sktech of their works at Columbus. My raid to Mayfield a few nights since has caused the advance of the enemy below towards that town and somewhat on this side. I hope they will come nearer. One of the Cavalry men who was wounded and taken prisoner whilst on outpost duty and exchanged for some one of your prisoners reports but from 10 to 15,000 at Columbus many heavy guns and three field batteries of 6 pieces each. That Genl. A. S. *Johnston* has gone to assist *Zollicoffer* at the gap, that *Hardee* left Columbus some 10 days ago with 10,000 supposed to Bowling green. I rejoice that your men at Ironton met with such success." ALS, DNA, RG 393, District of Southeast Mo., Letters Received. On Oct. 28, Lt. S. Ledyard Phelps reported to Capt. Andrew H. Foote concerning the expedition to Eddyville. ALS, *ibid.*, RG 45, Area 5. *O.R.* (Navy), I, xxii, 379–80. See also *O.R.*, I, iv, 215–19.

1. James F. Casey. See letter of May 10, 1861, note 8.
2. Caseyville, Ky., about eleven miles south of Shawneetown, Ill., on the Ohio River.

3. Princeton, Ky., about forty-two miles east of Paducah.

4. Eddyville, Ky., on the Cumberland River, about twenty-five miles south-east of Smithland by land.

To Col. Leonard F. Ross

———

Head Quarters Dist S. E. Mo
Cairo Oct 25th 1861

COLONEL

I am instructed by Gen Grant to inform you that he has heard with great satisfaction an unofficial but as he believes a reliable report of the recent battle near Fredericktown, and he deems it a pleasant duty to say to you that he congratulates you upon the brave and successful charge made by you and your command upon the enemy.

Not wishing to make any inviduos distinction when all of his forces seem to have done so nobly, he can not but acknowledge that the Post of Danger and of honor allotted to your regiment as leading the van in the contest was valiantly sustained.—

You will communicate to your command the high appreciation of their services, entertained by their commanding General and say to them for him that they have earned as they deserve the sincerest thanks of their countreymen

Very Respectfully
Your Obt Servt
W. S. HILLYER
Capt & Aid de Camp

To Col Ross
Comdg 17th Ills Vols

Copies, DLC-USG, V, 1, 2, 3, 79; DNA, RG 393, USG Letters Sent. *O.R.*, I, iii, 212. See letter to Col. Joseph B. Plummer, Oct. 27, 1861. On Oct. 28, 1861, Col. Leonard F. Ross prepared a report of the engagement at Fredericktown. *O.R.*, I, iii, 210–11. For more on Fredericktown, see Jay Monaghan, *Swamp Fox of the Confederacy: The Life and Military Services of M. Jeff Thompson* (Tuscaloosa, 1956), chap. III.

On Nov. 1, Ross wrote to USG. "My Regt was paid off yesterday—that is we recd three months pay when there was five months pay due—On getting their pay many of the officers and soldiers are making applications for leaves of absence and furloughs—In my opinion very many of the applications should be granted—We have in the Regt about 100 men of families who are desirous of going home and fixing up their business and making arrangements for winter—I have also in the Regt a large number of boys who were never from home until they volunteered into the U S Service—they have been on the sick list for a long time—They were good, obedient boys at home, loved their parents, brothers and sisters and are none in reality sick—*home sick* it may be said—But I am satisfied they will be no better until they obtain a sight ~~for~~ of the longed-for—'sweet home'—In most cases three or four days at home would effect a cure—would it not be cheaper, better and more humane to grant a short furlough, than to keep them laying around the hospital drawling out a miserable existence and of no benefit to the service whatever ?—In addition they have a *claim* for leave of absence that should be respected—When they first enlisted it was for three months only—but under the influences brought to bear on them were induced to volunteer for three years—this was in many cases with an express promise on the part of the Captain that a furlough should be granted for them to go home and arrange their business before winter—If consistent with the good of the service I would be much pleased with permission to grant leaves of absence and furloughs in all such cases In fact if we could be spared from the service for a couple of weeks I do not believe the service would lose in the end if the entire regiment was allowed to spend that length of time on *furlough*—I could remove them free of expense to the government, and could recruit and fill up to the full extent allowed—I thank you sincerely my dear sir for the very complimentary notice you have seen proper to take of my regiment—and of the flattering manner in which you speak of their services in the late engagement at Fredericktown I take pleasure in stating to you, as I have already stated in my official report—that 'all without exception performed their whole duty'—I am proud to be in command of a regiment of such true and reliable soldiers—" ALS, DNA, RG 393, Western Dept., Letters Received.

To Maj. James Simons

Head Quarters Dist S. E. Mo
Cairo Oct 25th 1861

Surgeon J. Simmons
Medical Director
Cairo Ills
Sir

On your arrival in Washington City, you are directed to have a personel interview with the Surgeon General[1] and secretary of War, if practicable and suggest to them a change in the method of keeping account of Hospital Fund.—The present method is too complicated for utility in the Volunteer Service and a change such as suggested by yourself, to the Department would, in my opinion be attended with the most happy results.

You are also directed to communicate freely on the subjects of the wants of the ~~people~~ ~~Hospital~~ Medical Department at this place, with which from your connection you are thoroughly acquainted.

U. S. GRANT
Brig Genl Com

Copies, DLC-USG, V, 1, 2, 3, 77; DNA, RG 393, USG Letters Sent. On Oct. 28, 1861, Capt. John A. Rawlins issued two special orders. "Leave of absence for seven days is hereby granted Surgeon James Simmons U. S. A. at the expiration of which his leave granted by the commander of the Western Department for twenty days will commence" Copies, DLC-USG, V, 15, 77, 82; DNA, RG 393, USG Special Orders. "Surgeon James Simmons U. S. A. Medical Director, having received leave of absence, Surgeon John H. Brinton is appointed to act in his place. He will be obeyed and respected accordingly." LS, McClernand Papers, IHi; DNA, RG 94, Letters Received. On Nov. 20, Col. Clement A. Finley endorsed the latter copy of the orders. "The within order of General Grant giving leave of absence to Surgeon Simons, the Medical Director at Cairo is referred to the Adjutant General as a practice embarrassing to this Office, and which should be prohibited. In this case, it substitutes an inexperienced Medical Officer for the performance of very important duties without giving any reason for Dr. Simon's leave of absence." ES, *ibid.*

1. Col. Clement A. Finley, surgeon-general.

To Mary Grant

———

Cairo, October 25th 1861

DEAR SISTER;

I have gone longer this time without writing to you than I intended and have no good excuse for it. I have rec'd two letters, at least, from you and father since my last one of which wanted special answer. As I have not got that letter before me I may fail to answer some points. As to my not taking Columbus there are several reasons for it which I understand perfectly and could make plain to anyone else but do not feel disposed to commit the reasons to paper. As to the needlessness of the movements of troops I am a better judge than the newspapaper reporters who write about it. My whole administration of affairs seems to have given entire satisfaction to those who have the right to judge and should have the ability to judge correctly. I find by a little absence for the few last days[1] (under orders) that my whole course has received marked approbation from citizens & soldiers, so much so that many who are comparitive strangers to me are already claiming for me promotion. This is highly gratifying but I do not think any promotions should be made for the present. Let service tell who are the deserving ones and give them the promotion. Father also wrote about a Mr. Reed! He is now here and will probably be able to secure a position. I do not want to be importuned for places. I have none to give and want to be placed under no obligation to anyone. My influance no doubt would secure places with those under me but I become directly responsible for the suitableness of the appointee, and then there is no telling what moment I may have to put my hand upon the very person who has confered the favor, or the one recommended by me. I want always to be in a condition to do my duty without partiality, favor or affection.—In the matter of making harness I know that a very large amount is wanted. Maj. Robert Allen, Chief Quartermaster for the Western Department, stationed in St. Louis has the letting of a greatdeel. Father remembers his father well. He is a son of old Irish Jimmy as he used to be called about Georgetown to distinguish him from the other two Jimmy Allens. He is a friend of mine also.—This letter has proven so far more one to father than to yourself but I direct to you that you may reply. I write in great haste having been engaged all evening in writing orders, and still having more to do.—I send you, with this the likenesses of myself and staff.[2] No 1 you will have no difficulty in recognizing. No 2 is Capt. J. A. Rawlins, A. A. Gen. Nos 3 & 4 Capts. Lagow & Hillyer Aides-de-Camps, No 5 Dr. Simons Medical Director. A good looking set aint they? I expect Julia here the latter part of next week. I wish you could come at the same time and stay a week or two. I think it would pay you well. Wont you try and come? If it was atall necessary I would pay the expense myself to have you come. Give my love to all at home. I think I will send you several more of my Photographs, one for Uncle Samuel,[3] one for Aunt Margaret,[4] one for Aunt Rachel[5] and one for Mrs. Bailey.[6]

Your Brother ULYS.

ALS, deCoppet Collection, NjP.

1. See letter to Capt. Chauncey McKeever, Oct. 25, 1861.
2. See illustrations in *PUSG*, 2.
3. Samuel Simpson, brother of USG's mother. *PUSG*, 1, 7n–8n.
4. Margaret Grant Marshall, sister of USG's father.
5. See letter to Mary Grant, April 29, 1861.
6. Mrs. George B. Bailey of Georgetown, Ohio. *PUSG*, 1, 3n, 27–29.

To Brig. Gen. John A. McClernand

Head Quarters, Dist. S. E. Mo.
Cairo, October 26th 186[1]

GEN. J. A. MCCLERNAND
COMD.G POST
CAIRO ILL.
GEN.

Will you be kind enough to order the release of Dr. Boggs who was confined last night by my order and oblige

Yours Truly
U. S. GRANT
Brig. Gen Com

ALS, McClernand Papers, IHi.

To Capt. Chauncey McKeever

Head Quarters Dist S. E. Mo
Cairo Oct 27th 1861

CAPT CHAUNCEY MCKEEVER
A. A. GENL. WESTERN DEPT
ST LOUIS, MO
CAPTAIN

The health of the 2d Iowa Regiment is such that I have thought it both prudent and humane to send them to Saint Louis to recruit their health.[1]—Col Tuttle the Commander is desirous of returning to this place as soon as it ~~is~~ will be prudent to do so and I have directed him to report to Dept Hd Quarters when he thinks the health of his Regiment sufficiently recovered.

As this District is but weakly garrisoned I would respectfully request that a Regiment be sent here to replace the Iowa 2d ~~and~~ All ~~the~~ troops you can send will be gladly received.

Such draughts have been made upon the force at Columbus lately for the Green River country[2] and possibly other parts of Kentucky, that if Genl Smith, and my command were prepared it might now be taken.[3] I am not prepared however for a forward movement. My Cavalry are not arme[d] nor my Artillery equipped. The Infantry ~~are~~ is not well armed and transportation is entirely inadequate to any forward movement.

I shall make this evening a requisition on the Quartermaster in St Louis for 8000 Bed sacks.

They are highly essential for the comfort and health of the men and I hope the commander of the Department will order their immediate delivery.

I am Sir Very Respectfully
Your obt Servt
U. S. GRANT
Brig Genl Com

Copies, DLC-USG, V, 4, 5, 7, 8, 78, VIA, 2; DNA, RG 393, USG Hd. Qrs. Correspondence. *O.R.*, I, iii, 556–57.

1. On Oct. 27, 1861, Capt. John A. Rawlins wrote to Col. James M. Tuttle. "In consequence of the existing state of health in your command, you will proceed to day by steamer to St Louis and there report to Head Quarters Western Dept for orders. When the health of your command has sufficiently recovered to justify its return to this place you will report the fact to Hd Qrs Western Dept. All transportation in charge of Regl Quartermaster will be left in charge of a suitable person for use here untill the return of your Regiment. All other baggage will accompany you." Copies, DLC-USG, V, 1, 2, 3, 77, VIA, 2; DNA, RG 393, USG Letters Sent.

2. The Green River generally furnished the dividing line between U. S. A. and C. S. A. forces in central Ky.

3. C. S. A. Maj. Gen. Leonidas Polk reported his force as 17,230 at Columbus, Ky., for Oct., 1861. USG reported his force at 11,161 as of Oct. 31, including 2,348 at Cape Girardeau. On Oct. 10, Brig. Gen. Charles F. Smith had 6,821 at Paducah. *O.R.*, I, iii, 530, 558, 730.

To Col. Joseph B. Plummer

Head Quarters Dist S. E. Mo
Cairo Oct 27th 1861

Col J. B. Plummer
Comdg U. S. Forces
Cape Girardeau, Mo
Col

Your report of the expedition under your command[1] is received. I congratulate you and the Officers and Soldiers of the expedition upon the result.

But little doubt can be entertained of the success of our arms when not opposed by very superior numbers, and in the action of Fredericktown they have given proof of courage and determination which shows that they would undergo and fatigue or hardships to meet our rebellious brethren even at great odds.

Our loss small as it is, is to be regretted, but the friends and relatives of those who fell can congratulate themselves in the midst of their affliction, that they fell in maintaining the cause of Constitutional freedom and the integrity of a Flag erected in the first instance, at a sacrifice of many of the noblest lives that ever graced a nation.

In conclusion say to your troops they have done nobly. It goes to prove that much more may be expected of them when the country and our great cause calls upon them

>Yours &c
>
>U. S. GRANT
>
>Brig Genl Comdg

Copies, DLC-USG, V, 1, 2, 3, 79; DNA, RG 94, War Records Office, Union Battle Reports; *ibid.*, RG 393, USG Letters Sent. *O.R.*, I, iii, 209.

1. On Oct. 26, 1861, Col. Joseph B. Plummer wrote to USG. "Pursuant to your order of the 16th inst I left this Post on the 18th inst with about fifteen hundred men and marched upon Fredricktown, via Jackson and Dallis where I arrived at 12 O.Clock on Monday the 21st inst. Finding there Col Carlin with about three thousand men who had arrived at 9. O.Clock that morning. He gave me a portion of his Command which I. united with my own, and immediately started in pursuit of Thompson, who was reported to have evacuated the town the day before and retreated towards Greenville. I found him however occupying a position about one mile out of town on the Greenville road which he had held since about 9 O.Clock. A. M. and immediately attacked him, The battle lasted about two and one half hours, and resulted in the total defeat of Thompson, and route of all his forces, consisting of about three thousand five hundred men. Their loss was severe, ours very light. Among their killed was Lowe, On the following day I pursued Thompson twenty two miles towards Greenville for the purpose of capturing his train, but finding further pursuit useless, and beleiving Pilot Knob secure—and the object of the expedition accomplished I returned to this Post, where I arrived last evening, having been absent seven days and a half. I brought with me forty two prisoners, and one iron twelve pound field piece, a number of small arms and horses taken upon the field I will forward a detailed report of the battle, as soon as reports from Colonels of Regiments and Commanding Officers of Corps are received" ALS, DNA, RG 94, War Records Office, Union Battle Reports; *ibid.*, RG 393, Western Dept., Letters Received. *O.R.*, I, iii, 206. On Oct. 31, Plummer sent to USG's hd. qrs. a more detailed report and submitted eight sub-reports, all printed *ibid.*, pp. 206–16, 221–23. The LS is in DNA, RG 94, War Records Office, Union Battle Reports.

To Capt. Chauncey McKeever

Head Quarters Dist S. E. Mo
Cairo Oct 28th 1861

CAPT CHAUNCEY MCKEEVER
ASST ADJT GENL WESTERN DEPT
SAINT LOUIS MO
SIR

When I assumed command of this Military District I found a large block of buildings in Mound City occupied for army purposes. Supposing it to be by authority I made no inquiries as to authority or price paid. I now learn that no contract has ever been entered into binding upon Government and as some day a large claim may be based upon occupancy I would recomend that the Property be condemned for military purposes. It is said that the greater interest is owned by southern seccessionists.

The Buildings were put up during a real estate excitement when it was supposed that Mound City was to be a rival to St Louis. The city proving a failure the property has no intrinsic value except for army purposes. To us it is indispensable.

The large number of sick require greater Hospital accomodations than we have without these buildings, and for this it is well adapted. It will accomodate well one thousand men. I have ordered it used as indicated and would as indicated reccomend that the property be condemned. The Board called for the purpose being instructed to set the prices according to its present value, and fixing a rent, giving owners their option to sell or recieve the rent.

Respectfully
Your obt Servt
U. S. GRANT
Brig Genl Comdg

Copies, DLC-USG, V, 4, 5, 7, 8, 78; DNA, RG 393, USG Hd. Qrs. Correspondence. On Oct. 31, 1861, Capt. Chauncey McKeever endorsed the letter. "The within proposition to convene a Board to appraise the property is approved. The property cannot be purchased, but may be rented." Copy, *ibid.*, Western Dept., Endorsements. On Nov. 2, Capt. John A. Rawlins issued special orders. "By directions from Head Quarters Western Department, a Board of survey to consist of the following members Viz: Col James. D. Morgan 10th Ill Vols Major John Tillson 10th Ill Vols Franklin, Brigade Surgeon is is hereby appointed to meet at Mound City Illinois, on Monday the 4th day of November inst. or as soon thereafter as practicable, to condemn for Military purposes a large block of buildings now used as a Hospital. The Board will assess the value per month of said buildings to be paid during the time it may be occupied by Government, taking into account all facts that may exist, the inconvenience to owners, if any is experienced, what the property would probably bring them if not used by Government &c" Copies, DLC-USG, V, 15, 16, 77, 82; DNA, RG 393, USG Special Orders. See letter to H. C. Howard, Nov. 18, 1861. USG's attention may have been drawn to this matter during his visit to Mound City on Oct. 27 to witness the launching of the gunboat *Mound City.* Letter of "Horatio," Oct. 27, 1861, in *Missouri Democrat*, Oct. 30, 1861.

To Brig. Gen. John A. McClernand

Head Quarters, Dist. S. E. Mo
Cairo, October 28th 1861

Carson should be questioned as to losing Shaler's money, and discharged from our service, and if ~~th~~ Shaler's statement is found correct, in this respect, he should be liberated at once, and, if he desires it, permited ~~him~~ to pass our lines.

U. S. GRANT
Brig. Gen. Com

AES, McClernand Papers, IHi. Written on a letter of Oct. 26, 1861, from Capt. William H. Parish, 29th Ill., provost marshal, and Capt. James H. Williamson, 31st Ill., to Brig. Gen. John A. McClernand. "We have had before us to day, Charles Shaler arrested some two or three days since by Capt. Carson on charge of being a spy. This young man is but about seventeen years of age quite a youth and evidently of gentle blood—The young man tells his simple unvarnished story thus. That he lives in Pittsburg—that he served thee months in Twelfth regiment Pa. Volunteers, and was third sergeant, in Company "I"—That he had his discharge with him in his pocket at the time he was arrested—that he gave it together with his money $30 to Capt Carson—That the Capt lost his pocket book & money—The young man wished to go south to see a brother whom he, honestly enough says is in Jeff Thompsons Army, and wounded. That he started at the earnest request of an allmost heartbroken mother—He states that his brother has long resided in the South—hense took up arms against us. Granted, and yet we cannot find in our hearts to condemn this young man for daring danger & braving death, to learn the fate of his erring brother, or minister to his sufferings, especially when urged by his mother to make the effort. We unhesitatingly repudiate the idea that he is a spy—We think he has been overreached—and that his anxeity to see his brother may have led him far beyond the path of safety. While we cannot reccommend him to be discharged we hope every facility will be afforded him to vindicate himself from the charge of being a spy, and to be restored to his friends if not clearly proven guilty." LS, *ibid.* McClernand then sent the letter to USG. "As I am not clear as to the propriety of permitting Mr Shaler to pass our lines, I refer the question to Gen'l Grant." AES, *ibid.* On Oct. 30, Secretary of War Simon Cameron telegraphed to USG. "Release Chas Shaler Jr. a young man from Pittsburg, who was arrested yesterday at Cairo as a spy; and give him safe conduct to proceed to his home in Pittsburg." Copies, DLC-USG, V, 4, 5, 7, 8; DNA, RG 393, USG Hd. Qrs. Correspondence.

To Capt. Chauncey McKeever

BY TELEGRAPH FROM Cairo Oct 29 *1861*

To CAPT C McKEEVER

I find a deficency in muster & pay Rolls Send a Quantity at once

U S GRANT

Telegram received, DNA, RG 107, Telegrams Collected (Unbound); copies, *ibid.*, RG 393, Western Dept., Telegrams; DLC-USG, VIA, 2.

To Lt. S. Ledyard Phelps

Head Quarters Dist S. E. Mo
Cairo Oct 29th 1861

Capt.

You will proceed to Mound City with the Barge captured by you in the Cumberland River, and then have her appraised by competent persons and repaired for the use of this command

U. S. Grant
Brig Genl Comdg

To Capt S. L. Phelps U. S. N.
Comdg G B Conestoga
off Cairo Ills

Copies, DLC-USG, V, 1, 2, 3, 77; DNA, RG 393, USG Letters Sent. On Oct. 29, 1861, Lt. S. Ledyard Phelps wrote to USG. "I yesterday seized the barge 'Kentucky,' 5 miles above the mouth of the Cumberland River, and have brought her to this place. It is the property of a Company in Memphis, Tennessee. The person in whose charge I found it, stated that the barge belonged to the Memphis Company, but that he had a bill of sale of her to secure him in a debt due from that Company. I do not know to what extent this would effect the condition of the property with respect to its liability to seizure under acts of Congress relating to the present rebellion. Enclosed are two statements and a copy of this paper for the use of the District Attorney at this place." ALS, *ibid.*, District of Southeast Mo., Letters Received. Phelps also sent USG two statements concerning the barge. "The barge now lying on the right bank of the Cumberland, about five miles above Smithland, was towed there by the Steamer Granit State for the purpose of taking stone to Memphis, Tennessee, to be used by a Company in that City, in the construction of a wharf. The 'Granit State' had been employed several months before the blockade of the river in towing barges, to the point above referred to, on the Cumberland, and in taking them back to Memphis, loaded with Stone.—To the best of my knowledge and belief the said barge is the property of parties residing in Memphis, Tennessee.—Elijah Carroll Note: George Sey (Sea? Cey? manner of spelling name not known) of Caseyville, was a pilot on board Granit State at the time the barge was towed to the point where she lies on the Cumberland. John A. Duble, 1st Master Gun Boat Conestoga, knows the barge and has employed her at Memphis. S. L. Phelps." "I hereby certify I know the Barge 'Kentucky' now lying some five miles up the ~~Tennessee~~ Cumberland River belonged to the Company building the Memphis Wharf and has been used for the purpose of transporting rock from the Ohio River to Memphis for that purpose. I further certify I have had occasion to use the Barge Kentucky to lift the St. Bt. W W. Thomas off the Bar at the foot of Island 40. above Memphis and got her from Memphis towed up to me for that purpose, John Lowden of Memphis Ten. being at the head of the Company to pave the Memphis Wharf and now a

resident of that place JNO. A DUBLE" DS, *ibid.* On Oct. 30, Brig. Gen. Charles
F. Smith telegraphed to USG. "The barge Kentucky can be docked & caulked at
Paducah for four hundred & fifty dollars including her decks. If the Decks are
not caulked, the Price will be three hundred & fifty dollars." Telegram received
(punctuation added), *ibid.*, Dept. of the Mo., Telegrams Received.

To Capt. Chauncey McKeever

Head Quarters, Dist. S. E. Mo.
Cairo, October 30th 1861

CAPT. CHAUNCEY MCKEEVER
A. A. GEN. WESTERN DEPT.
ST. LOUIS, MO.
SIR:

To-day I sent a flag of truce to near Columbus, bearer of
Capt. Whitfield, who had been sent here in charge of Capt. J. W.
Gosnold of the 13th Mo. Vols. to be delivered up to the Southern
Army.

Capt. G.'s conduct was such as to induce me to direct that he
should not accompany the expedition. He showed such anxiety
however that I consented to him going along but not to be
recognized in any official capacity. His subsequent conduct shows
that my first judgment was right.

I refer you to Capt. Hillyer's report, herewith accompanying,[1] for further information.

Your Obt. Svt.
U. S. GRANT
Brig. Gen. Com.

ALS, DNA, RG 393, Western Dept., Letters Received. *O.R.*, II, i, *514.* On
Oct. 27, 1861, Col. Joseph B. Plummer wrote to USG's hd. qrs. asking what
should be done with prisoners taken at Fredericktown. *Ibid.*, p. 513.

1. On Oct. 30, Capt. William S. Hillyer wrote to USG. "In pursuance of
your orders I left Cairo on the Steamer W. H. B. at 10 o'clck to day having in
charge Capt Whitfield of the rebel army and went down the river with a flag of
truce. A mile this side of Columbus I was met by the Steamer Yazoo having on

board Gen Polk and Staff of the rebel army—Upon the invitation of Gen Polk I went aboard the Yazoo, stated to Gen Polk the object of my mission and deliverd the prisoner—While on board the Yazoo Gen Polk informed me that Capt Gosnold (who accompanied the expedition) had solicited him to be permitted to go to Columbus and that he had told Gosnold that his request must be proferred through me before it could receive his consideration—I thereupon ordered Gosnold on board our Steamer and started back to Cairo—A few minutes afterward Capt Gosnell jumped overboard and (as I believe) was drowned. No other incident worthy of report occured—I arrived at Cairo at four o'clock—" ALS, DNA, RG 393, Dept. of Kansas, Letters Received; LS, *ibid.*, Western Dept., Letters Received. *O.R.*, II, i, 514.

To Brig. Gen. John A. McClernand

Head Quarters, Dist. S. E. Mo.

Cairo, October 30th 1861.

It is my opinion that the authority granted does not authorize a greater number of men than the maximum of a Cavalry Company unless a larger number was specified in the permission.

U. S. GRANT

Brig. Gen. Com

AES, McClernand Papers, IHi. Written on a letter from Brig. Gen. John A. McClernand to USG, Oct. 30, 1861. "In pursuance of authority from Major General John C. Fremont, to Captain F. Evans to raise a cavalry company to guard Big Muddy bridge he has raised a cavalry force of one hundred and twenty-four mounted men,—all, or most, of whom have been at that place for some two or three weeks past. I write to inquire whether he will be permitted to retain ~~all of them~~ so large a force or required to reduce ~~the number~~ it to the legal maximum of a cavalry company He is awaiting an answer before he leaves, to night." LS, *ibid.* Capt. Finis Evans commanded an Ill. State Guards cav. co. named the Egyptian Guards. State Guards, Commission Records, I-ar. On Oct. 20, McClernand wrote to USG. "I have the honor to report as the result of my visit ~~yesterday~~ to and inspection of Big Muddy river bridge, yesterday, and the guard there stationed, that I found all safe. The bridge is undergoing repairs by the Central Rail Road Company, and Capt. Finis Evans is guarding it with a Company of Cavalry numbering about one fifty men, rank and file. I gave them special instructions to keep up an active vigilence to prevent injury to the bridge and ~~sup~~ surprize of his Command." Copy, McClernand Papers, IHi.

On Dec. 26, McClernand wrote to USG. "Herewith please find certain papers, which according to our understanding today, I enclose to you for transmission to Head Quarters of the Dept of the Mo at St Louis" Copy, *ibid.* The papers concerned the recruitment and organization of his brigade, and included a request to authorize Capt. William Boyle to recruit two cos. of art. Copies, *ibid*. On Dec. 26, McClernand wrote to Boyle. "Your proposal, as above set forth, is accepted, subject to the approval of Maj Genl H. W. Halleck, Com'g Dept of the Mo, and Brig Genl U. S. Grant, Comg Dist of Cairo." Copy, *ibid*. Below this letter, USG wrote: "approved." Also on Dec. 26, McClernand wrote to USG enclosing copies of five documents relating to the Egyptian Guards. Copies, *ibid*. On Dec. 30, Capt. John C. Kelton wrote to USG. "Major General Halleck directs me to say to you, that the Company to which you gave referrence in a Communication of the 26th inst., evidently comes under the style of 'Home Guards' referred to in General Orders No. 25—They will therefore be mustered in and out to cover services rendered away from their homes, if any has been so rendered. A company of regularly mustered in volunteers will, if necessary be put in their place. Attention will be given that they give up all arms and public property. You will appoint a mustering officer and give him the proper instructions." Copy, DNA, RG 393, Dept. of the Mo., Letters Sent (Press).

On Jan. 2, 1862, Capt. John A. Rawlins issued Special Orders No. 4. "In pursuance of directions from Head Quarters Dept. of the Mo. of Dec. 30th 1861, Captain W. S. Hillyer Aid De. Camp and Mustering Officer, will proceed, as soon as practicable, to Big. Muddy Bridge, and muster in Capt. Finess Evans Company of Cavalry, and immediately muster them out of service. All Arms, Ammunition, Camp and Garrison Equipage, and other public property, in their possession, will before being mustered for pay, be turned over to the property Officer at Cairo, and receipts taken. Capt. Brinck, Ordnance, and Capt. R. B. Hatch, Asst. Qr. Mr., will accompany the Mustering Officer, and receive & receipt for property pertaining to their respective Departments. Rations on hand, will be turned over to the company sent, to relieve them, and will be deducted, from the stores to be received, on their next provision return. Brig. Genl. J. A. McClernand Comdg. Cairo, will designate a Company of Cavalry or Infantry, to relieve the command at Big Muddy Bridge" Copies, DLC-USG, V, 15, 16, 82, 87, 89; DNA, RG 393, USG Special Orders.

On Jan. 3, McClernand wrote to USG. "Your Special Order No 4 of yesterday, has been received, and the execution of so much of it as relates to my command directed. I can not refrain from expressing my regret, that it is found necessary to remove Capt. Evans from the duty heretofore assigned him—and still more, that his company is to be mustered out of the service. When I was charged with the command of this Post, and the forces connected with it, I found the guarding of the Bridge across Big Muddy River, confided to an infantry company from the 8th Regiment, Col Oglesby. It was very desirable, and seemed for the good of the service, that on the removal of that Regiment to Birds Point, the company thus detailed, should be restored to Col Oglesby's command. The defense of Big Muddy Bridge being an imperative necessity and Capt. *Finis Evans*, a man of high character, of wealth, and great influence in the community surrounding the point to be guarded, having tendered a cavalry company for the purpose of protecting it as long as required, and for other service afterwards, on the 14th of September last I accordingly, addressed Major Genl. Fremont recommending the acceptance of his company for that purpose, urging among other reasons—'that while cavalry would be quite as well suited for the protection of the bridge as Infantry, they would be preferable, as having greater facility for extending their reconnoissances to, or near the Ohio and Mississippi rivers.' The authority thus solicited, was granted by Genl. Fremont on Sept. 20th, the company to serve under the requirements of the act of Congress No 24 dated July 31st 1861. By this order, their muster into the U. S. Service was dispensed with. On the first day of October Capt. Evans reported his company to me for duty: and by my special Order No 748, he was placed in charge of Big Muddy Bridge, relieving the infantry there stationed. Since that time to the present, Capt. Evans has performed faithfully the duty assigned him—being recognized, and furnished supplies from the United States and the State of Illinois. He is regarded as one of the most valuable of our volunteer officers, and commands a full company of good men, well mounted. They are nearly all heads of families, having homes and estates in the vicinity and consequently entirely reliable under all circumstances. His influence in his neighborhood in preventing mischief and restraining disaffection, has been great. Your order mustering him out of service, also requires me to designate another company to perform the same duty. This makes it necessary to break up existing arrangements, and introduce into a regiment now compact, that disorder and inconvenience which is necessarily attendant upon its partial disruption, and owing to reasons peculiar to that locality, I am persuaded that no other company can perform the service so effectually, or with so salutary an influence upon the people among whom they are placed. In addition to these considerations I will add, that the company can perform the necessary police and scouting service, as far as the Ohio and Mississippi rivers, rendering unnecessary the frequent details from this, more distant point. All the reasons which prevailed with me in recommending the organization of the company for this service, and with Gov. Yates and Genl. Fremont in authorizing and giving success to the measure, still prevail, and with additional force. I therefore respectfully urge, that the company refered to, be mustered into the service of the United States, in the usual manner; and that its fitness for the duty in which it is now engaged be recognized by its further detail at that place—" Copies, DLC-Robert T. Lincoln; McClernand Papers, IHi.

The copy sent to President Abraham Lincoln was probably an enclosure in a letter of Jan. 3 from McClernand to Lincoln. "Herewith you will find a copy of the letter of authority executed by you to me.

'Executive Mansion.
Aug. 7th, 1861.

Hon John A McClernand
My Dear Sir.

You having been appointed a Brigadier General of Illinois Volunteers.

Your Brigade will consist of four regiments—if convenient and desirable—*one* company of cavalry in *each* regiment and *two* artillery companies. Any four regiments which will be agreeable to you and to one another, will be agreeable to me. One Regt of Hon John. A. Logan, One of Hon P B Fouke, one of Hon I. N. Coler, and one of Hon B. C. Cook, will be entirely satisfactory to me—or if any one of these Regiments fail, take any other that is agreeable to you and to the regiment—In all this, I think it will conduce to harmony for you to confer with Major General Fremont.

A. Lincoln.'

Am I to understand that this authority has been in any way revoked? I inquire because I have yet a vacant Cavalry and Light Artillery company to form. But for the order which sent me, without previous notice, to this Post, and the consequent labors that have engrossed my whole time and attention, I would have long since filled up these two companies. I have an opportunity to do it now; and ask of you a declaration in regard to it—trusting that it will be favorable to so desirable and proper an object. Through your kindness my batteries, (which are of the first class,) have been received, and I only need an assurance to enable me to man the remaining one. If I am left to the process of recruiting through general officers assigned to that service, I may never succeed in securing the two companies required. With these companies the organization and efficiency of my brigade will be completed. As a recompense for so many favors received at your hands, accept my heartfelt thanks, and the sincere assurance that all of them have been asked, as I am sure they have been granted in the interest of that Country, whose just cause I hold worthy of the sacrifice of fortune and life, if need be." LS, DLC-Robert T. Lincoln.

On Jan. 4, Rawlins wrote to McClernand. "I am instucted by the General Commdg to inquire if you have designated a Company to relieve the one stationed at Big Muddy Bridge, as per Special Order No 4, Jany 2nd 1862" Copies, DLC-USG, V, 1, 2, 3, 85; DNA, RG 393, USG Letters Sent. On Jan. 4, McClernand wrote to Rawlins. "Genl. McClernand advises Genl. Grant that he has detailed one Company out of the 4th Regt Cavalry to relieve Capt Evans' Co. at Big Muddy Bridge." Register of Letters, McClernand Papers, IHi. On Jan. 5, Rawlins wrote to Capt. Reuben B. Hatch. "You will provide Rail Road transportation for one Company of Cavalry, Camp and Garrison Equipage and two teams to Big Muddy Bridge to be in readiness tomorrow the 6th inst. at 9 O'clock, A. M. One Platform Car will be required, in making up the train." Copies, DLC-USG, V, 1, 2, 3, 85; DNA, RG 393, USG Letters Sent. On Jan. 6, Rawlins wrote to Hatch. "Yesterday orders were given for a train of Cars to be in readiness at 9 O'clock, A. M. this morning to transport a Company of Cavalry to the Big Muddy Bridge. It is now after the hour and the Company is waiting whilst the Cars, are not ready and no explanation given" Copies, ibid. On Jan. 7, McClernand wrote to Capt. William S. Hillyer. "Capt Wm D Hutchins having reported to me that he had raised a Company of Cavalry for one of the Regiments of my brigade pursuant to previous authority given by me, and having tendered said Company for acceptance, You will please proceed to Big Muddy Bridge and muster the same into the service of the United States, if the rank and file are equal to the Minimum number required by law, for such a company, the act of mustering them also to enure as the completion of my acceptance of the company." Df, McClernand Papers, IHi. On Jan. 7, Hillyer wrote to McClernand. "I will start on the early train Thursday morning for 'Big Muddy' to muster out Capt Evans Company & will be happy to fulfill your commands at that time—" ALS, ibid.

Testimony

Cairo, Illinois, October 31, 1861.

ULYSSES S. GRANT, being duly sworn, was examined as follows:

Question. Will you state the official position you occupy in the United States army?

Answer. I am brigadier general, commanding the district of southeast Missouri, to which is attached Cairo, Fort Holt, and Mound City. It extends to Cape Girardeau, but did not take in Ironton until recently.

Question. Have you any knowledge of a lot of Austrian muskets sent to the fort at Cairo? If so, please state what time they were sent, where they were sent from, the nature of the arm, and everything relating thereto.

Answer. Some arms, called the Austrian musket, were in the hands of a portion of my troops before I came here, I presume. They have been the subject of complaint wherever the troops have had them, first, because in firing them the greater portion of them would miss fire; and, secondly, the recoil is so severe that it militates very much against the effectiveness of the arm. Men would hold them very tight, shut their eyes, and brace themselves to prepare for the shock. Such are the complaints made to me.

Question. How many of them have been sent here?

Answer. I think about 2,000, but I cannot state positively.

Question. What action was taken by you in regard to them?

Answer. I reported them several times to the commander of the western department as being useless, and I also called for a board of survey to examine into and report upon the quality of the arms with which the troops here were dissatisfied, including both those I have mentioned and any others, if such there were. That report having been filed with General McClernand at this post, he can furnish a copy of it.[1]

Question. What other special objections are there to its use?

Answer. Another special objection is, they carry a ball of a different calibre from that of the musket in our service. A confusion in relation to ammunition might occur by the two kinds getting mixed.

Question. Is there any objection to the primers?

Answer. The caps we use for our regular muskets are too small for this gun.[2]

(A musket was here shown the witness.)

Question. Is the gun which we now present to you the gun you have had in your mind in your previous testimony?

Answer. It is not.

Question. State to the committee if it should turn out that the Austrian muskets which have been referred to in the questions already asked are of the kind of which this is a sample, what would your judgment of it be?

Answer. I would have to make up a hasty judgment upon it, because I have never seen one of this kind before. I should not, however, like to receive an arm like this for men in the field, because such a different ammunition is required for it. And then it is a heavy and awkward arm. It would take as long to prime this gun as it would to load an ordinary musket. It consumes too much time to get out these little wire primers, and open and shut the pan. I can say nothing in regard to the effectiveness of the arm. I am not prepared to say that it would recoil, or that it would not carry well.

Question. When you speak of the Austrian musket, do you mean what is called the needle musket, or do you speak of a musket the lock of which is formed upon the same principle as the American musket with the ordinary percussion primer?

Answer. I got my impression of the Austrian musket when Colonel Walters[3] drew some muskets, and which they called the Austrian muskets, but I am sure they could not have got such an outlandish arm as this you have shown me with this little wire primer. The muskets on which I ordered a board of survey I thought all the time were Austrian muskets.

Question. Have you examined the Austrian needle musket?

Answer. I have looked at the arm you have shown me and which you designate by that name. It requires a special ammunition, the bore being larger than that of our musket, and it also requires a special ammunition for its discharge.

Question. State your opinion of that weapon as a weapon to be used in the American army.

Answer. I have not examined it until to-day, and upon a slight examination I am most decidedly opposed to its use. The ground of objection would be the weight of the weapon; their requiring a special ammunition different from that in ordinary use; the time which would be consumed in priming it; and the using a primer which is not manufactured in this country.

Question. Do you think these objections are sufficient to make it entirely unwise to depend upon such arms at all in our ordinary military operations?

Answer. I do not think they should be used one moment beyond the time when they can be replaced by a better arm?

Question. Has this arm, in fact, been used, so far as you know, by any portion of your command?

Answer. I have never seen it in the hands of any of my men, and it has not been used, so far as I know.

Question. Where was the musket obtained to which you referred in the first part of your testimony?

Answer. In St. Louis.

Question. How is beef furnished to the district you are commanding?

Answer. By contract made before I took command of the district.

Question. Who has that contract, and at what price is the beef furnished?

Answer. I have forgotten the name of the contractor, though I have seen him.

Question. Do you know the terms of the contract?

Answer. I cannot be certain as to the price.

Question. What quality of beef has been furnished your district since you have been here?

Answer. The quality has been very good until quite recently. Within the last two or three weeks we have been getting light and poor beef, so much so, that on seeing the cattle myself, I directed the commanding officer at Bird's Point to order a board of survey.

Question. Has that board held a meeting?

Answer. Yes, sir. The proceedings of that board have not been yet reported to me. I gave orders if the board condemned them, as I was confident they would, that the contractor should be ordered to drive the cattle away.

Question. Upon what information did you order that board of survey?

Answer. Upon seeing the cattle myself. I saw they were small, lean cattle—many of them cows—which, in my judgment, would not make over 250 pounds of beef, net weight, each, if even that.

Question. Did you consider the beef unfit for the use of the army?

Answer. I did, most decidedly.

Question. If the board of survey reports against the beef, what shall you do with the cattle?

Answer. Throw them back upon the hands of the contractor, and refuse to receive them from him.

Question. Do you know anything about the contract for the hay which is furnished at this post?

Answer. That is received from St. Louis, and is receipted for to the quartermaster there. A great deal of it has been poor hay, and some of it was common prairie hay. I reported the fact to the quartermaster at St. Louis.

Question. How recently?

Answer. Within the last three weeks.

Question. What reason, if any, is there that hay should be sent here from St. Louis, instead of being bought in this vicinity?

Answer. I know of none. My own opinion is, that it should be bought here, directly, as it can be had cheaper than in St. Louis. I have now permission to purchase it here.

Question. At what price can you purchase a good quality of hay here?

Answer. I cannot say, not having to make the purchases myself. I am credibly informed that it can be bought upon the line of the railroad for $5 a ton, and that would bring it here, in my judgment, at not more than from nine to ten dollars a ton.

Question. What is the organization of the quartermaster's department in your division?

Answer. There is the post quartermaster, Mr. Hatch, and the brigade quartermaster, Captain Dunlop.[4] Then there are regimental quartermasters to each regiment. They are not authorized to make purchases, but draw all their supplies from Captain Hatch.

Question. By whom have the purchases in your department been made?

Answer. Since I have been in command here there have been no purchases of any consequence made. Everything has been brought from St. Louis.

Question. By whose direction has that been done?

Answer. Major McKinstry issued orders to Captain Hatch requiring him to draw all his supplies from St. Louis.

Question. Is that order still in existence?

Answer. I presume it can be furnished by Captain Hatch.

Answer. In what respect, in your judgment, is the public interest subserved by such an order?

Answer. In my opinion it is not subserved at all; on the contrary, it would be subserved by making the purchases here, as articles can be bought cheaper in this vicinity. I have represented that fact to the department in St. Louis.

Question. Has any notice been taken of your representations?

Answer. Yes, sir. Major Allen, the present quartermaster there, and the adjutant general, have ordered a change.

Question. So at the present time the articles are being purchased here?

Answer. They are not purchased here, for the reason that we have neither money nor credit.

Question. Why, so far as you know, has not the government furnished money to purchase these supplies?

Answer. Any answer I could make would be mere surmise. I know of no reason which I am prepared to state.

Question. Do you know the amount to which the quartermaster's department in this division is indebted?

Answer. I cannot inform you exactly. It seems to me that it is in the neighborhood of $600,000.

Question. Do you know for what that indebtedness was incurred chiefly?

Answer. They are indebted for horses, mules, lumber, forage, and for everything used in fitting up this military post; also, for coal consumed by our transports, and for the hire of persons, and, I presume, for the hire of boats, &c.

Question. How many of the boats in the service of the government here are under your command?

Answer. The number is changing constantly. When boats go up the St. Louis they are out of my command; while here they are all under my command. The moment they pass out of my district they are beyond my control. There are here some small captured boats which will be confiscated. They cost the government nothing, and there are chartered boats.

Question. Have you had the chartering of these boats?

Answer. No, sir. They were chartered in St. Louis. I am under the impression that the "Chancellor" has been chartered here without my knowledge. I would have approved the charter, but it is improper to do so without my previous sanction.

Question. By whom?

Answer. If at all, by the quartermaster. No contract should be made without my approval, and I do not intend to allow anything of that kind to be done.

Question. Have there been any contracts for boats made without your approval?

Answer. I have never approved of the contract for any boat except the wharf boat.

Question. What was the contract price for that?

Answer. $1,000 a month. That looked to me like $600 too much; but when I came to look into it, I saw that we were paying more than that for storage. That boat will store 2,500 tons. However, that is a temporary arrangement, and whenever we can dispense with it it will be done.

Question. When does this contract expire?

Answer. We are to pay at that rate as long as we use the boat. We could not get along without it. It saves more than its charter in storage, and if we move south, it would be convenient for the transportation of commissary stores.

Question. Are there a number of boats here which have been taken from the rebels; and if so, what number, and in what condition are they?

Answer. Several were taken previously to my coming here, and four have been taken since.

Question. In whose hands are they, and what measures have been taken to confiscate them?

Answer. One of them in our possession is hardly fit for use except as a hospital. We have another which we use constantly, and which has never been claimed by anybody.

Question. Where was she taken?

Answer. Up the Tennessee or Cumberland rivers. Those which have been taken since I have been here are in the hands of the civil authorities. I have ordered one or two of them to be used, to be returned to the civil authorities when called for.

Question. Can you make any use of those boats for the government service?

Answer. O yes; we are using them.

Question. Has the government in its employ, including those hired in St. Louis, more than are necessary?

Answer. I cannot say what number of boats are in the service at St. Louis, but they never send a boat here from that point unless they have something to send upon it. I keep no more boats here than are absolutely necessary for the service; and if there was danger of being attacked, we would need more boats than we have. But I think we could charter at any moment, if it were necessary, boats sufficient for our purposes—boats now lying up and doing nothing. I do not propose to charter them until we require their services.

Question. How many gunboats are now in the service of the government at this post; in what manner are they employed; what is the number of their officers and crews; and by whom are they supplied?

Answer. We have four gunboats here and at Paducah. Sometimes two of them are here and sometimes three. They carry, on an average, 100 men each. They are all officered by regular officers of the navy, and, in my opinion, very fortunately commanded.

Question. State the names of the various boats, under whose command they are, and the number of officers.

Answer. You can get the number of officers correctly from Commander Foot, as he has command of them, and they make no report to me. Commander Foot commands the entire fleet, and for the present he remains at St. Louis, having charge of those new gunboats which are being built, their armament, and the making of all the appointments, &c.

Captain Porter commands the *New Era*; Captain Walker[5] commands the *Taylor*; Captain Stembel commands the *Lexington*; and Captain Phelps the *Conestoga*.

Question. What was the grade of those officers in the navy, and what is their grade here?

Answer. I think Foot, Porter, and Walker are captains in the regular navy; that Stembel was a commander, and Phelps a lieutenant.

Question. State, as nearly as you can, the number of officers employed, besides the commanders of the vessels.

Answer. I cannot tell you, as it is so much out of my line.

Question. Do you know in what manner those vessels are supplied?

Answer. I have tried to get a solution of that question myself from the commanding general of this district, but I have never received a reply to my communication upon that subject. I have supplied them here from the army commissary stores, because it was a necessity that they should be supplied, as they are doing valuable service.

HRC, 37-2-2, part 2, 1–6. This testimony was given to the House Select Committee on Government Contracts, authorized on July 8, 1861, which included Elihu B. Washburne. On Oct. 31, Washburne wrote from Cairo to Secretary of the Treasury Salmon P. Chase. "Genl. Grant, who is in command of this whole section, is one of the best officers in the army, and is doing wonders in bringing order out of chaos. He is as incorruptible as he is brave. Genl. McClernand, in command of this particular post is doing admirably. But they complain they have no money, and are greatly deficient in arms." *Annual Report of the American Historical Association for the Year 1902* (Washington, 1903), II, 507–8. See letter to Elihu B. Washburne, Nov. 20, 1861.

1. The board was actually ordered by Brig. Gen. John A. McClernand. *HRC*, 37-2-2, part 2, 9.
2. See letters to Maj. Gen. John C. Frémont, Sept. 12, 15, 1861.
3. Perhaps a reference to Col. William H. L. Wallace, 11th Ill.
4. Capt. James Dunlap.
5. Commander Henry Walke.

To Brig. Gen. John A. McClernand

Head Quarters, Dist. S. E. Mo.
Cairo October 31st 1861

Gen. J. A. McClernand
Comd.g Post, Cairo Ill.
Gen.

Capt. Fullerton[1] 2d Ill. Cavalry has brought some wheat, and other property taken from one Price, a Kentucky rebel, which it is necessary to make some disposition of.

I would recommend that the wheat be sent to the mill and exchanged for flour and that turned over to the Post Commissary.

The other property being claimed by other parties their claims should be investigated and if not found valid the property should go into the hands of the Quartermaster.

Respectfully &c.

U. S. GRANT

Brig. Gen. Com

ALS, McClernand Papers, IHi.

1. Capt. Hugh Fullerton of Havana, 2nd Ill. Cav.

To Commander Henry Walke

Headquarters District Southeast Missouri,
Cairo, October 31, 1861.

CAPTAIN:

Commodore Foote has written to me to send the gunboat *Conestoga*, or some other, to Paducah to relieve the *New Era*, which is to return to St. Louis.[1] Will you be kind enough to distinguish the boat that is to go?

I would be pleased to have you make a reconnoissance to-day with your gunboat as far as it is secure to go. It is not my desire that you should throw any shell, unless you should discover the enemy away from their encampments and think you could do good execution.

It is not absolutely necessary that the gunboat should go to Paducah before to-morrow.

Yours, respectfully,

U. S. GRANT,

Brigadier-General, Commanding.

Captain Walke,
Commanding Fleet, Cairo, Ill.

O.R. (Navy), I, xxii, 389; Goodspeed's Catalogue 510, April 10, 1963. On Oct. 31, 1861, Commander Henry Walke wrote to Capt. Andrew H. Foote. "I made a reconnoissance down the river this morning, under instructions from General Grant, as far as the extreme end of Lucas Bend and below Island No. 4. Found no apparent change in the appearance of the country and saw no movements of the enemy this side of Columbus. Many of their camp tents seem to have disappeared from the Iron Banks, and there were no new indications of works or anything else going on. We returned to Cairo by 3. General Grant having referred the subject of Commander Porter's being relieved from duty at Paducah to me, I designated the *Conestoga* as best adapted for that service, and this vessel will take her place to-morrow at Mound City; the *Lexington* remaining at Cairo and vicinity." *O.R.* (Navy), I, xxii, 389–90.

1. After remodeling in St. Louis, the gunboat *New Era* was renamed *Essex.*

To Capt. John P. Hawkins

Head Quarters Dist S. E. Mo
Cairo Oct 31st 1861

SPECIAL ORDER

Capt J. P. Hawkins Act Chief Qr Mr & Comsy Dist S. E. Mo. will proceed to Springfield Ill. and St Louis Mo. for the purpose of procuring Blankets for Hospitals and other purposes connected with his department

U. S. GRANT
Brig Genl Comdg

Copies, DLC-USG, V, 15, 16, 77, 82; DNA, RG 393, USG Special Orders. See letter to Brig. Gen. Lorenzo Thomas, Oct. 20, 1861.

To Capt. Reuben B. Hatch

———

Head Quarters Dist S. E. Mo
Cairo ~~Oct~~ Nov 1st 1861

CAPT R. B. HATCH
POST Q. M.
CAIRO ILLS
SIR

You are directed to purchase a lot of corn now at the Levee for the use of Government, provided the same can be got for a sum not to exceed thirty cents per bushell.

U. S. GRANT
Brig Genl Comdg

Copies, DLC-USG, V, 2, 16, 77, 82; DNA, RG 393, Letters Sent.

To Capt. Reuben B. Hatch

———

Headquarters Dist. S. E. Mo.
Cairo, Nov. 1, 1861

CAPT R. B. HATCH
POST Q. M.
CAIRO ILLS
SIR

You are directed to turn over to Col J. A. Logan[1] all the muskets in your possession and take receipt for the same

U S. GRANT
Brig Gnl Comdg

Copies, DLC-USG, V, 1, 2, 3, 77; DNA, RG 393, USG Letters Sent.

1. Col. John A. Logan, 31st Ill., was concurrently U.S. Representative from the Ninth Congressional District of Ill., comprising the southernmost part of the state. Logan's pro-southern stance in the prewar Congress created doubt concerning which side he would favor when war began. His first public speech for

the Union was made to USG's 7th Congressional District Regt. See letter to Julia Dent Grant, June 27, 1861, note 2. USG believed that Logan's vigorous support of the Union cause influenced all of southern Ill. See letter to Elihu B. Washburne, Feb. 22, 1862; *Memoirs*, I, 244–46. See also James P. Jones, "*Black Jack:*" *John A. Logan and Southern Illinois in the Civil War Era* (Tallahassee, 1967), chaps. v–vi.

To William S. Hillyer

———

Head Quarters District South East Mo.
Cairo, Nov 1st 1861

To ALL WHOM IT MAY CONCERN
By virtue of the authority in me vested I do nominate and appoint
Master Willie S. Hillyer
Pony Aid de Camp with the rank of major to be attached to my staff.

All stable boys will take due notice and obey him accordingly —Done at Cairo this Novr 1, 1861

U. S. GRANT
Brig. Gen. U. S. A.

Attest
JNO. A. RAWLINS
Assistant Adj General

DS, Palmer Collection, OClWHi. For an indication of the family troubles which may have brought the young son of Capt. William S. Hillyer to Cairo, see letter to Julia Dent Grant, Sept. 20, 1861.

To Capt. Chauncey McKeever

———

BY TELEGRAPH FROM Cairo [*Nov.*] 2d *186*[*1*]
To CAPT MCKEEVER
Your telegraph recd   I will send two (2) regts cavalry & artillery at once.

U S GRANT

Telegram received, DNA, RG 107, Telegrams Collected (Unbound); copies, *ibid.*, RG 393, Western Dept., Telegrams; DLC-USG, VIA, 2. On Nov. 2, 1861, Capt. Chauncey McKeever had telegraphed to USG. "Jeff Thompson is at Indian Ford of the St. Francis river, twenty five miles below Greenville, with about three thousand men. Colonel Carlin has started with force from Pilot Knob. Send a force from Cape Girardeau and Birds Point to assist Carlin in driving Thompson into Arkansas." Copies, *ibid.*, V, 4, 5, 7, 8; DNA, RG 94, Letters Received; *ibid.*, RG 393, USG Hd. Qrs. Correspondence. *O.R.*, I, iii, 268.

To Brig. Gen. John A. McClernand

Head Quarters, Dist. S. E. Mo.
Cairo, November 2d 1861

GEN. J. A. MCCLERNAND
COMD.G POST
CAIRO ILL.
GEN.

I am directed, by a despatch just receive, to send a force to Indian Ford, on the St. Francois river.[1] I have thought of sending Cols. Lawler & Logan as a part of the command if there is no valid reason for not doing so.

I should like to see those Cols. to-night and give directions so that they may prepare for an early start.

Your Obt. Svt.
U. S. GRANT
Brig. Gen.

ALS, McClernand Papers, IHi.

1. Indian Ford, on the St. Francis River in Mo., about sixty-two miles west of Cairo. See preceding telegram.

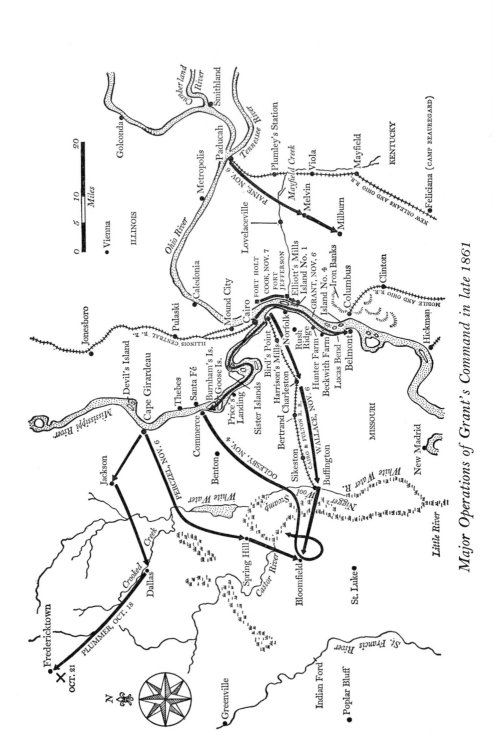

Major Operations of Grant's Command in late 1861

To Col. Richard J. Oglesby

———

Head Quarters Dist S. E. Mo
Cairo Nov 2d 1861

Col

A dispatch just recieved requires me to send a force to the St Francis River to destroy Rebels congregated there.[1]

I have determined to give you the command and will require your Regiment and three ~~questions~~ companies of Cavalry from Birds Point to prepare for as early a move tomorrow as ~~possible~~ practicable.

The balance of your command will be sent from this side of the River.

You will require fourteen days rations and about four days forage this latter article being heavy must be supplied by the country through which you pass.

Thirty or thirty five Teams must be supplied from your side of the River and to get them you will have to draw upon the Regimental transportation of the whole command there.

Detailed instructions will be drawn up for you before starting.[2]

U. S. Grant
Brig Genl Comdg

To Col Oglesby
Birds Point Mo

Copies, DLC-USG, V, 1, 2, 3, 77; DNA, RG 94, Letters Received; *ibid.*, War Records Office, Union Battle Reports; *ibid.*, RG 393, USG Letters Sent. *O.R.*, I, iii, 257. On Nov. 13, 1861, Col. Richard J. Oglesby wrote to USG. "I have to report that upon receiving your order at 12 O'clock at night Nov. 2d., I immediately organized the expedition to move in-land from this point, and in the direction of the St Francis river. On Monday morning the ~~entire~~ forces Consisting of the 18th Reg't Ills Vols Commanded by Col Michael Lawler the 29th Reg't Ills Vols Commanded by Col James Reardon, and One Section of Captain Schwartz, Light Artillery, Commanded by Lieut Cumbert from Brig Genl McClernand's Brigade Cairo Ills, and the 8th Reg't Ills Vols Lieut Col Frank L. Rhoads Com'dg, One Battalion 11th Reg't Ills Vols Lieut Col P. E. G. Ransom Com'dg, Captain Pfaffs, Cavalry; and Captain Langens Cavalry Lieut Hansen Com'dg and Capt Nolemans Centralia Cavalry, Lieut Tufts Com'dg, were landed at Commerce

Mo. The day was occupied ~~by~~ in unloading supplies and arranging transportation for the March; Bearing in mind your order to pursue ~~Jeff. Thompson~~ the Rebel forces under Jeff Thompson—wherever they might be found, and to destroy the same, if found—I marched directly for Bloomfield Mo, at which point I was reliably informed the Rebel forces were encamped, to avoid delay I moved the column directly towards the 'Nigger Wool' Swamp, and crossed it, and the Swamp between it and Little River at Stringer's ferry—7 miles in one day. to do this it became necessary to construct several bridges, and to cut out a new road in several places. The Rebel pickets were met by my advance guard on the bridge, over the Lake in the Swamp, a Slight skirmish ensued, an effort was made by the Rebels to burn the bridge, it was soon repaired under the direction of Dr John M. Phipps Ass't Surgeon of the 8th Reg't. In the afternoon of Thursday, seven miles from Bloomfield, I received a note from Col Perczel of the 10th Reg't Iowa Vols, informing me that he had taken possesion of the town, without resistance. The forces under Genl Thompson retreated in the direction of New Madrid on the night of the 6th Inst.—At Bloomfield I received your order to turn the Column in the direction of New Madrid; I had already sent forward on the road towards New Madrid, Col Perczel with his Reg't about 6 miles, when Col. Wm H. L. Wallace came up with the remaining Companies of his Regiment and took command of the 11th Reg't in person; Through Col Wallace I received your verbal order to return to Birds Point. To avoid the terrible Swamp in front of Bloomfield I returned by Cape Girardeau Col's Lawler and Reardon marched to Cape Girardeau in two days The 8th and 11th Ills and 10th Iowa following the next day. The whole force arrived at Birds Point on Tuesday the 12th, having marched over 100 miles, and embarked and debarked twice and travelled by water 85 miles besides—in less than nine days. I detained the forces one day at Bloomfield out of the nine. The chief object of the expedition having failed, I have to inform you that the information derived about the Country and of the feelings of the inhabitants, and the purposes of the rebellion have fully compensated all the labor it has required.—A more unhappy and deluded people I have never seen— Wherever the Column moved, Consternation filled the whole Community, and the fact that—without regard to sex or age, the whole people were not outraged and destroyed, seemed to Stupify them. I have to report the wanton destruction of property in one or two instances. Otherwise the March through the Country was most exemplary and satisfactory. My orders were obeyed with cheerfulness and alacrity. After four days, I obtained forage from the people of the Country for all the Mules and horses. Four fifths of the Inhabitants are ready to return to the Union, whenever the Government can assure them from punishment by the Rebel Army.—The Yoke of Jeff Thompson is a heavy One; and the people are becoming disgusted at his arbitrary Sway. The Scrip he has substituted for a good currency is totally worthless. His brutality in murdering in Cold blood so many good citizens of Mo, and suffering them to rot unburied in full view of the public, has met its just return, in the horror with which he and his whole Command are beginning to be appreciated by the people of South E. Mo" Copies, DNA, RG 94, Letters Received; *ibid.*, War Records Office, Union Battle Reports; *ibid.*, RG 393, District of Southeast Mo., Letters Received. *O.R.*, I, iii, 256–57.

1. See telegram to Capt. Chauncey McKeever, Nov. 2, 1861.
2. See letter to Col. Richard J. Oglesby, Nov. 3, 1861.

To Maj. Joseph D. Webster

Head Qrs Dist So. E. Mo
Cairo Nov 2d 1861.

COL J D WEBSTER
CHIEF OF ENGINEERS
CAIRO ILLS

You will commence as soon as possible revetting the outer embankments of Fort Prentiss with planks or such materials as in your judgment, may be the best suited.

You are authorized to purchase such materials as may be requisite for that purpose

U. S. GRANT
Brig Gen Comdg

Copies, DLC-USG, V, 1, 2, 3, 77; DNA, RG 393, USG Letters Sent. See letter to Capt. Chauncey McKeever, Oct. 17, 1861.

To Capt. Reuben C. Rutherford

Head Quarters Dist S. E. Mo
Cairo Nov 2d 1861

CAPT RUTHERFORD

will fill all orders of Col A. H. Waterman,[1] for subsistence Stores without regard to the usual forms of Provision Returns —in compliance with the order of Genl J. C. Fremont Comdg Western Dept.

U. S. GRANT
Brig Genl Comdg

Copies, DLC-USG, V, 15, 16, 77, 82; DNA, RG 393, USG Special Orders.

1. Col. A. H. Waterman had been appointed superintendent of the Cairo and Fulton Railroad. See letter to Col. A. H. Waterman, Nov. 15, 1861.

To Capt. Chauncey McKeever

BY TELEGRAPH FROM Cairo [*Nov.*] 3 *186*[*1*]
To CAPT CHAUNCEY McKEEVER
Send me one or two 2 Regiments from St Louis in place
Second Iowa. Authorize me to order Eight 8th Missouri from
Paducah. We have not got land transportation.
U. S. GRANT

Telegram received (punctuation added), DNA, RG 107, Telegrams Collected
(Unbound); copies, *ibid.*, RG 393, Western Dept., Telegrams; DLC-USG, VIA,
2.

To Col. Richard J. Oglesby

Head Quarters Dist S. E. Mo
Cairo Nov 3d 1861

COL R. J. OGLESBY
COMDG U. S. FORCES
BIRDS POINT, MO
You will take command of an expedition, consisting of your
Regt four companies of the 11th Ill. all of the 18th and 29th
Cols Lawler and ~~Logan~~ Reardon[1] Comd.g, three companies of
Cavalry from Birds Point, to be selected and notified by yourself,
and a section of Schwartz Battery of artillery,[2] and proceed by
steamers to Commerce Mo. From Commerce you will strike for
Sikeston, Mr Cropper acting as guide. From there you will go
in pursuit of a Rebel force understood to be 3000 strong under
Jeff Thompson, and now at ~~St Francios~~ Indian Ford on the St
Francois River.
An expedition has already left Ironton Mo. to attack this
force. Should you learn that they have left that place it will not
be necessary for you to go there but pursue the enemy in any

direction he may ~~choose~~ go, always being cautious not to fall in with an unlooked for foe too strong for the command ~~for~~ under you.

The object of the expedition is to destroy this force, and the manner of doing it is left largely at your discretion beleiving it better not to trammel you with instructions. Transportation will be furnished you for fourteen days Rations and four or five days forage. All that you may require, outside of this must be furnished by the country through which you pass.

In taking supplies you will be careful to select a proper officer to press them, and require a receipt to be given, and the articles pressed accounted for the same as if purchased.

You are particularly enjoined to allow no foraging by your men. It is demoralizing in the extreme and is apt to make open enemies where they would not otherwise exist.

Yours &c

U. S. GRANT

Brig Genl Com

Copies, DLC-USG, V, 1, 2, 3, 77; DNA, RG 94, Letters Received; *ibid.*, RG 393, USG Letters Sent. *O.R.*, I, iii, 268. On Nov. 3, 1861. Capt. John A. Rawlins wrote to Brig. Gen. John A. McClernand. "I am directed by Brig Genl U. S. Grant Comdg to request that you have ready for moving from here by 4 o.clock P. M. by Boat the 18th and 32nd Regts Ill Vols They will take with them all their land transportation, forty rounds of Ammunition in Cartridge Boxes and as many more in Wagons, fourteen days Rations, and five days Forage for teams and Horses. orders have been given to Capt Schwartz, to have one section of his Battery ready to move at the same time." LS, McClernand Papers, IHi. In letterbook copies, the 18th and 29th Ill. are designated. DLC-USG, V, 1, 2, 3, 77; DNA, RG 393, USG Letters Sent. On the same day, Rawlins wrote to Capt. Reuben B. Hatch. "You will furnish to the 29th Regt Ill Vols seven or eight teams for their transportation, and forage for five days." Copies, *ibid.* Also on Nov. 3, Capt. William S. Hillyer wrote to George W. Graham. "You will furnish steamboat transportation for three Regiments of Infantry, three companies of Cavalry a section of artillery, and the transportation for the whole command to be ready at 12 o.clock to day.—let the 'Scott' go to Birds Point, to take one Regiment of Infantry & three companies of Cavalry.—the rest will load here—" Copies, *ibid.* On Nov. 4, Col. Richard J. Oglesby wrote to USG. "I have just completed the Loading of my Supply Train—will start in the morning at 6½ Oclock. My Scouts in from Benton bring three Prisoners—from them as well as from other more reliable sources I learn the road from Sykeston to Bloomfield is nearly impassable—my impression to night is that I shall go to Abe Hunters farm tomorrow night as I get plenty of water there from there I will go to [.....] Waughs—Confederate Col—5 miles and then 8 miles to Little River—The swamp is more accessible by this route and I will be able to reach Bloomfield one day or nearly so earlier There is no special object in going to Sykeston—unless to cut Him—Jeff—off. I gain nothing in that view—since He could as well fall back towards the Arkansas Line across the St Francois—He has 2000 Men of all sorts—but Himself is yet absent at Memphis or was Saturday—I shall pay my respects to Col Hunters & Col Waughs Beef at an early day—I fear I shall have trouble with Col Lawlers Men—whilst He seems very anxious to do His whole duty He seems not to be able to check the Licentious habits of His Soldiers—they have committed some small depredations to day on citizens near Town—'' ALS, *ibid.*, District of Southeast Mo., Letters Received.

    1. Col. James S. Rearden, 29th Ill.
    2. On Nov. 3, Rawlins wrote to Capt. Adolph Schwartz. "You will have one section of your artillery with what ammunition they can carry, together with Fourteen Days rations ready for moving from here by boat by 4 o.clock this P. M also 4 days forage for Horses" Copies, DLC-USG, V, 1, 2, 3, 77; DNA, RG 393, USG Letters Sent.

To Col. Joseph B. Plummer

Head Qrs Dist S. E. Mo
Cairo Nov 3d 1861

Col J. B. Plummer
Comdg U. S. Forces
Cape Girardeau, Mo
Sir

    The Question has been asked me if leaves of absence may not be granted sick men from your command. You may grant suitable leaves to all men who are unfit for duty, and in case of three months volunteers who have since enlisted for three years, and not previously been on leave you can do the same.

Yours &c
U. S. Grant
Brig Genl Comdg

Copies, DLC-USG, V, 1, 2, 3, 77; DNA, RG 393, USG Letters Sent.

To Capt. Chauncey McKeever

——

By Telegraph from Cairo [*Nov. 4*] *186*[*1*]
To Capt C McKeever
    Sir. I have sent three (3) regts & battalion of Infantry three
(3) companies of cavalry & section of artillery as ordered
                                            U S Grant

Telegram received, DNA, RG 107, Telegrams Collected (Unbound); copies,
ibid., RG 393, Western Dept., Telegrams; DLC-USG, VIA, 2. See telegram to
Capt. Chauncey McKeever, Nov. 2, 1861.

To Col. Joseph B. Plummer

——

                            Head Quarters District S. E. Mo
                                    Cairo Nov 4th 1861

Col J. B. Plummer
Comdg U. S. Forces
Cape Girardeau, Mo
Sir
    In pursuance of directions from Head Quarters Western
Department you will send out on an expedition towards Bloomfield the 10th Iowa Vols.
    Send with them four days rations and four days forage.
    Caution the commanding officer of the Expedition, in your
instructions that no marauding or foraging is to be allowed under
any circumstances. Private Houses are not to be entered,
against the will of the people, except in pursuance of orders of
the Commanding officer of & then, only on business to carry
out the object of the expedition.
    When it becomes necessary to have forage for the trans-
portation of teams it will be taken and vouchers given at a fair
valuation, and accounted for.

On the return of this Regiment it will be ordered here unless otherwise directed.

You will also send to this place as soon as practicable, so much of the Engineers force as can be spared from your command.

Yours &c

U. S. GRANT

Brig Genl Comdg

Copies, DLC-USG, V, 1, 2, 3, 77; DNA, RG 393, USG Letters Sent. *O.R.*, I, iii, 259. On Nov. 5, 1861, Col. Leonard F. Ross, Cape Girardeau, wrote to USG. "An order from Head Qrs West Dept dated Nov 1st/61 and directed to Col J B Plummer instructing him to make demonstrations against Bloomfield with part of the forces here, was received last evening I shall move in that direction at 5. O clock A M. this morning with about 1600 Infantry 40 Cavalry and one section of Artillery It is reported here that five or six thousand troops from Cairo landed at Commerce to day, and are moveing towards Benton" Copy, DNA, RG 393, Post of Cape Girardeau, Letters Sent. On Nov. 6, Col. Joseph B. Plummer wrote to Capt. John A. Rawlins. "I have the honor to report that on my return to this Post last evening I found Col. Ross had marched yesterday morning with the three Regts Stationed here, a Section of Artillery, and all of the Fremont Rangers. I immediatly despatched a messenger with an order for the 17th Ill. and 11th Mo. to return to this Post and instructed the 10th Iowa to move on towards Bloomfield in Compliance with the orders of the Genl. Comd'g" LS, *ibid.*, District of Southeast Mo., Letters Received. Also on Nov. 6, Plummer again wrote to Rawlins. "Pursuant to the Genls instruction I send down on the Steamer "B" One Company of the Engineer troops under the Command of, 2d Lieut Hasie, being all that can conveniently spaired from the Post at this time. Major Hasie who was Captain of the Co. and has been notified of his promotion, I retain here in Command of the remainder of the Detachment The 1st Lieut is absent but will be ordered to join his Company as soon as he returns to this Post" Copy, *ibid.*, Post of Cape Girardeau, Letters Sent. On Nov. 7, Plummer telegraphed to USG. "A Short time after I despatched my Letter of this morning to Genl. Grant, Col. Ross arrived here with his command. Col. Percell is ~~all ready~~ already in Bloomfield or Near there. I will direct Col. Ross to Start back for Bloomfield this Evening, Should the Genl. Still deem it necessary." Telegram received (punctuation added), *ibid.*, Dept. of the Mo., Telegrams Received. On Nov. 12, Col. Nicholas Perczel reported the results of his expedition to Plummer. ALS, *ibid.*, RG 94, War Records Office, Union Battle Reports. *O.R.*, I, iii, 258–59. See letter to Col. Joseph B. Plummer, Nov. 7, 1861.

To Brig. Gen. John A. McClernand

Head Quarters, Dist. S. E. Mo.
Cairo, November 5th 1861

GEN. J. A. MCCLERNAND
COMD.G POST
CAIRO, ILL.
GEN.

In pursuance of directions from Head Quarters Western Department ~~in~~ a reconnoisance, in force, will be made from this command commencing to-morrow evening.

You will please notify one regiment from your command,[1] and any Cavalry that may be effectively armed, to hold themselvs in readiness with two days rations in their haversacks and forty rounds of Ammunition in Cartridge box.

I should be pleased to have a consultation with you this evening, after ten, on the subject if you are at leasure.

Yours &c—
U. S. GRANT
Brig. Gen. Com.

ALS, McClernand Papers, IHi.

1. On Nov. 5, 1861, Brig. Gen. John A. McClernand ordered Col. Napoleon B. Buford, 27th Ill., to prepare his regt. to move "at a moments warning." *The Collector*, LXXVII, 1–3 (1964), 9.

To Brig. Gen. Charles F. Smith

———

Head Quarters, Dist. S. E. Mo.
Cairo, November 5th 1861

Gen. C. F. Smith
Comd.g U. S. Forces
Paducah Ky.
Gen.

In pursuance of directions from Head Quarters, Western Dept. I have sent from here a force of about 3.000 men, all arms, towards Indian Ford, on the St. Francois river, and also a force of one regiment from Cape Girardeau in the same direction.

I am now, under the same instructions, fitting out an expedition to menace Belmont and will take all the force proper to spare from here, probably not more than 3000 men.

If you can make a demonst[ration] towards Columbus, at the same time, with a portion of your command it would probably keep the enemy from throwing over the river much more force than they now have there, and might enable me to drive those they now have out of Missouri.

The principle point to gain is to prevent the enemy from sending a force to fall in the rear of those now out from this command.

I will leave here to morrow night, by boat, and land some twelve miles below.

Respectfully
Your Obt. Svt.
U. S. Grant
Brig. Gen. Com.

ALS, DNA, RG 94, Letters Received. *O.R.*, I, iii, 273. On Nov. 6, 1861, Brig. Gen. Charles F. Smith forwarded this letter to Brig. Gen. Lorenzo Thomas as an enclosure in a letter printed *ibid.*, I, iv, 339–40. On Nov. 6, Smith wrote to USG. "I have ~~responded~~ responded by telegraph just now that I meant to send a force to threaten Columbus. Genl. *Paine* with 2000 men of all arms will leave here at 2 o'c this afternoon & will be about 3 days, going to *Melvin*. I shall also send to

Plumley's Station on the rail-way (12 miles) a regt. & section of art." ALS, DNA, RG 393, District of Southeast Mo., Letters Received.

To Col. C. Carroll Marsh

Head Quarters Dist S. E. Mo.
Cairo Nov 5th 1861

Col. C. C. Marsh
Comdg Brigade
Birds Point, Mo
Sir

In pursuance of directions from Head Quarters Western Department, a reconnoisance in force will be made starting probably tomorrow evening.

The able bodied of the 22d Ill and 7th Iowa Vols. together with Taylors Battery of Light Artillery, and all the Cavalry at Birds Point, will be required on the expedition.

You will give the necessary instructions to such of these troops as belong to your Brigade to hold themselves in readiness, with two days rations in their Haversacks, and forty rounds of ammunition.

U. S. Grant
Brig. Gen. Com

LS, DNA, RG 94, War Records Office, Dept. of the Mo. This letter appears in the USG letterbooks addressed to Col. C. Carroll Marsh and also Col. Henry Dougherty, indicating the probability that an identical letter was sent to Dougherty. Copies, DLC-USG, V, 1, 2, 77; DNA, RG 393, USG Letters Sent. The copy in vol. 77 bears a notation by John W. Resor, secretary. "An order in substance the same as this has this day been forwarded to Brig Genl McClernand of which there is no true copy."

To Col. C. Carroll Marsh

———

Head Quarters Dist S. E. Mo
Cairo Nov 5th 1861

COLONEL

I am instructed by Genl Grant Comdg to extend to you and your command, a cordial welcome on your return from the field of Battle and of victory.

The reports that have reached him from Fredericktown, have filled him with the highest admiration of the valor and patriotism displayed, by you and your command in that engagement.

Amid the gloom that filled the country on the announcement of the reverses of our arms at "Leesburg,"[1] Fredericktown arose and threw athwart the clouds its bow of promise.

I[*t*] was your privilege to be among the foremost of that gallant band who raised our drooping banner and emblazoned it with victory.

The importance of that success cannot be measured by any ordinary standard.—It gave new life to tens of thousands of our discouraged Soldiers.—It crushed out the Rebellion in South East Missouri.—It sustained the prestige of victory to our flag, and not the least of your Generals Congratulations is that you have brought back your entire command.

Yours &c
U. S. Grant
WM. S. HILLYER
Aid de Camp

To Col C. C. Marsh
Comdg 20th Ill Vols

Copies, DLC-USG, V, 1, 2, 3, 79; DNA, RG 393, USG Letters Sent. *O.R.*, I, iii, 214. For the official report of Col. C. Carroll Marsh, see *ibid.*, pp. 212–13.

1. The U. S. defeat near Leesburg, Va., Oct. 21, 1861, is better known as the battle of Ball's Bluff or Edwards' Ferry.

To Capt. Reuben B. Hatch

———

Head Quarters Dist S. E. Mo
Cairo Nov 5th 1861

Capt. R. B. Hatch
Post Quartermaster
Cairo Ills.
Sir
   You will please make out requisitions for Axes, spades, Picks, and all tools likely to be required by this command, and not now on hand, and have the same forwarded to Saint Louis, as soon as possible.
Yours &c
U. S. Grant
Brig Genl Comdg

Copies, DLC-USG, V, 1, 2, 3, 77; DNA, RG 393, USG Letters Sent.

To Richard Yates

———

Brigade Head Quarters
Camp Cairo Nov. 5th 1861

His Excellency
Richd Yates
Govr. of Illinois
Sir:
   A Committee of respectable and leading citizens of Jefferson County Illinois, Consisting of Maj. Noah Johnson,[1] Hon Wm Anderson, Wm Dodd Esqr., Harvey T. Pace Esq. T. B. Tanner

Esq and others, waited upon us, at this place, on the 31st ulto, for the purpose of making and asking explanations.

They informed us that the arrest of one or more persons in their neighboring County of Hamilton, by order of the Military authorities at Shawneetown Illinois,[2] had excited much apprehension and uneasiness among the people of Jefferson County for their own personal safety; and protesting the loyalty of the people of that County, asked if any assurance could be given which would allay the disquietude refered to.—We answered that the arrests alluded to were not made by our order, or with our knowledge, and that no arrest or molestation of a citizen of the State was contemplated by us in any case cognizable by the Civil authorities and wherein our authority was not clear for the purpose.

We stated to them that you, as Governor, of the State and Commander in Chief of the Militia of the State, ~~was~~ were the proper person to hear their representations and to afford such relief as the case might require, and that we doubted not you would do so.

We suggested that we had heard of the existence of a secret political order known as the "Knights of the Golden Circle" in Some portions of Illinois, which, in the begining had aided and abetted the rebellion in the South and whose ultimate aim,—in the North—was incompatible with good Citizenship, and the fulfillment of patriotic duty,—and that the order Should be discontinued and if necessary repressed—[3]

The members of the Committee, respectively, denied that they were members of, or privy to the order: and concluded the interview by requesting us to report the result of it to you,—hoping as they said that you would take such steps as you might think proper to quiet the apprehensions of those in whose behalf they spoke—and pledging themselves, at the same time, that if suspicion Should attach to any one of them, or to any of those for whom they Spoke, upon notification of the fact, he would be immediately sent by them before any tribunal having cognizance of his case.

Having complied with this request, we close this communication.

> Your Obt Servt—
> U. S. GRANT
> Brig. Gen. Com.
> Dist. S. E. Mo.
> JOHN A. McCLERNAND
> Brig. Genl. Comg.

LS, ICHi. Dateline, style, and handwriting all indicate that the letter was prepared at the hd. qrs. of Brig. Gen. John A. McClernand. Governor Richard Yates
outlined his answer on the back of the letter. "A cautious article should be written
this Committee—saying that no arrests made had been directly authorized by me
—but that I was well advised of the movements of the 'Knights of the Golden
Circle'—that their objects were fully understood—that arrests would be discouraged except in clear cases—but that all traitors and secessionists had better
seek a more congenial and could not live in Illinois while there was power in the
government to ~~put them down~~ inflict the punishment their treason deserved."

 1. Noah C. Johnson appears to have acted as an investigator for USG. On
Oct. 8, 1861, R. B. Stinson, Anna, Ill., reported Johnson to the provost marshal,
St. Louis, as a suspicious person making extensive inquiries. ALS, DNA, RG 109,
Records of the U. S. War Dept. Relating to Confederates, Union Provost Marshal's Citizens File. On Oct. 21, Johnson wrote to USG. "I took passage on the
Steamer Louissiana on the 18th inst Landed on Burnhams Island 8 oclock Same
evening Stayed there untill next Morning Crossed over to Commerce and found
the Business Men Selling to every person Calling on them, without regard to
politics the Same thing Done in Santifee on the opposite Side to Commerce on
the Illinois Side—the Same thing Done at the Town of Thebes five Miles above
Santifee on the Illinois Side they all promised to do Better and that they would
Sell nothing more to a Secessionest how fare the[y] will regard their promises I
Cannot tell I Would here remark that there is a Store in the Town of Benton 8
Miles West of Commerce that is furnishing Supplies to the Secessionest Scercely
a Union family in the place or neigh Bourhood—I also Learn upon good authority
that there has Ben Severil persons known to Cross the Mississippi River ten
Miles above this place taking with them a Quanty of arms" ALS, *ibid.*, RG 393,
District of Southeast Mo., Letters Received.
 2. On Oct. 25, Col. Robert Kirkham, Shawneetown, Ill., wrote to USG.
"There are one or two companies forming in Hamilton and Jefferson Co.s of this
state with the intention of going into the Southern Confedercy. I have here about
30 guns, and it is actually necessary to have a larger number so that I can go into
to these counties for the purpose of capturing the Ringleaders and others that are
interested in Rendering any assistance in the way of getting up Companies. Could
you not send me 100 guns or more. I can make good use of them. I have just
Returned from an Expedition, and succeeded in capturing four men (one a captain) who were interested in getting up a company for the purpose of moving into
Kentucky and connecting themselves with the Southern Rebels. If you could send

me guns, until some can Reach me Springfield you will confer a great favour"
ALS, *ibid.* On Oct. 25, Lt. S. Ledyard Phelps wrote to Capt. Andrew H. Foote.
"I did not receive the dispatch till noon yesterday, having gone down below
Shawneetown in hope of taking prisoners Some 70 K. G. C,s about leaving Illinois
to join the rebels in Kentucky. The person who had gone out to ascertain exactly
the movements of these people, and who had joined their order for this purpose,
failed to return, and I, therefore, could effect nothing." ALS, *ibid.*, RG 45, Area 5.
O.R. (Navy), I, xxii, 378. "A squad of Uncle Sam's boys passed through Mc-
Leansboro in Hamilton county, and took in charge eight of the Grand Lights of
the Circle." Letter of L. O. M. Butler, Fairfield, Ill., Oct. 30, 1861, in *Missouri
Democrat*, Nov. 4, 1861.

    3. The nature and extent in Ill. of secret societies such as the Knights of the
Golden Circle aiding the C. S. A. has always been disputed. After a survey of the
evidence, Frank L. Klement concluded that "the subversive society bogey-man
was a political apparition intended solely to aid Republicans in defeating Demo-
crats at the polls." "Copperhead Secret Societies in Illinois during the Civil
War," *Journal of the Illinois State Historical Society*, XLVIII, 2 (Summer, 1955),
180.

To Brig. Gen. Charles F. Smith

———

By Telegraph from Cairo [*Nov.*] 6th *1861*
To Gen Smith

    I move tonight with all my available force, about four
thousand, if necessary I can send an express to two columns now
moving towards Bloomfield & add nearly five thousand more
Gen Grant

Telegram received, DNA, RG 94, Letters Received. On Nov. 6, 1861, Brig. Gen.
Charles F. Smith forwarded this telegram to Brig. Gen. Lorenzo Thomas as an
enclosure in a letter printed in *O.R.*, I, iv, 339–40.

To Col. John Cook

———

Head Quarters, Dist. S. E. Mo.
Cairo, November 6th 1861

Col. J. Cook
Comd.g U. S. Forces
Fort Holt Ky.
Sir:

Hold Sixteen Companies of your command in readiness to march, at an hours notice, with two days rations in their Haversacks.

You will require no transportation except for tents sufficient to accommodate your command for one night.

Yours &c.
U. S. Grant
Brig. Gen. Com.

ALS, ICarbS. See following letter.

To Col. John Cook

———

Head Quarters Dist S. E. Mo
Cairo Nov 6th 1861

Col. J. Cook
Comdg U. S. Forces
Fort Holt, Ky.

In pursuance with instructions sent this morning, you will march tomorrow morning, with the command directed to Elliotts Mills, taking two days rations.

Should you recieve no further instructions by 2 o.clock P. M. the day after tomorrow you will return to Fort Holt.

Take with you no more transportation than is absolutely necessary to the limited amount of tents and baggage for one night.

U. S. Grant
Brig Genl Comdg

Copies, DLC–USG, V, 1, 2, 3, 77; DNA, RG 393, USG Letters Sent. *O.R.*, I, iii, 273. See preceding letter. In a telegram dated only "Nov. 1861," but probably sent Nov. 8, 1st Lt. Leroy R. Waller, adjt., 7th Ill., reported to USG. "your order for the retreat of the 7th & 28th Infantry to Island No 1 has been complied with & will make fort holt at 12 oclock" Telegram received, DNA, RG 393, Dept. of the Mo., Telegrams Received.

To Cols. Jacob G. Lauman and Henry Dougherty

Head Quarters Dist S. E. Mo
Cairo Nov 6th 1861

Cols. Lauman & Dougherty
Hold your commands ready to go aboard of Steamers this evening as directed in orders yesterday

U. S. Grant
Brig Genl Comdg

Copies, DLC–USG, V, 1, 2, 3, 77; DNA, RG 393, USG Letters Sent. On Nov. 6, 1861, Capt. John A. Rawlins wrote to Cols. Jacob G. Lauman and Henry Dougherty. "On arrival of Steamers Belle Memphis and Montgomery you will have all the troops ordered to leave Birds Point by steamer, go aboard. Have all ready to commence going aboard by 4 o.clock P. M. of to day, when aboard of the Steamers, will lay there untill embark and then await the arrival of steamers from Cairo, when they you will follow." Copies, *ibid.*

Henry Dougherty, born in N. Car., brought as a boy to Carlyle, Ill., served in the Mexican War as a private, 1st U. S. Dragoons. In 1861 he enlisted in the 22nd Ill. as a private, but was soon elected col. Although not formally discharged until May 7, 1863, Dougherty never actually commanded the 22nd Ill. after losing his leg at the battle of Belmont, Nov. 7, 1861. For Lauman, see letter to Col. Jacob G. Lauman, Sept. 21, 1861.

To Col. C. Carroll Marsh

————

Head Quarters Dis. S E Mo
Cairo Nov 6th 1861

Col C C Marsh
Comdg 20th Ill Vol.
Sir

On tomorrow I want an Infantry reconoisance made out to Charleston to return in the evening.

Take such number as can be accommodated by the Cars making one trip, not to exceed however your regiment

Yours &c
U. S. Grant
Brig. Genl. Comdg.

Copies, DLC-USG, V, 1, 2, 3, 77; DNA, RG 393, USG Letters Sent. *O.R.*, I, iii, 274.

To Col. Richard J. Oglesby

————

Head Quarters, Dist. S. E. Mo.
Cairo, November 6th 1861

Col. R. Oglesby
Comdg. Expedition
U. S. Forces [. . . . .]

On receipt of this turn your column towards New Madrid. When you arrive at the nearest point to Columbus from which there is a road to that place communicate with me at Belmont.

Yours &c.
U. S. Grant
Brig. Gen. Com.

ALS, Oglesby Papers, IHi. *O.R.*, I, iii, 269. See following letter. On Nov. 7,
1861, Col. Richard J. Oglesby, "Nigger Wool Swamp on Castor River," wrote
to USG. "I have just rec'd your message of the 6th Inst—diecting me to turn the
column towards New Madrid, and one from you—verbally through Col W. H.
L. Wallace of a later date—to turn to Belmont—and join you there—I have one
Reg't at Bloomfield tonight and will go there tomorrow from there I will start in
the morning the Regiment there towards Buffington and Sykeston, and will
follow next day with main Column, Col Wallace will join me near Sykeston, I
cannot recross this Swamp here—it is terrible to encounter—Jeff Thompson fled
from Bloomfield Yesterday and was encamped at St Lukes, 10 miles S. West—
from ~~here~~ there to day—as soon as I turn back he will likely return—I am getting
along very well thus far—the train begins to work well—I think I could march to
Memphis on this side and exterminate Jeff—by the way—Col ———— 10th Iowa
took posession of Bloomfield to day at noon—There is a good road from Sykeston
to New Madrid you know—My total effective force now is about 3,300—I get
all the forage I want so far" ALS, DNA, RG 393, District of Southeast Mo.,
Letters Received.

To Col. William H. L. Wallace

———

Head Quarters Dist S. E. Mo
Cairo Nov 6th 1861

Col W. H. L. Wallace
Birds Point, Mo
Col.

Herewith I send you an order to Col Oglesby[1] to change the
direction of his column towards New Madrid halting to communicate with me at Belmont from the nearest point on his road.

I desire you to get up the Charleston expedition, ordered for
tomorrow, to start to night, taking two days rations with them.
You will accompany them to Charleston and get Col Oglesbys
instructions to him by a messenger if ~~possible~~ practicable and
when he is near enough you may join him.

For this purpose you may substitute the remainder of your
Regiment in place of an equal amount of Col Marshs.

The two days rations carried with your men in Haversacks
will enable you to join Col Oglesbys command and there you will
find rations enough for several days more, should they be necessary.

You may take a limited number of tents and at Charleston press Wagons to carry them to the main ~~channell~~ column; There you will find sufficient transportation to release the pressed wagons.

Yours &c
U. S. GRANT
Brig Genl Comdg

Copies, DLC-USG, V, 1, 2, 3, 77; DNA, RG 393, USG Letters Sent. *O.R.*, I, iii, 269.

1. See preceding letter.

Special Orders

Head Quarters Dist. S. E. Mo
On Board Steamer Memphis
Nov. 7th 1861

SPECIAL ORDER No

The troops composing the expedition now in transit at this point, will sail at 6 O'clock A. M., the Gun Boats in advance.

They will be followed by the 1st Brigade Commanded by Brigr Genl. McClernand.

The 1st Brigade will consist of all the troops from Cairo, Fort, Holt, and Taylers Battery

The 2nd Brigade, consisting of the remainder of the expedition, will be commanded by Col. Dougherty and will follow

The whole will be landed at the lowest point on the Mo. shore, that can be reached in security from the rebel Batteries, and where a landing can be effected.

From this point orders will be communicated for the disposition of the entire command. The point for ~~disem~~ debarkation will be designated by Capt. Walke Comdg. Naval Forces

U. S. GRANT
Brig. Genl Comdg.

FEDERAL FORCES AT BELMONT, MO.,
NOV. 7, 1861
U. S. GRANT, COMMANDING

FIRST BRIGADE, BRIG. GEN. J. A. McCLERNAND
27TH ILL., COL. N. B. BUFORD
30TH ILL., COL. P. B. FOUKE
31ST ILL., COL. J. A. LOGAN
DOLLINS' CO., ILL. CAVALRY,
   CAPT. J. J. DOLLINS
DELANO'S CO., ILL. CAVALRY,
   LIEUT. J. K. CATLIN
BATTERY B, 1ST ILL. LIGHT ARTILLERY,
   CAPT. E. TAYLOR
SECOND BRIGADE, COL. H. DOUGHERTY
22ND ILL., LIEUT. COL. H. E. HART
7TH IOWA, COL. J. G. LAUMAN

Corn Field

22

7 IOWA

TRANSPORTS

7 IOWA

27

LEXINGTON

TYLER

31

30

27

Field

Field

HOSPITAL

Corn Field

7 IOWA

22

31 IOWA

30

27

Corn Field

31

30

31

Field

30

31

7 IOWA

TYLER

LEXINGTON

22

30

31

7

FERRY
BOAT

27

22

7

27

Mississippi River

Missouri

Kentucky

N

CONFEDERATE CAMP

Belmont

FEDERAL INFANTRY
FEDERAL CAVALRY

CONFEDERATE CAMPS

UNION BATTERIES
CONFEDERATE BATTERIES

Columbus

0   ½   1

Approximate Scale of Miles

Engagement at Belmont, Missouri, Nov. 7, 1861

Copies, McClernand Papers, IHi; DLC-USG, V, 15, 16, 77, 82; DNA, RG 94, War Records Office, Union Battle Reports; *ibid.*, RG 393, USG Special Orders. *O.R.*, I, iii, 270; *O.R.* (Navy), I, xxii, 402.

To Col. Joseph B. Plummer

Headquarters Dist. S. E. Mo.
On board Transport
Near Columbus Ky Nov. 7 1861

COL J. B. PLUMMER COMDG FORCES.
CAPE GIRARDEAU MO.

Yours of yesterday just received.[1] When I gave directions for the expedition from Cape Girardeau, I expected the force from Birds Point to protect them from the South and the whole to meet at Bloomfield or be within striking distance. Requiring Colonel Oglesby's command with me however I have sent a messenger after it to turn it in this direction.

This will leave your command wholly unprotected from this quarter, hence the necessity of having it stronger than first designed. Receiving a report from Colonel Ross[2] but a few minutes after you left Cairo of the force he would take with him and knowing that he had started the morning before you left, I felt that he was strong enough, and did not think of a portion of his command being withdrawn.

I should have despatched to you immediately to prevent the expedition from continuing as it was.

You will restore the command to as near what it was, as a due regard for the security of your own position will permit, and allow it to proceed as originally designed.

Charge them to keep scouts well to the south and if they get in pursuit of Thompson in conjunction with the force from Ironton, chase him to Arkansas.

They should not venture far however, unprotected.

U. S. GRANT
Brig Genl.

Copies, DLC-USG, V, 1, 2, 3; DNA, RG 94, War Records Office, Union Battle Reports; *ibid.*, RG 393, USG Letters Sent. *O.R.*, I, iii, 259–60.

1. See letter to Col. Joseph B. Plummer, Nov. 4, 1861.
2. *Ibid.*

To Capt. Chauncey McKeever

———

Cairo Nov 7, 1861.

CAPT C. McKEEVER A. A. G.

We met the rebels about nine oclock this morning two & half 2½ miles from Belmont, drove them step by step into their camp & across the river. We burned their tents & started on our return with all their artillery but for lack of transportation had to leave four pieces in the woods. The rebels recrossed the river & followed in our rear to place of embarkation. Loss heavy on both sides.

U. S. GRANT
Brig. Gen.

Telegram, copy (punctuation added), DNA, RG 393, Western Dept., Telegrams. *O.R.*, I, liii, 506. News of Belmont also reached St. Louis through a telegram of Nov. 7, 1861, from Commander Roger Perry to Capt. Andrew H. Foote. "Gen. Grant at the Head of a force of observation, accompanied by the gun boats Lexington & Taylor, Charged and took the Rebel batteries at Belmont, destroying their tents. The enemy being reinforced from Columbus, Gen. Grant returned to the transports, bringing off sixty eight (68) Prisoners. The loss on both sides is great. The gun boats done their duty. Not arrived on their way up. Gen. Grant's horse was Shot." Copy (punctuation added), DNA, RG 45, Area 5. *O.R.* (Navy), I, xxii, 398.

To Brig. Gen. Charles F. Smith

Cairo

Nov. 7th [*1861*]

Gen Smith

Attacked the rebels this morning at nine oclock drove them out of Belmont & destroyed their encampment; loss heavy on both sides—they had eleven regts against our 3000 men[1]—if you have an opportunity communicate with Gen Paine our arrival here this evening—

U. S. Grant

Telegram received, DNA, RG 94, Letters Received. *O.R.*, I, iv, 346. On Nov. 7, 1861, Brig. Gen. Charles F. Smith forwarded this telegram to Brig. Gen. Lorenzo Thomas as an enclosure in a letter printed *ibid.*, pp. 345–46.

On Nov. 7, Capt. William S. Hillyer wrote to Smith. "I am instructed by Genl. Grant to inform you that he left Cairo Wednesday night, and landed his troops early Thursday morning, about five miles above Columbus on the Missouri side, under the protection of our two Gun Boats. He marched his troops down and met the enemy about two miles this side of Belmont. We immediately formed and gave them Battle, after hard fighting we drove the enemy back to his Camps and finally routed and dispersed him, took and destroyed his Camp, and took his Guns. We then marched our forces in return bringing with us *two* of the enemies Guns a number of Horses and 115 prisoners Our troops behaved handsomely.—Our loss is about 250 Killed wounded and missing The enemies loss must have been two or three times as great as ours. The prisoners report the enemies force at thirteen Regiments and one Battery We had about three thousand men and two Batteries" ALS, DNA, RG 94, Letters Received. Two days later, Smith forwarded this letter to Maj. Gen. George B. McClellan.

1. USG's original report stated that he had 2,850 men at Belmont; the revised report placed the total at 3,114. See letter to Brig. Gen. Seth Williams, Nov. 10, 1861. C.S.A. forces at Belmont were approximately 2,500 when the battle began and 5,000 by the end of the day, with ten C.S.A. regts. participating. Robert Underwood Johnson and Clarence Clough Buel, eds., *Battles and Leaders of the Civil War* (New York, 1887), I, 355*n*–56*n*; William M. Polk, *Leonidas Polk: Bishop and General* (New York, 1915), II, 42–44; *O.R.*, I, iii, 304. U.S. losses were 80 killed, 322 wounded, and 54 missing. See letter to Brig. Gen. Seth Williams, Nov. 20, 1861, note 2. C.S.A. losses were 105 killed, 419 wounded, 117 missing. *O.R.*, I, iii, 310.

To George W. Graham

Head Quarters Dis. S. E. Mo
Cairo Nov 7th 1861

COMMODORE GRAHAM

You will have a Boat (the W H B if convenient) at an early hour in the morning to go with a flag of truce to Columbus

Also send the accompaning dispatch to Col. Marsh[1] as soon as possible

By order Genl Grant
WM S HILLYER
Aid de Camp

Copies, DLC-USG, V, 1, 2, 3, 77; DNA, RG 393, USG Letters Sent.

1. On Nov. 7, 1861, Capt. William S. Hillyer wrote to Col. C. Carroll Marsh. "You will send the accompaniing dispatch to Col Wallace as soon as possible in the morning to Charleston by rail If Col. Wallace is not at Charleston the messenger must find him and deliver the dispatch" Copies, *ibid.*

Orders

Head Quarters Dis. S. E. Mo
Cairo Nov. 8th 1861

ORDERS

The General Comdg. this Military Distict, returns his thanks to the troops under his command, at the Battle of Belmont on yesterday

It has been his fortune, to have been in all the Battles fought in Mexico, by Genls. Scott and Taylor, save *Buena-Vista*, and never saw one more hotly contested, or where troops behaved with more gallantry.

Such courage will insure victory wherever our Flag may be bourne, and protected by such a class of men

To the many brave men who fell, the sympathy of the country is due, and will be manifested in a manner unmis[*ta*]kable

U. S. GRANT
Brig. Genl. Comd'g.

Copies, DLC-USG, V, 12, 13, 14, 80; DNA, RG 393, USG General Orders. *O.R.*, I, iii, 274; *O.R.* (Navy), I, xxii, 398.

To Maj. Gen. Leonidas Polk

Cairo November 8th 1861

GENL COMDG. FORCES
COLUMBUS KY.
SIR

In the skirmish of yesterday, in which both parties behaved with so much gallantry, many unfortunate men were left upon the Field of Battle who it was impossible to provide for.

I now send in the interest of humanity, to have these unfortunates collected and medical attendance secured them.

I at the same time return sixty four prisoners taken by our forces who are unconditionally released. Col. Webster Chief of Engineers Dis S. E Mo goes bearer of this, and will express to you my views upon the course that should be pursued under circumstances such as those of yesterday

I am sir very respectfully
Your Obt. Svt.
U. S. GRANT
Brig. Genl. Comd'g

Copies, DLC-USG, V, 1, 2, 3, 77, 79; DNA, RG 393, USG Letters Sent. *O.R.*, II, i, 515. On Nov. 8, 1861, Maj. Gen. Leonidas Polk replied to USG. "I have received your note in regard to your wounded and killed left on the battle field after yesterdays engagement. The lateness of the hour at which my troops returned to the principal Scene of the action prevented my bestowing the care upon your wounded which I desired. Such attentions as were practicable were shown them; and measures were taken at an early hour this morning to have them all brought into my hospitals. Provision also was made for taking care of your dead. The permission you desire under your flag of Truce to aid in attentions to your wounded is granted with pleasure under such restrictions as the exigencies of our service may require. In your note you say nothing of an exchange of prisoners though you send me a private message as to your willingness to release certain wounded men and some invalids taken from our list of sick in Camp, and expect in return a corresponding number of your prisoners. My own feelings would prompt me to waive again the unimportant affectation of declining to recognize these States as belligerants, in the interests of humanity, but my Government requires all prisoners to be placed at the disposal of the Secretary of War. I have dispatched him to know if the case of the severely wounded held by me would form an exception." ALS, DNA, RG 393, Dept. of the Mo., Letters Received. *O.R.,* II, i, 515–16. On Nov. 9, Maj. Joseph D. Webster wrote to USG. "I have the honor to report the result of the expedition sent under a flag of truce to Columbus yesterday.—On our arrival in the vicinity of the place, a steamer carrying Capt. Blake, Ass't Adj't Gen'l. of General Polk met us.—I delivered to him your letter, and offered him unconditionally the sick and wounded prisoners whom I had in charge.—He informed me that orders had been recently received by Genl. Polk respecting the exchange of prisoners, and declined accepting those I offered until he could receive further instructions.—He then left, saying that we had permission to bury our dead on the field of battle.—I placed a working party under command of Lieut. Col. Hart of 22d Illinois Reg't, and sent them to the field where they were employed for the remainder of the day, in caring for the wounded, some of whom were found yet there, and in burying the dead.—It was near sunset when Capt. Blake again came on board our boat, and handed me the communication from Gen'l Polk which I gave you last night on my return.—He informed me that a dispatch had been sent to their 'Secretary of War' in regard to the exchange of prisoners, but that they had received no reply.—During the interval between the two visits of Capt. Blake, several parties of the enemy visited our boat, General Cheatham among them.—He informed me that he had directed four of our wounded to be brought to us, and asked if I would give four of theirs in exchange.— I told him that I would give him four or any other number he would accept unconditionally, but that I had no authority to negotiate an exchange,—and that as to the four of ours which he sent on board, I would await the decision of Gen'l. Polk. Several more of our wounded had also been given into the care of our party on the field by Major Mason, Quarter Master at Columbus.—These facts I mentioned to Capt. Blake and told him that those thus put in our care awaited his orders, as I wished to avoid any appearance even of doing anything not in strict accordance with our obligations under the flag of truce.—He replied that he did not wish to interfere with any arrangements made by others—and I thought that under this state of the case it would be putting an unnecessarily fine point on the matter to decline to take back the wounded men so politely offered by Gen'l. Cheatham and Major Mason.—It is due to the latter gentleman particularly to say that his disposition to do every thing in his power to aid us in our mission of humanity was conspicuous during our entire stay there, and certainly deserves our warmest appreciation.—At the second visit of Capt. Blake to our boat, he received the sick and wounded prisoners whom I again offered to him unconditionally, and they were put on board his boat.—The number of our wounded as above stated from General Cheatham and Major Mason and brought up by me, was thirteen.—I inclose herewith a list of our men in the hands of the enemy given me by Captain Blake, which he thought to be nearly complete. The number reported by our party as buried by them on the field yesterday was sixty eight.—" LS, DNA, RG 94, Letters Received. *O.R.*, II, i, 516–17. See letter to Maj. Gen. Leonidas Polk, Nov. 12, 1861.

To Capt. Chauncey McKeever

—————

Cairo, Nov 8, 61.

CAPT C. MCKEEVER
A. A. G.

Our loss yesterday was about two hundred & fifty 250 killed wounded & missing, about one half killed or mortally wounded. The victory was complete. We carried off the field all the rebels' artillery, but had to leave in the woods several of their guns for want of teams. One hundred & thirty prisoners were brought to this place. Gen. McClernand & myself had a horse shot under us. Prisoners taken report that a large force were prepared to start [*to*] join Price.[1] This move will no doubt defeat this move. Pillow was on the field & is reported killed.[2]

U. S. GRANT

Telegram, copy (punctuation added), DNA, RG 393, Western Dept., Telegrams. *O.R.*, I, liii, 507.

1. Sterling Price, born in Va., settled in Mo. as a young man and soon began a successful career in Democratic politics. On Aug. 12, 1846, he resigned from the U.S. House of Representatives to serve as col., 2nd Mo., in the Mexican War. He was governor of Mo., 1853–57. During the winter of 1860–61 he maintained a conditional Union position, but after the seizure of Camp Jackson he offered his services to pro-secession Governor Claiborne F. Jackson and was appointed maj. gen., Mo. State Guard. Albert Castel, *General Sterling Price and the Civil War in the West* (Baton Rouge, La., 1968), pp. 3–15; *DAB*, XV, 216–17.

2. Brig. Gen. Gideon J. Pillow was unharmed. C.S.A. Maj. Gen. Leonidas Polk heard that USG had been killed. *O.R.*, I, iii, 304.

To Brig. Gen. John A. McClernand

———

Head Quarters, Dist S. E. Mo.
Cairo, November 8th 1861

GEN.

Will you please order detailed twelve men, under a suitable officer, to accompany the flags to Columbus this morning.

They can report to Capt. Graham and go aboard the Flag Steamer at once.

Your Obt. Svt.
U. S. GRANT
Brig. Gen. Com

To Gen. J. A. McClernand
Comd.g Post
Cairo Ill.

ALS, McClernand Papers, IHi.

To Brig. Gen. Charles F. Smith

———

BY TELEGRAPH FROM Cairo [*Nov.*] 8th *1861*

TO GEN SMITH.

We drove the Rebels completely from Belmont, burned their tents, & carried off their artillery, for want of horses to draw them, we had to leave all but two pieces on the field. The victory was complete. Our loss is not far from 250 Killed, wounded, & missing. The Rebel loss must have been from five to six hundred including 130 prisoners brought from the field—

U S GRANT

Telegram received, DNA, RG 94, Letters Received. *O.R.*, I, iv, 346. On Nov. 8, 1861, Brig. Gen. Charles F. Smith forwarded this telegram to hd. qrs., U.S. Army, as an enclosure in a letter printed *ibid*. On Nov. 8, Smith had telegraphed to USG. "Please let me have some particulars of the affair at Belmont What was your loss. Do you propose to carry out the idea & when" Telegram received, DNA, RG 393, Dept. of the Mo., Telegrams Received.

To Col. C. Carroll Marsh

Head Quarters Dis. S. E Mo
Cairo Nov 8th 1861

COL C C MARSH
COMDG. FORCES, BIRDS POINT
SIR

Move your Regiment to Charleston tomorrow and hold that point until Col. Oglesby reaches there. When he arrives inform him of the purport of my order of this date and all return together

Keep the R. R. transportation with you well guarded to avoid against the possibility of having your retreat cut off

Take with you two days rations

U. S. GRANT
Brig Genl. Comdg.

Copies, DLC-USG, V, 1, 2, 77; DNA, RG 393, USG Letters Sent. On Nov. 9, 1861, Col. Richard J. Oglesby wrote to USG. "Your order to return to birds Point recd at Midnight last night—I immediately recalled my advanced guard six miles on the road to Sykeston.—In view o̶ t̶h̶e̶ of the heavy rain Last night in the direction of the swamps before me and of your return to Cairo—I will move the Column back [. . .] of Cape Girardeau—I will be there Monday noon or by 4 P. M. ready to go on board Boats for Cairo—be good enough to send enough Boats to relieve me from uncoupling wagons about six will answer Jeff. Thompson Has f̶ left the state anyhow, I had only to return—but I would like to have done so by Belmont. Col Wallace here—Regt will be by noon" ALS, *ibid.*, District of Southeast Mo., Letters Received.

To Capt. Reuben B. Hatch

Head Qrs Dist S. E. Mo.
Cairo Nov. 8th 1861

CAPTAIN

You will continue to supply this post with Fuel, Forage, Straw and Stationery by purchase or otherwise, You will procure and retain at this post a sufficient quantity to guard against any ordinary circumstance. You will purchase as soon as practicable not less than 100 tons of straw for bedding for the soldiers at, and in the vicinity of this post

U. S. GRANT
Brig. Gen. Com.

Capt R B Hatch
Asst. Q. M.

Copies, DLC-USG, V, 1, 2, 3; DNA, RG 92, Consolidated Correspondence, Cairo Fraud Investigation; *ibid.*, RG 393, USG Letters Sent.

To Jesse Root Grant

Cairo, November 8th 1861

DEAR FATHER,

It is late at night and I want to get a letter into the Mail for you before it closes. As I have just finished a very hasty letter to Julia[1] that contains about what I would write, and having something els to do myself, I will have my clerk copy it on to this.

Day before yesterday, I left here with about 3000 men in five steamers, convoyed by two Gun Boats, and proceeded down the river, to within about twelve miles of Columbus. The next morning the Boats were dropped down just out of range of the enemies Batteries, and the troops debarked—

During this operation our Gun-Boats exercised the rebels by throwing shells into their Camps and Batteries—

When all ready we proceeded about one mile towards Belmont opposite Columbus: where I formed the troops into lines, and ordered two Companies from each Regiment to deploy as skirmishers, and push on through the woods and discover the position of the enemy. They had gone but a little way when they were fired upon and the *Ball* may be said to have fairly opened.

The whole command with the exception of a small reserve, were then deployed in like manner with the first, and ordered forward. The order was obeyed with great alacrity, the men all showing great courage. I can say with gratification that every Colonel without a single exception, set an example to their commands that inspired a confidence that will always insure victory when there is the slightest possibility of gaining one. I feel truly proud to command such men. From here we fought our way from tree to tree through the woods to Belmont, about 2½ miles, the enemy contesting every foot of ground. Here the enemy had strengthened their position by felling the trees for two or three hundred yards, and sharpening the limbs making a sort of Abattis. Our men charged through making the victory complete, giving us possession of their Camp and Garrison Equipage Artillery and every thing else.

We got a great many prisoners, the majority however succeeded in getting aboard their Steamers, and pushing across the river We burned every thing possible and started back having accomplished all that we went for, and even more. Belmont is entirely covered by the Batteries from Columbus and is worth nothing as a Military Position. Cannot be held without Columbus

The object of the expedition was to prevent the enemy from sending a force into Missouri to cut off troops I had sent there for a special purpose, and to prevent reinforcing Price

Besides being well fortified at Columbus their numbers far exceed ours, and it would have been folly to have attacked them. We found the Confederates well armed and brave. On our return stragglers that had been left in our rear, *now front,* fired into us and more recrossed the river and gave us Battle for full a mile and afterwards at the Boats when we were embarking. There was no hasty retreating or running away. Taking into account the object of the expedition the victory was most complete. It has given me a confidence in the Officers and men of this command, that will enable me to lead them in any future engagement without fear of the result. Genl. McClernand, (who by the way acted with great coolness and courage throughout, and proved that he is a soldier as well as statesman) and my self each had our Horses shot under us. Most of the Field Officers met with the same loss, besides nearly one third of them being Killed or wounded themselves. As near as I can ascertain our loss was about 250 Killed wounded and missing I write in great haste to get this in the Office tonight

U. S. GRANT

AL, PPRF. Everything after the first paragraph is in another hand. The entire letter, except for the first paragraph and the last sentence, was printed in the *Cincinnati Gazette,* Nov. 11, 1861, identified as a letter from USG to his father.

1. The letter to Julia Dent Grant has not been found.

To Capt. Reuben B. Hatch

———

Head Quarters Dis. S. E Mo.
Cairo Nov 9th 1861

SPECIAL ORDER NO

The Post Quarter Master will issue to Capt. McCalister Light Artillery twelve (12) of the captured Horses in his possession for the use of his Battery

U. S. GRANT
Brig. Genl Comdg.

To Capt R. B. Hatch
Post Quarter Master
Cairo Ill

Copies, DLC-USG, V, 15, 16, 77, 82; DNA, RG 393, USG Special Orders.

To Capt. Reuben B. Hatch

————

Head Quarters Dist S. E. Mo
Cairo Nov 9th 1861

SPECIAL ORDER NO
The Post Quarter Master will issue to Capt Taylor Light
Artillery, Fourteen (14) of the Captured Horses taken at the
Battle of Belmont, the same being required to complete his Bat-
tery.

U. S. GRANT
Brig Genl Comdg

To Capt R. B. Hatch.
Post Q. M.
Cairo, Ills

Copies, DLC-USG, V, 15, 16, 77, 82; DNA, RG 393, USG Special Orders.

To Maj. Gen. Leonidas Polk

————

Cairo, Ill., November 10, 1861.

MAJ. GEN. L. POLK, COMMANDING AT COLUMBUS, KY.
GENERAL:
It grieves me to have to trouble you again with a flag of truce
but Mrs. Colonel Dougherty whose husband is a prisoner with
you is very anxious to join him under such restrictions as you may

impose, and I understand that some of your officers expressed the opinion that no objections would be interposed. I will be most happy to reciprocate in a similar manner at any time you may request it.

I am, general, very respectfully, your obedient servant,

U. S. GRANT,

Brigadier-General, U. S. Army.

O.R., II, i, 517. USG's letter was carried to Columbus and delivered to Maj. Gen. Leonidas Polk by Capt. Reuben B. Hatch, accompanied by a correspondent of the *Missouri Democrat*. Letter of "Horatio," Nov. 10, 1861, in *Missouri Democrat*, Nov. 12, 1861. On Nov. 10, 1861, Polk replied to USG. "I am in receipt of your note under cover of your flag of truce asking for Mrs. Dohirty the privalege of joining her husband who was unfortunately wounded in the affair of the 7th. It gives me pleasure to grant her the opportunity of rendering such grateful service and I hope through her attentions the Col may speedily be restored to such a condition of health as is compatible with the loss he has been obliged to sustain." ALS, DNA, RG 393, District of Southeast Mo., Letters Received. *O.R.*, II, i, 517. On Dec. 6, Polk wrote to USG. "I have pleasure in returning to you Col Dougherty, the last of your Command who was wounded in the battle of the 7th ult, and who has so far recovered as to allow of his removal. I also return to you Lt. Smith who has been the attendant and nurse of Col Dougherty and whose devoted services may still be necessary to his comfort and ultimate recovery. He is released on parole. The memorandum here with sent you will Show that in the exchange or release of prisoners heretofore made, exclusive of that made through Col Buford in the first instance, I have released one hundred and fourteen, against one hundred and twenty four released by you. I will send you so soon as the arrangements can be made the difference between these numbers with the understanding that henceforth these exchanges shall be made with a distinct regard to the numbers and grade of the prisoners exchanged." ALS, DNA, RG 393, District of Southeast Mo., Letters Received. *O.R.*, II, i, 529. Polk's memorandum is *ibid.*

To Brig. Gen. Seth Williams

————

Head Quarters, Dist. S. E. Mo.
Cairo, November 10th 1861.

S Williams
Asst: Adjt: Gen.
Washington D. C.
Sir;

On the evening of the 6th instant~~ant~~ I left this place with 2850 men, all arms, to make a reconnoisance towards Columbus. The object of the expedition was to prevent the enemy from sending out reinforcements to Prices Army in Mo. and also from cutting off two small Columns that I had been directed to send out, from this place, and Cape Girardeau, in pursuit of Jeff. Thompson.[1]

Knowing that Columbus was strongly garrisoned I asked Gen. Smith, Comd.g at Paducah Ky. to make demonstrations in the same direction.[2] He did so by ordering a small force to Mayfield and another in the direction of Columbus, not to approach nearer however than twelve or fifteen miles. I also sent a small force on the Kentucky side with orders not to advance nearer than Elliott's Mills, some twelve miles from Columbus.[3]

The expedition under my immediate command were stopped about nine miles below here, on the Kentucky shore, and remained until morning. All this served to distract the enemy and lead him to think that he was to be attacked in his strongly fortified position.—At day light we proceeded down the river to a point just out of range of rebel guns and debarked on the Mo. shore. From here the troops were marched by a flank for about one miles towards Belmont and then drawn up in line, one battalion having been left as a reserve near the transports. Two companies from each regiment, five skelitons in number, were then thrown out as skirmishers to ascertain the position of the enemy.—It was but a very few minuets before they met him and a general engagement ensued. The balance of my force, with the exception of the reserve, was then thrown forward, all as skirmishers, and the enemy driven foot by foot and from tree to tree back to their encampment on the river bank a distance of over two miles.

Here they had strengthened their position by felling the timber for several hundred yards around their camp and making a sort of Abattis.

Our men charged through this driving the enemy over the banks and into their transports in quick time leaving us in possession of evrything not exceedingly portable.

Belmont is on low ground and evry foot of it commanded by the guns on the opposite shore and of course could not be held for a single hour after the enemy become aware of the withdrawel of their troops.

Having no wagons with me I could not move any of the captured property consequently gave orders for its distruction. —Their tents blankets &c. were set on fire and we retired taking their Artillery with us.—Two pieces being drawn by hand, and one by an insufficient team, were spiked and left in the woods bringing two to this place.

Before geting farely under way the enemy made his appearance again and attempted to surround us. Our troops were not in the least discouraged but charged the enemy and again defeated him.

Our loss was about eighty five killed, One hundred & fifty wounded, many of them slightly, and about an equal number missing. Nearly all the missing from the 7th Iowa regiment who behaved with great gallantry and suffered more severely than any other troops.—I have not yet been able to get in the reports from sub commanders but will forward them as soon as received.

All the troops behaved with great gallantry much of which is to be attributed to the coolness and presence of mind of the officers, particularly the Colonels.

Gen. McClernand was in the midst of danger throughout the engagement and displayed both coolness and judgement. His horse was three times shot. My horse was also shot under me.

To my Staff, Capts. Rawlins Lagow & Hillyer, and volunteer Aides, Capts. Hatch & Graham I am much indebted for the assistance they gave.—Col. Webster, acting chief Engineer also accompanied me and displayed highly soldierlike qualities. Col. Daugherty 22d Ill. Vols. was three times wounded; and taken prisoner.

The Seventh Iowa regiment lost their Lieut. Colonel, (killed) and Col. and Major severely wounded. The reports to be forwarded will detail more fully the particulars of our loss.

Surgeon Brinton was on the field during the entire engagement and displayed great ability and efficiency in providing for the wounded and organizing the Medical Corps.

The Gun boats Taylor & Lexington, Capts. Walke & Stembel U. S. N. commanding, convoyed the expedition and rendered most efficient service. Immediately upon our landing they engaged the enemies batteries and protected our transports throughout. For particulars see accompanying report of Capt. Walke.[4]

> I am sir very respectfully
> Your Obt. Svt.
> U. S. GRANT
> Brig. Gen. Com.

ALS, DNA, RG 94, Letters Received. This report appeared in some newspapers with the date Nov. 12, 1861, and was reprinted several times with the erroneous date: for example, in Frank Moore, ed., *The Rebellion Record* (New York, 1861–68), III, 278–79.

For some unexplained reason, USG prepared a second report of Belmont several years after the battle. On April 27, 1864, Brig. Gen. John A. Rawlins wrote to his wife. "Colonel Bowers and myself finished yesterday General Grant's report of the battle of Belmont." James Harrison Wilson, *The Life of John A. Rawlins* (New York, 1916), p. 425. The revised report was not sent to the War Dept. until more than a year later. See letter to Edwin M. Stanton, June 26, 1865. The revised report was addressed to Brig. Gen. Seth Williams, dated Nov. 17, 1861. "The following order was received from Headquarters, Western Department:

Saint Louis, Nov: 1st 1861

General Grant.
Commanding at Cairo:
You are hereby directed to hold your whole command ready to

march at an hours notice, until further orders, and you will take particular care to be amply supplied with transportation and ammunition. You are also directed to make demonstrations with your troops along both sides of the river towards Charleston, Norfolk and Blandville; and to keep your columns constantly moving back and forward against those places, without however, attacking the enemy.

Very Respectfully &c.,
Chauncey McKeever.
Asst Adjt Gen'l.

At the same time I was notified that similar instructions had been sent to Brig. Gen. C. F. Smith, commanding Paducah, Ky., and was directed to communicate with him freely as to my movements, that his might be cooperative.

On the 2d of the same month, and before it was possible for any considerable preparation to have been made for the execution of this order, the following telegraphic dispatch was received:

Saint Louis, Novemb. 2d 1861

To Brig. Gen. Grant:

Jeff Thompson is at Indian Ford, of the St. Francois river, twenty-five miles below Greenville, with about three thousand men. Col. Carlin has started with forces from Pilot Knob. Send a force from Cape-Girardeau and Birds Point to assist Carlin in driving Thompson into Arkansas.

By order of Maj. Gen. Fremont
C. McKeever
Asst Adjt Gen'l.

The forces I determined to send from Birds Point were immediately designated and Col. R. J. Oglesby, 8th Ills. Vols., assigned to the command under the following detailed instructions:

Headquarters, Dist. S. E. Mo.
Cairo, November 3d, 1861

Col. R. J. Oglesby, Comd'g &c.
Birds Point, Mo.

You will take command of an expedition consisting of your regiment, four companies of the 11th Illinois, all of the 18th and 29th, three companies of cavalry from Birds Point, (to be selected and notified by yourself,) and a section of Schwartz' battery, artillery; and proceed by steamboats to Commerce, Mo. From Commerce you will strike for Sikeston, Mr Cropper acting as guide. From there you will go in pursuit of a rebel force, understood to be 3000 strong, under Jeff Thompson, now at Indian Ford on the St Francis river.

An expedition has already left Ironton, Mo., to attack this force. Should they learn that they have left that place it will not be necessary for you to go there, but pursue the enemy in any direction he may go, always being cautious not to fall in with an unlooked for foe, too strong for the command under you.

The object of the expedition is to destroy this force, and the manner of doing it is left largely at your discretion, believing it better not to trammel you with instructions. Transportation will be furnished you for fourteen days rations, and four or five days forage. All you may require outside of this, must be furnished by the country through which you pass. In taking supplies you will be careful to select a proper officer to press them, and require a receipt to be given, and the articles pressed accounted for in the same manner as if purchased.

You are particularly enjoined to allow no foraging by your men. It is demoralizing in the extreme, and is apt to make open enemies where they would not otherwise exist.

U. S. GRANT
Brig. General.

Col. J. B. Plummer, 11th Missouri Volunteers, commanding Cape Girardeau, was directed to send one regim't in the direction of Bloomfield, with a view to attracting the attention of the enemy.

The forces under Col. Oglesby were all got off on the evening of the 3d.

On the 5th a telegram was received from Headquarters, St Louis, stating that the enemy was reenforcing Price's Army from Columbus by way of White river, and directing that the demonstration that had been ordered against Columbus, be immediately made. Orders were accordingly at once given to the troops under my command that remained at Cairo, Birds Point and Fort Holt. A letter was also sent to Brig Gen. C. F. Smith, commanding at Paducah, requesting him to make a demonstration at the same time against Columbus.

To more effectually attain the object of the demonstration against the enemy at Belmont and Columbus, I determined on the morning of the 6th, to temporarily change the direction of Col. Oglesby's column towards New Madrid; and also to send a small force under Col. W. H. L. Wallace, 11th Ills. Vols., to Charleston, Mo., to ultimately join Col. Oglesby. In accordance with this determination I addressed Col Oglesby the following communication:

Cairo, November 6th, 1861

Col. R. J. Oglesby
commanding Expedition.

On receipt of this turn your column towards New Madrid, When you arrive at the nearest point to Columbus from which there is a road to that place, communicate with me at Belmont.

U. S. GRANT
Brig. General.

which was sent to Col. Wallace with the following letter:

Cairo, November 6th, 1861

Col. W. H. L. Wallace,
Birds Point, Mo.

Herewith I send you an order to Col. Oglesby to change the direction of his column towards New Madrid, halting to communicate with me at Belmont from the nearest point on his road.

I desire you to get up the Charleston expedition ordered for to morrow, to start to night, taking two days rations with them. You will accompany them to Charleston and get Col. Oglesby's instructions to him by a messenger, if practicable, and when he is near enough you may join him. For this purpose you may substitute the remainder of your regiment in place of an equal amount from Col. Marsh's. The two days rations, carried by your men in havresacks, will enable you to join Col. Oglesby's command, and there you will find rations enough for several days more, should they be necessary. You may take a limited number of tents, and at Charleston press wagons to carry them to the main column. There you will find sufficient transportation to release the pressed wagons.

U. S. GRANT
Brig. General.

On the evening of the 6th, I left this place in steamers, with

McClernands Brigade, consisting of: 27th Reg't Illinois Vols., Col N. B. Buford, 30th Reg't Illinois Vols., Col. Philip B. Fouke, 31st Regt Illinois Vols., Col. Jno. A Logan, Dollins Company Independent Illinois Cavalry, Capt J. J Dollins Delano's Company Adams County Illinois Cavalry, Lieut. J. R. Catlin.

Dougherty's Brigade, consisting of: 22d Regt Illinois Vols., Lieut Col. H. E. Hart, 7th Reg't Iowa Vols., Col. J. G. Lauman,

amounting to three thousand, one hundred and fourteen (3114) men of all arms, to make the demonstration against Columbus. I proceeded down the river to a point nine miles below here, where we lay until next morning, on the Kentucky shore, which served to distract the enemy, and lead him to suppose that he was to be attacked in his strongly fortified position at Columbus.

About two o'clock on the morning of the 7th I received information from Col. W. H. L. Wallace, at Charleston (sent by a messenger on steamer 'W. H. B') that he had learned from a reliable union man that the enemy had been crossing troops from Columbus to Belmont the day before, for the purpose of following after and cutting off the forces under Col. Oglesby. Such a move on his part seemed to me more than probable, and gave at once a twofold importance to my demonstration against the enemy, namely: the prevention of reenforcement to General Price, and the cutting off of the two small columns that I had sent, in pursuance of directions, from this place and Cape Girardeau, in pursuit of Jeff Thompson. This information determined me to attack vigorously his forces at Belmont, knowing that should we be repulsed, we would reembark without difficulty under the protection of the gunboats. The following order was given:

On board steamer 'Belle Memphis.'
November 7th, 1861,—2 o'clock a.m.

Special Order.

The troops composing the present expedition from this place, will move promptly at six o'clock this morning. The gunboats will take the advance and be followed by the 1st Brigade under command of Brig. Gen. John A. McClernand, composed of all the troops from Cairo and Fort Holt. The 2d Brigade, comprising the remainder of the troops of the expedition, commanded by Col John Dougherty, will follow. The entire force will debark at the lowest point on the Missouri shore where a landing can be effected in security from the rebel batteries. The point of debarkation will be designated by Captain Walke, commanding Naval Forces.

By order of Brig. Gen. U. S. Grant
JNO A. RAWLINS.
Asst. Adjt. Genl.

Promptly at the hour designated, we proceeded down the river to a point just out of range of the rebel batteries at Columbus, and debarked on the Missouri shore. From here the troops were marched, with skirmishers well in advance, by flank for about one mile towards Belmont, and there formed in line of battle. One battalion had been left as a reserve near the transports. Two companies from each regiment were thrown forward as skirmishers to ascertain the position of the enemy, and about 9 o'clock met and engaged him. The balance of my force, with the exception of the reserve, was promptly thrown forward, and drove the enemy foot by foot, and from tree to tree, back to his encampment on the river bank, a distance of over two miles. Here he had strengthened his position by felling the timber for several hundred yards around his camp, making a sort of abattis. Our men charged through this, driving the enemy under cover of the bank, and many of them into their transports in quick time, leaving us in possession of every thing not exceedingly portable.

Belmont is situated on low ground and every foot is commanded by the guns on the opposite shore, and of course could not be held for a single hour after the enemy became aware of the withdrawal of his troops. Having no wagons with me I could move but little of the captured property, consequently gave orders for the destruction of every thing that could not be moved, and an immediate return to our transports. Tents, blankets, &c., were set on fire and destroyed, and our return march commenced, taking his artillery and a large number of captured horses and prisoners with us. Three pieces of artillery being drawn by hand and one by an inefficient team, were spiked and left on the road; two were brought to this place.

We had but fairly got under way when the enemy, having received reenforcements, rallied under cover of the river bank, and the woods on the point of land in the bend of the river above us; and made his appearance between us and our transports, evidently with a design of cutting off our return to them.

Our troops were not in the least discouraged but charged the enemy and again defeated him. We then, with the exception of the 27th Illinois, Col N. B. Buford commanding, reached our transports and embarked without further molestation. While waiting for the arrival of this regiment, and to get some of our wounded from a field hospital near by, the enemy, having crossed fresh troops from Columbus, again made his appearance on the river bank and commenced firing upon our transports. The fire was returned by our men from the decks of the steamers, and also by the gunboats, with terrible effect, compelling him to retire in the direction of Belmont. In the mean time Col. Buford, although he had received orders to return with the main force, took the Charleston road from Belmont and came in on the road leading to Birds Point where we had formed the line of battle in the morning. At this point to avoid the effect of the shells from the gunboats that were beginning to fall among his men, he took a blind path direct to the river, and followed a wood road up its bank, and thereby avoided meeting the enemy, who were retiring by the main road. On his appearance on the river bank, a steamer was dropped down and took his command on board, without his having participated or lost a man in the enemy's attempt to cut us off from our transports.

Notwithstanding the crowded state of our transports, the only loss we sustained from the enemy's fire upon them was three men wounded, one of whom belonged to one of the boats.

Our loss in killed on the field was eighty-five, three hundred and one wounded (many of them however slightly) and ninety-nine missing. Of the wounded a hundred and twenty-five fell into the hands of the enemy. Nearly all the missing were from the 7th Iowa Regiment, which suffered more severely than any other. All the troops behaved with great gallantry which was in a great degree attributable to the coolness and presence of mind of their officers, particularly the Colonels commanding.

General Mc.Clernand was in the midst of danger throughout the engagement, and displayed both coolness and judgment. His horse was three times shot under him.

Col Dougherty (22d Ills. Vols., commanding the 2d Brigade, by his coolness and bravery entitles himself to be named among the most competent of officers for command of troops in battle. In our second engagement he was three times wounded and fell a prisoner in the hands of the enemy.

Among the killed was Lieutenant Colonel A. Wentz, 7th Iowa Vols., and among the wounded were Col. J. G. Lauman and Major E. W. Rice, of the 7th Iowa.

The reports of sub-commanders will detail more fully particulars of the engagement, and the conduct of both officers and men.

To my staff, Captain John A. Rawlins, Asst Adjutant General, Lieutenants C. B. Lagow and Wm S. Hillyer, Aides de Camp, and Captain R. B. Hatch, Assistant Quartermaster, I am much indebted for the promptitude with which they discharged their several duties.

Surgeon J. H. Brinton, U. S. Vols., Chief Medical Officer, was on the field during the entire engagement, and displayed great ability and efficiency in providing for the wounded, and in organizing the Medical Corps.

Major J. D. Webster, acting Chief Engineer, also accompanied me on the field, and displayed soldierly qualities of a high order.

My own horse was shot under me, during the engagement.

The gunboats 'Tyler,' Captain Walke, and 'Lexington,' Captain Stembolt, convoyed the expedition and rendered most efficient service. Immediately upon our landing they engaged the enemy's batteries on the heights above Columbus, and protected our transports throughout. For a detailed account of the part taken by them, I refer with pleasure to the accompanying report of Captain H. S. Walke, senior officer.

In pursuance of my request, General Smith, commanding at Paducah, sent on the 7th inst., a force to Mayfield, Ky., and another in the direction of Columbus, with orders not to approach nearer, however, than twelve or fifteen miles of that place. I also sent a small force on the Kentucky side towards Columbus, under Col. John Cook, 7th Illinois Volunteers, with orders not to go beyond Elliotts Mills, distant some twelve miles from Columbus. These forces having marched to the points designated in their orders, returned without having met serious resistance.

On the evening of the 7th, information of the result of the engagement at Belmont, was sent to Col. Oglesby, commanding expedition against Jeff Thompson, and orders to return to Birds Point, by way of Charleston, Mo. Before these reached him however, he had learned that Jeff Thompson had left the place where he was reported to be when the expedition started, (he having gone towards New Madrid or Arkansas) and had determined to return. The same information was sent to the Commanding Officer at Cape Girardeau, with directions for the troops to be brought back, that had gone out from that place.

From all the information I have been able to obtain since the engagement, the enemy's loss in killed and wounded was much greater than ours. We captured 175 prisoners, all his artillery and transportation, and destroyed his entire camp and garrison equipage. Independent of the injuries inflicted upon him, and the prevention of his reenforcing Price, or sending a force to cut off the expeditions against Jeff Thompson, the confidence inspired in our troops in the engagement, will be of incalculable benefit to us in the future." LS, DNA, RG 94, War Records Office, Union Battle Reports. *O.R.*, I, iii, 267–72. Brig. Gen. Seth Williams of Me., USMA 1842, had served in the capacity of adjt. continuously since 1850, and was first assigned to duty under Maj. Gen. George B. McClellan on June 17, 1861.

1. In this sentence, USG apparently refers to the letter from Capt. Chauncey McKeever, Nov. 1, copied in the revised report on Belmont. LS, DNA, RG 393, District of Southeast Mo., Letters Received. On Nov. 9, McKeever telegraphed to Maj. Gen. John C. Frémont. "Genl. Grant did not follow his instructions no orders were given to attack Belmont or Columbus." Copy, *ibid.*, Western Dept., Telegrams. *O.R.*, I, liii, 507. Some time in Nov., probably close to Nov. 10, Brig. Gen. Samuel R. Curtis telegraphed to USG. "I will see to having Regt. sent as soon as arms can be furnished. Hope your Gallant G̶a̶ assault on the Rebels may do good. Col. Fiala says Fremont ordered it on the first. McKeever says you had no orders. Who ordered troops from P̶l̶a̶t̶ Pilot Knob & Cape Girardeau. What are the limits of your command? Genl. Hunter assumed command on the fourth & assigned me command down Iron Mountain R. R. & I wish to avoid confusion of command." Telegram received (punctuation added), DNA, RG 393, Dept. of the Mo., Telegrams Received. On Nov. 8, Curtis telegraphed to Col. Edward D. Townsend, AGO. "General Fiala's telegraph is from one on Frémont's staff, and seems to flourish the premature movement on Belmont as a Frémont victory, which I sincerely hope it was, although improperly addressed and coming from an irregular source three days after General Hunter's order was published. After sending a copy to General Hunter, I have concluded not to delay it, but allow it to go on the wires to you." *O.R.*, I, iii, 566–67. On Nov. 9, Curtis telegraphed to Townsend. "Yesterday Colonel Fiala sent report of General Grant's movement on Belmont, as ordered by General Frémont to-day. Captain McKeever telegraphs from Cincinnati to General Frémont that General Grant had no orders from Frémont to attack Belmont or Columbus." *Ibid.*, p. 567.

In USG's revised report dated Nov. 17, printed above, he referred to a telegram of Nov. 5 from hd. qrs., St. Louis, informing him that Maj. Gen. Sterling Price's army in Mo. was being reinforced from Columbus and ordering him to make a demonstration against it. This telegram has not been found and it may be that in preparing the revised report, USG's staff extrapolated its existence from USG's Nov. 5 orders to Brig. Gen. Charles F. Smith, Brig. Gen. John A. McClernand, and Col. C. Carroll Marsh. These orders were probably based on telegrams of Nov. 1 and 2 from St. Louis which ordered USG to make demonstrations along both sides of the Mississippi and to send troops in order to disperse Brig. Gen. M. Jeff Thompson's troops reported to be at Indian Ford on the St. Francis River. It is unlikely that St. Louis hd. qrs. would have issued orders for an offensive on Nov. 5 because a change in command had just taken place. On Nov. 2, near Springfield, Mo., Frémont received orders relieving him from command of the Western Dept. His temporary replacement, Maj. Gen. David Hunter, assumed command in the field on Nov. 3. The news of the change apparently reached Cairo some time on Nov. 6. Depts. were reorganized on Nov. 9 when Maj. Gen. Henry W. Halleck was appointed to command the Dept. of the Mo. *Ibid.*, pp. 553, 559, 561, 567; *Missouri Democrat*, Nov. 6, 1861.

It is unlikely that Frémont sent orders on Nov. 5 since he had already been removed from command and, furthermore, he would have sent them through McKeever, who later asserted that USG had no orders. It is equally unlikely that Hunter issued such orders since his advent to command was so recent that he had no staff in St. Louis. Because of delay in telegraph service, Frémont's removal was not even officially known in St. Louis on Nov. 5. On the following day Curtis was ordered to "take at once the control of affairs in and around Saint Louis." *O.R.*, I, iii, 560; Kenneth E. Colton, ed., "With Fremont in Missouri in 1861: Letters of Samuel Ryan Curtis," *Annals of Iowa*, 3rd Series, 24 (1942), 153–54. Since nobody in St. Louis had authority to send orders to USG on Nov. 5, and no mention of a telegram appears either in the records of the Western Dept. or in those kept by USG, the telegram of Nov. 5 is probably imaginary.

USG later recalled that he did not have orders to attack and did not expect to do so when he left Cairo aboard the transports. He wrote that once the expedition was underway, "I saw that the officers and men were elated at the prospect of at last having the opportunity of doing what they had volunteered to do—fight the enemies of their country." Consequently, when he learned at 2 a.m. on Nov. 7 that troops were crossing from Columbus to Belmont, apparently to intercept Col. Richard J. Oglesby's column in Mo., USG decided to land, "capture Belmont, break up the camp and return." In addition to protecting Oglesby, USG believed that actual combat would improve the discipline and morale of the men in his command. *Memoirs*, I, 271–72. In reports made after the battle of Belmont, USG wrote that the purpose "of the expedition was to prevent the enemy from sending out reinforcements to Prices Army in Mo. and also from cutting off two small Columns that I had been directed to send out, from this place, and Cape Girardeau, in pursuit of Jeff. Thompson." There is no mention of orders authorizing an attack and USG noted that he specifically directed Smith's forces to come no closer to Columbus than "twelve or fifteen miles." See letter to Brig. Gen. Seth Williams, Nov. 10, 1861. A week later, USG again indicated that his purpose had been "to prevent the enemy from reinforcing Price, in Missouri, and from cutting off two small Columns I had been directed to send towards the St. Francois river . . ." See letter to Brig. Gen. Seth Williams, Nov. 20, 1861. In his report to Williams dated Nov. 17, but probably written later, USG repeated that the purpose had been "the prevention of reenforcement to General Price, and the cutting off of the two small columns that I had sent in pursuance of directions . . . in pursuit of Jeff Thompson." The decision to attack came after receiving information from Col. William H. L. Wallace that troops had crossed from Columbus to Belmont the day before in order to cut off Oglesby.

No mention of the 2 a.m. message from Wallace appears in any USG account written soon after the battle; no contemporary documentary record has been found; and it is not listed in USG's register of letters received. It is not clear from USG's revised report dated Nov. 17 whether the message was verbal or written. C.S.A. sources clearly indicate that there had been no movement from Columbus to Belmont or against Oglesby; additional troops were sent to Belmont only when Maj. Gen. Leonidas Polk learned of USG's approach. *O.R.*, I, iii, 306; William M. Polk, *Leonidas Polk: Bishop and General* (New York, 1915), II, 38.

USG's comments in the weeks before Belmont provide possible motives for his actions. In private letters he revealed concern about his rank and command and a desire to engage the enemy in action. Throughout Sept., USG had exhibited an impatience to move downriver. In late Sept., he wrote that he would like to take Columbus but lacked sufficient forces. He stated that if he did not move quickly he probably could not do it at all, for "There are to many Generals who rank me that have a commands inferior to mine for me to retain it." See letters to Julia Dent Grant, Sept. 22, 25, 1861. A month later he was still thinking about Columbus and lamented that delay in moving had allowed it to be so strongly occupied by the rebels that it could not now be taken. USG was impatient with being forced to remain at Cairo and wrote that "What I want is to advance." See letter to Julia Dent Grant, Oct. 20, 1861. USG informed McKeever a week later that the forces at Columbus had been reduced for service elsewhere, and that if he and Smith had adequate arms and equipment it could be taken. See letter to Capt. Chauncey McKeever, Oct. 27, 1861. Meanwhile, Frémont was pursuing Price in central Mo. while Thompson was reported active in southeast Mo. Consequently, on Nov. 1 and 2, McKeever sent orders directing USG to menace Columbus and send an expedition after Thompson. Acting on these orders, USG sent troops from Bird's Point and Cape Girardeau after Thompson and at the same time prepared for a demonstration against Columbus.

Capt. Andrew H. Foote's report to Secretary of the Navy Gideon Welles, Nov. 9, implied that USG intended to attack Belmont when he left Cairo. Foote charged that USG, contrary to an express promise, failed to inform the naval commander of the intended action. "General Grant, however, on my arrival this morning, called upon me and expressed his regret that he had not telegraphed as he had promised, assigned as the cause that he had forgotten it, in the haste in which the expedition was prepared, until it was too late for me to arrive in time to take command. . . ." *O.R.* (Navy), I, xxii, 399–400. See also *ibid.*, p. 397. In discussing the battle before the first reunion of the Army of the Tennessee, Rawlins implied that the attack may have come without higher authority by omitting mention of the Nov. 5 telegram. *Report of the Proceedings of the Society of the Army of the Tennessee, at the first Annual Meeting, held at Cincinnati, O., November 14th and 15th, 1866* (Cincinnati, 1877), p. 28.

A soldier who was in Oglesby's columns doubted that USG ever intended simply to menace Columbus. "I think the Paducah forces were to take Columbus, Grant was going to swallow Belmont, we were to drive all the guerrillas before us to New Madrid, and then with Paducah forces and Grant's we were to take Madrid and probably go on to Memphis or maybe join Fremont with our Army of say 15,000 men." See letter of Nov. 13, 1861, in Charles W. Wills, *Army Life of an Illinois Soldier, Including a Day by Day Record of Sherman's March to the Sea: Letters and Diary of the Late Charles W. Wills*, Mary E. Kellogg, ed. (Washington, 1906), pp. 42–43. Another soldier later recalled that the troops who left Cairo expected to attack Columbus. John Seaton, *The Battle of Belmont, November 7, 1861* (n.p., [1902]), p. 6.

A Cairo correspondent for the *Missouri Democrat*, Nov. 13, 1861, in a dispatch dated Nov. 10, wrote that USG originally intended to land his troops in Ky. for a demonstration against Columbus but was waiting until Oglesby arrived at Belmont before taking further action which reconnaissance might indicate was possible. USG changed plans and determined to attack Belmont after learning that troops had crossed the river in order to cut off Oglesby's columns. In testimony before the Committee on the Conduct of the War, Frémont indicated that he was preparing a general offensive to drive the rebels out of Mo. and then move to clear the Mississippi all the way to Memphis. Testimony of Jan. 30, 1862, *HRC*, 37-3-108, part 3, 74–75. McKeever, however, before the same committee, testified that he had ordered USG to send out troops to intercept Thompson, but made no mention of any other instructions. Testimony of March 8, 1862, *ibid.*, pp. 251–52.

USG's motives in attacking Belmont have received varied treatment from his biographers. Adam Badeau, *Military History of Ulysses S. Grant* (New York, 1868–81), I, 13–21, generally followed the revised report, but stressed the importance of the battle for the morale of the troops, concluding that USG, "even if he had not received the information on which his attack was based, would nevertheless have made the assault." *Ibid.*, p. 21. Augustus W. Alexander, *Grant as a Soldier* (St. Louis, 1887), pp. 41–47, used the inconsistencies in USG's accounts of Belmont as grounds for a bitter indictment; but A. L. Conger, *The Rise of U. S. Grant* (New York, 1931), pp. 81–101, 365–77, used the late dates of the revised report and the *Memoirs* as the basis for an interpretation based on the earlier letters, concluding that before leaving Cairo USG planned to attack Belmont in order to drive C.S.A. forces from the Mo. bank of the Mississippi. *Ibid.*, p. 372. Kenneth P. Williams, *Lincoln Finds a General* (New York, 1949–59), III, 75–100, relied largely on the revised report, criticized Conger for his reading of the letter of Nov. 6 to Oglesby as indicating early plans to attack Belmont, but admitted that he found the wording "somewhat enigmatic." *Ibid.*, p. 78. Bruce Catton, *Grant Moves South* (New York, 1960), pp. 70–84, also accepted the revised report, concluded that USG had several purposes in attacking Belmont, and emphasized the effect on morale.

Because of the contradictory nature of the sources, it appears impossible to reconcile the divergent interpretations of USG's motives in attacking Belmont. A close look at the documentary evidence, however, casts such doubt on the alleged telegram of Nov. 5 and the message of 2 a.m., Nov. 7, as to suggest that no satisfactory explanation can be found by examining the orders of USG's superiors or the actions of his opponents. The answer must be found in USG himself, and no simple answer will do.

2. See letter to Brig. Gen. Charles F. Smith, Nov. 5, 1861.

3. See letter to Col. John Cook, Nov. 6, 1861.

4. On Nov. 9, Commander Henry Walke wrote to USG. "Agreeable to your instructions I proceeded on the evening of the 6th, in company with the U S GunBoat Lexington under Commander Stembel, down the Mississippi convoying a number of Transport Steamers, as far as opposite Norfolk and near the Ky shore, where we all anchored for the night. At 3 o'clock the following morning, the GunBoats Taylor and Lexington proceeded down the river with the intention of engaging the enemy at Iron Banks, but after running a short distance we were met by such a dense fog as to render any further progress hazardous and unfeasible. We therefore rounded to and returned to the point from whence we started. I received your special order and at 6 o'clock we all started, the two GunBoats taking the lead, we proceeded to the extreme end of Lucas's Bend where I supposed we were out of the range of their guns. After your troops were disembarked and under marching orders—about 8½ oclock. The two Gun Boats proceeded to engage the batteries on Iron Banks, we each expended several rounds of shell with seemingly good effect, but their balls from the rifled cannon flew by and over us to a great extent, some of the shot going half a mile beyond the

transports, fortunately however they did us no damage and we returned to the Transports where they kept firing at us for a considerable length of time. I finally requested the Capts of the Transports to move above and out of the range of their guns, which subsequently they did, we ourselves doing likewise. At ten o'clock, hearing the battle at Belmont, our two Boats again proceeded down to engage their batteries, this time expending more shell, and receiving no injury. After an Engagement of about 20 minutes, in the meantime the shots flying thickly about us, we again returned to the Transports, continuing our fire as long as our shells reached them. At noon hearing the continued firing at Belmont, the two GunBoats made their third attack upon the enemy's Batteries, this time going nearly a quarter of a mile nearer. We opened a brisk fire of shell directing many of them to the enemy's camp at Belmont. Their rifled balls still passing beyond and around us, but one of their 24 pnds. struck us on the Starboard Bulwark, continuing obliquely through the spar deck and in its course taking off the head of one man, and injuring two others, one quite seriously. After firing a few more rounds we returned keeping up our fire from the Stern guns till out of reach It is truly miraculous that we have in all our engagements escaped with so little damage After nearly all the Troops had reembarked and were about ready to start, a sudden attack was made upon the Transport Vessels, by an apparently large reinforcement of the Rebels, our Boats being in good position we opened fire with our grape, cannister and 5 second shells, and completely routed them we learn with great slaughter. After silencing the enemy, we continued our fire with the broadside guns throwing shell on the Banks ahead with the bow gun to protect the Transports and throwing shell from the stern gun upen the enemy's ground so long as we were in reach. After passing a few miles up the river we met the Chancellor with Brig Gen McClerland on board who stated that some of their Troops had been left behind, and by his direction both GunBoats returned some distance picking up between us all there were to be seen together with a large number of Prisoners some wounded and sick. Every attention was paid to alleviate the sufferings of the wounded, Act Surgeons Kearney and Goddard dressing their wounds and the crew of the ship furnishing them with their own hammocks and bedding We then returned to Island No 1 met the RobRoy with instructions from you, turned over to her all our soldiers and Prisoners, and remained there till an hour after Col McCooks return from a reconnoisance down the Ky side, we then weighed anchor and proceeded to Cairo Commander Stembel with the Lexington as consort supported me in all the duties of the day with most commendable energy and in an effective manner." LS, DNA, RG 94, War Records Office, Union Battle Reports. *O.R.*, I, iii, 275–76. A copy of the same letter is dated Nov. 8. DNA, RG 45, Naval Records Collection, Area 5. *O.R.* (Navy), I, xxii, 402–4. Additional information on naval aspects of Belmont is in a letter of Nov. 9 from Capt. Andrew H. Foote to Secretary of the Navy Gideon Welles. LS, DNA, RG 45, Area 5. *O.R.* (Navy), I, xxii, 398–400.

USG may also have forwarded two other reports written before Nov. 10. On Nov. 8, Capt. Ezra Taylor wrote to USG. "I have to report the following causialities &c. during the expedition and fight which occured at Bellmont yesterday. Three men seriously wounded, 1st Segt. Chas. W. Everett, musket shot in the head, Segt. David F. Chase shot in the arm Private Geo Q. White lost right hand and badly wounded in the face. Slightly Wounded,—Privates C. R. Vanhorn and Wm. DeWolfe, Horses Lost. three shot on the field. Horses Wounded, Two in the legs, several others slightly wounded. Left on the field, Two Caissions, One

Baggage Wagon Two Sets Artillery Lead Harness, 1000 Ball Catridge for Colts Revolvers two hundred rounds ammunition for Six Pdr Guns, Twenty-five double Blankets, Twenty Canteens, Five Coats, 3 Caps Five Colts Revolvers, Five Horse Blankets, Six Sabers, Five Lanterns, Three Shovels, One Overcoat, Two Curry Combs & Brushes, Two Fuse Gouges, Sixty Friction Primers, Two Camp Kettles, Twenty Cups, One Leg Guard, One Sponge & Rammer, Six Whips, Twenty Havesacks, Two Pick Axes, Four Felling Axes One Trail Handspike,—Captured from the Enemy—Twenty Horses, One Mule, One Six Pdr Brass Gun, One 12 Pdr Brass Howitzer and some fragrements of Artillery Harness and sundry small articles captured by individuals, not of any perticular value to the service. My force consisted of Four 6 Pdr Field Guns, Two 12 Pdr Howitzers with Gun Limbers and Caissions complete, Eighty One Horses and Fourteen Mules One Thousand rounds ammunition for Guns and Howitzers, One Thousand Pistol Catridges, One Hundred and Fourteen Men with rations and forage for two days.—Number of rounds fired on the field, Four Hundred,—Number lost—Two Hundred. Number brought off the field Four Hundred. I have to regret the loss off my Caissions and Baggage Wagon but trust that the Government is amply repaid in the capture of two guns from the Enemy. I am highly gratified to be able to report that the officers and men under my command conducted themselves in a manner to deserve my highest commendation and praise as soldiers, I take pleasure in mentioning in perticular Leut. P. H. White and the men under his immediate command for the bravery displayed in driving the enemy from his position, silencing his Battry and under a galling fire from his infrantry, capuring two of his Guns, and although the result of the battle is anything but satisfactory to me yet I cannot forbear to say that considering the ground fought over, and the extreme difficuly experienced in handling Artillery in the woods that I am satisfied that no man could have effected more under the Circumstances." LS, DNA, RG 94, War Records Office, Union Battle Reports. *O.R.*, I, iii, 290.

On Nov. 10, Col. Jacob G. Lauman, 7th Iowa, wrote to USG. "I herewith hand you the report of the movements of my regiment, with the official List of killed and wounded at the Battle of Belmont as follows: On the fifth inst I recieved your order to hold my regiment in readiness to march at 4 Oclock P. M. on the following day with 24 hours rations in haversacks. It was dark, however, before we embarked on the Steamer Montgomery, and we soon after got under way. We proceeded but a short distance down the River when we tied up for the night. Early on the moring of the 7th preceeded by the gun boats Tyler & Conestoga, we proceeded on our way and soon after landed on the west bank of the Mississippi about 3 miles above Belmont, which is opposite Collumbus Ky. We immediately formed in line in the corn field on the bank of the river, about half past Eight Oclock and were soon after ordered by you to form on the left of McClernands brigade, which had already crossed the field. At this time I was joined by Col Dougherty with the 22nd Ills. We remained in this position untill Taylors battery had disembarked and taken their position, when we recieved orders to march, which we did in the following order. The first Brigade consisting of three regiments of Infantry and Taylors battery, then followed the Second Brigade, consisting of Eight companies of my regiment and Seven companies of the 22nd Ills,. Col Dougherty in command of the Brigade. Two companies of my regiment and three companies of Col Doughertys having previously been detached to guard the boats. The Cavalry were sent in advance, scouting. In this order we marched a mile or more, when we formed in line of battle in front of a cornfield. The

battery taking position in the field. We remained in this position but a short time
when we advanced in line of battle across a dry slough, and immediately in front
of heavy timber. There I recieved orders to throw forward two companies as
skirmishers. Which I complied with by sending Co "A" commanded by Lieut
De-Hew and Co "F" commanded by Captain Kittredge from my right wing. I
soon after sent forward Co "B," Captain Gardner from my left wing. These
companies were not long in finding the enemy, whome they found in force in front
and to the left of our position, and the heavy and continued firing convinced me
that we now had work to do I therefore dispached Lieut Col Wentz to ascertain
the force of the enemy and their exact position, but before he had time to return,
I recieved through your aid, Captain Rawlings, an order to advance to their support which I did, bringing my men under fire at double quick time. From this
time, about 11 Oclock, we fought the rebels Slowly but steadily, driving them
before us at every volley, our advance at this point was slow in consequence of
the obstructions in our way, caused by felling timber and under brush, but we
crept under and over it, at times lying down to let the fire of the artillery and
musketry pass over us, and then up an onward again until we arrived at the
field to the left of the rebel camp, here we were joined by our skirmishers who had
succeeded, after a severe struggle in driving back the enemy, and forming our line
immediately, we poured volley after volley on the retiring foe across the field
in front, and on the battery which was stationed at the head of of the encampment
on our right. Our fire was so hot the guns were soon abandoned, the enemy about
800 flying across the field in the greatest consternation. By a flank movement to
the right I brought my men into the open space in front of the battery, which was
immediately taken possession of, I believe by Lieutenant De-Heus, Co "A"
whose flag was soon seen flying from one of the captured pieces.—We were now
immediately in rear of the encampment, and were here joined by a portion of Col
Doughertys regiment, 22nd Ills. The rebels kept up a sharp and galling fire upon
us, but a few well directed volleys induced them to abandon their camp suddenly.
It was here whilst the firing was heaviest that 1st Sergeant Waller of Co "I"
seized the regimental colors and bore them aloft, and in front of the regimental
line, directing the attention of the boys to a fine large flag floating over the encampment decorated on one side with twelve stars and on the other with the
'Harp of Erin,' on a green silk ground, they with loud huzzas went forward and
secured it. It was in making this charge that my horse was shot. I. followed the
regiment on foot until we reached the lower end of the encampment, when I. was
supplied with an other horse, which had just been captured by one of the men.
When immediately ordering an other charge we drove all the remaining rebels
over the bank of the river (at this point some twelve feet high) and dashed up
the river road until we arrived at the log house, which constitutes the city of
Belmont. At this place there was considerable random firing, the rebels firing
from the cover of trees and the bank of the river, and it was here, ~~that~~ whilst giving
Captain Parrott of Co "E," orders to bring off two field pieces, which had been
abandoned by the enemy, or to throw them into the river, so as to render them
useless against us, that I recieved a ball through my left thigh, which for a time
disabled me. I was assisted by Capt Parrott to the rear of the tents, where I
remained but a short time, as one of the guns of Captain Taylors battery coming
along, they placed me on it and took me to the rear of the encampment. In the
meantime our men had recieved orders to burn and destroy the camp and property,
which had fallen into our hands, and in a very short time the destruction was

complete. The rebels had however not been idle, having several large Steamers in the river at Collumbus they were loaded down with fresh troops, which were thrown betwene us and our place of Debarkation, so as in a measure to cut off our retreat. Those of them also who had been driven from their guns in the early part of the fight, seeing us falling back towards our boats took fresh courage and commenced closing in on us : and as all the Illinois troops had now either left or were leaving except the Ills 22nd Col Dougherty, we were in danger of being surrounded and cut off. I was apprised of this state of affairs by Col Dougherty; to whose bravery I desire to bear testimony, and who lost a limb in his effort to bring off safely the rear of his Brigade as well as to that of his noble regiment, which fought side by side with us on that memorable day. I immediately gave orders to my regiment to retire, myself leading the way, but by this time we were subjected to an enfilading fire which caused us heavy losses. The men behaved in the most gallant manner, deliberately loading and firing as they retired and although every other man was either killed or wounded they scarcely accelerated their step, but coolly and deliberately loading and firing as they retired made their way to the boat. It was after the retreat had commenced that Lieut Col Wentz was killed; he died on the field of battle like a true soldier. He was a truely brave man and did his duty well and nobly. Lieut Dodge of Co "B" was killed and Lieut Gardiner who commanded Co "I" and Lieut Ream of Co "C." mortally wounded. Among my officers more or less severely wounded you will find the names of Major Rice, Captains Harper, Parrott, Kittridge and Gardner, and 1st Lieut de-Hews (who commanded company "A") of whose bravery I desire to speak in the most emphatic manner. I. desire also to direct your attention to to Capt Crabb, who was taken prisoner and who behaved in the most gallant manner, but I. might go on in this way and name nearly all my entire command for they all behaved like heroes, but there is one or two more, I feel it my duty to name as deserving special mention   Lieut Bowler, adjutant of the regiment and Lieut Estle, whose conduct was worthy of all praise, and and private Lawrence gregg, whose thigh was broken and he left on the field, he was taken prisoner and his leg amputated, but he died the same day telling his captors with his dying breath, that if he ever recovered so as to be able to move he would shoulder his musket again in his countrys service   Under cover of the fire from the gunboats we finally reached our boat betwene five and six Oclock and at about 8 Oclock arrived in Cairo   My entire loss in killed wounded prisoners and missing is as follows, out of an aggregate of somewhat over 400

killed	51	died of wounds	3
missing	10	Prisoners	39
	wounded	124	
		Total	227"

LS, NHi; copies, DNA, RG 94, 7th Iowa, Letterbook; *ibid.*, War Records Office, Union Battle Reports. *O.R.*, I, iii, 296–98. See letter to Brig. Gen. Seth Williams, Nov. 20, 1861.

Steamer "B"
Near Cairo, Ill,
November 12th/61

General,

Your note is just received. I am very happy to know that your Secretary of War has left the disposal of the prisoners taken at Belmont at your descretion.

Tomorrow at 12 O'Clock M. I will have a boat meet one from Columbus on the river between the two points, when all the prisoners in my possession will be transfered to you.

I cannot give the exact number now having relieved some thirty odd already without keeping an exact record.

I am Gen. Very respectfully
Your Obdt. Sevt.
U. S. Grant
Brig. Gen. U.S.A.

To
Maj. Gen. L. Polk
Comdg. Confederate Forces
Columbus Ky.

A letter from Grant to Maj. Gen. Polk, November 12, 1861.
Courtesy National Archives.

Cairo, Illinois, in 1861 : looking north up the Ohio River. Wharfboats are in the center of the photograph.

Another view of Cairo in 1861: looking south down the Ohio River. The Mississippi River is on the right, and Fort Prentiss stands at the confluence of the two rivers. *Courtesy Cairo Public Library.*

Gun crew at Fort Prentiss. *Courtesy Cairo Public Library.*

A contemporary sketch of Fort Prentiss. Fort Prentiss occupied the extreme point of the peninsula of Cairo at the confluence of the Mississippi and Ohio rivers, commanding both rivers. *Frank Leslie's Illustrated Newspaper, September 28, 1861.*

The ironclad gunboat *U.S.S. Cairo. U.S. War Department General Staff photo No. 165-C-630, National Archives.*

The gunboat U.S.S. *New Era* — later renamed U.S.S. *Essex* — "sketched by a correspondent." *Harper's Weekly, October 12, 1861.*

Cairo, Illinois, in 1856, as shown in *Ballou's Pictorial Drawing-Room Companion, August, 1856.*

To Col. Joseph P. Taylor

Head Quarters, Dist. S. E. Mo.
Cairo, November 10th 1861.

GEN. J. P. TAYLOR
COM.G GEN. U. S. A.
WASHINGTON, D. C.
GEN.

I wish to represent to you that the duty of Commissary for this District has been performed by R. C. Rutherford who originally held the position of Regimental Quartermaster in the three months volunteer service. He now holds no commission but is continued in his position.

I can honestly say that Mr. Rutherford must be continued in his present position, if the interest of the service is consulted, and hope that an appointment in your Department may be sent him at once.

I feel no personal interest in securing this appointment, but having command here I have turned my attention wholly to the interest, and economy, of the Government, and would have ordered Mr. Rutherford relieved some time since if I had not felt that it would have been a serious loss to have done so.

I am Gen., Very respectfully
Your Obt. Svt.
U. S. GRANT.
Brig. Gen. Com

P. S. (Reuben C. Rutherford)

ALS, DNA, RG 94, Letters Received. Col. Joseph P. Taylor of Ky. served as commissary gen. of subsistence Sept. 29, 1861 to June 29, 1864. On Nov. 15, 1861, Taylor replied to USG. "Yours of the 10th Inst is received. The appointments of Brigade Commissaries are made by the Secretary of War—to whom your letter will be referred Capt B. Du Barry C. S. now stationed at Harrisburg, Pa will be ordered to report to you as Commissary." Copy, *ibid.*, RG 192, Letters Sent. USG's letter was forwarded to the War Dept. on Nov. 14, then transmitted to the AGO. *Ibid.*, RG 107, Registers of Letters Received. See letter to Brig. Gen. Lorenzo Thomas, Oct. 20, 1861.

To Brig. Gen. Seth Williams

RECEIVED Nov 11 *1861*.
FROM Cairo Ill

To G. WILLIAMS

A special Dispatch to Memphis Appeal dated Atlanta Nov 8th states our fleet had captured three (3) forts in South Carolina at Port Royal Hilton Head & Bayou Point. Our forces had possession of the Town of Pt Royal twenty (20) miles from Savannah & were within ten (10) miles of the Charleston & Savannah Railroad   Rebels admit their loss very great. New Orleans Papers speak of the presence of an immense fleet off Ship Island.[1]

N. S. GRANT.
Br Gen U S A

Telegram received, DNA, RG 393, Army of the Potomac, Telegrams Received. On Nov. 11, 1861, the War Dept. sent a copy of this telegram to President Abraham Lincoln with a notation. "For the information of His Excellency, the President." DLC-Robert T. Lincoln. On Nov. 7, a fleet commanded by Flag Officer Samuel F. Du Pont and an army commanded by Brig. Gen. Thomas W. Sherman captured Port Royal, S. Car., and also nearby Forts Walker and Beauregard. C.S.A. losses were reported to be eleven killed, forty-eight wounded, three captured, and four missing. *O.R.*, I, vi, 12.

1. Ship Island, seventy miles east of New Orleans, was evacuated by C. S. A. forces on Sept. 17, but not occupied by U. S. forces until Dec. 3, 1861.

To Col. Jacob G. Lauman

Head Quarters Dis. S. E Mo
Cairo Nov 11th 1861

SPECIAL ORDER No

Leave of absence is hereby granted Col Lauman 7th Iowa Vols. to return to his home until his recovery from wounds received in the engagement at Belmont on the 7th inst.

Col. Lauman carries with him the congratulations of the

comdg. Genl. for the gallantry displayed by himself and the troops under his command, and the hope that they may soon be restored to such a state of health and numbers, as will enable them to do like efficient service in another field

U. S. GRANT Brig. Genl Comd'g

To Col Lauman 7th Iowa Vols

Copies, DLC-USG, V, 15, 16, 77, 82; DNA, RG 393, USG Special Orders. On Nov. 14, 1861, Capt. John A. Rawlins issued special orders. "The 10th Regiment Iowa Vols Col Perczell commanding are hereby assigned to the 2d Brigade Col Oglesby commanding. They will occupy the Grounds now occupied by the 7th Iowa   The 7th Iowa will proceed by the same transportation that brought the 10th to Saint Louis Mo and report to Genl Curtiss for duty. They will take with them all their Camp & Garrison equippage, but will leave their transportation which will be receipted for by Capt Hatch Post Quartermaster" Copies, *ibid.*

To Maj. Gen. Leonidas Polk

Steamer "B"
Near Cairo, Ill.
November 12th/61

GENERAL,

Your note is just received. I am very happy to know that your Secretary of War has left the disposal of the prisone[rs] taken at Belmont at your descretion.[1]

To-morrow at 12 O'Clock M. I will have a boat meet one from Columbus on the river between the two points, where all the prisoners in my posession will be transfered to you.

I cannot give the exact number now having relieved some thirty odd already without keeping an exact record.

I am Gen. Very respectfully
Your Obt. Svt.
U. S. GRANT
Brig. Gen. U. S. A.

To Maj. Gen. L. Polk
Comd.g Confeterate Forces
Columbus Ky.

ALS, DNA, RG 109, Documents Printed in *O.R. O.R.*, II, i, 518. On Nov. 12, 1861, Maj. Gen. Leonidas Polk wrote to USG. "In pursuance of my note of the 8th Inst I have to say, that, I have received from the Secy of War discretionary power as to the disposition of our prisoners. I have therefore concluded to return to you the whole of your wounded—one hundred and five in number—as to the details of this disposition I refer you to Brig Genl J P McCown to whom I have intrusted the safe conduct and delivry of the prisoners and who will communicate to you fully my views upon the whole subject—" Copy, DNA, RG 109, Documents Printed in *O.R.*; *ibid.*, RG 393, Dept. of the Mo., Letters Received. *O.R.*, II, i, 518. See letter to Maj. Gen. Leonidas Polk, Nov. 8, 1861. On Nov. 13, Capt. John A. Rawlins wrote to Brig. Gen. John A. McClernand. "In pursuance of an understanding between my self and General Polk, arrived at last evening, at the interview under his *flag of truce*, that he should release the remainder of our prisoners, taken in the engagement at Belmont on the 7th inst, and I should release theirs. You will have all the prisoners taken by us in said engagement, put on board the Steamer *Aleck Scott* by 12 Oclock 'M' of today" Copies, DLC-USG, V, 1, 2, 3, 77; DNA, RG 393, USG Letters Sent. *O.R.*, II, i, 519.

On Dec. 19, Polk wrote to USG. "In pursuance of my agreement I have had at my earliest convenience ten privates of the prisoners I hold selected to send up to you, that being the difference between the number released by you (124) and the number released by me (114) and agreed upon by yourself & Gen'l McCown. This does not include Lt Smith, Col Doughertys attendant, who was released by me on parole. These men were chosen by lot and sent up from Memphis, since their arrival I find one of them declines to return. I must therefore send you another at a future day in his place. I send you also your servant, the terms on which he is restored, you have already discussed with Col Tappan—" Copy, DNA, RG 109, Miscellaneous Confederate Papers. *O.R.*, II, i, 530. A list of prisoners sent on Dec. 19 is printed *ibid*.

1. On Nov. 11, C. S. A. Act. Secretary of War Judah P. Benjamin wrote to Polk. "Exchange your prisoners on the best equal terms you can get. An unconditional exchange preferred. If you cannot exchange give up all that are seriously wounded after taking a strict parole." *Ibid.*, p. 541.

To Maj. Gen. George B. McClellan

———

RECEIVED Nov 13th *1861*.
FROM Cairo 13th

To MAJ GEN G B McCLELLAN

I will report our strength condition &c. by first mail   we want arms clothing & quarter master funds badly   the credit of Gov't has been exhausted to such an extent that Economy would demand a speedy transmission of funds to Pay at least a part of our standing accounts

U S GRANT
Brig Gen'l

Telegram received, DNA, RG 92, Consolidated Correspondence, Ulysses S. Grant. On Nov. 10, 1861, Maj. Gen. George B. McClellan had telegraphed to USG. "Inform me fully of the number & condition of your command. Tell me your wants & wishes. Give positions numbers & condition of enemy. Your means of transportation by land and water Size and armament of gun boats. Communicate fully & often" ALS, CSmH. *O.R.*, I, liii, 507. On Nov. 13, in response to USG's telegram, Bvt. Col. Ebenezer S. Sibley, deputy q. m. gen., telegraphed to USG. "Your despatch to General McClellan received. Specify the articles of clothing most needed at this time." Telegram, copies, DLC-USG, V, 4, 5, 7, 8; DNA, RG 107, Telegrams Collected (Unbound); *ibid.*, RG 393, USG Hd. Qrs. Correspondence. See letter to Elihu B. Washburne, Nov. 20, 1861.

To Brig. Gen. John A. McClernand

———

Head Quarters, Dist. S. E. Mo.
Cairo, November, 13th/61

SPECIAL ORDER NO

The 48th Ill. Vols. Col. Haney[1] Commanding is assigned to duty at Cairo.

The Commanding officer will report for position and duty to Brig. Gen. J. A. McClernand, Comd.g Post.

U. S. GRANT
Brig. Gen. Com.

To Brig. Genl J. A. McClernand
Comdg. Post
Cairo Ils

ALS, McClernand Papers, IHi. On Nov. 11, 1861, Governor Richard Yates telegraphed to USG. "Col Haynes Regt are under marching orders for Cairo without arms if you Cannot use them they will go into Camp at Shawneetown" Telegram received, DNA, RG 393, Dept. of the Mo., Telegrams Received.

1. Col. Isham N. Haynie, 48th Ill., served as 1st lt. in the Mexican War, and was judge of the court of common pleas at Cairo at the outbreak of the Civil War.

To Brig. Gen. John A. McClernand

——————

Head Quarters Dist. S. E Mo.
Cairo Nov. 13th 1861.

If in the Judgement of the Medical Director the patients called for cannot be removed without danger of being injured by it they will not be removed—The object of having a Medical Director is that a responsible and competent person may have supervision over the sick and to do so properly he must have controle over them within fair limits

U. S. GRANT
Brig General Comdg

Copies (2), McClernand Papers, IHi. This endorsement is written on Special Orders No. 1609, Nov. 13, 1861, of Brig. Gen. John A. McClernand. "Col. John A. Logan of the 31st Regiment will take charge of and remove to his own Regimental Hospital all the wounded brought up from Columbus belonging to his Regiment. The Officers now having them in charge will please deliver them to him." Copy, *ibid*. Below McClernand's orders, Col. John A. Logan wrote to Maj. Mason Brayman. "Please deliver all my men to Parson Cole immediately" Copy, *ibid*. See letter to Brig. Gen. John A. McClernand, Nov. 15, 1861.

To Commander Henry Walke

———

Head Quarters Dist. S. E. Mo.
Cairo, Nov 13th, 1861

CAPT. WALKE
COMDG FLOTILLA
CAIRO, ILLS.
SIR
    Will you please send as soon as possible a statement of the
condition and armament of your Gun Boats.
                            Very Respt
                            Yours &c
                            U S GRANT
                            Brig Genl Comdg

Copy, DNA, RG 45, Area 5. *O.R.* (Navy), I, xxii, 428. On Nov. 13, 1861, Commander Henry Walke replied to USG. "I have the honor to state in reply to your
instructions, just received, That the Gun Boat Taylor is ready for action, with
two bow Guns, and four broadside guns, (64 pdrs) and one stern gun (32 pdr),
With small arms for the crew." Copy, DNA, RG 94, Letters Received.

To Brig. Gen. Lorenzo Thomas

———

Head Quarters, Dist. S. E. Mo.
Cairo, November 14th 1861

GEN. L. THOMAS
ADJT. GEN. U. S. A.
WASHINGTON D. C.
SIR:
    Enclosed please find report of Capt. Brinck, Act. Chief of
Ord. in the case of Sgt. W. T. Morgan who has proven himself
a worthless and useless soldier.
    I would respectfully recommend that Sgt. Morgan be dis-
honorably discharged from the service.

I am well aware that in the regular service he might be brought before a General Courtmartial on the charge of *Utter Worthlessness* and sentenced to be discharged but before Volunteer Courts I have not had an instance, to my recollection, where a sentence of the kind has been given for any offence.

> Very respectfully
> Your Obt. Svt.
> U. S. GRANT
> Brig. Gen. Com.

ALS, DNA, RG 393, Dept. of the Mo., Letters Received. Enclosed was a report of Nov. 14, 1861, from Capt. Wilbur F. Brinck to USG. "I have the honor to report that William. T. Morgan, formerly of Col Lawlers Regiment, from which he was transfered to the Artillery, and by Col Waagner (then chief of Artillery) ordered to Capt Swartz Battery. On account of drunkenness and neglect of duty, Capt Swartz made an application to have him discharged. Yesterday he showed me an order from John Loomis Assistant Adjutant General of the state of Illinois addressed to him as Captain, and authorising him to raise a company of Artillery. Morgan has not the ability for the position in any particular and on account of his drunkenness is *totally unfit* I have taken the liberty of informing you of these facts from a sense of duty" ALS, *ibid*.

William S. Morgan of Anna, Ill., enlisted in Co. F, 18th Ill., on May 30, 1861. After serving as sgt. he was reduced to private on Aug. 1. Three days later he was transferred as an act. 2nd lt. to the art. On Oct. 13, he was returned to the 18th Ill., but on Nov. 1 was authorized by 2nd asst. Ill. AG John S. Loomis to recruit a co. of art. Unsuccessful in accomplishing this, Morgan rejoined the 18th Ill. in Feb., 1862, and fell sick. On April 18, not having received pay for eight months, Morgan wrote an account of his services to Col. Michael K. Lawler, and USG endorsed the letter on April 26. "Respectfully forwarded to Head Quarters of the Dept." AES, *ibid*., RG 94, Completed Service Records. Morgan deserted two days later, returned May 26, and was detached as post engineer, Jackson, Tenn., on Aug. 27, where he served until killed in an accident on the Mississippi Central Railroad, June 15, 1863.

To Brig. Gen. Seth Williams

Head Quarters, Dist. S. E. Mo.
Cairo, November 14th 1861.

GEN. S. WILLIAMS
A. A. GEN. U. S. A.
WASHINGTON D. C.

In conformity with telegraphic dispatch from Maj. Gen. McClellan received yesterday asking a full number of my command, their condition, wants, position &c.[1] I have directed a full Monthly report made out to be sent to your office. Owing to the activity with which troops under my command have been kept moving since the first of the Month full reports are not yet in.

My command extends to Cape Girardeau, Mo. and includes the following posts.

Cape Girardeau Mo. garrisoned with three regiments of Infantry, one Comp.y Light Artillery, one Engineer Company, one Company mounted Home Guards & one Siege Company both the latter anxious to be mustered into the service of the United States. The post commanded by Col. J. B. Plummer 11th Mo. Vols.

Birds Point Mo. garrisoned with six regiments of Infantry, two companies Light Artillery, one Engineer Company, & Eleven companies Cavalry.

One company of Artillery have just received their pieces but have not yet been supplied with horses or harness. Four companies of the Cavalry arrived yesterday.

Fort Holt Ky. garrisoned with two regiments of Infantry, on[e] Comp.y each of Cavalry & Light Artillery, the Artillery with but four pieces (two of them taken at Belmont) and neither horses nor harness.

I was very much opposed to occupying Fort Holt at the begining but now a great deel of labor has been expended in fortifying and strengthening the position, and the troops there have partially built huts for Winter accommodation.

Mound City Garrisoned with one regiment of Infantry.

Cairo with six regiments of Infantry, one Company Light Artillery and nine companies of Cavalry. One regiment of Infantry and all the Cavalry but one Comp.y without arms.

My whole command numbers less than eighteen thousand of which about two thousand two hundred are sick. But for the measels however the health of the command would be comparitively good.

We are deficient in land transportation, arms and clothing. The latter two are deficient both in quantity and quality.

This post has been carrid on so long without funds in the Quartermaster's Department that nothing can be procured at current cash rates, and not atal except with difficulty. I would urge the necessity of sending a supply of funds for the use of this post soon.

I think also that the interest of the service demands that a regular Quartermaster be sent here.

I have under my command two Gunboats one of which remains at Mound City to guard the new boats being built there, the other here.

I shall hope to have ready by to-morrow a Monthly report showing the exact condition of my whole command and accompanied by reports of the various departments.

Very respectfully
Your Obt. Svt.
U. S. GRANT
Brig. Gen. Com

ALS, DNA, RG 94, Letters Received; LS (addressed to Brig. Gen. Lorenzo Thomas), *ibid*. *O.R.*, I, iii, 570–71. Relevant items among the fifteen enclosures in the letter to Thomas are printed elsewhere. On Nov. 13, 1861, Capt. Wilbur F. Brinck wrote to USG. "In pursuance of your order for a report of the heavy and Field Ordnance within your command and the amount of ammunition I have the honor to submit the following. Eight Twelve Pounder Howitzers Twenty one Six Pounder Field Pieces Of the above number Captain Taylor stationed at Birds Point Missouri has Two Twelve Pounder Howitzers and Four Six Pounder Pieces his Battery is not complete. Requisitions for everything necessary have been sent to Saint Louis a number of times but as yet remain unfilled. Captain Houghtaling stationed at Birds Point Missouri has Two Twelve Pounder

Howitzers and Four Six Pounder Pieces, when his Horses (which are expected daily) are received his Battery will be complete. Captain Schwartz stationed at Cairo has a complete Battery of Two Twelve Pounder Howitzers and Four Six Pounder Pieces, but requires about Seventy more men. Capt McAllister stationed at Camp Holt Kentucky has Two Twelve Pounder Howitzers and Three Six Pounder Pieces (one each Howitzer and Six Pounder Field Piece was *captured at Belmont*) none of these Pieces are fit for field Service. Captain Campbell stationed at Cape Giraradeau Missouri has Six Six Pounder Pieces, this Battery is not fit for Field Service without considerable repairing. At Cairo (*unmounted*) we have one Eight inch Columbiad (Model 1859) and one Twenty four Pounder Gun with Siege Carriage. *Mounted At Mound City* one Twenty four Pounder Gun on Siege Carriage. At *Fort Prentiss Cairo* one Eight inch Morter, one Eight inch Howitzer Two Eight inch Columbiads mounted on Columbiad Carriages—Two Twenty four Pounder Guns on Siege Carriages   Four Thirty two Pounders on Barbette Carriages   *At Birds Point Missouri* Seven Twenty four Pounders on Barbette Carriages, Three Twenty four Pounder Howitzers on Siege Carriages   *At Camp Holt Kentucky* (upper Battery) Three Navel long Thirty two Pounders on Barbette Carriages—one Twenty four Pounder Garrison Gun on Barbette Carriage (Lower Battery) one Eight inch Columbiad on Columbiad Carriage   At *Cape Giraradeau* Missouri Nine Thirty two Pounders on Barbette Carriages   Exhibit No 1 gives amount of perfect Infantry ammunition on hand. Exhibit No 2—gives amount of Field and Siege Ammunition, all of the Six and Twelve Pounder ammunition has been condemned this afternoon by the Commission appointed by you. Therefore we have none on hand but a small lot in the hands [*of*] Captains Schwartz and Houghtaling our supply of Siege ammunition is small   Requisitions have been made but remain unfilled. I have furnished the Gun Boats some for their Columbiads as they cannot draw from the stores at Saint Louis, all the ordnance there being of different model from that on the Boats stationed at this place. I have Requisitions in St Louis for Two Hundred Thousand Rounds Infantry Ammunition and will add that our wants are never supplied promptly. I've also drawn for Six, Twelve and Twenty four Pounder ammunition about one eighth has been received. Much of the Infantry ammunition is very imperfect Three different Calibres of Ball being put in one box of Musket Cartridges— Twenty four Thousand imperfect Infantry Cartridges were returned to me to day. I am of the opinion that there is a discrepancy in the bore of some of the Muskets in which the Cartridges (Cal 69) is used, as many Musket Barrells burst at the skirmish at Belmont. The Cartridges issued for use at that time have not been reported to me as imperfect." LS, DNA, RG 94, Letters Received.

On Nov. 13, Capt. John A. Rawlins wrote to Capt. Reuben B. Hatch. "You will send to these Head Qrs immediately a statement of the means of Transportation (by land and water) of this Military District" Copies, DLC-USG, V, 1, 2, 3, 77; DNA, RG 393, USG Letters Sent. On Nov. 13, Hatch wrote to USG. "In obedience to your order of this date I have the honor to submit the enclosed reports of Land & Water transportation in this Military District." ALS, *ibid.*, RG 94, Letters Received. Hatch reported water transportation as follows:

		tons	capacity
"Steamer 'Alex Scott'	(Cairo)	1200	2000 men
" Memphis	(")	1000	1500 "
" Montgomery	(")	800	1000 "
" Chancellor	(")	600	1200 "

"	Keystone	(")	300	600	"
"	W. B. Terry	(")	200	500	"
"	Rob Roy	(")	200	400	"
"	W. H. B.	(")	100	400	"
"	Wilson	(")		400	"
"	Lake Erie	(Paducah)	100	300	"
"	Illinois	(Cape Girardeau)	1200	2000	"

3 boats at the landing can be ready
in 5 hours (not chartered)   5000   "
                                                        ——————
        Total capacity   15.300   "
Nov 13th 1861"

Hatch reported land transportation consisting of 121 teams of six mules, 13 teams of four mules, 8 teams of two mules, 19 teams of four horses, and 100 teams of two horses.

1. See telegram to Maj. Gen. George B. McClellan, Nov. 13, 1861.

To Surgeon John H. Brinton

————

Head Quarters Dist S. E. Mo
Cairo Nov 14th 1861

SPECIAL ORDER No

Surgeon J Brinton Medical Director will proceed as soon as practicable to Cape Girardeau Mo. to inspect the Hospital and make such changes and orders as he may deem nescessary for the benefit of the sick

U. S. GRANT
Brig. Genl Comdg.

To Surgeon J Brinton
Medical Director
Cairo Ills

Copies, DLC-USG, V, 15, 16, 77, 82; DNA, RG 393, USG Special Orders. See *Personal Memoirs of John H. Brinton* (New York, 1914), pp. 95–96. John H. Brinton of Pa. was appointed surgeon of vols. on Aug. 3, 1861. Although he hoped to be assigned to the command of his cousin, Maj. Gen. George Brinton McClellan, he was ordered on Sept. 4 to the Western Dept. *Ibid.*, p. 29. After some time at the hospital at Mound City, he was reassigned as act. medical director, District of Southeast Mo. See letter to Maj. James Simons, Oct. 25, 1861.

General Orders No. 15

Head Quarters Dist S. E. Mo
Cairo Nov 15th 1861

GENERAL ORDER NO 15

It is reported to the General Commanding this Military District that Soldiers of his command are known to have bartered away Horses and other property captured at the Battle of Belmont.

They are again informed that all captured property becomes property of the United States and as such must be turned over to the Post Quartermaster and accounted for.

It is the special duty of all Commanders of Regiments Companies and Detachments to see that this order is complied with.

Citizens who purchase such property knowing it to be captured violate the Law and will be made to loose the property purchased by them in every instance where it can be proven.

Commissioned officers who permit members of their command to retain property, commit a grave Military offence which it is hoped they will speedily correct

By order
U. S. GRANT
Brig Genl Comdg

Copies, DLC-USG, V, 12, 13, 14, 80; DNA, RG 393, USG General Orders. Two earlier orders related to property captured at Belmont. On Nov. 8, 1861, Capt. John A. Rawlins issued special orders. "All the property of every description, taken by the Officers and Soldiers at the Battle of Belmont, on the 7th inst, will be turned over to Capt. R. B. Hatch Asst. Quarter Master, U. S. A. who will receipt for the same. Such of the property as the Captors may desire to keep as trophies, or in lieu of property of same kind lost by them in the engagement, upon application in writing to these Head Quarters, will be returned to them, so far as may be consistent with, and conformable to the Army regulations. The commandants of Regiments and of Companies will see that the requirements of this order are immediately complied with" Copies, DLC-USG, V, 15, 16, 77, 82; DNA, RG 393, USG Special Orders. On Nov. 11, Rawlins again issued special orders. "There will be delivered to no Officers or Soldiers, any of the Horses captured in the skirmish at Belmont on the 7th inst., except to such Officers as lost their Horses in the engagement and are entitled to receive pay from the Government for the same, and to such Soldiers as are entitled to be furnished Horses by the Government and to draw forage for the same, or such of said Soldiers who had furnished their own Horses and lost them in the engagement. And upon the delivery to such Officers and Soldiers of Horses in lieu of those they have lost, a receipt will be taken from them in full of claims they now have or may hereafter have against the Government for such lost property" Copies, *ibid.*

On Nov. 12, Brig. Gen. John A. McClernand wrote to USG. "The Dun Stallion, with white mane and tail, captured by my servant in the battle of Belmont, together with some other captured horses—have been turned over to my Brigade Quarter Master, Captain Dunlap, as public property, and are subject to any transfer of possession or disposition you may be pleased to order. I have instructed Capt Dunlap to report to me the number of horses, and the quantity and kinds of other property, in his possession, captured at Belmont, of which I will advise you at an early date." LS, *ibid.*, District of Southeast Mo., Letters Received; ADf, McClernand Papers, IHi.

On Nov. 20, Capt. William S. Hillyer wrote to Capt. Reuben B. Hatch. "You will sell at public vendue to the highest bidder for Cash, all captured property, now in your custody not suitable for Government purpose, first giving public notice by printed hand bills of the time, terms, and place of sale, and the property to be sold" Copies, DLC-USG, V, 1, 2, 3, 77; DNA, RG 393, USG Letters Sent.

On Jan. 11, 1862, Hatch wrote to USG. "All the stock taken at the Battle of Belmont which was returned to me was sold by your order and the proseeds for them accounted for to Government Such stock as I have now on hand which I have reported to you not having been informed whether taken in battle or otherwise I have turned over to U S marshall Philips This was done upon your communication this morning dilivered to me by marshall Philips—I have no doubt of its correctness. I would mention that the property was reported to me, as captured property and not taken from citizens" ALS, *ibid.*, District of Cairo, Letters Received.

To Brig. Gen. John A. McClernand

———

Head Quarters Dist. S. E. Mo
Cairo November 15th 1861

GENL. J. A. McCLERNAND
COMDG. POST
CAIRO ILL
GENL.

Your note dated yesterday, relative to the removal of wounded men from Mound City Hospital is just received.

In reply, I would state, that the matter was refered to me by the Medical Director of this Military District, and I gave a decision according to my judgement, and known usage in the regular service

As a rule when a soldier gets into Hospital, he cannot be removed except, at the instance of the Surgeon in charge.

The rule seems to be a fair one, the Surgeon being the best judge of what is ~~best~~ for the health of their patients.

In the present instance, it was reported to me, that one of the wounded men was shot through the Lungs, and could not be removed without manifest injury to the man, and possibly, at the peril of his life.

I feel no desire General, to in the slightest degree, interfere with your administration of the affairs of this Post, further than my duties as District Commander absolutely require.

Reading Col. Logans. communication to you,[1] shows me, that I was laboring under a misapprehension, when I gave my decision to Surgeon Brinton. From this it would appear, that your order for the removal of Col. Logans wounded was given before they had been taken into Hospital. The Surgeon was evidently wrong in disobeying then.

The last clause in Col. Logans communication, characterizing the Medical Director as a *brute* is altogether wrong, such charges should only be made, in a way to bring proof of the fact before a Court Martial.

I regret that any difficulty should occur, and therefore am sorry that I was not advised before your last order was put in execution. I regret it more, that a part of the difficulty has grown out of the fact that I did not think at the time of giving my decision, of your first order having been given, as stated above, before the wounded men had been taken into Hospital

I am Ever
Your Obt Svt
U. S. GRANT
Brig. Genl. Comdg.

LS, McClernand Papers, IHi. On Nov. 14, 1861, Brig. Gen. John A. McClernand wrote to USG. "The copy of my order to Col. Logan, to receive, and transfer his wounded men, to his own Regimental Hospital, together with your indorsement, to me thereon, is received Predicating my order to Col Logan, upon the accompanying, responsible, communication to me from him, I felt not only that I was justified, but required, as the Commandant of the Post, responsible for its proper administration, both to make it and to see that it was executed. Col Logan, in a personal interview this morning, having again invoked the aid of my authority to obtain possession of his wounded men, and not understanding you to have ordered otherwise, I have directed him to cause an examination to be made respecting his men, and if, in his judgment nescessary, to send a detail to Mound City to recover them, and to arrest, and bring before me, any one who may resist my order. Prompted, equally by a sense of duty and self respect, I hope my action in this behalf will be satisfactory to you." LS, DNA, RG 393, District of Southeast Mo., Letters Received; ADfS, McClernand Papers, IHi. See endorsement to Brig. Gen. John A. McClernand, Nov. 13, 1861.

1. Not found.

To Col. A. H. Waterman

Head Quarters Dist S. E. Mo
Cairo November 15th 1861

SPECIAL ORDER No

Col. A. H. Waterman, Superintendent of Cairo & Fulton R. R. will proceed to St Louis Mo. for the purpose of adjusting his account, and obtaining the approval of the Genl. Comdg. the Western Department, to the Muster Roll of employees thereon

U. S. GRANT
Brig Genl Comdg

To Col. A. H. Waterman
Supt. Cairo & Fulton R R.
Birds Point Mo

Copies, DLC-USG, V, 15, 16, 77, 82; DNA, RG 393, USG Special Orders. On Nov. 25, 1861, USG issued special orders. "Comdg Officers at Birds Point will furnish Col Waterman from time to time such details of men as may be required to keep up communication by Rail, between that post and Charleston. All Citizens having been discharged by orders from these Head Quarters, the entire work will be performed by details" Copies, *ibid.* See letter to Capt. John C. Kelton, Dec. 8, 1861.

To Commander Henry Walke

———

Head Quarters, Dist. S. E. Mo.
Cairo, November 15th 1861.

CAPT. H. WALKE
COMD.G G. B. TAYLOR
MOUND CITY, ILL.
CAPT.

The Lexington requiring some work done which will require the putting out her fires, and requiring here, at all times an available Gunboat, I would be pleased to have you bring down the Taylor until the Lexington is again ready for service.

Yours &c.
U. S. GRANT
Brig. Gen. Com.

ALS, ICarbS. *O.R.* (Navy), I, xxii, 431.

To Capt. Reuben B. Hatch

———

Head Quarters Dist. S. E. Mo
Cairo November 15th 1861

CAPT. R. B. HATCH
POST QUARTERMASTER
CAIRO ILLS
SIR

You will send a Boat up the river, to points above Paducah, and purchase from fifty, to two hundred tons of hay, for immediate use. The quantity purchased must depend on the price at which it can be procured

U. S. GRANT
Brig. Genl Comdg.

Copies, DLC-USG, V, 2, 16, 77, 82; DNA, RG 393, USG Letters Sent. On Nov. 16, 1861, Capt. John A. Rawlins issued special orders. "Major Mudd Capt. T. J. Larison of 2d Ill. Cavalry and Capt. Delano of same Regt. at Fort Holt, Ky., are hereby appointed a *Board* of *Survey* to inspect, and make report immediately, of the quality and condition of a lot of Hay, forwarded by G. W. Cochram, to Capt. R. B. Hatch asst. Q. M. U. S. A. Cairo Ill under Government contract" Copies, DLC-USG, V, 15, 16, 77, 82; DNA, RG 393, USG Special Orders. The arrival of hay of questionable quality under regular contract probably explains USG's decision to purchase hay locally.

To Capt. Reuben B. Hatch

————

Head Quarters Dist. S. E. Mo
Cairo Nov. 15th 1861

Special Order No

The Post Quartermaster will put up with as little delay as possible, a building for Hospital purposes in accordance with the plan submitted by Asst. Surgeon Taggart,[1] Medical Purveyor

U S. Grant
Brig. Genl Comdg.

To Capt. R. B. Hatch
Post Quartermaster
Cairo Ils

Copies, DLC-USG, V, 15, 16, 77, 82; DNA, RG 393, USG Special Orders. On Nov. 25, 1861, USG issued special orders. "Asst. Surgeon J. P. Taggart U. S. A. Medical Purveyor, will procure with as little delay as practicable, Two Hundred Hospital Cots, for the use of the sick of this command" Copies, *ibid.*

1. Asst. Surgeon J. P. Taggart was announced as medical purveyor, District of Cairo, in General Orders No. 22, Dec. 23, 1861.

To Brig. Gen. M. Jeff Thompson

———

Head Quarters Dist. S. E. Mo
Cairo Nov 16th 1861

Gen. J Thompson
Comdg. Mo. Forces
New Madrid Mo.
Sir

I have been requested to intercede in behalf of Judge David R. Conrad, who I understand is now a prisoner in your Camp.

Judge Conrad as I understand, is in no way connected with the belligerents on either side, but from his age and respectability, if I can lend a helping hand for his release, I will be most happy to do so

I am not aware of the charges under which the Judge rests, and cannot say therefore what success my appeal in his behalf is likely to meet with. My propostion however, is to release any four of your prisoners, you may designate of those now in my possession, on the return of Judge Conrad to this place

I am sir Your Obt. Svt.
U. S. Grant
Brig. Genl Comdg.

Copies, DLC-USG, V, 1, 2, 3, 79; DNA, RG 393, USG Letters Sent. *O.R.*, II, i, 521. On Nov. 2, 1861, Maj. Montague S. Hasie sent to USG a "Statement in case of Judge Conrad taken prisoner by the rebels and under sentence of death." DLC-USG, V, 10; DNA, RG 393, USG Register of Letters Received. On Nov. 12, Brig. Gen. M. Jeff Thompson wrote to Col. Joseph B. Plummer. "I have Judge David Conrad, of Bollinger County, still a prisoner he having violated his parole a few days after he was arrested." *O.R.*, II, i, 519. On Nov. 15, Capt. George P. Edgar, asst. adjt. gen. for Plummer, replied to Thompson. "We understand that Colonel Killian, of the Missouri State Militia, has released George and Thomas Sepaugh, Clandfelter and two Becks with others on parole conditional upon the release of Judge David Conrad, of Bollinger County, Mo. If there is any misapprehension in regard to the matter please let it be known immediately at these headquarters. We hope that the years of Judge Conrad will secure him attention and comforts which perhaps a younger man would not have the right to expect under the circumstances which to you warrant his detention." *Ibid.*, p. 520.

On Nov. 19, Thompson replied to USG. "Your communication of the 16th

—inst, in relation to Judge Conrad is at hand—Judge Conrad has been released for several days, from confinement and has been staying with some of his personal friends—(officers in my army) awaiting a safe escort to his home—Judge Conrad was arrested by some of my scouts as a member of the Home Guard, and would have been released by me in a few days, or probally at once, had I not just been starting on my expedition to the Iron Mountain Rail Road. On my return from that expedition I found that Smith and Conrad had been allowed the limits of the town of Bloomfield on Parole, and had both violated their Parole and escaped. Conrad was recaptured and I felt disposed to punish him severely, but he has so many friends among my men that I defered the matter for investigation and it now seems that he did not know that it was wrong to try to escape in the manner he did—In a communication from Capt George P. Edgar A. A. G. at Cape Girardeau in reference to Judge Conrad, he says that Col Killian has already released several men on Parole conditioned upon the release of Conrad—I mention this that I may not get more in the exchange than you consider him worth. Not knowing, personally, which of my men have families, you can let them determine among themselves which shall be released—I am requested to mention John L. Clark, of Capt Hales Co—2nd Regt Cavalry, and W A. Presnel of Wilsons Co. 2nd Regt Cavalry—David Spradnel of Higdons company of the 3rd Regt Infantry, and Nathan Sutton of Higdons company—as being men with large families—These men are reported at the Cape—You will please place to my credit Capt T. J. Larrison and Lieutenant J. B. Tanney of the 2nd Regt Illinois Cavalry, whom I captured on the S. B. Platte Valley, on the 18th inst—and several (Eight) soldiers, a list of whose names I have not at hand, but who will probably report themselves, as Paroled—Hoping that Judge Conrad will give a better account of us than that which Madam Rumer has given" ALS, WHi. *O.R.*, II, i, 521–22. USG endorsed the letter. "Refered to Comd.g Officer Cape Girardeau. I promised to release four men for Judge Conrad and if that number has not already been released, without consideration, you may make up the deficiency. You can also release ~~four~~ eight for Capt. Larrison and ~~two~~ four for Lieut. Tanny who were captured off the Platte Valley and were paroled. Send one of the number released to Gen. Thompson with a letter stating what has been done." AES, WHi. On Nov. 20, Thompson wrote a pass for Conrad. *O.R.*, II, i, 522. See letter to Brig. Gen. M. Jeff Thompson, Dec. 4, 1861.

To Brig. Gen. Samuel R. Curtis

Head Quarters Dist. S. E. Mo
Cairo November 16th 1861

Genl. S. Curtis
Comdg. U. S. Forces
St Louis Mo
Genl.

Several persons have come to this Post, with safe conduct through signed by yourself.

I regard this as one of the most exposed Posts, in the Army, at this time, and would much prefer that the number sent South, should be made as limited as possible, or, be sent by some other route

Although I shall accommodate whenever it seems to me consistent with the interest of the Public service, I shall in future exercise my own judgement, about passing persons through my lines, unless the authority comes from a Senior, and one who exercises a command over me

I am very respectfully Your Obt. Svt
U. S. Grant
Brig. Genl. Comdg.

Copies, DLC-USG, V, 1, 2, 3, 79; DNA, RG 393, USG Letters Sent. *O.R.*, I, iii, 571. On Nov. 19, 1861, Brig. Gen. Samuel R. Curtis replied to USG. "Yours concerning passes is just received. Of course you being on the great highway between St Louis and New Orleans, must have these matters before you My passes only convey persons through my command and beyond I merely give suggestions. I have never given enough to speak of until the matter of Exchanges came up. On these I am acting under Genl Fremonts orders.—In all cases I design to avoid the least intrution on your command" ALS, DNA, RG 393, District of Cairo, Letters Received. See letter to Jesse Root Grant, Aug. 31, 1861, note 2.

To Brig. Gen. John A. McClernand

Head Quarters, Dist. S. E. Mo.
Cairo, November 16th 1861

GEN.

Can you inform me if Col. Dunlap[1] has received any public funds within the last few days.

I enquire because Capt Hatch informs me that he understood so, and if he has it will make a change in the disposition to be made of money received to-day.

I promised the Col. to have $5.000 00 placed to his credit should he not receive money independently.

Respectfully Your Obt. Svt.
U. S. GRANT
Brig. Gen. Com

ALS, McClernand Papers, IHi. On the bottom of this letter Brig. Gen. John A. McClernand noted: "(Ansd Negative, Nov 16 1861)."

1. Capt. James Dunlap was appointed asst. q. m. of vols. on Aug. 8, 1861, and served as brigade q. m. for McClernand.

To Col. Napoleon B. Buford

Head Quarters, Dist. S. E. Mo.
Cairo, November 16th 1861

COL. N. B. BEAUFORD
27TH ILL. VOLS.
CAIRO, ILL.
COL.

The object of the present Flag of Truce is merely to return to the South three prisoners who have been exchanged. I have at the same time authorized Mr. Schanute, who is a citizen of Alton, but wishes to go South on important business, which he will make known to you to accompany you.

Permit no outsiders to accompany the expedition unless Capt. Parish[1] should apply. He may be made an exception.

You may mention casually that I expected, after the conversation between Gen. Polk and myself, and the understanding ~~between~~ with Gen. McGown[2] the day before, that our prisoners would be returned.

They sent our wounded unconditionally as I had sent their sick & wounded before, and I returned over one hundred able bodied men, unconditionally it is true, yet a voluntary offer was made to at least return an equal number of ours.

I have no doubt but that it is Gen. Polk's intention to send them, and should they not come I would attribute the fact to interferance on the part of higher authority.[3]

I also return to day one prisoner who was not sent back before.

Yours Respectfully
U. S. GRANT
Brig. Gen. Com

ALS, IHi. Col. Napoleon B. Buford of Ky., USMA 1827, who resigned from the U. S. Army on Dec. 31, 1835, had become a prominent merchant and manufacturer of Rock Island, Ill., where he also served as president of a bank and a railroad before the Civil War. On Aug. 10, 1861, he was appointed col,. 27th Ill.

1. Capt. William H. Parish, 29th Ill., served as provost marshal, then resigned as of Oct. 26, 1861. See endorsement to Brig. Gen. John A. McClernand, Oct. 28, 1861.
2. C. S. A. Brig. Gen. John P. McCown.
3. This message resulted in a letter from C. S. A. Maj. Gen. Leonidas Polk to USG, Nov. 16, 1861. "I regret there should have been any misapprehension on your part as to the Exchange of prisoners at our last interview. My intention was to say to you that while I did not desire to press you to the recognition of the principle of exchange as usually recognized by belligerents I was yet willing to adopt it, and it was that principle on which I proposed to act in surrendering the prisoners turned over to you. My impression was and is that taking into the account the rank of those turned over to you I have made a fair exchange. If on examination it should appear otherwise I am willing to add to the list of those surrendered." ALS, DNA, RG 393, District of Southeast Mo., Letters Received. O.R., II, i, 520–21.

To Capt. Reuben B. Hatch

———

Head Quarters Dist S. E. Mo
Cairo Nov 16th 1861

SPECIAL ORDER NO
The Post Quartermaster will turn over to Capt Brinck,
Ordnance Officer, all arms & accoutrements in his possession
U. S. GRANT
Brig Genl Comd,g

To Capt R. B. Hatch
Post Q. M.
Cairo Ills

Copies, DLC-USG, V, 15, 16, 77, 82; DNA, RG 393, USG Special Orders.

To Brig. Gen. Lorenzo Thomas

———

Head Quarters, Dist. S. E. Mo.
Cairo, November 17th 1861.

GEN. L. THOMAS
ADJT. GEN. U. S. A.
WASHINGTON D. C.
SIR:

By the last mail, whilst I was out of my office for a few
minuets, a Trimonthly report of this command was forwarded
without a letter of advice accompanying.

I now respectfully acknowledge the omission.

Since the first of the month a portion of this command have
been kept so actively moving that the Regl. Monthly Reports
were late coming in, and when in many of them were wrong and
had to be returned for correction.

I will use evry endeavor to get the consolidated report completed as soon as possible.

> I am Gen Very respectfully
> Your Obt. Svt.
> U. S. GRANT
> Brig. Gen. Com.

ALS, Haskell Collection, MiU-C. The same letter appears in the USG letter-books addressed to Brig. Gen. Seth Williams. Copies, DLC-USG, V, 4, 5, 7, 8, 78; DNA, RG 393, USG Hd. Qrs. Correspondence. A notation on the copy in vol. 78 reads: "A copy of this letter was also sent to the Adjt Genl of the Army. J. W. R." On Nov. 13, 1861, Brig. Gen. Lorenzo Thomas had telegraphed to USG. "You will forward immediately to this office, a complete return of your ~~full~~ whole command." Telegram sent, *ibid.*, RG 107, Telegrams Collected (Unbound); copies, *ibid.*, RG 393, USG Hd. Qrs. Correspondence; DLC-USG, V, 4, 5, 7, 8.

To Brig. Gen. Seth Williams

> Head Quarters, Dist. S. E. Mo.
> Cairo, November 17th 1861

GEN. S. WILLIAMS
A. A. GEN.
WASHINGTON D. C.
GEN.

In the Battle of Belmont on the 7th of this month a number of Forage Officers lost their horses, killed in action.

I would respectfully recommend that in all such cases, by fully authenticating the loss, they be allowed to draw from the Quarter Masters Department, horses of equal value.

Many of the officers would be relieved by this course, and by reporting the names of all who are supplied in this way to the

Adj. Gen. of the Army, or to the Quartermaster Gen. it would prevent compensation being paid hereafter.

> I am Gen
> Very respectfully
> Your Obt. Svt.
> U. S. GRANT
> Brig. Gen. Com.

ALS, Mrs. Walter Love, Flint, Mich. The same letter appears in the USG letter-books addressed to Brig. Gen. Lorenzo Thomas. Copies, DLC-USG, V, 4, 5, 7, 8, 78; DNA, RG 393, USG Hd. Qrs. Correspondence. For a possible explanation, see letter to Brig. Gen. Lorenzo Thomas, Nov. 17, 1861.

To Capt. Chauncey McKeever

———

> Head Quarters, Dist. S. E. Mo.
> Cairo, Nov. 17th 1861.

A. A. GEN.
WESTERN DEPARTMENT
ST. LOUIS, MO.
SIR:

Enclosed herewith I send you a letter just received from Cape Girardeau which fully explains itself.[1]

I have also been called upon to-day by a lady from Bloomfield who states that the Union people of that destrict are not only depridated upon but their lives are constantly in danger. Many have already been murdered for entertaining Union sentiments, and people of this class are not permitted to leave on pain of death.

She urges, on behalf of the Union people, that troops be sent there either to garrison the place perminantly, or for a stated period, giving the citizens notice of the length of time they intend to remaining so that they might take advantage of their protection to get away.

Bloomfield is Geographically a commanding position and if troops could be spared I would earnestly recommend the occupation of it.

> Very respectfully
> Your Obt. Svt.
> U. S. GRANT
> Brig. Gen. Com.

ALS, DNA, RG 393, Dept. of the Mo., Letters Received. *O.R.*, I, iii, 571.

1. The enclosure is a letter of Nov. 15, 1861, from Lt. Col. Enos P. Wood, 17th Ill., to USG. "Mr. Bacon a gentleman from Stoddard County in this State, and who has been selling goods there for some years, has lately been compelled to leave his home in Bloomfield, by the return of Jeff Thompsons scouts to that town. He informs me that there is in that County large quantities of corn and wheat, as well as stock, which the Rebels are rapidly converting to their own use —he has himself between two & three thousand Bushels of corn and four or five hundred of wheat; and other parties in the immediate neighborhood of Bloomfield & most of whom are rabid Secessionists; have nearly as much, and some of them, larger amounts of grain than this   Indeed the farmers generally, he tells me; have raised unusually good crops; The Rebels are now and will no doubt continue to avail themselves of these supplies to sustain their own forces   But if these supplies could be converted to more loyal purposes or entirely destroyed, would they not be compelled to leave this portion of the State   Being transiently in command at this Post I have deemed this information sufficiently important to communicate to District Head Quarters" ALS, DNA, RG 393, Dept. of the Mo., Letters Received.

To Brig. Gen. John A. McClernand

> Head Quarters, Dist. S. E. Mo.
> Cairo, November 18th 1861.

GEN. J. A. MCCLERNAND
COMD.G POST
CAIRO ILL.
GEN.

Please designate a regiment of Infantry to accompany the expedition to Cape Girardeau.

We will get off at as early an hour as practicable.
                              Your Obt. Svt.
                              U. S. Grant
                              Brig. Gen. Com.

ALS, McClernand Papers, IHi. Also on Nov. 18, 1861, Capt. John A. Rawlins wrote to Brig. Gen. John A. McClernand. "I am instructed by the Brig. Genl. Comdg. to request that you designate two of the best armed Cavalry companies of your command, for tempory service at Cape Girardeau, they will probably be absent about one week, if needed some Carbines can be furnished them here, they will take with them such rations only as have been issued to them and are now in hands, drawing rations and forage at Cape Girardeau, and will be ready to leave on *Steamer* at 8. oclock A. M. of tomorrow the 19th inst." LS, *ibid.*

To Brig. Gen. John A. McClernand

                              Head Quarters, Dist. S. E. Mo.
                              Cairo, November 18th 1861.

Gen. J. A. McClernand.
Comd.g Post
Cairo, Illinois
Gen.

Col. Haynie[1] has made such representations to me as to in-duce me to believe that from one thousand to twelve hundred men, with five days rations, could do good service for the Union people of Crittenden County Ky.[2] if sent there soon.

I also received a letter from there this morning making similar representations.[3]

I shall be too busy ~~this~~ to-day to attend to any details having notified the troops at Birds Point that I shall review them at 2 O'Clock p. m.

It will meet with my approbation if you will have the expedition fitted out.

                              Yours Respectfully
                              U. S. Grant
                              Brig. Gen. Com.

ALS, McClernand Papers, IHi.

    1. Col. Isham N. Haynie, 48th Ill.
    2. Crittenden County, Ky., on the Ohio River opposite Ill., east of Paducah.
    3. On Nov. 15, 1861, John Mitchell, Cave in Rock, Ill., wrote to USG. "Permit me to represent the condition of this section of the border and ask the necessary aid   This point on the south shore of Illinois derives its importance in a strategic sense from being the main crossing of the Nashville and St Louis road or line of travel—The county in Kentuckey opposite this place (Crittenden) is one of the strongest Union counties in South Western Ky   her people have sent 300 men into the Federal army, and her best men are the strong supporters of the Governme[nt]—the Southern troops at Hopkinsville have given them great trouble, driving them from their homes, taking them prisoner, stealing their goods, Horses &c and as many as 150 have come over to this place at different times and sojourned with us returning home when the rebel rovers have returned to Hopkinsville this place and its people though fiew in number have given such aid to our Union neighbours of Ky that repeated threats have been made to come over here and sink our Ferry boat and thus cut off the retreat of the Union men. Now should they do this they would find a quantity of goods in the stores and boats at this place   it is desirable to prevent this and ask that this point be mad[e] a military post   it is a strong natural point and a fiew men will effectually controul the enemy in the opposite county and much encourage and strengthen the hands of the Union men in that county—Furthermore the Ferry four miles above this place is in the hands of one Levi Rikey a stron[g] sessesionist and we fear may be used to cross over a force above us that may do us mischief. Our condition is rendered more hazardous from the fact that all our appeals for arms have been disregarded   We are defenceless while this small county has sent near half of her voting population to the Federal aid and the presence here of Ky union men attracts the hatred and ire of those troopers   We ask earnestly that a camp be formed here or some aid sent   there is now to day 2200 Rebels on their way (through Marion the co seat of Crittenden) to attack Smithland   this I have from a reliable source   they was stealing Wagons teams &c and say the[y] want 1200 wagons   what aid is sent ought to be sent quickly" ALS, *ibid.* On Nov. 18, Lt. Col. John Olney, 6th Ill. Cav., from Camp Mather, near Shawneetown, Ill., wrote to USG. "The Bearer, Mr. John Mitchell of Cave in Rock visits Cairo, to get assistance for the Union people of Illinois & Kentucky at and opposite the Cave. We are not able to furnish him—men—arms or ammunition. Mr. M. is thoroughly reliable—any statements he makes will be correct." ALS, *ibid.* Cave in Rock, Ill., is opposite Crittenden County, Ky.
    On Nov. 15, Brig. Gen. Charles F. Smith telegraphed to USG. "I will Send the Conestoga to Union" Telegram received, DNA, RG 393, Dept. of the Mo., Telegrams Received. On Nov. 18, Smith telegraphed to USG. "I heard today the report of the 2000, but do not credit it. I am inclined to think that 200 Cavalry would be nearer the number after Hogs. The Conestoga is or was at Uniontown. I know not what is being done." Telegram received (punctuation added), *ibid.* On Nov. 18, Smith again telegraphed to USG. "The Conestoga just in, nine Oclock P. M. No rebels within 25 miles of Uniontown. About 100 Cavalry marauding. 2000 Rebels with three small iron guns reported at Princeton with the object to take Cattle & Hogs. Conestoga had a brush with Enemy at Clinton—" Telegram received (punctuation added), McClernand Papers, IHi.

See report of Lt. S. Ledyard Phelps, Nov. 19, *O.R.* (Navy), I, xxii, 435–36.

On Nov. 23, Ill. AG Allen C. Fuller telegraphed to USG. "The Governor being confined to his bed, I have been faithfully trying to send an armed regt. to Cave in the Rocks. Genl. Hunter had ordered to St. Louis four Regts. nearly full. These orders have, at my request, been suspended by Genl. Halleck. With Genl. Halleck consent, I can send you an armed Regt. early next week." Telegram received (punctuation added), DNA, RG 393, Dept. of the Mo., Telegrams Received. See *O.R.*, I, viii, 372–73.

To Col. Richard J. Oglesby

———

> Head Quarters Dist S. E. Mo
> Cairo November 18th 1861

Col R J Oglesby
Comdg. Forces U.S.
Birds Point Mo
Sir

The Steamer Platte Vally was attacked this afternoon, by one or two hundred of Jeff Thompsons men, commanded by Jeff in person, and two officers of the 2nd Cavalry who were on leave were taken prisoners. They were paroled, and one returned here and gave the information. This took place at Prices Landing at 4 o'clock P. M. today. I want all the Cavalry that is well armed, sent out tonight, by the river road, and seven or eight hundred Infantry sent at the same time, by rail to Charleston. I will go from here, tomorrow morning, with Infantry and Cavalry and try to catch him   Let these two commands be got off as early as possible tonight.

No Baggage is to be taken and only two days rations in Haversacks.

I would like Col. Wallace to go in command of the expedition, and if he knows of a passable road from Charleston to Benton, let the command be doubled, & one half taken that route

> Yours &c
> U. S. Grant
> Brig Genl Comdg.

Copies, DLC-USG, V, 1, 2, 3, 79; DNA, RG 94, War Records Office, Union Battle Reports; *ibid.*, Dept. of the Mo.; *ibid.*, RG 393, USG Letters Sent. *O.R.*, I, iii, 367–68.

The capture of the *Platte Valley* correlates better than any other incident of the period with an account by USG of an attempt at his capture. USG states that several paroled Camp Jackson prisoners in his office one day learned of USG's plan to visit Cape Girardeau the following day. Although USG's plans changed, a government steamer twenty miles above Cairo was stopped the next day, and one of the officers who had been in USG's office demanded USG's surrender. *Memoirs*, I, 268. USG spoke of plans to go to Cape Girardeau in his letter to Brig. Gen. John A. McClernand, Nov. 18, 1861. In two separate letters written the day before the seizure of the *Platte Valley*, Brig. Gen. M. Jeff Thompson acknowledged orders but denied his ability to capture "any particular boat." *O.R.*, I, iii, 368. If the attack on the *Platte Valley* was an attempt to capture USG, the details are not completely clear: Camp Jackson prisoners were not passing through USG's office at that time. See letter to Capt. William McMichael, Nov. 23, 1861, note 1. Flag Officer Andrew H. Foote, on the other hand, believed that Thompson's objective was the *Maria Denning*, which left St. Louis on Nov. 19 loaded with equipment for the gunboat fleet. Robert Means Thompson and Richard Wainwright, eds., *Confidential Correspondence of Gustavus Vasa Fox* (New York, 1918–19), II, 15.

To Commanding Officer, Cape Girardeau

Head Quarters Dist S E. Mo
Cairo Nov. 18th 1861

COMDG. OFFICER
CAPE GIRARDEAU MO
SIR

Jeff Thompson with a portion of his command are now at Prices landing, with Artillery to sink all Gov. Boats.—Warn Steamers now on their way down

I send out this night to cut off his retreat south. Send from the Cape by daylight, at furthest, a Regiment to Benton Send them with two days rations in their Haversacks, and without Wagons or Baggage. Let the troops sent to Benton drop down the river to Commerce on the Steamer Illinois. During their

absence the Steamer should be taken to the opposite side of the
river

> Yours &c
> U. S. GRANT
> Brig Genl Comdg.

Copies, DLC-USG, V, 1, 2, 3, 79; DNA, RG 393, USG Letters Sent. On Nov. 20
1861, Lt. Col. Enos P. Wood, 17th Ill., wrote to USG. "In compliance with your
order of the 18th inst., received on the morning of the 19th I embarked the 17th
Illinois Regiment, with squad of Fremont Rangers and one gun & artillery squad
from Campbells Battery; on Board the Steamer Illinois, all under command of
Maj. Smith of the 17. Ills. Regt. The expedition landed at Commerce about noon
& immediately proceeded to Benton where they took up position for the night,
but without being able to obtain any information of the enemy—This morning
on receiving your notice of the flight of Thompson, the expedition returned to the
Boat and landed here, without any casualty, this afternoon—Maj. Smith reports
the capture of one secess. negro, who started off from Commerce in hot haste in
advance of our forces spreading the news 'that the abolitionists were coming to
steal all their horses—' after a chase chase he was overtaken just beyond Benton,
and is brot in as a prisoner—his Mistress or owner a widow woman is reported
as a staunch Unionists—" ALS, *ibid.*, District of Southeast Mo., Letters Received.

To Capt. Reuben B. Hatch

——————

> Head Quarters Dist. S. E. Mo
> Cairo Nov. 18th 1861

CAPT. R. B. HATCH
POST QUARTERMASTER
CAIRO ILL
CAPT.

On Saturday I signed an order for two horses to be dlivered
for the use of two Cavalry soldiers who had lost their Horses

On reflection the law requires in such cases that these soldiers
should serve on foot until they supply themselves again, and
shall not receive the 40 cts. per day until they do supply themselves

You are directed therefore to demand the return of said Horses if they have been issued, and not to let them go if not already gone.

U. S. Grant
Brig. Genl Comdg.

Copies, DLC-USG, V, 1, 2, 3, 77; DNA, RG 393, USG Letters Sent.

To H. C. Howard

Head Quarters Dist. S. E. Mo
Cairo November 18th 1861

Mr H. C. Howard
Mound City Ill
Dear Sir

I have recommended the allowance of your claim for damages caused, or that will be caused, by moving your goods from the building, they now occupy—That account has gone on to Head Quarters, Western Department, and will no doubt be allowed, in the full sum asked by yourself

The building is an absolute nescessity for the wounded and sick of this command and must be speedily surrendered to our use

After your own offer I hope it will not be nescessary to do more than notify you ~~that~~ but the building we must have by this day week

Your truly
U. S. Grant
Brig Genl. Comdg.

Copies, DLC-USG, V, 1, 2, 3, 79; DNA, RG 393, USG Letters Sent. On Nov. 5, 1861, H. C. Howard and Co. wrote to USG. "Your petitioners, H C Howard, James Y. Clemson and O Wilson residents of Mound City Illinois, and doing business at said place as Copartners under the firm name of H. C. Howard & Co would respectfully represent that on or about the 1st day of August 1860, your petitioners leased of one Dr Talbott the[*n*] a resident of Lexington Ky now on a visit or tour to Europe for a period of 4 years, a certain building situate in and composeing a part of what is known and designated as Union Block in Mound City Illinois which said building and tenement is described as No 5 in said block, that said building and tenement is 22 ft front and Seventy or Seventy five feet back & three Stories high. That since that time to wit; the term of leasing said premises your petitioners have occupied the same in carrying on their said Copartnership business, which is the manufacture and sale of Furniture, that said building and premises are well adapted to said business, that the said Dr. Talbott at the time he leased said premises, haveing special confidence in your petitioners that they would take special care of the same and being desirous of encourgeing Manufactures and business in the said Mound City with a view of enhancing the value of property there, let your petitioners have the same at all most a nominal sum; to wit: the sum of fifty Dollars a year, that at the time your petitioners leased said premises as aforesaid they required divers and sundry improvements and additions in order to fit and prepare them for carrying on your petitioners said business, which your petitioners agreed to do and have since done at their own costs and charges, That said improvements and additions so made as above stated have been done by at a cost of at least ($200.) Two Hundred Dollars. Your petitioners would further show, that there is not another building to be had in said Mound City, that can be had suitable or adapted to the carrying on of their said business   That if rooms and buildings could be procured by them at all, in number and capacity sufficient to carry on their said business they would cost at the present prices of rent in said Mound City, not less than four or five Hundred dollars a year; So your petitioners charge and show that their said lease is now worth at least exclusive of the nominal rent to be paid by them ($350) Three Hundred & fifty Dollars per Annum   In addition thereto your petitioners would further show that they now have on hand in said building a stock of furniture ready for sale amounting in value to at least Eight or Ten Thousand Dollars That said furniture could not be removed and re-stored even for a short distance and with the utmost care, without defaceing and impairing it to a considerabe extent that it would neccessarily have to be revarnished. Your petitioners would therefore say that it is their opinion that the actual costs of moveing said furniture even to some other place in Mound City and the probable damages neccessarily occuring to the furniture in moveing it would be at least four Hundred Dollars Your petitioners would further show that on the 4th of this inst. they were notified by the Government of the United States through its Agent Dr Franklin at Mound City, to give immediate possession of said premises, the same being wanted for Government purposes, and that your petitioners will in obedience to said notice give possession of the same   In view of the premises your petitioners would ask that your Honor will afford them such releif as may be just and consistent with the law and public good" AD, *ibid.*, RG 109, Records of the U. S. War Dept. Relating to Confederates, Union Provost Marshal's Citizens File. On the same day, USG endorsed the petition. "Respectfully refered to Head Quarters, Western Dept. The charges made by Mr. Howard I do not think unreasonable and therefore have no hesitation in recommending that they be allowed." AE, *ibid.* See letter to Capt. Chauncey McKeever, Oct. 28, 1861. Additional information on the claim of H. C. Howard is available in his testimony before the Commission on War Claims at St. Louis (Davis-Holt-Campbell Commission). DNA, RG 217.

To Col. William H. L. Wallace

————

Prices Landing Mo.
3½ o'clock P. M
[*Nov. 19, 1861*]

Col.

Your dispatch is just received. We learn that Thompson left an hour before sundown yesterday I shall return to Cairo to-night and you can do the same.

I look upon it as hopeless to run after Jeff when he has ~~more~~ none but friends in front. I hope however you may succeed in capturing his artillery of which I understand he has two pieces.

Yours &c.

U. S. Grant.

Brig. Gen'l.

To Col. W. H. L. Wallace
Comd'g Expedition
Charleston Mo.

Copy, Wallace-Dickey Papers, IHi. See letter to Col. Richard J. Oglesby, Nov. 18, 1861.

To Brig. Gen. Seth Williams

————

Head Quarters, Dist. S. E. Mo.
Cairo, November 20th 1861

Gen. S. Williams
A. A. Gen. U. S. A.
Washington, D. C.

General.

Enclosed I send you the report of Brig. Gen. J. A. McClernand,[1] commanding 1st Brigade in the late engagement at Belmont Missouri. Also the report of Surgeon Brinton,[2] Medical Director, who accompanied me on that occasion.

The 7th Iowa and 22d Illinois Volunteers were the only troops in the engagement not included in Gen. McClernand's command. Each of these lost their commanders, wounded, and consequently I have no official report of them. Being on the field myself during the entire engagement I can answer for the gallantry of officers & men of both these regiments.

The 7th Iowa lost their Colonel (Lawman) wounded severely, and Lieut. Col. (Wentze)[3] killed, and Major (Rice)[4] severely wounded. Lieuts. Dodge & Gardner[5] and twenty-three rank and file were killed; wounded Capts. Gardner, Harper Parrott & Lt. Reams[6] and seventy-four others.

Of the 22d Illinois Col. Daugherty was badly wounded and taken prisoner. Twenty-one rank & file were killed. Capts. Hubbard & McAdams[7] and seventy-four men were wounded.

Information received since the engagement through the Southern press, and from persons coming from the South since, show the enemies force, on the field, to have been over 9000 men, and their loss in killed and wounded alone not less than 600. My own impression is their loss was much greater.

The city of Memphis was thrown into mourning for the dead & wounded taken there. Great apprehension is said to have prevailed lest the blow should be followed up with an attack upon them.

The officers and men, with rare exceptions, showed great personal courage and I have every reason to be satisfied with their conduct.

The lesson, though severe, will be of great advantage to the entire command.

The object aimed at, to-wit, to prevent the enemy from reinforcing Price,[8] in Missouri, and from cutting off two small Columns I had been directed to send towards the St. Francois river was accomplished to the fullest extent.

The enemy have entirely abandoned Belmont, and have been receiving reinforcements in Columbus continuously since the engagement.

> I am Gen. Very respectfully
> Your Obt. Svt.
> U. S. GRANT
> Brig. Gen. Com.

ALS, DNA, RG 94, War Records Office, Union Battle Reports. *O.R.*, I, iii, 272–73. With this letter USG submitted the remainder of the reports received by him on Belmont except that of Col. Henry Dougherty, 22nd Ill., prepared in Dec. "In pursuance of your order Issued on the 6th of November I embarked the 22nd Reg't Ill Vols numbering 562 men rank and File with 2 days rations, on board the Transport Belle Memphis. Everything being on board the Steamer we moved out into the Stream and after a short trip laid to on the Kentucky shore near the head of Island No 1, where we remained through the night in company with other Transports from Cairo and Birds Point, aboard of which were troops comprising the 7th Iowa commanded by Col Larhman, 27th Illinois Col Buford 30th Ill Col Foulk, 31st Ill Col Logan. Also Capt Taylors Battery of light Artillery together with a small force of Cavalry. The Gun Boats Lexington and Tylor accompanying us which took position in the Stream were anchored below the Transports   Our Officers and men being comfortably provided for soon retired for the night, impressed with the probability of realizing their most ardent wishes for by this time all on board were fully impressed with the opinion that we were bound for Belmont which the Sequel proved to be true. Having received orders from you during the night through the hands of A A Genl Rawlins I assertained that had placed me in command of the 2d Brigade, I immediately transferred the command of the 22nd Ill to Lt. Col H. E. Hart who in accepting it remarked that he felt satisfied that the Officers and men would do their duty, which I am proud to say they did to my and I hope to your entire satisfaction. Early on the morning of the 7th the Transports proceeded by the Gun Boats moved down the River until within sight of the Rebel forces on the summit of the Iron Banks immediately above Columbus on the Kentucky Shore and as afterward proved to be the case within range of some of the enemies Batteries of heavy artillery   After the disembarkation of the forces and formation of the 22d Illinois and 7th Iowa Regiments into line, three Companies of the former and two Companies of the latter were ordered to remain with the Transports, being placed under the Command of Captain Detrich of the 22d Ill who was ordered by you to protect the Transports and engage any forces of the enemy which might approach them. His Report is herewith submitted. Having passed through a field near where we disembarked and reached the timber we formed in line of battle. The First Brigade ~~composing~~ consisting, of the 27th 30th and 31st Illinois Volunteers under the command of Brigadier Genl Jno A. McClernand taking the right a little in advance of the Second Brigade composed of the 22d Ill and the 7th Iowa Reg'ts under my command and the whole force under your command in person. As soon as the line of battle was formed the order to advance was received and promptly obeyed. The 22d Illinois and 7th Iowa advanced for about 500 yards to the margin of a slough, where an order was given to halt and wait for further orders   Here Companies 'C' and 'B' of the 22d Illinois under the command of Captain Teaton and one company of the 7th Iowa were deployed as skirmishers to ascertain and if possible to discover the position of the enemy   Soon the order of advance was again given and from this point the Second Brigade encountered heavy timber much of which had been felled by the enemy in order to impede the progress of any attacting force. Regardless of the obstacles thus encountered the Second Brigade advanced as rapidly as possible for about half a mile passing over much of the distance at double quick march. Hearing firing on the right while the skirmisher[s] of the Second Brigade remained silen[t] on the left we advanced by a flank movement to the right through almost impenetrable woods, climbing over felled trees and filing around tree tops in the direction of the firing. Halting a few moments to form a line we again advanced and encountered the enemy behind logs and among tree tops and at this point the firing commenced on the left, which now seemed to be general along the whole line. The whole force being apparently engaged in action. The enemy for some time obstinately resisted any advance at this point & a storm of musketry raged along the whole line of the Second Brigade. Shell and Shot from the Artillery of the enemy along the Iron Banks and the field pieces at Belmont fell thick and fast and a perfect storm of bullets from their his small arms was here encountered. Many of our brave men were wounded at this point and some fell to rise no more sealing their patriotism with their hearts blood, but their valor forced the enemy to yield at last, and again the Second Brigade advanced, pressing on over their enemys dead and wounded— many of wheom implored our men not to murder them being evidently under the belief of the false and wicked impressions so industriously sought to be made by many of the leaders of this curssed rebellion that we were barbarians and savages but instead of murdering them some of our men ministered to their wants and conveyed them to places of safety   Step by step we drove them until they reached a secondary bank such as abound through the river bottoms of the west under which they were protected from our fire and where they made another desperate stand for about thirty minutes, where our fire became so hot that they retreated precipitately to some open ground near their encampment covered by a rude abatis of felled timber. Strewing the ground as they went with guns, coats and canteens   our brave troops followed them with shouts pouring volley after volley into them. Here the enemies movements at this point gave unmistakeable evidence of being panic stricken and defeated retreating to the river and up the river bank behind the shelter of some brush and timber   On gaining the open ground near their encampment opposite to and in sight of the lower part of Columbus the relative positions of the different commands for the first time since the commencement of the battle became visible. The Second Brigade being on the left had a shorter distance to march in order to reach the enemy than the first and consequently reached the open ground in front of the enemies camp in advance of the right wing. In a few minutes one section of Capt Taylors battery of artillery emerged from the timber on the right and took position when the 7th Iowa and 22d Illinois fell back and supported the battery which opened a fire on the retreating rebels and their camp   The battery was well served and evidently disconcerted the rebels accelerating their retreat and spreading consternation amongst them. From that point the Second Brigade advanced with the battery entered the encampment of the enemy and captured three pieces of their his Artillery one piece being taken possession of by Company 'B' Capt Seaton and one by Company 'E' Capt McAdams both of the 22nd Illinois and the third by a part of our forces unknown to me. Two of the pieces were placed in charge of Capt Tayor who gallantly brought them away from the field to be used in a better cause in future After assisting in the destruction of the Rebel camp and property not moveable as long as was prudent under the fire of the rebel batteries in and about Columbus which commanded the whole ground the order to retire to the transports was received but not before the rebel flag had been hauled down and the Stars and Stripes, the flag of our Fathers still bright with the glorious memories of the past was exhibited to their view   After it had been displayed and the field music had played our national air, within hearing of the rebels the order to retire was received from you and our weary forces were called from the camp which they had distroyed   In the meantime the Rebels had transported a large force of fresh troops across the River seven Regiments according to their own statement contained in a Memphis paper. These were formed in the timber and in some corn fields between their destroyed camp and our transports. On the return the Second Brigade encountered these fresh forces and at once engaged them and opened a passage through them. At this time the 7th Iowa was in the rear of the 22d Ill and was somewhat confused all the field officers and many of the company officers of that brave Regiment being either killed, wounded or taken by the enemy. I told the men that as we had fought our way in we could fight our way out again and and ordered them to keep up a Steady fire on the left which they did with a will notwithstanding their exhaustion opening the ranks of the enemy and forcing their way through in order to reach the transports at the same place we had debarked On reaching the transports which were safe and in waiting for us. Meeting Lt. Col. H. E. Hart who had conducted himself through the entire battle with the coolness and bravery of a soldier I And ordered him to embark the 22d Ill Reg't on board the Belle Memphis while I returned to fetch up the rear of the Brigade on my return I found many of the Iowa 7th considerably scattered   while chearing them up and hurrying them forward I received a small shot in the Shoulder and one on the elbow and shortly after wards a ball through the ankle   My horse was also shot in several places who fell with me and soon expired   I found myself unable to travel and was consequently captured by the rebels who treated me with respect and kindness. The loss of the 22d Reg't Illinois Vols during the day was 23 killed 74 wounded and 37 missing   Total loss 134. Captains Challenor and Abbott were severely wounded and left upon the field where they were afterward taken by the enemy. Captain Hubbard was slightly wounded. Lieut Adams was severely wounded in the left arm and taken prisoner   Capts Challenor and Abbott and Lieut Adams have since been returned together with all the non-com. officers privates who were wounded   The loss of the 7th Iowa Regiment during the action was 26 killed 80 wounded and 137 missing   Total 243 making the whole loss of th[e] Second Brigade 377 among them were Col Larhman severely wounded Lt Col Wentz killed together with most of their company Officers who fought gallantly until stricken down by the enemy   This Regiment through out the entire battle fought like Veterans dealing death to the Rebels wherever they encountered them. Iowa may well feel proud of their her Sons who fought at Belmont   Many of the missing nearly all in fact were taken prisoners but some of which there is no certain information it is fered were killed   I am informed that as soon as the Steamer Memphis got out of the fire of the enemy every attention and care was paid to the wounded of which there was quite a number on board. Many of the Officers were very active in ministering to their wants and Surgeons Stearns and Woodward attended them faithfully performing their duties dressing their wounds and extracting many balls while under way to Cairo   Dr. Hamilton Quarter Master of the 22d Ill Vols also assisted and rendered most efficient aid. I am further informed that only one Two Horse wagon belonging to the Quarter Masters Department of the 22d Reg't Ills was left. It contained nothing but could not be got aboard because of the bank of the River where the Memphis lay was so perpendicular that a road had to be made with shovels, which consumed too much time   All the Horses including those captured from the enemy were got on board   Many instances of individual heroism and bravery occured during the day but where all acted so gallantly it would be unjust to discriminate   The whole force under your command acted like Veterans and you justly feel proud of the manner in which they conducted themselves on the well contested Battle field of Belmont" ALS, DNA, RG 94, War Records Office, Union Battle Reports. *O.R.*, I, iii, 291–94.

1. On Nov. 12, 1861, Brig. Gen. John A. McClernand wrote to USG. "I have the honor to report the part taken by the forces under my command in the action before Columbus, Ky. on the 7th inst. These forces consisted of a portion of my own brigade, viz, The 27th Regiment, Col N. B. Buford; The 30th, Philip B. Fouke; The 31st Col John A. Logan; including one Company of cavalry under Capt J. J. Dollins—the strength of the 27th being 720, rank and file; that of the 30th 500; that of the 31st 610; exclusive of 70 mounted men, making in all 1900, rank and file. To this force you added, by your order, of the 6th inst, Capt Delano's company of Adam's County cavalry, 58 men, under Lieut. J. R Catlin; and Capt Ezra Taylor's battery of Chicago Light Artillery, consisting of 4 six pound guns; 2 twelve pound howitzers, and 114 men. The total disposable force under my command being, 2,072, rank and file—all Illinois Volunteers. Having embarked on the steamer 'Scott' with the 30th and 31st Regiments, on the evening of the 6th inst, I left Cairo at 5 oclock, and proceeded down the Mississipi to the foot of Island No 1, and lay to for the night on the Kentucky shore, eleven miles above Columbus, as previously instructed by you. Posting a strong guard for the protection of the boat, and those that followed to the same point, I remained until 7 o'clock on the following morning. At that hour, preceded by the Gun boats Tyler and Lexington, and followed by the remainder of the transports, I proceeded down the river to the designated landing, on the Missouri Shore, about two and a half miles, in a direct line from Columbus and Belmont. By 8½ oclock, the rest of the transports had arrived, and the whole force was disembarked, and marching beyond a collection of cornfields, in front of the landing, was formed for an advance movement, and awaited your order. I ordered Dollins' and Delano's cavalry to scour the woods along the road to Belmont, and report to me from time to time. The remainder of my command followed the cavalry—the 27th in front, the 30th next, supported by a section of Taylor's battery; the 31st and the remainder of Taylor's battery next; succeeded by the 7th Iowa Col Lauman, and the 22d Illinois Col Dougherty, who had been assigned, by you, to that portion of the command. When the rear of the column had reached a road intersecting our line of march, about a mile and a half from the abatis surrounding the enemy's camp, the line of battle was formed on ground which I had previously selected. The 27th on the right and the 30th on its left, forming the right wing. A section of Taylor's battery was disposed on the left of the 30th, and two hundred feet in rear of the line. The 31st formed the centre, the 7th and 22d forming the left wing, masking two sections of artillery. By this time Dollins' cavalry was skirmishing sharply with the enemy's pickets to the right and in advance of our line, the enemy, in the meantime, having shifted the heavy fire of his batteries, at Columbus, from our Gun boats to our advancing line, but with out serious effect. With your permission, I now ordered two companies from each Regiment of my command to advance, instructing them to seek out and develope the position of the enemy— the 22d and 7th pushing forward similar parties, at the same time. A sharp firing having immediately commenced, between the skirmishing parties of the 30th and 31st and the enemy; I ordered forward another party to their support, rode forward, selected a new position and ordered up the balance of my command—the 27th to pass around the head of a pond, the 30th and 31st with the Artillery

crossing the dry bed of the same pond in their front. On their arrival, I reformed the line of battle, in the same order, as before; expecting that the 7th and 22d would resume their former position on the left wing. This disposition would have perfected a line sufficient to enclose the enemy's camp on all sides accessible to us, thus enabling us to command the river above and below him, and to prevent the crossing of reinforcements from Columbus insuring his capture as well as defeat. The 30th and 31st and the Artillery moving forward promptly relieved the skirmishing parties, and soon became engaged with a heavy body of the enemy's infantry and cavalry. This struggle, which was continued for half an hour with great obstinacy, threw our ranks into temporary disorder, but the men promptly rallied under the gallant example of Cols. Fouke and Logan, assisted by Major Brayman acting Assistant Adjutant General of my brigade; also by Capt Schwartz acting Chief of Artillery; Capt Dresser of the Artillery; Lt Babcock of the 2d Cavalry and Lt. Eddy of the 29th Illinois Regiment who, had upon my invitation kindly joined my staff. Our men pressed vigorously upon the enemy and drove him back, his cavalry leaving that part of the field and not appearing again, until attacked by Capt Dollins, on the river bank, below his encampment some time after, and chased out of sight. Advancing about a quarter of a mile farther, this force again came up with the enemy who by this time had been re-inforced in this part of the field, as I since learn by three regiments and a company of cavalry. Thus strengthened, he attempted to turn our left flank, but ordering Col Logan to extend the line of battle by a flank movement, and bringing up a section of Taylor's battery, commanded by 1st Lieut P. H. White, under the direction of Capt Schwartz, to cover the space thus left between the 30th and 31st, the attempt was frustrated. Having completed this disposition, we again opened a deadly fire from both infantry and Artillery, and after a desperate resistance drove the enemy back the third time—forcing him to seek cover among thick woods and brush, protected by the heavy guns at Columbus. In this struggle, while leading the charge, I received a ball in one of my holsters which failed of harm by striking a pistol. Here Cols. Fouke and Logan urged on their men by the most energetic appeals; here Capt Dresser's horse was shot under him, while Capt Schwartz's horse was twice wounded. Here the projectiles from the enemy's heavy guns, at Columbus and their Artillery at Belmont, crashed through the woods over and among us; here again all my staff, who were with me, displayed the greatest intrepidity and activity; and here too many of our officers and privates were killed or wounded. Nor should I omit to add, that this gallant conduct was stimulated by your presence and inspired by your example. Here your horse was shot under you. While this struggle was going on, a tremendous fire from the 27th which had, under the skilful guidance of Col Buford, approached the abatis on the right and rear of the tents, was heard. About the same time the 7th and 22d, which had passed the rear of the 30th and 31st, hastened up, and closing the space between them and the 27th poured a deadly fire upon the enemy. A combined movement was now made upon three sides of the enemy's defences, and driving him across them, we followed, upon his heels, into the clear space around his camp. The 27th was the first seen, by me, entering upon this ground. I called the attention of the other regiments to the fact, and the whole line was quickened with eager and impatient emulation. In a few minutes our entire force was within the enclosure. Under the skillful direction of Capt Schwartz, Capt Taylor now brought up his battery, within three hundred yards of the enemy's tents, and opened fire upon them. The enemy fled with precipitation from the tents, and took shelter behind some buildings, near the river, and into the woods above the camp, under cover of his batteries, at Columbus. Near this battery I met Col. Dougherty, who was leading the 7th and 22d through the open space towards the tents. At the same time our lines upon the right and left were pressing up to the line of fire from our battery, which now ceased firing, and our men rushed forward, among the tents and towards some buildings near the river. Passing over to the right of the camp, I met with Col Buford, for the first time, since his arduous and perilous detour around the pond, and congratulated him upon the eagerness of his men to be the first to pass the enemy's works. During the execution of this movement Capt Alexander Bielaski, one of my Aids-de-camp, who had accompanied Col Buford during the march of the 27th separate from the main command, having dismounted from his horse, which had been several times wounded, was shot down while advancing with the flag of his adopted country in his hand, and calling on the men in his rear to follow him. His bravery was only equalled by his fidelity as a soldier and patriot. He died making the stars and stripes his winding sheet. Honored be his memory. Near him, and a few minutes afterward, Col Lauman fell severely wounded, in the thigh, while leading his men in a daring charge. About the same time Capt. Wm. A Schmidt of the 27th, was also wounded, while striving for the advance. Galloping my horse down to the river, I found Capt Bozarth of Company 'K.' 27th Regiment, supported by squads of men who had joined him, sharply engaged with a detachment of the enemy, whom he drove into the woods above the camp. Here the firing was very hot; my own head was grazed by a ball; my horse was wounded in the shoulders and his caparison torn in several places. Here, too, one of the enemy's caissons fell into my hands, and a capture of artillery was made by Capt Schwartz—a portion of the 7th Iowa gallantly assisting in achieving this result. Having complete possession of the enemy's camp, in full view of his formidable batteries, at Columbus, I gave the word for three cheers for the Union, to which the brave men around me responded with the most enthusiastic applause. Several of the enemy's steamers, being within range above and below, I ordered a section of Taylor's battery, under the direction of Capt Schwartz, down near the river, and opened a fire upon them, and upon Columbus itself, but with what effect, I could not learn. The enemy's tents were set on fire—destroying his camp equipage, about 4000 blankets and all his means of transportation. Such horses and other property as could be removed, were seized, and four pieces of his artillery and one caisson were brought to the rear. The enemy, at Columbus, seeing us in possession of his camp, directed upon us the fire of his heavy guns, but ranging too high inflicted no injury. Information came, at the same time, of the crossing of heavy bodies of troops above us, amounting, as I since learn, to five regiments, which joining those which had fled in that direction, formed rapidly in our rear with the design of cutting off our communication with our transports. To prevent this, and having fully accomplished the object of the expedition, I ordered Capt Taylor to reverse his guns, and open fire upon the enemy in his new position, which was done with great spirit and effect, breaking his line and opening our way to the main road. Promptly responding to an order to that effect, Col Logan ordered his flag in front of his regiment, prepared to force his way in the same direction, if necessary. Moving on, he was followed by the whole force, except the 27th and the cavalry companies of Captains Dollins and Delano. Determined to preserve my command unbroken, and to defeat the evident design of the enemy to divide it, I twice rode back across the field to bring up the 27th and Dollins cavalry, and also dispatched Major Brayman for the same purpose, but without accomplishing the object, they having sought, in returning, the same route by which they advanced in the morning. On passing into the woods, the 30th, the 7th, and 22d encountered a heavy fire on their right and left successively, which was returned with such vigor and effect as to drive back the superior force of the enemy and silence his firing, but not until the 7th and 22d had been thrown into temporary disorder. Here Lt. Col Wentz, of the 7th, a gallant and faithful officer and Capt Markley of the 30th, with several privates were killed, and Col Dougherty of the 22d, and Major McClurken of the 30th, who was near me, seriously wounded. Here my body servant killed one of the enemy by a pistol shot. Driving the enemy back on either side, we moved on, occasionally exchanging shots with straggling parties, in the course of which my horse received another ball, being one of two fired, at me, from the corner of a field. Capt Schwartz was at my right when these shots were fired. At this stage of the contest, according to the admission of rebel officers, the enemy's forces had been swelled by frequent reenforcements from the other side to be over thirteen regiments of infantry and something less than two squadrons of cavalry, excluding his artillery; four pieces of which were in our possession; two of which, after being spiked, together with part of one of our own caissons, were left on the way for want of animals to bring them off. The other two with their horses and harness were brought off. On reaching the landing, and not finding the detachments of the 7th and 22d which you had left behind in the morning to guard the boats, I ordered Delano's Cavalry, which was embarking, to the rear of the fields to watch the enemy. Within an hour all our forces which had arrived were embarked, Capt Schwartz, Capt Hatch Asst Quarter Master, and myself being the last to get on board. Suddenly the enemy, in strong force, whose approach had been discovered by Lt Col John H. White of the 31st—who had been conspicuous through the day for his dauntless courage and conduct—came within range of our Musketry, when a terrible fire was opened upon him, by the Gunboats, as well as by Taylor's battery, and the infantry from the decks of the transports. The engagement thus renewed, was kept up with great spirit and with deadly effect upon the enemy until the transports had passed beyond his reach. Exposed to the terrible fire of the Gunboats and Taylor's battery, a great number of the enemy were killed and wounded in this the closing scene of a battle of six hours duration. The 27th and Dollins' cavalry being yet behind, I ordered my transport to continue in the rear of the fleet; excepting the Gunboats, and after proceeding a short distance, landed and directed the Gunboats to return and a[wa]it their appearance. At this moment Lt. H. A. Rust Adjutant of the 27th, a brave & enterprising officer, hastened up and announced the approach of the 27th and Dollins Cavalry. Accompanied by Captains Schwartz and Hatch, I rode down the river bank and met Col Buford with a part of his command. Informing him that my transport was waiting to receive him, I went further down the river and met Captain Dollins, whom I also instructed to embark; and still further down met the remainder of the 27th, which had halted on the bank where the Gunboat Tyler was lying to—the Lexington lying still further down. The rest of the boats having gone forward, Capt Walke of the Tyler, at my request, promptly took the remainder of the 27th on board—Capt Stembel of the Lexington covering the embarkation. Having thus embarked all my command, I returned with Captains Schwartz and Hatch to my transport and re-embarked, reaching Cairo about midnight, after a day of almost unceasing marching and conflict. I can not bestow too high commendation upon all whom I had the honor to command on that day.

Supplied with inferior and defective arms, many of which could not be discharged, and others bursting in use, they fought an enemy in woods with which he was familiar; behind defensive works which he had been preparing for months; in the face of a battery at Belmont, and under his heavy guns at Columbus; and although numbering three or four to our one, beat him—capturing several stand of his colors, destroying his camp and carrying off a large amount of property, already mentioned. From his own semi-official accounts, his loss was 600 killed, wounded and missing—including among the killed and wounded a number of officers, and probably among the missing, 155 prisoners who were brought to this post—To mention all who did well, would include every man in my command who came under my personal notice. Both officers and privates did their whole duty; nobly sustaining the enviable character of Americans and Illinoians. They shed new lustre upon the flag of their country, by upholding it, in triumph, amid the shock of battle and the din of arms. The blood they so freely poured out, proved their devotion to their country, and serves to hallow a just cause with glorious recollections. Their success was that of citizen soldiers. Major Brayman, Captains Schwartz and Dresser, and Lieutenants Eddy and Babcock, all members of my staff, are entitled to my gratitude for the zeal and alacrity with which they bore my orders in the face of danger and discharged all their duties, in the field. Cols Buford, Fouke and Logan, repeatedly led their regiments to the charge and as often drove the enemy back in confusion, thus inspiring their men with kindred ardor, and largely contributing to the success of the day. Col Logan's admirable tactics not only foiled the frequent attempts of the enemy to flank him, but secured a steady advance towards the enemy's camp. Col Fouke and his command, exposed throughout to a galling fire from the enemy, never ceased to press forward. His march was marked by the killed and wounded of the foe mingled with many of his own men. Accomplishing a difficult circuit, Col Buford, active, eager and emulous, was the first to throw his men within the enemy's defences. Capt Taylor and Lt. White managed the battery attached to my command with admirable skill and most successful effect. Capt J. J. Dollins with his company of cavalry, displayed unsurpassed activity and daring. Having been early detached from his regiment (the 31st) he found his way in company with the 27th, to the enemy's camp, on the lower side, charging his line with an impetuosity characteristic of himself and his brave followers. Our victory, though signal and and extraordinary cost many valuable lives. Of the 27th 11. were killed, 42. wounded; and 28 are missing. Among the wounded was Capt. Schmidt already honorably mentioned, and Lieut Wm Shipley of Company 'A' a gallant and promising young officer, who has since died. Of the 30th, 9. were killed, 27. wounded, and 8 are missing. Among the killed, is Capt Thomas. G. Markley of Company 'D,' a brave and valuable officer, who died true to his trust. Major Thomas McClerken an accomplished and effecient officer, whose services were conspicuous on the field, was severely, and I fear mortally wounded. Of the 31st 10 were killed, 61 wounded, and four (4.) are missing. Capt John W. Rigby of Company 'F.' a veteran and faithful officer, being among the wounded; also Capt Wm. A. Looney, of Company 'C,' and Alexander. S. Somerville of Company 'K,' both bold and exemplary officers. Of Dollins cavalry 1 was killed, and 2 wounded. Of Taylor's battery of Light Artillery, 5 were wounded; among whom was 1st Sergeant Chas. W. Everett. In closing this report, unavoidably somewhat imperfect, I can not refrain from bearing testimony to the gallantry and good conduct of every arm of your whole force. Each did well; and rejoicing in it, I cannot but sympathize in in the just

pride with which their valor has inspired you, as their victorious commander—
P. S. Herewith you will find a diagram of the field covered by the operations of
the forces commanded by you, in the battle of Belmont, prepared, at my request,
by Captain A. Schwartz Acting Chief of Artillery." LS, DNA, RG 94, War
Records Office, Union Battle Reports; Brayman Papers, ICHi; (Printed) Mc-
Clernand Papers, IHi; DLC-Robert T. Lincoln. *O.R.*, I, iii, 277–83.

2. On Nov. 18, Surgeon John H. Brinton wrote to USG. "I have the honor
to submit the following list of soldiers wounded in the recent fight at Belmont.
Mo: The total number of injured as yet reported to this office amounts to *Two
hundred & forty seven*. Of these as will be seen by reference to the subjoined statement, *ten* have already died—It should however be stated that from one regiment
(viz the 7th Iowa volunteers) no report has as yet been rendered. The number
of casualties to this corps have been more in number then to any other regiment;
and when the report of the Surgeon Dr. Witter—shall have been received, the
list as already submitted, will doubtless be somewhat augmented—The reason of
the delay with regard to the report of the wounded of the 7th Iowa regiment arises
from the fact that immediately after the battle of the 7th Inst: that regiment was
ordered to Benton Barracks, Mo:—a portion of the wounded being left behind
at this place, & in Mound City, whilst another portion were conveyed northward
with their regiment—Many of the wounded at present in our depot and general
Hospitals are cases of unfavorable nature—This is owing to the circumstance
that they fell into the hands of the enemy and were left exposed on the field of
battle for at least eighteen or twenty-four hours—They were subsequently
returned to us by their captors—Had the Medical department of your command
been provided with the proper ambulance train, that disastrous and mortifying
result might have been avoided. The only means of transportation which I pos-
sessed, consisted of some two or three ordinary army wagons, obtained from the
Quartermaster's department—These being destitute of springs, and the country
over which they passed being wooded and rough; our wounded suffered much unnecessary anguish—I would also state that Surgeon Gordon of the 30th regiment
Ills: vols; and Assistant Surgeon Whitnall of the 31st Ills. Vols: were captured
by the enemy, and still remain in their hands.—It affords me pleasure to notice
the ability and efficiency of Brigade Surgeon Stearns, and the Corps of Surgeons
generally—I would especially instance the conduct of Assistant Surgeon Kendall
of [Capt.] Delano's Cavalry who freely exposed himself to the fire of the enemy,
in his efforts to rescue and aid our wounded—" LS, DNA, RG 94, War Records
Office, Union Battle Reports. *O.R.*, I, iii, 274–75. Brinton later prepared a more
detailed report for the Medical Dept., listing 80 killed, 322 wounded (of which
35 died subsequently), and 54 missing. *The Medical and Surgical History of the
War of the Rebellion* (Washington, 1870–88), I, part 1, appendix, 18–22.

3. Lt. Col. Augustus Wentz, 7th Iowa, was killed at Belmont.

4. Maj. Elliott W. Rice later succeeded Jacob G. Lauman as col., 7th Iowa.

5. 2nd Lt. George W. S. Dodge, 7th Iowa, was killed in action at Belmont;
1st Lt. Charles Gardner died Nov. 10, 1861, of wounds received at Belmont.

6. Capts. Gideon Gardner, James P. Harper, and James C. Parrott, 7th
Iowa, recovered; 2nd Lt. Benjamin Reams died Nov. 22, 1861, of wounds received at Belmont.

7. Capts. James A. Hubbard and Samuel G. McAdams, 22nd Ill.

8. Maj. Gen. Sterling Price, Mo. State Guard.

To Maj. Gen. Henry W. Halleck

By Telegraph from Cairo [*Nov.*] 20 *1861*
To Maj Gen Halleck

Can I have authority to call upon you in St Louis with the view of making known in person the wants & condition of this command

U S Grant
Brig Genl
Comdg

Telegram received, DNA, RG 94, Generals' Papers and Books, Telegrams Received by Gen. Halleck. Henry W. Halleck of N.Y., USMA 1839, resigned from the U.S. Army on Aug. 1, 1854 with the rank of capt. His book, *Elements of Military Art and Science* (1846), though largely a translation of the work of Baron Henri Jomini, established his position as a military theorist, while his success as a lawyer and businessman in San Francisco demonstrated his abilities as an administrator. Stephen E. Ambrose, *Halleck: Lincoln's Chief of Staff* (Baton Rouge, La., 1962), chap. I. On Aug. 19, 1861, Halleck was appointed maj. gen., and on Nov. 9 was assigned to command the major part of what had been the Western Dept. On Nov. 19, Halleck assumed command of the Dept. of the Mo.

On Nov. 21, Halleck telegraphed to USG. "You will send reports, in writing, of wants and condition of your command. Cannot just now be ordered to St. Louis." Copies, DNA, RG 94, Generals' Papers and Books, Telegrams Sent by Gen. Halleck in Cipher; *ibid.*, RG 393, Dept. of the Mo., Telegrams Sent; *ibid.*, USG Hd. Qrs. Correspondence; DLC-USG, V, 4, 5, 7, 8.

To Col. Richard J. Oglesby

Head Quarters Dist. S. E. Mo
Cairo Nov. 20th 1861

Col. R J Oglesby
Comdg. 2d Brigade
Birds Point Mo
Col.

You will cause an immediate investigation to be made of the property, now illegally held by Officers and soldiers of your command.

All Officers found with captured property, taken at Belmont or on your recent expedition, without written authority from these Head Quarters, will be placed in arrest, and soldiers so holding will be put in confinement.

Conduct of such an infamous character has been reported to me as to call for an investigation. If incorrect it is well that the matter should be set right. If true the guilty should be punished, in order that the innocent may not suffer for the acts of others.

Knowing that your views in this matter accord with mine, I trust you will have this matter thoroughly investigated

Yours truly

U. S. GRANT

Brig. Genl Comdg.

Copies, DLC-USG, V, 1, 2, 3, 77; DNA, RG 393, USG Letters Sent. *O.R.*, I, viii, 369–70. On Nov. 23, 1861, Capt. John A. Rawlins wrote to Col. Richard J. Oglesby. "I am instructed by the Genl. Comdg. to say, your Report of recent expedition after Jeff Thompson, dated the 20th inst. is received. The Negro captured by Major Smith, as mentioned therein, you will put on board first Govt. Steamer bound for this place, and send him ashore at Commerce, with permission to go to his Mistress she being reported a staunch Unionist" Copies, DLC-USG, V, 1, 2, 3, 79; DNA, RG 393, USG Letters Sent. On Nov. 27, Rawlins wrote to Oglesby. "I am instructed by the Genl Comdg. to inform you, that your letter of date 25th inst., enclosing report of Committee, appointed under your order No 9, was duly received, and direct that Committee be discharged, their report being appro ved" Copies, *ibid.*

To Capt. Reuben B. Hatch

Head Quarters Dist. S. E. Mo

Cairo Nov. 20th 1861

SPECIAL ORDER NO

The Post Quarter Master will cause to be fitted up as a store House, with as little delay as possible, the Mill & surrounding buildings at Birds Point Mo.

He will when these buildings are completed, keep an issuing Agt. at Birds Point and issue from that point to all troops there

U. S. GRANT

Brig Genl Comdg.

To Capt. R. B. Hatch
Post. Quarter Master
Cairo Ils

Copies, DLC-USG, V, 15, 16, 77, 82; DNA, RG 393, USG Special Orders.

To Elihu B. Washburne

Cairo Illinois
November 20th 1861.

HON. E. B. WASHBURN
GALENA ILL.
DEAR SIR:

Your two letters, one from Washington the other from Galena, were received, the last several days ago.[1] You have placed me under renewed obligations by your exertions in behalf of my command[.] The very day, or day after, your Washington letter was written I received telegraphic despatches from Gen. McClellan & Quarter Master Sibley, the first calling for a full report of all my wants as well as evrything connected with this command, and announcing that 3000 stand of arms were to be sent. The latter enquiring the articles of clothing most needed.[2]

I saw through the press of the country the new assignment of Military Departments and knew that it would defeat the plan proposed by Gen. McClernand and myself.[3]

I asked for nothing for myself. I believed that Cairo should be the Head Quarters of the Department called upon to act South: 1st Because supplies can reach here from all the cheap markets of the West more cheaply than by the any other point near where they are to be consumed; 2d Because Illinois, from the great number of troops she has supplied, is more entitled to the few benefits that arise from this war than states that really have absorbed our Army by their disloyalty and discontent.

The very flattering interest you have taken in my personal welfare and advancement I know of but one way of repaying. That is, to exert my utmost ability to the end that you may not be disappointed in your appreciation. I promise the country my undivided time and exertions and any fault shall be from an error in judgement, not of heart.

The battle of Belmont, as time passes, proves to have been a greater success than Gen. McClernand or myself at first thought. The enemies loss proves to be greater and the effect upon the Southern mind more saddening. Their loss was near three to our one, by accounts which we have since received, whilst their force bore about the same ratio. to ours I do not wish to trespass upon your time but shall always be pleased to hear from you.

Yours Truly

U. S. GRANT

P. S. We have here an Illinois man that I want to call your attention to. I mean Col. W. H. L. Wallace. He is not aware that I feel any personal interest in him but if I could be instrumental in calling the attention of the country to him sufficiently to secure him the appointment of a Brigadier Generalship I should feel that I had done the country a greater service than himself.

Col. Wallace is evry inch a soldier. A gentleman by nature and a man of great modesty and great tallent. He served in Mexico and now since the first call for three months troops. But few such soldiers have been called to the higher positions in our Army.[4]

U. S. G.

ALS, Mrs. Walter Love, Flint, Mich.

1. The letter from Galena has not been found. On Nov. 12, 1861, Elihu B. Washburne wrote to USG from Washington. "I have been here since Saturday doing all in my power to forward the interests of our gallant troops at Cairo. I have the positive promise that three thousand stand of arms shall go to you at once, and also that all other matters shall be attended to as soon as possible. The unfortunate administration of matters by Genl. Frémont in the Western Depart-

ment, has disarranged all plans and thrown everything into utter confusion. Halleck goes to that Department to-day, and things will improve from this day. Steps will be immediately taken, I think, to inaugerate the expedition down the river. I have no time to write you fully, as I am on the eve of starting for home, and I will write you fully from there in regard to matters of interest to you. We have only meagre details of the battle of Belmont, and all concur that the most brilliant fighting was done there that has been done during the war, and that our troops covered themselves all over with glory, and, further, that you and McClernand have won undying laurels. My regards to Capt. Rawlins." ALS, DNA, RG 393, District of Southeast Mo., Letters Received.

2. See telegram to Maj. Gen. George B. McClellan, Nov. 13, 1861. On Nov. 11, Asst. Secretary of War Thomas A. Scott telegraphed to USG. "Mr Washburne call this morning to secure arms for your Command. We have strong hopes of getting 3000 stand in New York today which shall be sent at once by Express in order to supply your men" Copy, DNA, RG 107, Telegrams Sent.

3. No other USG correspondence relating to this plan has been found. Apparently USG had discussed it when Washburne was in Cairo. See Testimony, Oct. 31, 1861. On Nov. 10, after an interview with Washburne, President Abraham Lincoln wrote to Brig. Gen. John A. McClernand congratulating him on the battle of Belmont and asking him to be patient about arms. "It would be agreeable to each division of the army to know its own precise destination: but the Government cannot immediately, nor inflexibly at any time, determine as to all; nor if determined, can it tell its *friends* without at the same time telling its *enemies.*" Lincoln, *Works*, V, 20. On Nov. 22, McClernand replied to Lincoln. "Accept my grateful acknowledgements for your kind commendation of the conduct of our troops at Belmont. It is the more acceptable because it forms a generous and just contrast with the hasty and unwarranted animadversions of others. It is due to our troops, to say that they, unquestionably, out-fought those of the enemy. For many of the particulars of the battle, allow me to refer you to my report, herewith, inclosed. I think there has been a want of military unity in this portion of the Western Department. The disadvantage of insufficient numbers has been much aggravated by dividing them into distinct and independent commands. A combined and simultaneous attack by our forces at Paducah, Cairo and Cape Girardeau, upon Columbus, as well as Belmont, would, probably, have resulted in the reduction of both of the latter places. I would suggest the organization of a new Military Department, to comprise the immediate ~~valley~~ valley of the Lower Mississippi, including Southern Missouri and South Western Ky. An energetic, enterprising and judicious commander would early redeem this department from the thraldom of rebellion. I say this, of course, upon the assumption that he would be ~~supported by~~ supplied with an adequate army. Pardon me for again asking you [*to*] assign Lt. J. H. Wilson (now, probably in Baltimore or Anapolis) to duty in my Staff. I think I can make his services as valuable to the country here as they are where he may now be. Your compliance with this request will greatly oblige me both personally and officially. I am yet without a commissary: indeed there is none here: an intruder, without either appointment or commission—or legal obligation to the Government is acting as such. I allude to a Mr Rutherford; whose continuance or appointment I do not recommend. Please assign some commissary already appointed to this Post; and if there be none unassigned; I believe your old friend Henry Kreigh would accept if appointed." ALS, DLC-Robert T. Lincoln.

Additional light on McClernand's plans is shed by his Washington correspondents. On Dec. 9, U.S. Representative Samuel S. Cox, an Ohio Democrat, wrote to McClernand. "I was very glad to hear from you; and you guessed well that I would heed your counsel & wishes. I shall, if no one else does, make a speech, at the proper time, for the *practical and complete rescue of the Mississippi from the treacherous and treasonable foes*." ALS, McClernand Papers, IHi. On Dec. 27, Col. John A. Logan, again occupying his seat in Congress, wrote to McClernand. "This evening I had an interview with the President and am satisfied that he is favorable to establishing a department at Cairo. he told me that he would have a conference with McClellan as soon as he can be fit to see since McClellan is now quite sick." ALS, *ibid*. On Jan. 14, 1862, Logan wrote to McClernand. "I have on all occasions been pressing the necessity of a separate Dept at Cairo and at one time thought there was a fair prospect for success. but am fearful that there is too much West Point controlling things here. it does appear to me that the red tape will finally destroy the Country if the Rebels don't. . . . we get no credit for what we do, and really I feel like desperation, as I see death staring us all in the face (of our command) sooner or later, as we will get no help we must do all ourselves. I was four days here before I could get to see the secty of war, ~~and~~ *but* thank god he is now out of the office—I shall see Lincoln again to morrow and will again urge our claims   I think if a dept could be established there your promotion would be almost certain as the Prest. is certainly your true friend." ALS, *ibid*.

4. On Nov. 23, 1861, Washburne forwarded USG's letter to Lincoln along with a letter of his own. "I want you to take a moments' time to read this letter of Genl Grant, and note what he says of the battle of Belmont, and particularly what he says of Wallace. No higher testimony can be borne to the ~~testimony~~ merit of Wallace, than this borne by the brave and modest Grant, his associate in arms. I well recollect what you told me about your desire to appoint Wallace. Is it not too bad that such men as Hurlbut and Strong and McKinstry are brigadiers, while Wallace, in active service in the field from the very start, is still only a colonel?" ALS, DNA, RG 94, Letters Received. Washburne also enclosed a message to Lincoln from Ill. Congressman Owen Lovejoy. "I earnestly recommend the appointment of Col Wm. H. L. Wallace as one of the Brigadier Generals for the State of Illinois" ALS, *ibid*.

To Capt. John C. Kelton

Head Quarters, Dist. S. E. Mo.
Cairo, November 21st 1861.

A. A. GEN. DEPT. OF MO.
ST. LOUIS, MO.
SIR;

General Order No 1 of the 19th inst. Dept. of the Missouri is just received.[1]

During the temporary absence of Head Quarters from St. Louis I made a report to Maj. Gen. McClellan and was directed by him to make a full report of all my command, how located, their wants &c.[2] This has been done but no requisitions forwarded.

My command embraces the posts of Cape Girardeau & Birds Point Mo. Fort Holt, Ky. and Cairo & Mound City Ill. For strength of each command see Tri-monthly report which will be forwarded within a day or two.[3]

Paducah & Smithland compose a seperate District.

Since the affair of Belmont on the 7th inst. quite a number of Northern men have made their escape from the South, not a few of them soldiers. From this source I have got what I believe to be a reliable statement of the strength of the enemy, the position of his batteries, number of his troops &c. There is now at Columbus forty-seven regiments of Infantry & Cavalry, ten companies of Light Artillery, and over One hundred pieces of heavy Ordnance. All the statements I have received coroborate each other.

In addition to these there is at Camp Beaurigard, on the road about half way between Mayfield and Union City, some eight thousand more, all arms, under command of Col. Bowen, of Camp Jackson notoriety.[4]

The position of this camp may have been changed since I last heard from them but they are exclusive of those enumerated above.

The enemy are working night and day upon their fortifications, and the greatest consternation has prevailed for the last ten days lest Columbus should be attacked.

Finding they are let alone they may be induced to act on the offensive if more troops are not sent here soon.

A Gun boat reached Columbus the night of the 19th and another is expected within a few days. ~~from below~~.

The condition of this command is bad in every particular, except discipline. In this latter I think they will compare favorably with almost any Volunteers.

There is a great deficiency in transportation. I have no Ambulances. The clothing received has been almost universally of an inferior quality, and deficient in quantity. The arms in the hands of the men are mostly the old Flint Lock, altered, the Tower musket and others of still more inferior quality. My Cavalry force are none of them properly armed, the best being deficient in Sword Belts, and having the old pattern Carbines. Eight Companies are entirely without arms of any description.

The Quarter Master's Department has been carried on here with so little funds that Government credit has become exhausted. I would urgently recommend that relief in this particular be afforded at as early a day as practicable.

> Respectfully
> Your Obt. Svt.
> U. S. GRANT
> Brig. Gen. Com.

P. S. The facts relative to arms, clothing, Quarter Masters Department &c. have been frequently reported and requisitions made.

U. S. G.

ALS, James S. Schoff, New York, N.Y. *O.R.*, I, vii, 442. John C. Kelton served as col., 9th Mo., Sept. 21 to Nov. 21, 1861. In becoming asst. adjt. gen., Dept. of the Mo., on Nov. 24, he apparently reverted to his U.S. Army rank of capt. until appointed a staff col., Jan. 4, 1862.

1. In General Orders No. 1, Nov. 19, 1861, Maj. Gen. Henry W. Halleck assumed command of the Dept. of the Mo. *O.R.*, I, viii, 369.
2. See telegram to Maj. Gen. George B. McClellan, Nov. 13, 1861.
3. See letter to Capt. John C. Kelton, Nov. 22, 1861.
4. On Nov. 30, Col. John S. Bowen, commanding Camp Beauregard, reported his aggregate force, present and absent, at 4,794. *O.R.*, I, vii, 728.

To Commanding Officer, Cape Girardeau

———

Head Quarters Dist. S. E. Mo
Cairo Nov. 21 1861

Sir

I am directed by the Commanding General, to inform you that General Jeff Thompson, took from the Platte Valley on Tuesday and has now confined, in New Madrid, two men, named Wm McMillen and James Meekle—

These men are citizens of Illinois and were employed in Memphis, before the commencement of this war, and had been there ever since. They are Mechanics and were employed there as such.

Not being able to procure passes, they escaped to Paducah Ky. took a boat ~~there~~ for this place, and immediately on their arrival here, took passage on the Platte Valley for St Louis, *enroute* to Quincy Illinois their home.

They were never employed as spies and never acted as such. They had no interview with the Commanding General, here, and did not *volunteer* any information—and did not come here for that purpose

They can in no just sense be considered *spies*—They were simply northern men, who had availed themselves, of an opportunity to escape to their homes and families.

If Thompson will release them and give them safe escort to our lines, you will release such number of his men as he may think just, and give them safe escort beyond our lines. In communicating with Thompson, you will send him a copy of this letter

By order Genl Grant Comdg.
Wm S Hillyer
Capt. & Aid de Camp

To Commanding officer U. S. Forces
Cape Girardeau Mo

Copies, DLC-USG, V, 1, 2, 3, 79; DNA, RG 393, USG Letters Sent. *O.R.*, II, ii, 144–45. On Nov. 26, 1861, Col. Joseph B. Plummer wrote to Brig. Gen. M. Jeff Thompson enclosing the letter from Capt. William S. Hillyer. *Ibid.*, II, i, 523–24. On Dec. 1, Thompson replied to USG. "Yours of the 21st through Col. J. B. Plummer Commandant of Cape Girardeau is at hand. The prisoners Wm. McMillan and James Merkle, were immediately forwarded to Genl Polk at Columbus & I will send your letter, in reference to them directly to him. I will state in referance to these men, that when I examined the S. B. Platte Valley, I found drawing purporting to be plans of the Fortifications of Columbus and upon enquiring found McMillan & Merkle had either made the drawings or furnished the information—& from *some* parties on the Boat, I learned they had been very boastful of their success & the value of the information they had acquired. I understand they have been sent to Memphis, but I will immediately lay your statement before Genl. Polk & although he may object to their leaving the Confederacy at this time (as they also worked at Columbus), yet I believe your statement will be sufficient to have them released from confinement." Copies, DNA, RG 109, 1st Div., Mo. State Guard, Letters Sent; *ibid.*, RG 393, Post of Cape Girardeau, Letters Sent. *O.R.*, II, ii, 145.

On Nov. 21, the capt. and two clerks of the *Platte Valley*, then under arrest, were sent to the U.S. Arsenal at St. Louis under orders of USG. *Ibid.* II, i, 136–37. See letter to John C. Kelton, Nov. 29, 1861, note 1.

To Capt. John C. Kelton

Head Quarters Dist. S. E. Mo
Cairo Nov 22nd 1861

A. A. GENL DEPT. OF THE MO
ST LOUIS MO
SIR

I have frequently reported to the Western Department that the line of Steamers plying between St Louis and Cairo, by landing at points on the Missouri shore were enabled to afford aid and comfort to the enemy

I have been reliably informed that some of the officers, particularly the Clerks, of these Boats, were regularly in the employ of the Southern Confederacy, so called

The case of the Platte Valley, a few days since, confirms me in this belief

I have heretofore recommended that all the carrying trade between here and St Louis, be performed by Government, charging uniform rates. I would respectfully renew the suggestion, and in consideration of the special disloyalty of South East Missouri I would further recommend, that all commerce be cut off from all points south of Cape Girardeau.

There is not a sufficiency of Union sentiment left in this portion of the state to save Sodom

This is shown from the fact, that Jeff Thompson, or any of the Rebels, can go into Charleston and spend hours or encamp for the night, on their way north to depridate upon Union men, and not one loyalist is found to report the fact to our Picket, stationed but one & a half miles off

> Very Respectfully
> Your Obt Servt
> U. S. GRANT
> Brig Genl Comdg

Copies, DLC-USG, V, 4, 5, 7, 8, 9, 78; DNA, RG 393, USG Hd. Qrs. Correspondence. *O.R.*, I, viii, 373–74. On Nov. 24, 1861, Capt. John C. Kelton wrote to Brig. Gen. Samuel R. Curtis. "The Major General commanding directs that you carry into effect the recommendations of Brig.r Gen'l. U. S. Grant, conveyed in a communication to these Head Quarters, dated Nov. 22d, concerning the river navigation of the Missouri as far as you may deem necessary and practicable." Copy, DNA, RG 393, District of Southeast Mo., Letters Received. *O.R.*, I, viii, 375.

To Capt. John C. Kelton

> Head Quarters Dist. S. E. Mo
> Cairo Nov 22nd 1861

ASST. ADJT. GENERAL
DEPT. OF THE MISSOURI
ST LOUIS MO
SIR

I have the honor herewith to transmit to you my Trimonthly Return of the troops of my command, for the first third of the present month, a copy of which at the date thereof, there being no Head Quarters in this Department, I forwarded to the Head Quarters of the Army at Washington.

The Trimonthly Return due the 20th inst. will be sent you as soon as Sub Reports are received from which to compile them

I am very respectfully—Your Obt Svt

U. S. GRANT—Brig. Genl. Comdg.

Copies, DLC-USG, V, 4, 5, 7, 8, 9, 78; DNA, RG 393, USG Hd. Qrs. Correspondence.

To Flag Officer Andrew H. Foote

Cairo, November 22, 1861.

To COMMODORE FOOTE.

I would inform you that the Mississippi is falling, with scant six feet. Would it not be well to send the gun-boats while it is possible?

U. S. GRANT.

Telegram, James Mason Hoppin, *Life of Andrew Hull Foote, Rear-Admiral United States Navy* (New York, 1874), p. 162. On Nov. 19, 1861, Flag Officer Andrew H. Foote wrote to James B. Eads, St. Louis, urging him to send the gunboats to Cairo immediately because of the falling of the Mississippi River. *O.R.* (Navy), I, xxii, 439. The *St. Louis* arrived at Cairo on Nov. 28, the *Pittsburg* on Nov. 29. The *Carondelet* and *Louisville* reached Cairo by Dec. 5. *Ibid.*, pp. 444–45, 451–52. The *Benton* and *Essex* ran aground. *Ibid.*, pp. 453, 459.

To Brig. Gen. John A. McClernand

Head Quarters, Dist. S. E. Mo.
Cairo, November 22d 1861.

Gen. J. A. McClernand,
Comd.g U. S. Forces
Cairo Illinois.
Gen.

It is my desire that you should proceed to Springfield Illinois, at as early a period as practicable, for the purpose of laying before the Governor of the State the importance of filling regiments now actually in service, and arming them, as far as possible, in prefference to regiments yet to be called out.

Respectfully &c.
U. S. Grant
Brig. Gen. Com.

ALS, McClernand Papers, IHi. On Nov. 23, 1861, Capt. John A. Rawlins wrote to Brig. Gen. John A. McClernand. "The General commanding directs me to inform you that he goes to Cape Girardeau tonight on business connected with this district, and to request that you defer your departure to Springfeild and remain in command until his return." LS, *ibid.* On Nov. 30, McClernand wrote to USG. "In pursuance of your order of the 23d inst, I proceeded to Springfield Ill, for the purpose of urging His Excellency Richard Yates Governor of said state to fill up deficient regiments and other military organizations stationed at this post. Upon reaching Springfield I immediately called upon Col A. C. Fuller Adjt Genl of the State, at his office, and in a personal interview, set forth the necessity for prompt compliance with the request I made in your behalf. Among other things, I stated that being isolated as a military camp, under strict military government, it was impracticable, either for officers or privates here, to leave their posts for the purpose of recruiting, without serious detriment to the public service. That from the peculiar relation of Cairo to Missouri and Kentucky and dependent posts in in those states, it was in fact, an important base of military operations, And as such, had to supply the Commissary and Quarter Master's Departments of a considerable number of troops here and elsewhere; And that in order to do this an exhausting and oppressive amount of fatigue duty was performed by the troops here.—The details for such service being daily very large, and that while this service was wearing out the men, it had also caused much sickness among them. That besides these details, others were made daily for the purpose of guarding our camp here upon a line some seven miles long. That in addition to this our whole force here, amounting to something over 5000 was threatened by an enemy of some 40.000 men, consisting of Infantry, Cavalry and light artillery, at Columbus, only twenty miles distant. And that in these circumstances, if we were not at the mercy of the enemy, we were certainly destitute of the means of aggresive operations and perhaps of effectual self defence. In short, that the inferiority of our force invited the invasion of the State. The Adjutant admitted that ~~our~~ the case was a strong one, but replied that he thought it would be unjust to detach from the regiments at Camp Butler, although incomplete, men for the purpose of filling up the deficient organizations at Cairo. I answered that the military necessity required it, and that all mere personal considerations should be subordinated to that necessity; and that less injury would result to the public service by delaying the completion of those regiments than by delaying the completion of those at Cairo; and that although late, now would be a good time to reform the evil of commissioning the field officers of regiments themselves in advance of filling up the ranks of the regiments themselves—That the men should be recruited first and the officers commissioned afterwards. Having procured an interview with the Governor, I found him convalescing from a severe illness, but still little able to discuss matters of business. He heard however what I had to say, which was a repetition, substantially, of the views I had expressed to the Adjutant. He also admitted the reason and force of those views, yet did not respond to them by definite action. Desiring, however, to see them carried into effect, he requested me to see several officers having incomplete corps at Camp Butler and urge upon them the propriety of allowing their men to be incorporated in the deficient organizations at Cairo. This I did, informing them, at the same time, that upon doing so they would be compensated by the assignment to them of such offices as were disposable. They declined to do so; of which I afterwards advised the Adjutant. He replied in terms of regret, and promised to do whatever he could to secure the accomplishment of the object of my mission; also the accomplishment of various other matters of minor importance; such as the issuing of commissions &c which in the press of business had been for some time delayed. Before we parted, in order to leave a permanent record of what I had said and place a proper responsibility I put into his hands a communication whereof the following is a copy. That communication you will see is a resume of what has been herein before ~~been~~ set forth

'Copy'

Springfield Ill
Nov 27th 1861

A. C. Fuller
Col & Adjt Genl
State of Ill
Sir—

I am here in obedience to my own sense of duty, as well as by the order of Brig Genl U. S. Grant, Comdg. Dist of South East Mo, to urge upon his Excellency, Gov. Yates the importance of filling up the different volunteer corps at Cairo. At all times small since the commencement of the war, the force now there is comparatively smaller than at any former period. The precise number of that force is shown by document marked 'A,' to which I respectfully refer you.

On the other hand, the enemy are assembled in formidable force at Columbus and other near points in Ky. It is almost certain that he has 47 Regts of Infantry, 10 Companies of Light Artillery and some 6000

Cavalry encamped at Columbus, alone; besides over 100 pieces of cannon in battery, and probably, by this time, 3 gun boats.

With this superiority of force he is in condition to assume the offensive and put us on the defensive; thus exposing Illinois to the danger of invasion. Hence the recent daring attempts of Jeff Thompson's band to seize loyal vessels, passing to and fro, between Cairo and St Louis, and the report of a meditated hostile movement upon Fort Holt and Bird's Point.

It is still more important to fill up those corps, if a forward movement against the enemy shall be soon made, for without it, such a movement could hardly eventuate otherwise than disastrously. Without it, a miracle only could insure our success. Again; those corps are already in the field and confronted with the enemy. They have gained military experience and comparative expertness—Have already rendered valuable service and afford greater promise of immediate usefulness than raw recruits. Less injury, therefore, would result from the delay of completing the latter than the former.

For these and other reasons given in our conversation yesterday, I venture to urge you to exert your influence with the Governor to fill up our incomplete organizations at Cairo, and I do so with the more confidence, since I am informed, that your own reasoning and opinion coincide with Genl Grant's and my own upon this subject.

The gratitude of the whole army at Cairo and the promotion of the public service will reward Gov. Yates for ~~the~~ a favorable response to this earnest appeal.

'A'

Infantry			Regts attached		
	Present No.	Deficy		Present No.	Deficy
27th Regt.	849	161	10th Regt.	705	305
29th "	867	143	18th "	873	137
30th "	758	252	48th "	793	217
31st "	923	87			
	3,397	643		2,371	659

Cavalry

	Present No.	Deficy
Capt. Carmichael's Co.	83	12
" O. Harnott's "	75	20
" Dollins' "	94	1
" Stewarts "	88	7
" Evans' "	94	1
	434	41

Artillery

	Present No.	Deficy
Capt. Schwartz's Co.	88	56
" Dresser's "	48	96
" "		144
	136	296

Hoping that this report will be received by you as affording satisfactory proof of the zeal and fidelity of my endeavors to accomplish your wishes in the premises, I beg to subscribe myself—" Copy, *ibid.*

To Capt. William McMichael

Head Quarters, Dist. S. E. Mo.
Cairo, November 23d 1861.

CAPT. WM McMICHAEL
A. A. GEN. DEPT. OF THE MO.
ST. LOUIS MO.
SIR:

Enclosed you will find report of Maj. Webster made in complyance with Gen. Order No 2 from Head Quarters Department of the Missouri.

I would remark in connection with this that the services of Maj. Webster cannot well be dispensed with at this time, and if not inconsistent with the good of the service, would respectfully request that he be continued in his present duties.

Respectfully
Your Obt. Svt.
U. S. GRANT
Brig. Gen. Com.

ALS, DNA, RG 393, Dept. of the Mo., Letters Received. William McMichael of Pa. was appointed capt. and asst. adjt. gen. of vols. on Aug. 15, 1861. For Maj. Joseph D. Webster, see telegram to Maj. Gen. John C. Frémont, Sept. 7, 1861, note 1.

USG enclosed a letter of Nov. 23 from Webster to McMichael. "I beg leave to report for the information of the General commanding the 'Department of the Missouri' that I have been acting as Engineer of the defensive works in this vicinity since the 27th day of August last, in obedience to an order from Major General Fremont lately commanding the Western Department, a copy of which I enclose.—Coming here on the 22d of April last with the State troops which first occupied this place in the capacity of Paymaster, I was on the first of May commissioned as Inspector of the First Brigade of Illinois Volunteers.—Under both these appointments I acted as Engineer by request of the officers in command.— On the 18th of June was appointed by the Governor of the State of Illinois 'Engineer in Chief' with the rank of Colonel.—As such my proper post was at Springfield, the seat of the State Government, in charge of the State Arsenal, magazine, arms, ammunition, &c. But at the particular request of Brig. Gen'l. Prentiss I was allowed to remain here as engineer of the Post.—The work on the redoubt at this point, and the intrenched camp at Bird's Point were going on under my orders, when on the 21st day of June I received and accepted an appointment as additional Paymaster—followed in a day or two by a telegram order from the Paymaster General to continue here till the works were completed.—I remained accordingly, until—on a request to have my official position and duty better defined, I received the order first noticed above under which I am now acting." LS, DNA, RG 393, Dept. of the Mo., Letters Received. On Nov. 26, Brig. Gen. Schuyler Hamilton wrote to USG. "I am directed by Major General Halleck to say Major Webster will be continued in his present duties until further orders." Copies, DLC-USG, V, 7, 8, 9; DNA, RG 393, Dept. of the Mo., Letters Sent; *ibid.*, USG Hd. Qrs. Correspondence.

To Capt. William McMichael

———

Head Quarters, Dist. S. E. Mo.
Cairo, Nov. 23d 1861.

CAPT. WM MCMICHAEL
A. A. GEN. DEPT. OF THE MO.
SIR:

I enclose herewith a remarkable document presented at our out guards to-day by Capt. George of the Rebel Army.

Capt. George is permitted to go to St. Louis, as a prisoner on Parole, to report to the Gen. Comd.g the Dept. for his decission.

Very respectfully
Your Obt. Svt.
U. S. GRANT
Brig. Gen. Com

P. S. Capt. George, since my writing the above, states that he is not nor has he been in the Confederate Army. He was a Camp Jackson prisoner since which he has not taken up arms. He now simply claims the right under the Price Frémont exchange[1] to return to his family in St. Louis, and should he desire to do so, to join Gen. Price and the Mo. state troops.

U. S. GRANT
Brig. Gen

ALS, DNA, RG 393, Dept. of the Mo., Letters Received. *O.R.*, II, i, 116. Enclosed was a statement written on Nov. 20, 1861, at Columbus, Ky., by Gus A. Henry, asst. adjt. gen. for Brig. Gen. Gideon J. Pillow. "Capt. James George and Lieut Henry Guibor, late prisoners of war and duly exchanged by agreement between Maj Gen. Freemont U. S. A. and Maj Gen. Price of the Missouri State troops as appears to me, now therefore I grant said officers Capt. George and Lieut Guibor this 'safe Guard' to pass the picket lines and videts of this army in thier Return to Saint Louis and back to this place." DS, DNA, RG 393, Dept. of the Mo., Letters Received. *O.R.*, II, i, 116–17. On Nov. 23, USG prepared a pass for Capt. James George. "Capt. George, one of the Camp Jackson prisoners, having presented himself to the grand guard of Fort Holt, Kentucky, is hereby permitted to pass all guards of the United States for the purpose of going to St. Louis, Mo., as a prisoner, there to report himself to the commanding officer of this military department, and to state his case in person. He will not be molested while on the journey direct, between Cairo and St. Louis." *Missouri Democrat*, Nov. 27, 1861.

On Nov. 26, Capt. John C. Kelton wrote to USG. "Your letter of the 23d inst. with enclosed safeguard to Captain George and Lieut Guibor, purporting to have been signed by order of General Pillow has been received. I am directed by the Commanding General of this Department to say that you did very wrong in permitting these officers to pass your lines under the authority of such a paper. Any person attempting hereafter to pass with such a document, will be immediately arrested and the case reported to these Headquarters for instructions." Copies, DLC-USG, V, 4, 5, 7, 8, 9; DNA, RG 393, Dept. of the Mo., Letters Sent; *ibid.*, USG Hd. Qrs. Correspondence. *O.R.*, II, i, 117–18. See letter to Capt. John C. Kelton, Nov. 28, 1861.

1. On Oct. 26, representatives of Maj. Gen. John C. Frémont and Maj. Gen. Sterling Price, Mo. State Guard, reached an agreement concerning the exchange of prisoners. *O.R.*, II, i, 548–58. By the time arrangements for implementation were complete, however, Frémont had been replaced in command of the Western Dept. by Maj. Gen. David Hunter, who refused to recognize the agreement. *Ibid.*, pp. 560–61. On Nov. 22, through General Orders No. 4, Maj. Gen. Henry W. Halleck authorized the passage through his lines of prisoners properly exchanged under the agreement. *Ibid.*, p. 562. On Nov. 26, through General Orders No. 10, Halleck clarified his earlier orders by forbidding exchanged prisoners to reenter his lines. *Ibid.* Most of the prisoners had been captured at Camp Jackson on May 10. See letter to Julia Dent Grant, May 10, 1861, note 15.

To Capt. William McMichael

———

Head Quarters, Dist. S. E. Mo.
Cairo, November 25th 1861.

CAPT. WM McMICHAEL
A. A. GEN., DEPT. OF THE MO.
ST. LOUIS, MO.
SIR:

Last evening a party of prisoners taken at Camp Jackson arrived here on the Steamer Platte Valley. I had them detained on the Steamer until this morning when they were put aboard one of the ferries and landed at Norfolk, Mo. about five miles below.

These prisoners are coming in squads from day to day and necessarily keep the enemy well informed of all movements it is possible for the community at large to know, as well as the secret plottings of the enemy in our midst. ~~are doing~~

I would again report to the Comd.g officer of this Department the almost certain disloyalty of the entire boating interest plying between St. Louis and this place. I am informed that the owners of the Packets complained of are generally enemies to the Government and their acts prove conclusively that the crews employed are.

Respectfully
Your Obt. Svt.
U. S. GRANT
Brig. Gen. Com

ALS, DNA, RG 393, Dept. of the Mo., Letters Received. *O.R.*, II, i, 117. On Nov. 27, 1861, Capt. William McMichael replied to USG. "The General directs me to acknowledge the receipt of your communication of November 25th, and to say that hereafter prisoners will be sent under escort. Brig. Gen. Curtiss has been directed to take charge of and regulate all boats running on the river between this place and Cairo. A copy of his orders are sent enclosed." Copies, DLC-USG, V, 4, 5, 7, 8, 9, VIA, 2; DNA, RG 393, Dept. of the Mo., Letters Sent; *ibid.*, USG Hd. Qrs. Correspondence. In the meantime, on Nov. 25, USG had taken action against the owners of the *Platte Valley*. "The Steamer Platte Valley by her evident disloyal inclinations having made it necessary to send an armed escort to accompany her on her last trip, and to strengthen said guard at Cape Girardeau, a post within this command the said reinforcement is positively prohibitted from giving a certificate of transportation for the same. It is further reccomended that the officer commanding the main Escort decline giving any certificate untill all the facts are laid before his immediate commanding officer and then act upon his decission." DS, ICHi.

To Capt. William McMichael

Head Quarters, Dist. S. E. Mo.
Cairo, November 25th 1861.

CAPT. WM MCMICHAEL
A. A. GEN. DEPT. OF THE MO.
ST. LOUIS, MO.
SIR;

Enclosed herewith I have the honor to submit copy of a special order[1] made with the view of ascertaining parties who have been guilty of Military offences.

I am well aware that in an Army long organized such an inquisition could not be tolerated, but believing the good of the service demands such an investigation I respectfully submit this for the approval of the Gen. Comd.g the Department.

Respectfully
U. S. GRANT
Brig. Gen. Com.

ALS, DNA, RG 393, Dept. of the Mo., Letters Received.

1. "It having been reported to these Head Quarters that a course highly prejudicial to good order and Military Discipline, and extremely demoralizing to troops, has been practiced at Cape Girardeau, Mo. 1st. In appraising captured property and permitting Officers to purchase at the appraised value. 2nd In turning expeditions through the country into Foraging and Marauding parties. 3d Most disgraceful and licentious conduct on the part of two or more Commissioned Officers, towards a female prisoner; The Genl Commanding has determined to have a full investigation. For this purpose the following detail is ordered, to wit;

Maj M. S. Hasie Engr Reg.t
Capt. G Taggart A. C. S.
and Capt. M. M. Warner 11th Mo Vols

They will have authority to send for Prisoners and take evidence. All persons proven to have speculated in public, or captured property, or to have purchased the same improperly, or to have in their possession such property will be reported. The Board will meet at Cape Girardeau on Thursday the 22d inst. and from day to day thereafter untill a full investigation is had of all the complaints enumerated herein." Copy, *ibid*. In letterbook copies, the date for meeting is given as Nov. 28, 1861. DLC-USG, V, 15, 16, 77, 82; DNA, RG 393, USG Special Orders. On Nov. 27, Capt. William McMichael wrote to USG. "The Commanding General directs me to say in answer to your communication of Nov. 25th, in relation to ascertaining parties who have been guilty of military offences, that no action will be taken on the subject at present." Copies, *ibid*., Dept. of the Mo., Letters Sent; DLC-USG, VIA, 2. On Nov. 29, Capt. John A. Rawlins wrote to the commanding officer, Cape Girardeau. "I am instructed by Brig Genl U. S. Grant to say, the Board ordered to convene on Thursday the 28th inst, in pursuance of Special Orders of these Head Quarters of date the 25th inst, will suspend all action until further orders." Copies, *ibid*., V, 1, 2, 3, 77; DNA, RG 393, USG Letters Sent.

To Brig. Gen. Don Carlos Buell

Cairo Ill Nov 25 [*1861*]

It is reported that the Secessionists are driving large numbers of hogs and Cattle from Union, Webster and Hopkins counties. The Command at Shawneetown think they can stop it, if they had a steamer to cross with. They want to charter the Bullet now laying up here. Being out of my jurisdiction I cannot authorize it, but refer the matter to you Will you authorize the charter

Telegram, copy, DNA, RG 393, Dept. of the Ohio, Telegrams Received. On Nov. 25, 1861, Brig. Gen. Don Carlos Buell of Ohio, USMA 1841, commanding Dept. of the Ohio, telegraphed to USG. "I assent to your troops Crossing the river for the purpose stated. For means of transportation your troops must depend on your authority." Telegram received (punctuation added), *ibid*., District of Southeast Mo., Letters Received; copy, *ibid*., Dept. of the Ohio, Telegrams Sent. See telegram to Brig. Gen. Don Carlos Buell, Nov. 26, 1861.

On Nov. 23, Col. Robert Kirkham, Shawneetown, Ill., wrote to USG. "Allow me to introduce my Lut Col W R Brown, whose business in your city is to bring up the Steamer Fanny Bullit, to, this place, if you can spare hi[m], one [siege] gun, Six Pounder let him have it. I have one Twelve and one Six lbs. gun, but no amunition or Balls for, the, Six lbs gun, you will please furnish him with amunition and Ball for about 100 Rounds[.] I have Telgraphed to Gov Yates for five hundred guns but as yet have not receivd them if I had them I could capture from Ky opposite us large quantites of [hogs] that have been sold on foot to be driven South, if you have any arms to spare please let him have them, and furnish him with coal to bring up the boat & please approve my action in the premises, and believe me your friend." ALS, DNA, RG 393, District of Southeast Mo., Letters Received.

To Col. Joseph B. Plummer

―――――――

~~Special~~ Head Quarters Dist S E Mo
Cairo Nov 25th 1861

SPECIAL ORDER No

The Commanding Officer at Cape Girardeau Mo will cause to be issued to Capt. Powels[1] Compy of Artillery & Capt Murdocks[2] company of Cavalry, such clothing as he may deem necessary for the health and comfort of their commands.

By order
U. S. GRANT
Brig Genl Comdg

To Col Plummer
Comdg U. S. Forces
Cape Girardeau Mo

Copies, DLC-USG, V, 15, 16, 77, 82; DNA, RG 393, USG Special Orders. On Nov. 25, 1861, Capt. John A. Rawlins wrote to the Commanding Officer, Cape Girardeau. "You will order the two companies of 2nd Ill Cavalry now under your command to return to this place by the same transportation which conveys Capt Langens and Pfaffs commands to that post, they being under orders to report to you immediately" Copies, DLC-USG, V, 1, 2, 3, 77; DNA, RG 393, USG Letters Sent. On the same day, Rawlins wrote twice to Col. Richard J. Oglesby. "You will designate of your command *one company of Cavalry*, who will proceed to Fort. Holt Ky. and there report to the commanding officer for duty." "You will detail four companies of Infantry from the 20th Ill Regt., with two days rations, to proceed on Steamer to Cape Girardeau and return, to act as an escort for Cavalry ordered there. They will be ready to move at 8 o'clock A. M. on the 26th inst" Copies, *ibid*. Also on the same day, Rawlins wrote to Capt. Ernest Pfaff, Benton Hussars, Mo. Cav. "You will hold your command with their Camp and Garrison Equipage in readiness to embark on Steamer at 8 o.clock A. M. on tomorrow the 26th inst. and in Company with Capt. Langens command, proceed to Cape Girardeau Mo and there report to the commanding Officer U. S. Forces

for duty The Steamer will be in waiting for you at Fort Holt Ky." Copies, *ibid*.
At the same time, Rawlins sent an almost identical letter to Capt. Edward Langen,
Benton Hussars. Copies, *ibid*.

1. See letter to Capt. Chauncey McKeever, Oct. 9, 1861.
2. Capt. Lindsay Murdoch or Murdock organized a cav. co., later Co. A,
12th Cav., Mo. State Militia.

To Col. Joseph B. Plummer

Head Quarters Dist S. E. Mo
Cairo Nov 25th 1861

SPECIAL ORDER No

Leave of absence for seven days ~~is hereby granted~~ with permission to apply for an extension of thirty days is hereby granted
Col J. B. Plummer 11th Mo Vols.

Col Plummer having filled the position of Colonel of Regiment and commander of an important post, most efficiently for
over two months while only holding a recognized commission of
Capt. I would particularly urge that the extension asked for be
granted.

I would further most heartily reccomend that Col Plummer
be returned to this command with his rank confirmed by competent authority—This I consider due him for gallantry displayed at the Battle of Wilsons Creek where he received a wound,
and for the entire credit which is due him for bringing on and
fighting the battle of Fredericktown when our arms were
crowned with an important victory

U. S. GRANT
Brig Genl Com

Copies, DLC-USG, V, 15, 16, 77, 82; DNA, RG 393, USG Special Orders;
(misdated Nov. 23, 1861), *ibid*., RG 94, War Records Office, Union Battle
Reports. *O.R.*, I, iii, 209–10. On Feb. 21, 1862, Joseph B. Plummer was nominat-
ed as brig. gen., and was confirmed on March 7 to rank from Oct. 22, 1861.
Senate Executive Journal, XII, 133–34, 157.

To Capt. John C. Kelton

——————

Head Quarters, Dist. S. E. Mo.
Cairo, November 26th 1861.

Capt. J. C. Kelton,
A. A. Gen. Dept. of the Mo.
St. Louis, Mo.
Sir:

One more of the Camp Jackson exchanged prisoners has arrived here this evening, on his way South. I have determined to retain him, and all others arriving in small squads, until the whole of them are here and discharge them together. I respectfully submit this plan for the approval of the Gen. Commanding the Department.

Respectfully
Your Obt. Svt.
U. S. Grant
Brig. Gen. Com.

ALS, DNA, RG 393, Dept. of the Mo., Letters Received. *O.R.*, II, i, 118. On Nov. 29, 1861, Capt. William McMichael wrote to USG. "In answer to your communication of November 26th announcing that you are retaining the Camp Jackson prisoners who arrive in small numbers, so that they will be sent to the enemy in large bodies, the Commanding General directs me to say that he approves of your action in this matter." Copies, DLC-USG, V, 4, 5, 7, 8, 9, VIA, 2; DNA, RG 393, Dept. of the Mo., Letters Sent; *ibid.*, USG Hd. Qrs. Correspondence. *O.R.*, II, i, 119. See letter to Capt. William McMichael, Nov. 25, 1861.

To Brig. Gen. Don Carlos Buell

——————

Cairo, Ill. Nov 26. [*1861*]

The troops that propose action within your departement are not of my command. They wish to charter a steamer now laying up here wich I do not feel authorized to sanction. Large droves of Stock are being droven to the southern army the design stopping.

Telegram, copy, DNA, RG 393, Dept. of the Ohio, Telegrams Received. On
Nov. 27, 1861, Col. James B. Fry, chief of staff to Brig. Gen. Don Carlos Buell,
telegraphed to USG. "The move proposed in your telegram of yesterday should
be referred to the genl Comdg the troops proposing it by Command Gen Buel"
Telegram received, *ibid.*, Dept. of the Mo., Telegrams Received; copy, *ibid.*,
Dept. of the Ohio, Telegrams Sent. See telegram to Brig. Gen. Don Carlos
Buell, Nov. 25, 1861.

To Capt. John C. Kelton

———

By Telegraph from Cairo [*Nov.*] 27 *1861*
To Capt J. C. Kelton

The rebels are fortifying New Madrid; have five hundred
(500) Negroes at work. A party of our Cavalry was yesterday
in Belmont. No enemy found on the Missouri side.

U. S. Grant

Telegram received (punctuation added), DNA, RG 94, Generals' Papers and
Books, Telegrams Received by Gen. Halleck; copy, *ibid.*, RG 393, Dept. of the
Mo., Telegrams Received. *O.R.*, I, viii, 383.

To Jesse Root Grant

———

Cairo, Illinois,
November 27th, 1861.

Dear Father:

Your letter enclosed with a shawl to Julia is just received.

In regard to your stricture about my not writing I think that
you have no cause of complaint. My time is all taken up with
public duties.

Your statement of prices at which you proposed furnishing
harness was forwarded to Maj. Allen[1] as soon as received and I
directed Lagow, who received the letter enclosing it, to inform
you of the fact. He did so at once.

I cannot take an active part in securing contracts. If I were not in the army I should do so, but situated as I am it is necessary both to my efficiency for the public good and my own reputation that I should keep clear of Government contracts.

I do not write you about plans, or the necessity of what has been done or what is doing because I am opposed to publicity in these matters. Then too you are very much disposed to criticise unfavorably from information received through the public press, a portion of which I am sorry to see can look at nothing favorably that does not look to a war upon slavery. My inclination is to whip the rebellion into submission, preserving all constitutional rights. If it cannot be whipped in any other way than through a war against slavery, let it come to that legitimately. If it is necessary that slavery should fall that the Republic may continue its existence, let slavery go. But that portion of the press that advocates the beginning of such a war now, are as great enemies to their country as if they were open and avowed secessionists.

There is a desire upon the part of people who stay securely at home to read in the morning papers, at their breakfast, startling reports of battles fought. They cannot understand why troops are kept inactive for weeks or even months. They do not understand that men have to be disciplined, arms made, transportation and provisions provided. I am very tired of the course pursued by a portion of the Union press.

Julia left last Saturday for St. Louis where she will probably spend a couple of weeks and return here should I still remain. It costs nothing for her to go there, and it may be the last opportunity she will have of visiting her father. From here she will go to Covington, and spend a week or two before going back to Galena.

It was my bay horse (cost me $140) that was shot. I also lost the little pony, my fine saddle and bridle, and the common one. What I lost cost about $250. My saddle cloth which was about half the cost of the whole, I left at home.

I try to write home about once in two weeks and think I keep it up pretty well. I wrote to you directly after the battle of Belmont, and Lagow and Julia have each written since.

Give my love to all at home. I am very glad to get letters
from home and will write as often as I can. I am somewhat
troubled lest I lose my command here, though I believe my
administration has given general satisfaction not only to those
over me but to all concerned. This is the most important command within the department however, and will probably be given
to the senior officer next to General Halleck himself.

There are not so many brigadier generals in the army as
there are brigades, and as to divisions they are nearly all commanded by brigadiers.

Yours,

ULYSSES.

J. G. Cramer, pp. 68–71.

1. See letter to Maj. Robert Allen, Oct. 7, 1861.

To Maj. Gen. Henry W. Halleck

Head Quarters, Dist. S. E. Mo.

Cairo, November 28th 1861.

Refered to Head Quarters Dept. of the Mo.

Maj. Shaler is now a prisoner at this place awaiting the
orders of Maj. Gen. Hallack. He is a cripple on cruches and not
likely to take up arms soon again.

U. S. GRANT

Brig. Gen. Com.

AES, DNA, RG 393, District of Southeast Mo., Letters Received. Written on a
letter of Nov. 25, 1861, from Brig. Gen. M. Jeff Thompson to USG. "The bearer
of this Major James R. Shaler, was and is Major of the 2nd Regiment of the
M. V. M. and was one of the Camp Jackson prisoners—and is one of the gentlemen included in the Treaty between Generals Fremont and Price—We hear that
these gentlemen are to be allowed to visit St Louis for the purpose of reporting
themselves to be regularly exchanged—If you understand the matter in this way,
you will please allow Major Shaler to pass to St Louis, and if not you will please
let him return—Major Shaler is now in no way, connected with the Missouri

State Guard or Confederate States Army, nor has he been" ALS, *ibid.* *O.R.*, II, i, 117. On Nov. 30, Capt. John C. Kelton endorsed the letter. "Major Jas. R Shaler will not be permitted to visit St Louis—He may return" AES, DNA, RG 393, District of Southeast Mo., Letters Received.

To Capt. John C. Kelton

———

Head Quarters, Dist. S. E. Mo.
Cairo, November 28th 1861.

CAPT. J. C. KELTON
A. A. GEN. DEPT. OF THE MO.
ST. LOUIS, MO.
SIR:

Yours of the 26th inst. in relation to Capt. Georges return to St. Louis is received.

Capt. George was arrested by the Picket to whom he presented himself and, as a prisoner, was brought before me. Being a Commissioned officer I confined him during his few hours stay here to the Hotel, on his own word not to leave it, and sent him a prisoner to report to the Gen. Comd.g the Department for his decission.

Altough the terms of the exchange of prisoners, entered into between Gens. Frémont and Price, would authorize the passage of Camp Jackson prisoners to the Army to which they might belong I did not interpret it as authority for them to return from the South to visit their friends and then pass our lines again.

The matter was simply refered to the Gen. Comd.g the Department, and the prisoner, a Commissioned officer, sent to St. Louis on his Parole.

Lieut. Guibor, whos name appears on the pass with Capt. Georges, did not accompany him.

I am very respectfully
Your Obt. Svt.
U. S. GRANT
Brig. Gen. Com.

ALS, DNA, RG 393, District of Southeast Mo., Letters Received. *O.R.*, II, i, 119.
See letter to Capt. William McMichael, Nov. 23, 1861.

To Capt. John C. Kelton

———

Head Quarters, Dist. S. E. Mo.
Cairo, November 28th 1861.

CAPT. J. C. KELTON
A. A. GEN. DEPT. OF THE MO.
ST. LOUIS, MO.
SIR:

I would respectfully report for the concideration of the Gen. Comd.g the Dept. that on Monday[1] last one of the two Gunboats[2] for service at this place was sent to meet two of the new ones then said to be ready to start for Cairo. None of this fleet have yet arrived.

As reported by me the rebels have one Gunboat at Columbus and are now expecting a fleet of them from New Orleans, under command of Capt. Hollins.[3] The arrival of this fleet without the floating means here of competing with them will serve materially to restore the confidance, and feeling of security, of the enemy, now, from best accounts, much shaken.

I have been much dissatisfied with the progress making upon the Gunboats being built at Mound City, and have expressed the fear that the detention upon those being built at Carondelet would prevent their being brought out this Winter. In view of the fact that the Mississippi river is usually very low in the month of December I would respectfully recommend that all the Gunboats at Carondelet be brought here as soon as practicable, and as light.

One point I would ask for information on. Many men representing themselvs as Northern men who happened to be South at the commencement of our present difficulties, and forced to enter their service, are deserting and pass our lines on their way North. Some enlist in our service but the majority make their way North. Many of them are without the means of paying their passage and I would ask, in such cases, if I am authorized to give them free passes ~~over~~ to their homes.

I am satisfied that every case that has come under my own observation the desertion has been for the purpose of escape and not to get within our lines for the purpose of gaining information.

> Respectfully
> Your Obt. Svt.
> U. S. GRANT
> Brig. Gen. Com.

P. S. Since writing the above one of the Gunboats from St. Louis has arrived.[4] The other is aground about fifteen miles above Cape Girardeau.

> U. S. GRANT

ALS, DNA, RG 393, Dept. of the Mo., Letters Received. *O.R.*, I, vii, 455.

1. Nov. 25, 1861.
2. The gunboat *Lexington. O.R.* (Navy), I, xxii, 440–42, 444.
3. C. S. A. Capt. George N. Hollins of Md., formerly U. S. Navy capt., was then commandant of the naval station at New Orleans and later commanded C. S. A. naval forces on the Mississippi River.
4. The gunboat *St. Louis*. See telegram to Flag Officer Andrew H. Foote, Nov. 22, 1861.

To Capt. John C. Kelton

> Head Quarters, Dist. S. E. Mo.
> Cairo, November 29th 1861.

CAPT. J. C. KELTON
A. A. GEN. DEPT. OF THE MO.
ST. LOUIS MO.
SIR:

I enclose you herewith a note from Gen. M. Jeff. Thompson of the Missouri State Guards, presented by his Aid-de-Camp Lt.

Col. Chappell.¹ Col. Chappell come here with a Flag of Truce sent by Gen. Polk, in charge of Col. de Russey of the so called Confederate Army.²

I informed Col. Chappell that he was at perfect liberty to return under the flag that brought him, but that he could not accompany me to Cairo except as a prisoner, to await the action of the Gen. Comd.g the Department. He chose to accompany me and is now a prisoner here.

He expressed a particular desire to visit St. Louis, as a prisoner or otherwise, under any restrictions, to bear dispatches which he has directed to Maj. Gen. Hallack.

The matter is respectfully refered to the Commander of the Department for his decission.

> Very respectfully
> Your Obt. Svt.
> U. S. GRANT
> Brig. Gen. Com.

ALS, DNA, RG 393, Dept. of the Mo., Letters Received. *O.R.*, II, i, 525. On Dec. 3, 1861, Capt. John H. Hammond wrote to USG. "I have the honor to inform you that Lieut. Colonel Chappell cannot be permitted to come to Saint Louis. He may be returned under a flag of truce, and any dispatches he may have for the Commanding General, you can forward in the usual manner." Copies, DLC-USG, V, 7, 8; DNA, RG 393, USG Hd. Qrs. Correspondence; *ibid.*, Dept. of the Mo., Letters Sent. *O.R.*, II, i, 527. Other copies of the same letter, misdated Dec. 30, are in DLC-USG, V, 4, 5, 7, 8, 9; DNA, RG 393, USG Hd. Qrs. Correspondence.

1. On Nov. 27, Brig. Gen. M. Jeff Thompson wrote to USG. "I send Lieut Col Wm C. Chappell with a letter to Major General Halleck, in reference to the Officers of the S. B. Platte Valley—Col Chappell carries also a letter to my Brother in Law, John J. Abell of St Joseph, Mo—This letter you will please peruse—I assure you that it is strictly on private family matters, and has no reference, directly or indirectly, to military or political affairs—and if it is consistent with your sense of duty please forward it to its direction—I would request that Col—Chappell be allowed to proceed to St. Louis, under such restrictions as you may see fit to impose, to bear the letter to Genl. Halleck—so that if my Wife shall be allowed to come to me, he may escort her You will find that he is strictly honourable, and will take no advantage of your confidence—" ALS, *ibid.*, Dept. of the Mo., Letters Received. *O.R.*, II, i, 525.
2. On Nov. 29, Maj. Gen. Leonidas Polk wrote to USG. "This will be handed you by Col De Russey of my Staff who is in command of the Flag of Truce

under which he goes to you. He is accompanied by other officers by my permission, and will present to you the gentleman who is the bearer of the particular subject of the Flag." ALS, DNA, RG 393, Dept. of the Mo., Letters Received. *O.R.*, II, i, 525.

To Capt. John C. Kelton

Head Quarters, Dist. S. E. Mo.
Cairo, November 29th 1861

CAPT. J. C. KELTON
A. A. GEN. DEPT. OF THE MISSOURI
ST LOUIS MO
SIR:

Enclosed herewith please find a letter sent me from Columbus this day by Flag of Truce, from Maj. Gen. Polk. The letter fully explains itself.

In view of the fact that Gen. Polk permitted the families of two of the officers wounded at Belmont to visit them I would respectfully recommend that the exchange asked for be made, if practicable.

Respectfully
Your Obt. Svt.
U. S. GRANT
Brig. Gen. Com.

ALS, Mrs. Walter Love, Flint, Mich. *O.R.*, II, i, 524. On Nov. 29, 1861, C. S. A. Maj. Gen. Leonidas Polk wrote to USG. "I hope that the courtesy shown to the families of two of your wounded Officers may furnish a justification for the application covered by the Flag of Truce now sent you. If consistent with your views of public duty, in any way to aid in the accomplishment of the object sought, it would be grateful to the feelings of the parties most deeply interested. I avail of the occasion to say, that there is a young man, a private, whose name is John Groves, who was wounded and taken prisoner at Cheat Mountain, who is now in Columbus Ohio, who I desire to exchange for; if this can be effected, I should be pleased to offer any one of like rank in my hands for him." LS, DNA, RG 94, Letters Received; ADfS, *ibid.*, RG 109, Polk Papers. *O.R.*, II, i, 524. On Dec. 3, Capt. John H. Hammond wrote to USG. "In reply to your favor of November 29th, enclosing letter from General Polk, I have the honor to inform you that your letter and enclosure, have been referred to the Commander in Chief at

Washington." Copies, DLC-USG, V, 7, 8, VIA, 2; DNA, RG 393, USG Hd. Qrs. Correspondence; *ibid.*, Dept. of the Mo., Letters Sent. *O.R.*, II, i, 527. Other copies of the same letter, misdated Dec. 30, are in DLC-USG, V, 4, 5, 7, 8, 9; DNA RG 393, USG Hd. Qrs. Correspondence. On Dec. 10, Brig. Gen. Lorenzo Thomas wrote to Maj. Gen. Henry W. Halleck. "The General-in-Chief desires that the proposition of General Polk, dated November 29, for the exchange of a young man named John Groves, detained as a prisoner at Columbus, Ohio, be acceded to. General Polk's letter was forwarded by Brig. Gen.l Grant from Cairo." Copy, *ibid.*, RG 94, Letters Sent. *O.R.*, II, i, 529. On Dec. 16, Capt. John C. Kelton sent Thomas' letter to USG. "General Grant will have this order carried into effect immediately." Copies, DLC-USG, V, 7, 79; DNA, RG 393, USG Hd. Qrs. Correspondence. See letter to Commanding Officer, Military Prison, Columbus, Ohio, Dec. 19, 1861.

To Capt. John C. Kelton

Head Quarters, Dist. S. E. Mo.
Cairo, November 29th 1861

Capt. J. C. Kelton
A. A. Gen. Dept. of the Missouri
St. Louis, Mo.
Sir:

I have here two prisoners arrested as Spies who are un-doubtedly guilty of the charge. One of them can be proven to have been engaged in carrying information from Sympathizers in Southern Illinois ~~and~~ to the troops at Columbus, Ky.[1]

As the evidence against these prisoners will be more easily obtained here than in St. Louis I would recommend that their trial take place here.

Information from Columbus to-day is to the effect that the rebels have three gunboats. They are small, carrying but four guns each, but I have no information as to their strength.

The state of Mississippi has called for 10,000 state troops, for sixty days, to assist in the defence of Columbus.[2] There seems to be a great effort making throughout the south to make Columbus impregnable.

I get this information from the Memphis Appeal of the 28th,

(yesterday), a copy of which I received this evening. I give the information for what it is worth.

> Respectfully
> Your Obt. Svt.
> U. S. GRANT
> Brig. Gen. Com.

ALS, DNA, RG 393, Dept. of the Mo., Letters Received. *O.R.*, I, vii, 460. On Dec. 4, 1861, Capt. John C. Kelton replied to USG. "In reply to your letter of the 29th ult., I have to inform you that Gen'l Halleck directs you to hold the two spies in close imprisonment at Cairo, till they can be tried by a military commission. You will prefer charges those spies, which, with a list of eight officers you may consider suitable for their trials, from which the General will select, you will forward to these Head Quarters." LS, DNA, RG 393, District of Southeast Mo., Letters Received; copy, *ibid.*, Dept. of the Mo., Letters Sent. Kelton's letter is misdated Nov. 4 *ibid.*, USG Hd. Qrs. Correspondence; DLC-USG, V, 7, 8, 9. See letter to Capt. John C. Kelton, Dec. 8, 1861.

1. The *Cairo Gazette*, Dec. 5, 1861, reported the recent arrest of B. F. Lowe of Williamson County, Ill., who was alleged to have made at least two trips between his home and Columbus, where he was at the time of the battle of Belmont. The *Gazette* reported that there was "sufficient evidence against him to prove him a spy."

2. On Nov. 21, Governor John J. Pettus of Miss. called for sixty day vols., not to exceed 10,000, to defend Columbus "or any other threatened position." *O.R.*, I, vii, 688–89.

To Col. Richard J. Oglesby

——

> Head Quarters Dist S. E. Mo
> Cairo Nov 29th 1861

COL R. J. OGLESBY
COMDG 2ND BRIGADE
BIRDS POINT, MO
COL

Capt Greenly[1] 31st Ill Vols has just made complaint that some of the men sent by your order to Sister Island for the purpose of getting logs, left their party and visited the house occupied by his family and abused a Girl living there; also killed some twenty hogs belonging to neighbors. Further they stopped some citizens and took from them their guns. These outrages must be punished. The senior officer of the expedition must be arrested, and charges preferred, and no more parties are to be sent without a Field Officers accompanying them.

The Officer in command will be held strictly accountable for the conduct of his men, and where they are caught in such acts, they should be shot upon the spot.

Yours &c

U. S. GRANT

Brig Genl Comdg

Copies, DLC-USG, V, 1, 2, 3, 79; DNA, RG 393, USG Letters Sent. On Nov. 29, 1861, Capt. John A. Rawlins wrote to Col. Richard J. Oglesby. "I am instructed, by the Brig. Genl. Comdg. to say, charges of a heinous nature, being prefered against Private Peter Kelly of Co "E" 8th Regt. Ill. Vols. you will cause him to be arrested, put in Irons, and sent to Cairo Ill *at once*, where in due time he will be turned over to the civil authorities for trial and punishment" Copies, DLC-USG, V, 1, 2, 3, 77; DNA, RG 393, USG Letters Sent. On the same day, Rawlins wrote to the officer of the day. "The Bearer of this order has in charge Private Peter Kelly Co "E" 8th Regt. Ill Vols, a prisoner, whom you will cause to be put in Irons, and closely guarded, until further orders from these Head Quarters" Copies, DLC-USG, V, 2, 77; DNA, RG 393, USG Letters Sent. On Dec. 1, Rawlins again wrote to the officer of the day. "The Bearer of this order has in charge, Private John Bachman of Company "I" 8th Regt. Ill. Vols, a prisoner whom you will cause to be put in Irons and closely guarded, until further orders from these Head Quarters. if you have no Irons, you will procure them as soon as practicable, for this prisoner and Peter Kelly of the same Regt." Copies, *ibid.* On Dec. 31, Rawlins wrote to Capt. Orsamus Greenlee. "If you desire to prosecute, Private Peter Kelly Co "E" 8th Ill Vols, and John Bachman Co "I" same Regt., said to have been guilty of offences, committed in this County, while engaged in getting out Logs for Winter Quarters, to which you called the attention of the General Commanding this District, about the 29th ult., you will give notice to this office to that effect '*immediately*,' otherwise they will be discharged from custody, they having been in confinement since the 29th ult." Copies, DLC-USG, V, 1, 2, 3, 79; DNA, RG 393, USG Letters Sent. Private Peter Kelly of Peoria, Ill., died at Cairo on Feb. 18, 1863; Private John Bachman of Peoria served until mustered out on July 30, 1864.

1. Capt. Orsamus Greenlee of Cairo, 31st Ill.

To Col. Leonard F. Ross

————

Head Quarters Dist. S. E. Mo
Cairo Nov 29th 1861

Col L Ross
17th Ill Vols
Cape Girardeau Mo
Col

Enclosed herewith I send you accounts made by your command, whilst at Fort Jefferson, for your approval or remarks

I would state that the Quarter Master of the command should have (if he did not) taken up the Corn destroyed, same as if purchased, and fed it out to the public animals in his charge and expended it same as forage procured by purchase or on receipts

Respectfully
Your Obt. Servt
U. S. Grant
Brig Genl Comg

Copies, DLC-USG, V, 1, 2, 3, 79; DNA, RG 393, USG Letters Sent.

To Capt. Thomas J. Haines

————

Head Quarters Dist. S. E. Mo
Cairo Nov 29th 1861

Capt. Haynes
A. C. S. St Louis Mo
Sir

The contract for baking bread for the troops of this command, expires tomorrow, but will be continued for a few days to see if a satisfactory arrangement can be made. I am assured that the contractor is losing money by the present arrangement. From my experience in the management of Bake Houses, as

Comy. in the Army,[1] I suppose, that at the present low rate of flour, making the savings from baking of but little value, the great cost of building ovens, and high wages of hands, this must be so.

If the present arrangement is broken up it will be nescessary to hire these bake houses at a high rent, buy them or build new ones.

On the whole I am firmly of the opinion, that the most economical course to pursue is to make such arrangement as will secure the present system of furnishing bread.

If we had entirely a regular army, or if the present supply was expected to be required for any great length of time, I would not recommend this course

> Respectfully &c.
> U. S. GRANT
> Brig Genl Comg

Copies, DLC-USG, V, 1, 2, 3, 79; DNA, RG 393, USG Letters Sent. Capt. Thomas J. Haines of N. H., USMA 1849, was appointed chief commissary, Dept. of the Mo., on Nov. 30, 1861. See letter to Capt. Thomas J. Haines, Dec. 17, 1861.

1. During the Mexican War, USG as commissary officer had rented a bakery to turn flour rations into bread at a considerable profit to the regt. fund. *Memoirs,* I, 180. In June, 1861, USG discussed the possibility of taking a contract for bread. *Garland,* pp. 168–69; J. L. Ringwalt, *Anecdotes of General Ulysses S. Grant* (Philadelphia, 1886), p. 25.

To Jesse Root Grant

Cairo, Illinois
November 29th 1861

DEAR FATHER,

Your letter asking if Mr. Leathers can be passed South, and also enclosing two extracts from papers is received.

It is entirely out of the question to pass persons South. We have many Union Men sacrificing their lives now from exposure, as well as battle, in a cause brought about by Secession and it is necessary for the security of the thousands still exposed that all communication should be cut off between the two sections.

As to that article in the Hawk Eye it gives me no uneasiness whatever. The Iowa Regiment done its duty fully and my report gives it full credit. All who were on the battle field know where Gen. McClernand and my self were and it needs no resort to the Public press for our vindication.[1] The other extract gives our loss in killed and wounded almost exactly correct. Our missing however is only three or four over one hundred. Recent information ~~information~~ received through deserters shows that the rebel loss from killed wounded and missing reaches about 2500. One thing is certain, after the battle about one third of Columbus was used for Hospitals and many were removed to houses in the country. There was also two Steamboat loads sent to Memphis and the largest Hotel in the city taken as a Hospital[.] The city was put in mourning and all business suspended for a day: and the citizen thrown into the greatest consternation lest they would be attacked.

I wrote to you two days ago[2] therefore it is not necessary to write a long letter.

I believe I told you that Julia had gone to St. Louis. Will pay you a short visit before returning to Galena.

ULYSSES.

ALS, PPRF.

1. On Nov. 9, 1861, the *Burlington* (Iowa) *Daily Hawk-Eye* complained editorially that the role of the 7th Iowa at Belmont had been slighted in newspaper accounts, a charge repeated in subsequent issues. On Nov. 22, the *Hawk-Eye* stated that "Generals Grant and McClernand, at the battle of Belmont, were never nearer the rebel battery than the Hospital, one and a half miles distant . . . that the shooting of Grant's horse was by three straggling secessionists, after the batteries had been taken and when there was no engagement going on."

The battle of Belmont provoked considerable newspaper debate as to whether it was a victory or a defeat. Newspaper coverage of USG is analyzed in Anna Maclay Green, "Civil War Public Opinion of General Grant," *Journal of the Illinois State Historical Society*, XXII, 1 (April, 1929), 1–64. This survey, which covers four New York City and three Ohio newspapers, can be supplemented by Barnard K. Leiter, "A Study of the Relationship between General Ulysses S. Grant and various Illinois Newspapers covering the period June, 1861, to March, 1864," (unpublished masters' thesis, Southern Illinois University, 1964).

2. See letter to Jesse Root Grant, Nov. 27, 1861.

To Capt. John C. Kelton

By Telegraph from Cairo Nov. 30 *1861*
To Capt J C Kelton
A letter received from Gov. Yates requests that the forty-eight (th) Ills. be sent to Shawneetown. This Regt was sent here at my request before being entirely full. Shall I pay any attention to the request of the Governor? We require all the troops we have and more.

U. S. Grant
Brig. Genl.

Telegram received, DNA, RG 94, Generals' Papers and Books, Telegrams Received by Gen. Halleck. On Nov. 25, 1861, Governor Richard Yates wrote to USG "in reference to ordering the 48th Ill. Inf. Vols. to Shawneetown to reorganize." *Ibid.*, RG 393, USG Register of Letters Received. On Nov. 30, Capt. John C. Kelton wrote to USG. "The Commanding General directs me to say in reply to your telegram of this date, to keep the 48th Illinois Regiment subject only to his or your orders." Copies, DLC-USG, V, 4, 5, 7, 8, 9; DNA, RG 393, USG Hd. Qrs. Correspondence. Kelton also telegraphed the same instructions. Copies, *ibid.* On Dec. 2, Capt. John A. Rawlins wrote to Col. Isham N. Haynie. "I am instructed by Brig. Genl Grant to say, in compliance with the following order received this morning by telegraph from Dept. Hd. Qrs. . . . Your command will remain here and not move to Shawneetown, as ~~requested by~~ previously contemplated" Copies, DLC-USG, V, 1, 2, 3, 77; DNA, RG 393, USG Letters Sent; *ibid.*, RG 94, 48th Ill., Letterbook.

To Flag Officer Andrew H. Foote

Cairo, November 30, 1861.
To Commodore Foote.
Two or three rebel gun-boats have made a reconnoissance down the Tennessee. General Smith[1] requests that a gun-boat from here be sent. I have none.

U. S. Grant.

Telegram, James Mason Hoppin, *Life of Andrew Hull Foote, Rear-Admiral United States Navy* (New York, 1874), p. 162. On Nov. 29, 1861, Brig. Gen.

Charles F. Smith wrote to USG. "The enemy's gunboats (two or three) are said to ~~having~~ have made a reconnaissance below Fort Henry on the Tennessee. By reconnaissance I suppose is really meant they were making a trial trip. If you can spare me a gun boat for a few days I should like to send her and the Conestoga to look after this river craft. If you cannot please send this to Flag Off.r *Foote*, also telegraph him. Our line to Cairo has not been in working order for two days. I wish you would do me the favor to speak to the Superintendent at Cairo about this." ALS, DNA, RG 393, District of Southeast Mo., Letters Received. On Nov. 30, Smith telegraphed to USG. "The Conestoga returned this morning from up the Tennessee; neither saw nor heard of Rebel Gunboats. She has gone with three Companies & a Howitzer to Cave in Rock to look after Rebels at Caseyville. I want another Gunboat." Telegram received (punctuation added), *ibid.*, Dept. of the Mo., Telegrams Received. On Nov. 30, Flag Officer Andrew H. Foote telegraphed to USG. "In case two Gunboats cannot be sent to the Tennessee River and the enemys boats are larger than ours, would it not be well to block up the river. Genl Smith & Lieut. Comdg. Phelps have formerly been consulted about these—I hope to leave for Cairo in the Benton last Gunboat on Tuesday or early on Wednesday. If two Gunboats can be sent please telegraph me. I am consulting with Genl. Halleck" Copy, *ibid.*, RG 45, Area 5. *O.R.* (Navy), I, xxii, 447–48.

1. Misprinted "Small" in Hoppin.

To Col. John Cook

Head Quarters Dist. S. E. Mo
Cairo November 30th 1861

Col. J Cook
Comdg. U. S. Forces
Fort Holt Ky
Col

You will please detail one commissioned, one non-commissioned [*officer*] & fifteen privates to accompany the Steamer D. G. Taylor to St Louis and back

Select a commissioned officer of efficiency, and sober well behaved men. There has been great complaint against the Guard sent down from St Louis

Send four days rations for the Guard

Yours &c
U. S. Grant
Brig. Genl. Comdg.

Copies, DLC-USG, V, 1, 2, 3, 77; DNA, RG 393, USG Letters Sent. On Nov. 30, 1861, Capt. John A. Rawlins wrote to Brig. Gen. John A. McClernand. "I am directed by the General Comdg. to request that you cause to be detailed at once forty (40) men to assist in unloading Commissary Stores, from Steamer D. G. Taylor, they will report to Capt. R. C. Rutherford ~~Post~~ asst. Commissary Cairo Ils" LS, McClernand Papers, IHi.

To Capt. Reuben C. Rutherford

———

Head Quarters Dist. S. E. Mo
Cairo Nov 30th 1861

Capt. R. C. Rutherford
Post Comy.
Sir

Send by Steamer Key Stone to Mr J Mitchell, Cave in Rock Ill the following articles of Comy Stores "to wit"

One barrel of Pork, 100 lbs Ham or Shoulders.

Two barrels of flour, 100 lbs Coffee, 200 lbs Sugar.

Mr J. Mitchell is running his Ferry night and day, to bring Union men, who are driven from their homes in Ky. and has at times, over fifty of these unfortunates people subsisting at his house, the majority of whom, have nothing to compensate him with

U. S. Grant
Brig. Genl Comdg.

Copies, DLC-USG, V, 1, 2, 3, 77; DNA, RG 393, USG Letters Sent. See letter to Brig. Gen. John A. McClernand, Nov. 18, 1861, note 3.

To Charles De Arnaud

———

Head Quarters, Dist. S. E. Mo.
Cairo, November 30th 1861

CHARLES DE ARNAUD,

SIR:

In reply to your request, and the note from Major Gen. Hallack, presented me by yourself, I can state that I took possession of Paducah, Ky. solely on information given by yourself, and to the effect that the rebels were marching upon that city with a large force. This information I afterwards had reason to believe was fully verified; first, because as we approached the city secession flags were flying, and the citizens seemed much disappointed that Southern troops, expected by them, were not in in advance of us. It was understood that they would arrive that day.

I also understood afterwards that a force of some 4,000 Confederate troops were actually on their way for Paducah when taken possession of by my order.

A point through which many valuable supplies were obtained, for the Southern Army, was cut off by this move, and a large quantity of provisions, leather &c. supposed to be for the use of the Southern Army captured.

For the value, and use to which these were put, I refer you to Gen. Paine who I left in command.—Only remaining in Paducah a few hours, and being busily engaged with other matters during that time, I can make no estimate of the cash value of the stores captured.

Yours &c.
U. S. GRANT
Brig. Gen. Com.

ALS, DNA, RG 94, Vol. Service Branch, No. 10086. See telegram to Maj. Gen. John C. Frémont, Sept. 5, 1861. On Oct. 6, and again on Oct. 23, 1861, Charles de Arnaud was paid $300 by order of Maj. Gen. John C. Frémont "for secret service." *SRC*, 56-2-2492, p. 9. On Nov. 18, de Arnaud wrote to Maj. Gen.

Henry W. Halleck stating that he had received funds for "traveling expenses," and asking, "what you think should be the amount of compensation properly my due." *Ibid.* On Nov. 20, Capt. William McMichael replied for Halleck "that any claims you may have for secret services rendered must be made to the officer who employed you." *Ibid.* The Halleck note to which USG refers has not been found.

De Arnaud also secured a letter of endorsement from Frémont, dated Jan. 2, 1862. "This is to certify that Mr. Charles d'Arnaud was employed by me from about the 1st of August in travelling throughout the rebel parts of Tennessee & Kentucky with the object of ascertaining the strength condition and probable movements of the rebel forces. He made under my direction many such journeys, reporting fully & in detail upon the force of the various encampments and the condition and strength of garrisons and various works in Tennessee & along the Mississippi river. He obtained this information at much personal risk & with singular intelligence, & performed the duties entrusted to him entirely to my satisfaction. He continued on this duty until the termination of my command in the Western Dept. His services were valuable to the government & I consider him entitled to the largest consideration that the government allows in such cases or to such agents." ALS, DNA, RG 94, Vol. Service Branch, No. 10086. On Jan. 6, Flag Officer Andrew H. Foote wrote to President Abraham Lincoln. "The bearer, Charles De Arnaud, has, to my knowledge, rendered important services to the Government. He, at the risk of his life, gave information which led to our capture of Paducah, Ky., in advance of the rebels; thereby he saved the country thousands of lives and millions of dollars. I fully indorse his certificate of Maj. Gen. J. C. Frémont. He is entitled to the largest remuneration the Government pays for such services." *SRC,* 56-2-2492, p. 11. On the same day, de Arnaud prepared a bill for $3,600. *Ibid.,* p. 10. USG's letter was endorsed by U.S. Representative Francis P. Blair, Jr. "I cannot see how the Government can avoid paying this claim Gen.l Frémont had authority to employ this gentleman & certifies as also does Grant to the rendition of important & valuable service, & the Government is bound to pay the sum claimed which is not considered unreasonable" On Jan. 13, Lincoln added his endorsement. "I have no time to investigate this claim; but I desire the accounting officers to investigate it, and if it be found just and equitable, to pay it, notwithstanding any want of technical legality or form." The following day, Secretary of War Simon Cameron added his endorsement. "I have considered this claim and cannot bring my mind to the conclusion that the sum charged is not exorbitant. I am willing to allow $2,000—in full of the claim & the Dis Clk War Dept. is authorized to pay Charles De Arnaud that sum." Accordingly, de Arnaud was paid "$2,000 in full for the above account." *Ibid.,* p. 11.

The nature of de Arnaud's services to USG and Frémont is obscured by his subsequent insanity and fantastic claims. On June 23, 1871, he wrote to USG, then President, from Cincinnati, discussing his services and asking additional compensation. *Ibid.,* pp. 32–33. No action resulted, and de Arnaud disappeared for fourteen years. In 1885, de Arnaud began an extraordinary campaign for compensation and recognition. At least nine times between 1887 and 1901 bills were introduced in Congress to provide him with either medals or money. During this time he was convicted of defrauding a widow in a real estate transaction and indicted in D.C. for claiming a pension under the name of Capt. Alfred Arnaud, 5th Mo., who was a completely different person. Evidence was introduced that, between 1862 and 1887, perhaps for nearly the entire quarter century, de Arnaud was in a mental asylum in Germany under the name of Roman Adolf

Schmideberg. He later claimed that his hallucinations resulted from wounds received in U.S. service, thus strengthening his claims for compensation. Numerous government records concerning de Arnaud are conveniently summarized in *SRC*, 56-2-2492. Because neither his honesty nor his sanity can be trusted, the nature of his services cannot be appraised. Available C. S. A. military records do not indicate plans for the occupation of Paducah.

To Capt. John C. Kelton

Head Quarters, Dist. S. E. Mo.
Cairo, December 1st 1861.

Capt. J. C. Kelton
A. A. Gen. Dept. of the Missouri,
St. Louis, Mo.
Sir:

Bishop Major General Polk's three gunboats made a Sundays excursion up to see us this evening, fired five or six shots when within about half a mile of range of the nearest point of the Camp at Fort Holt, and returned as soon as replied to. Our gunboats followed them seven or eight miles but could not get near enough to engage them.[1]

I would respectfully submit it to the Gen. Comd.g the Department whether the Hospital facilities at this place, and at Mound City, should not be increased in advance of the demand for more room. The Hospitals are sufficiently commodious for all that are sick at present, and have a very suitable supply of evrything required, except perhaps blankets. By adding bedsteads & bedding the accomodations can be given for about three hundred & fifty more.

I have received Invoice & Bill of Lading of 4000 stand of French Muskets, with accoutrement complete, for them, from the East. These with 4000 stand of improved arms which I understand are to be sent for Gen. McClernand's Brigade will supply this command, or nearly so.

There is much difficulty experienced here in finding storage for our Commissary supplies. I caused to be rented some months ago a very large and conveniently arranged Wharfboat for this purpose. It will store, conveniently for issue, two & a half millions of rations, with office room and apartments overhead sufficient for the A. C. S. and his assistants. This boat could be moved down the river at any time if required.

When the gun boat fleet began to receive their supplies Commodore Foote made application for this storage room and obtained an order for it.[2] At that time I looked upon it as necessary for their use. Now however they have a large receiving Steamer[3] which in my judgement will accommodate all their stores, and be quite, if not more convenient than the Wharfboat. For this reason, and the fact that a large amount of provisions are now on the way, or soon will be, I would recommend that the order transfering this boat be rescinded. Otherwise a large portion of the stores to arrive will have to be stored on the landing, without shelter.

If Commodore Foote was here in person I think he would not object to making the arrangement asked, without the issuing of an order.

Respectfully
Your Obt. Svt.
U. S. Grant
Brig. Gen. Com

ALS, DNA, RG 393, Dept. of the Mo., Letters Received. *O.R.*, I, vii, 462–63. On Dec. 1, 1861, USG also telegraphed to Capt. John C. Kelton. "We have just had a visit from three 3 Rebel Gun Boats exchanged four 4 or five 5 Shots" Copies, DNA, RG 94, Generals' Papers and Books, Telegrams Received by Gen. Halleck; *ibid.*, RG 393, Dept. of the Mo., Telegrams Received. On Dec. 4, Kelton replied to USG. "In reply to communication of 1st inst., I am directed to say that the requisition for Post Surgeon will be promptly attended to. The Commissary of Subsistence at St. Louis has been directed to furnish suitable accommodations for storage of supplies." Copies, DLC-USG, V, 4, 5, 7, 8, 9; DNA, RG 393, USG Hd. Qrs. Correspondence; *ibid.*, Dept. of the Mo., Letters Sent.

1. On Dec. 1, Commander Benjamin M. Dove, of the *Maria Denning*, telegraphed to Flag Officer Andrew H. Foote. "Three gunboats appeared below Bird's Point, exchanged shots with Fort Holt, but out of range. Went down with

General Grant; sent the *Lexington* to follow them up." *O.R.* (Navy), I, xxii, 448. Also on Dec. 1, Col. John Cook wrote to USG. "At 3.15 P. M. Lieut Mathie Comd'g. Co. F, 7th Ills, Officer of the Day, reported to these Head Quarters the approach of three Rebel Gun Boats, names unknown, which were allowed to reach a distance of four and a half miles from Fort Holt, when deeming it imprudent to allow them to progress further the batteries were ordered to open upon them, the first shot being fired from Fort Holt on the extreme right of the fortifications, for the purpose of drawing a fire from the enemy, in order to test the power of his Artillery, which having been done the sixty four pounder ('Lady Grant') in Battery on the extreme left returned his fire dropping the first Shot within two hundred yards in advance of the Boat. The second Boat returning our fire, plainly showing the inadequacy of both guns and Artillerists to Cope with us at any shorter distance. The 64 Pdr Comd by Lieut Woods (McAllisters Artillery) was managed with marked ability although laboring under great disadvantages, the pieces being only provided with ammunition for 32 pdrs. I am confident that had we been supplied with ammunition adapted to the Caliber of the Gun, we could have done much damage to the enemy before he could have retreated. To elevate to such an extent as would enable us to reach him with a shot, (there being no known rule to establish the Angle) caused us in two instances to overshoot him; the shot from the Gun Boats always falling greatly short of us. On the approach of these Rebel Crafts a detachment from Capt Delano's Cavalry together with one company from the 28th Ills were ordered to proceed (the former as far as Ft Jefferson) as a reconnoitering party, with instructions to report by messenger anything that would reveal the intentions of the enemy, and the latter beyond the picket line deployed as skirmishers to guard against an unexpected attack in the rear of the Fort. Both of which have returned assuring me of the entire absence of any armed force about or around the Camp. All of which is most respectfully submitted." ALS, DNA, RG 94, War Records Office, Union Battle Reports. *O.R.*, I, vii, 6–7. The demonstration may have been ordered by C. S. A. Brig. Gen. Gideon J. Pillow while temporarily in command at Columbus. On Dec. 2, Pillow suggested an attack on Bird's Point, Fort Holt, and Cairo. *Ibid.*, p. 731.

2. See telegram to Capt. Chauncey McKeever, Oct. 20, 1861.

3. The receiving ship *Maria Denning*, ordered from St. Louis to Cairo on Nov. 9, arrived on Nov. 20. *O.R.* (Navy), I, xxii, 433–37. On Nov. 20, Commander Roger Perry wrote to Foote. "*Maria Denning* arrived at 9 a. m.; all of her cargo is on the wharf boat except the guns, which await the movements of the commissary stores." *Ibid.*, p. 437. On Nov. 24, Capt. Chauncey McKeever wrote to Foote. "The order to give over the *Graham*, wharf boat, was not countermanded, but suspended until a place could be procured for the commissary stores. I have ordered that it be turned over to you immediately." *Ibid.*, p. 442.

On Dec. 6, Capt. John A. Rawlins wrote to Brig. Gen. John A. McClernand. "I am instructed by the Genl Comdg. to request that you cause to be detailed from your command, *forty men* for duty at the Graham Wharf Boat, for the removal of Commissary Stores—The detail will report to Commissary at Wharf Boat, tomorrow the 7th inst at 8"o.clock A. M. and will be continued from day to day until the Stores are removed. You will have detail ordered at once with directions to report promptly, at the hour above named, as it is absolutely nescessary that the Stores should be removed, as soon as the same can be done." LS, McClernand Papers, IHi. On the same day, Rawlins wrote to Capt. William W. Leland. "You will immediately turn over, and surrender to the Navy Department, at this place, the Graham Wharf Boat, now occupied by you for Storage of Commissary Stores and Officers All Commissary Stores, will be removed from the same at once" Copies, DLC–USG, V, 1, 2, 3, 77; DNA, RG 393, USG Letters Sent. On Dec. 7, Leland wrote to USG. "According to your Order, dated Dec. 6th, I have this day vacated the Graham Wharf Boat and Offices, heretofore occupied by the Commissary Department, and have surrendered them to the Navy Department. The Commissary Stores and office have been removed to the Steamer 'New Uncle Sam.' " LS, *ibid.*, District of Cairo, Letters Received.

To Capt. John C. Kelton

Head Quarters, Dist. S. E. Mo.
Cairo, December 2d 1861.

Capt. J. C. Kelton,
A. A. Gen. Dept. of the Missouri,
St. Louis, Mo.
Sir:

Enclosed herewith I send you a letter from Col. Ross on the subject of Winter Quarters, change of Cavalry, ordering a General Court Martial &c.[1] I would respectfully call the attention of the Gen. Commanding to the subject of Winter Quarters.

I received instructions from Gen. Frémont, whilst he was in command, on the subject.[2] Under instructions then received Winter Quarters for the command here are being rapidly completed.

I visited Cape Girardeau and gave such verbal directions as I thought would secure winter Quarters for the troops at that place at a very small outlay.

The Cavalry complained of belong to Gen. Sigel's[3] Brigade and such complaints have been made against them, for their Marauding propensities that I would recommend mustering them out of service.

There seems to have been no provision made in the Acts of Congress organizing our Volunteer System for manning our

Siege batteries other than to take Companies authorized as Light Artillery Companies. All these manifest a great desire to get their batteries and do not like to remain in fortifications.

In view of these facts I authorized Lieut. Powell of the 20th Ill. Volunteers, and Act. Engineer on the works at Cape Girardeau, to raise a Siege Company out of the Missouri Home Guards, that were on duty there.[4] I also authorized the Commanding officer of the Battalion of Home Guards, Colonel, now Capt. Murdock to raise another Company of Cavalry or Infantry from the same men, subject to the approval of higher authority.[5]

These men were at Cape Girardeau, by authority of the Commander of the Department, when I was assigned to this command. Most of them are Missourians who could not return to their homes, and who could not have ~~staid~~ remained at home from the first, and remained loyal.

These companies are about full and could be filled to the maximum, if authorized, in a very short time. They have never been mustered into the United States service but are ready to be whenever Authority to do so is given.

I would respectfully ask to have this act legalized and these troops received. They have already been in service some four or five months, as Home Guards, and under their present organization.

Since writing the above the J. D. Perry has arrived having landed at Prices puting ashore a large amount of freight. I understand that the authority to do so was given by the Provost Martial of St. Louis.

There is great danger of loosing our boats by making these landings and all the Union men from this section of the state have been driven out by Thompson and his band.

I have ordered the Capt. of the Steamer J. D. Perry to disregard all orders to land on the Mo. shore between Cape Girardeau & this place unless given by the Commanding officer of the Department or myself.[6]

Should it be necessary for freight to go to Charleston Mo. it can be landed at Birds Point and go out by rail more economically than by any other route.

I enclose herewith report of Col. Oglesby, Comd.g at Birds Point, just received.[7]

> Respectfully
> Your Obt. Svt.
> U. S. GRANT
> Brig. Gen. Com

ALS, DNA, RG 393, Dept. of the Mo., Letters Received. *O.R.*, I, vii, 464–65.

1. Apparently two letters. On Nov. 30, 1861, Col. Leonard F. Ross wrote to USG. "When Col—Plummer left here yesterday—he informed me that there was an order here from you—directing a 'Court Martial'—to convene at this place—I have been unable to find the Order—or any authority for calling a '*Court Martial*'—from you—There are charges on file here against some forty persons —most of whom are confined, awaiting trial—Will you not—At an early day— order a 'Court Martial'—that these cases may be disposed of" Copy, DNA, RG 393, Post of Cape Girardeau, Letters Sent. On Dec. 1, Ross again wrote to USG. "Your Order of the 26th Ult—for the return of two *Horses* to Mr Hawkins is recd.—and an Order issued on the Quartermaster for the return of the property— The Horses were taken—I am informed—by Lieut Wilson of the Mo 11th. But my information is that no blame should attach to him—As they were supposed to be a part of the same property that had been taken from the '*Hunter Farm*' near Benton—and secreted by the parties taking it with the intention—as was supposed—of applying it to their own use—A party under Lieut Wilson—was sent down by Col Plummer to seize the property—and turn it over to the Post— Hawkins Horses were taken at the time—under the impression that they were a part of the 'Hunter Horses.' Permit me—General—at this time to call your attention to the matter of *Winter Quarters*—for the troops—to winter at this place—Before Col Plummer left—he gave Orders for fitting up a couple of Mills, above town—one for seven Companies of the Mo—11th—The other for seven Companies of my Regiment—the remainder to be placed in, and about—the Forts—I have several objections to this arrangement—1st It will throw the main body of our troops—away from our lines of defences—2d It will be inconvenient, and laborious, to carry Wood, ~~and~~ Water, and provisions up five pairs of stairs— Then it will be dangerous on account of fire   It would be unhealthy for so many —to be thrown together in a building—It will be about as expensive to fit them up in good order—as to build them Barracks   The Floor in the Mill assigned to my Regt. is open—and would have to be relaid and the cracks covered—to prevent—dirt from falling through from the upper Stories   Our tents in my opinion would be preferable to the Mills—I understand from Col Plummer, that the objection to building Barracks—is the expense. It will not be expensive—Our men can do nearly all the work—The Lumber can be purchas[ed] at ten Dollars per thousand ft—So I am informed by Lieut Shields—Then a considerable portion

of the Lumber used for Barracks—could probably be sold at the end of the war for near what it would cost at this time   If you will allow me a little discretion—in this matter—I feel confident, there will be no objection taken to the work, on the score of expense—And the troops will be in the right place in case of attack—The first and second Stories of the mill might be occupied by troops—and might answer very well for the Cavalry—Permit me also to make a suggestion—in regard to the Cavalry force at this place—compos[ed] as it is exclusively of Germans—'Home Guards[']] and 'Fremont Rangers'—If the two German companies—could be exchanged for 'American' troops, it would be an advantage to the service here—and if the 'Guards' and 'Rangers' could be removed to some other field of labor—the loss would not be severely felt at this Post—I would earnestly request that Capt Stuarts Cavalry, be stationed for the winter at this point—Besides being good reliable men—the Captain and his men are well acquainted through this part of the Country—and would be of great service in gaining information—as to the movements of the enemy—I wrote to you yesterday in regard to calling a 'General Court Martial' at this place—I hope it will be ordered at an early day—" Copy, *ibid.* On Nov. 26, Capt. William S. Hillyer had written twice to the commanding officer, Cape Girardeau. "I am instructed by Genl Grant comdg to inform you that if the Lieutenant who took the Horses alluded to in the accompanying order does not produce them immediately you will cause him to be arrested—you will also inquire into the circumstances attending their taking and report the facts to these Head Quarters." "You will have two Horses returned to Mr Hawkins, which were taken from him by a Lieutenant of your command on or about the 14th inst." Copies, DLC-USG, V, 1, 2, 3, 77; DNA, RG 393, USG Letters Sent. On Dec. 9, Capt. John A. Rawlins wrote to Ross. "Your communication of the 6th inst. enclosing copy of your Note of Nov 30th 1861 is received, and in answer thereto, I am instructed by Brig. Genl. Grant, to say, under authority from Genl. Fremont he had directed Col. Plummer, to convene a Court Martial at Cape Girardeau, which not having been acted upon, is in his opinion now void, Genl. Fremont being superceded in command of Department. You will therefore forward to these Head Quarters the names of the required number of Officers, available for Court Martial Duty, designating one capable to act as Judge Advocate. You will also send charges and specifications against two or three of the persons to be tried, and they will be forwarded to Dept. Hd. Qrs with request that the Court Martial be immediately convened." Copies, DLC-USG, V, 1, 2, 3, 79; DNA, RG 393, USG Letters Sent. See *Calendar*, Sept. 4, 1861, and letter to Capt. John C. Kelton, Dec. 15, 1861.

2. See telegram to Capt. Chauncey McKeever, Oct. 21, 1861.

3. Brig. Gen. Franz Sigel, born in Baden, Germany, a military academy graduate, participated in the 1848 revolution as an associate of Friedrich Hecker. After the failure of the revolution, he became a teacher in the U.S., settling in St. Louis, where he organized and commanded the 3rd Mo. Inf. when the Civil War began.

4. See letter to Capt. Chauncey McKeever, Oct. 9, 1861.

5. See orders for Col. Joseph B. Plummer, Nov. 25, 1861.

6. On Dec. 2, USG wrote to John Reilly, capt. of the *J. D. Perry.* "Until directed by Maj. Gen. Halleck, commanding the Department or the Commander of this Military District, you will make no landings on the Missouri shore, between Cape Girardeau and Birds Point, except at Commerce. All orders to the contrary, failing in this authority, will be totally disregarded" Copies, DLC-

USG, V, 1, 2, 3, 77; DNA, RG 393, USG Letters Sent. See letter to Capt. John
C. Kelton, Dec. 4, 1861.
    7. Not found.

To Capt. John C. Kelton

———

Head Quarters, Dist. S. E. Mo.
Cairo, December 3d 1861.

CAPT. J. C. KELTON
A. A. GEN. DEPT. OF THE MISSOURI,
ST. LOUIS, MO.
CAPT.

By orders from the Governor of this state two regiments of
troops have been sent to Shawneetown. One of these have been
mustered into the service of the United States, and the A. A. C. S.
who is now here, represents to me that the state authority declines rationing them longer. Under these circumstances I have
caused to be turned over to the Commissary ten days rations for
his regiment.

In a few days I understand the other regiment will be mustered in also, and will probably be calling here for subsistence.

Troops are highly necessary at Shawneetown not only to
protect the citizens from marauding parties of secession troops
who are now collecting hogs, cattle and horses on the opposite
side of the river, but will serve to keep open the navigation of the
Ohio, and to prevent much of the smuggling now going on.—
Under these circumstances I would respectfully ask if it would
not be well to extend the limits of this Military District to the
Wabash, and give it limits North, in this state.[1]

If this is not done I would at least recommend that some command be required to take in these troops, where they can look
for supplies, and so that they may be properly restrained.

Constant complaints are coming here from citizens of Crittenden & Union Counties Ky. of depridations that are being committed by troops from Hopkinsville,[2] and as the troops at Shawneetown have a Steamer at their command they ~~will be making~~ may make excursions across the river that might be improper.

There are large quantities of stock, of all kinds, being driven from these counties to the Southern Army, and quite a trade is being carried on in salt, powder, caps & domestics. I have reported these facts as far as ~~convenient~~ could well be done in a limited telegraphic despatch to Gen. Buell.[3]

Respectfully
Your Obt. Svt.
U. S. GRANT
Brig. Gen. Com.

ALS, DNA, RG 393, Dept. of the Mo., Letters Received. *O.R.*, I, vii, 472.

1. For the limits of the District of Southeast Mo., see General Orders No. 2, Sept. 1, 1861, note 1. On Nov. 24, 1861, Col. Nathan B. Forrest, Tenn. Cav., began a week-long expedition along the Ohio River in western Ky. to encourage C. S. A. sentiment and to gather hogs and cattle. *O.R.*, I, vii, 4–6. U.S. defense of the region was discussed in correspondence between Maj. Gen. Henry W. Halleck and Brig. Gen. Charles F. Smith. *Ibid.*, pp. 444–46, 448–49, 461–64.

2. C. S. A. Brig. Gen. Charles Clark at Hopkinsville, Ky., about seventy miles southeast of Paducah, had an estimated aggregate force, present and absent, of 3,500 as of Dec. 12. *Ibid.*, p. 762. A report as of Dec. 31 listed 3,550 aggregate present and absent, of which 2,295 were present. *Ibid.*, p. 814.

3. On Dec. 3, Brig. Gen. Don Carlos Buell telegraphed to USG. "Have recd your dispatch   Did you get mine of last night on another subject"   Telegram received, DNA, RG 393, Dept. of the Mo., Telegrams Received.

To Brig. Gen. M. Jeff Thompson

Head Quarters Dist S. E. Mo
Cairo December 4th 1861

GEN. M. JEFF. THOMPSON
COMDG. MO. STATE TROOPS
NEW MADRID MO.
GEN.

In conformity with my proposition to you I directed that four of your prisoners at Cape Girardeau should be released for the safe return of Judge Conrad.[1]

My letter to the commanding officer at the Cape on this subject was intended for your perusal and was sent by Judge Conrad

In that letter I directed that four prisoners should be released for the Judge, four for the 2d Lieut. and eight for the Capt. you arrested on the Steamer Platte Valley.

I was in Cape Girardeau a day or two after and found that the Judge had not yet made his appearance. Whilst there I learned that we had of your men a Capt. and Lieut. prisoners. I therefore changed my directions and ordered that these two officers, should be exchanged in lieu of twelve men. My instructions were to release these officers, and I intended it to mean unconditionally, and send you a note to the effect that it had been done, and for what purpose

The officer in command of the Post reported to me that he had released them on Parole, to terminate the moment you expressed a willingness to release the Platte Valley officers of theirs

I regret that I have forgotten the names of these two officers, but hope nevertheless that Capt. Larison[2] and Lieut.   [3] will be released by you in return. You may have received a communication from Cape Girardeau on this subject since the departure of your Aid de Camp, Lieut Col. Chappell.

I also enclose herewith copy of letter written by me at the

same time my instructions to the Commander at the Cape was to be sent to you.

> I am Gen very respectful
> Your Obt Svt
> U. S. GRANT
> Brig. Genl Comg

Copies, DLC-USG, V, 1, 2, 3, 79; DNA, RG 393, USG Letters Sent. *O.R.*, II, i, 528.

1. See letter to Brig. Gen. M. Jeff Thompson, Nov. 16, 1861.
2. Capt. Thomas J. Larison of Lincoln, Ill., 2nd Ill. Cav.
3. 2nd Lt. Jerome B. Tenney of Atlanta, Ill., 2nd Ill. Cav. See letter to Capt. Thomas J. Larison, Dec. 16, 1861.

To Lt. Col. William C. Chappell

———

> Head Quarters Dist. S. E. Mo
> Cairo December 4th 1861

COL. W. C. CHAPPELL
A. D. C. TO GEN. THOMPSON
CAIRO ILL
COL

Your note of this date has just reached me. There must be a decided misapprehension some where and I discover you are laboring under an entirely mistaken view of your position. You was fully informed that the Flag under which you come, protected you so long as you chose to remain under it. You was at perfect liberty to go back with that Flag, but informed that if you chose to accompany me it would be as a prisoner of War. I told you that I would communicate with the commander of this Department and state your case fully and if he gave his consent you should have all the priveleges asked for. In the mean time you would remain here under such restrictions as I would impose which however would not be onerous.

I communicated that evening with Gen. Halleck and have

not yet received his reply.[1] Your note this afternoon is the first intimation I have had that you desired to return South before hearing the result of this correspondence.

Had I known that you desired going with the Flag of Truce today I would have freely given my consent, and if you still desire to go I will send you down tomorrow, unless orders should be received in the mean time directing otherwise   My contracting your limits was in accordance with general instructions received. I feel no disposition to place you under close confinement but if you desire it please inform me.

Yours &c.

U. S. GRANT

Brig. Gen Comdg.

Copies, DLC-USG, V, 1, 2, 3, 79; DNA, RG 393, USG Letters Sent. *O.R.*, II, i, 527–28. On Dec. 4, 1861, Lt. Col. William C. Chappell wrote to USG. "On the 29th Nov inst. I delivered to you certain Despatches, two being to General Halleck from Brig Genl M. Jeff Thompson, one to yourself from the same, also one to you from Maj Genl Leonidas Polk of the Confederate army. Being under a flag of truce, recognized by you, I came here under certain restrictions. Those restrictions I have carefully fulfilled. On yesterday, I was notified by Capt Lagow, your Aide de Campe, to confine myself to the hotel. I have done so. At the same time he told me that the Iatan Steamer was coming down and to prepare myself to go down on her. I have not heard one word from you Sir since then but taking for granted my mission had failed, I concluded you, sir, would deliver to me upon my departure, the official documents that are due me   This A. M. I was notified to prepare to go on board the Iatan, and that your dispatches to my commanding General would be given me. I accordingly proceeded to the boat, but was not allowed to go on board by Capt Lagow, your Aide de Campe. I now Sir claim the privilege of the flag under which you received me, and a safe conduct through your lines, also I claim as due my Government, your reasons for my detention under a flag of truce. I also demand from you if my ~~my~~ petition be not granted, that I may be allowed to be placed under restraint as I hold that upon your refusal to return me inside of our lines that the flag under which you received me is not recognized   P. S. Sir, if you allow me the privilege of returning, I would ask that, you send me this P. M." ALS, DNA, RG 393, District of Cairo, Letters Received. See letter to Capt. John C. Kelton, Nov. 29, 1861.

In an unaddressed and unsigned letter dated Dec. 1, 1861, Maj. Mason Brayman complained that Chappell was acting as a spy, and in an undated appendix stated that Chappell later reported his findings to Maj. Gen. Leonidas Polk. ADf, Brayman Papers, ICHi. A note in another hand indicates that the letter was intended for Mrs. Abraham Lincoln. Why the letter was written is unknown. See letter of "C.," Dec. 5, 1861, in *Chicago Tribune*, Dec. 6, 1861.

1. See letter to Capt. John C. Kelton, Nov. 29, 1861.

To Capt. John C. Kelton

Head Quarters, Dist. S. E. Mo.
Cairo, December 4th 1861.

CAPT. J. C. KELTON
A. A. GEN. DEPT. OF THE MISSOURI,
ST. LOUIS, MO.

I would respectfully report that the goods landed at Price's landing on Monday last, by Steamer Perry, was moved directly, by team, to Hickman Ky. and New Madrid Mo.—I learned these facts too late to capture it and the teams used in its transportation.

Eighty barrels of this freight was whiskey, a character of commerce I would have no objection to being carried on with the South, but there is a possibility that some barrels marked whiskey might contain something els more objectionable.

I would not be understood as saying that I would sanction-~~ing~~ the passage South of anything interdicted.

Respectfully
Your Obt. Svt.
U. S. GRANT
Brig. Gen. Com.

ALS, DNA, RG 393, Dept. of the Mo., Letters Received. *O.R.*, I, viii, 404. On Dec. 2, 1861, Capt. John A. Rawlins wrote to Col. Leonard F. Ross. "I am instructed by Brig. Genl. Grant to say your Note of today is received. In the prohibition of the landing of Merchandize in Missouri you will be governed by enclosed General Orders No 4, issued from Hd. Qrs. St Louis Dist. St Louis Mo Nov 27 1861. As to the great demand for Whiskey he agrees with you, and is of the opinion the more Whiskey they could get the better, but he has issued an order prohibiting the landing of Boats or any Mdze. whatever between Cape Girardeau and Birds Point except at Commerce on the Missouri side in future unless expressly commanded by the Genl. Comdg. the Dept. or Commander of this District." LS, MoSHi.

To Col. Leonard F. Ross

Head Quarters Dist. S. E. Mo
Cairo December 4th 1861

Col L Ross
Comdg. U. S. Forces
Cape Girardeau Mo
Col

Your communication of yesterday[1] is received, and the following instructions are given in reply

You will require Col. Murdoch[2] to give over to the Quartermaster, all property taken by them from citizens of Missouri, such as may be reclaimed by owners, you will direct to be returned, unless taken from persons, directly giving aid and comfort to the enemy

When you know of depredations being committed by armed bodies of rebels, within reach of you, you can use your own discretion about the propriety of suppressing them.

I know your views about allowing troops to interpret the confiscation laws,[3] therefore no instructions are required on this point. One thing I will add. In cases of outrageous marauding I would fully justify shooting the perpetrators down, if caught in the act. I mean our own men as well as the enemy

When you are satisfied that Thompsons men are coming in with honest intentions, you may swear them, but in this matter, I would advise great caution. As a rule, it would be better to keep them entirely out, of your Camp, or confine them as prisoners of war. A few examples of confinement would prevent others from coming in

Respectfully
Your Obt Sevt
U. S. Grant
Brig Genl Comg

Copies, DLC-USG, V, 1, 2, 3, 79; DNA, RG 393, USG Letters Sent. *O.R.*, I, viii, 404; *ibid.*, II, i, 233.

1. Not found.
2. See orders for Col. Joseph B. Plummer, Nov. 25, 1861, note 2.
3. Under the Confiscation Act of Aug. 6, 1861, all property used for insurrectionary purposes was subject to confiscation and condemnation in U.S. district or circuit courts. The same act forbade the return of any slave who had been employed for rebel military purposes. *U.S. Statutes at Large*, XII, 319. Although some property was confiscated, few, if any, slaves were freed under this act, which remained in force throughout the war. J. G. Randall, *Constitutional Problems under Lincoln*, rev. ed. (Urbana, Ill., 1951), pp. 276, 333–35, 357. See letters to Col. John Cook, Dec. 25, 1861, and to Col. Leonard F. Ross, Jan. 5, 1862; see also *Calendar*, Nov. 26, 1861.

To Maj. Gen. Leonidas Polk

Head Quarters Dist. S. E Mo
Cairo December 5th 1861

MAJ. GEN. L POLK
COMDG. CONFEDERATE FORCES
COLUMBUS KY.
GEN.

I return today Lieut. Col. Chappell Aid-de-Camp to Gen. J. Thompson, who would have been sent yesterday had I been made aware that he desired to go back[1]

I also permit Mrs.   [2] of Evansville Indiana to accompany the Flag, in the hope that you will permit her daughter Mrs Harris of Columbus, and her son, a boy of some fourteen years of age, to visit her on the Truce Boat. This lady also desires to bring back her son.

In this behalf I do not intercede, knowing nothing of any of the parties. Being disposed my self to visit as lightly as possible, the rigors of a state of war upon noncombatants, I have permitted this lady to go to you to plead her own case. I would prefer however, that she be not permitted to go ashore, but allowed to see her family, under the Flag of Truce, if it be your pleasure to grant her request

> I am Gen. with great respect
> Your Obt. Svt.
> U. S. GRANT
> Brig. Gen. Comdg.

Copies, DLC-USG, V, 1, 2, 3, 79; DNA, RG 393, USG Letters Sent. *O.R.*, II, i, 528–29.

1. See letter to Lt. Col. William C. Chappell, Dec. 4, 1861.
2. The name is omitted on all copies.

To Col. Richard J. Oglesby

———

> Head Quarters Dist. S. E. Mo
> Cairo Dec 6th 1861

COLONEL

Information having been received at these Head Quarters, that the enemy have some heavy pieces of Artillery at Belmont, or at the point on the river immediately this side, not yet mounted, with but a small Guard and working party to protect them. You will order the entire force of Cavalry at Birds Point Mo to make a reconnoisance towards Belmont tonight, and if the enemy are found in force *not too strong*, they will make a dash upon him, and *Spike all his Guns* they may find, after which they will immediately return to Birds Point.—They will observe great caution, not to be drawn into ambush, or engaged with a superior force of the enemy.

A detachment will be sent from Cairo, to act in concert with those of your command.

> By order
> Brig. Genl Grant
> JNO A RAWLINS
> A A Genl

To Col R. J. Oglesby
Comdg. at Birds Point Mo
P. S. The expedition will be in readiness to move, immediately
upon the arrival of the force from Cairo, between the hours of
six & seven o.clock

Copies, DLC–USG, V, 1, 2, 3, 79; DNA, RG 393, USG Letters Sent; McClernand
Papers, IHi. *O.R.*, I, viii, 410. On Dec. 6, 1861, Capt. John A. Rawlins wrote to
Brig. Gen. John A. McClernand. "Enclosed herewith I send you copy of Orders
sent Col. R. J. Oglesby Comdg. at Birds Point   I have instructed Com. Graham
to have Steamers in readiness, to transport Cavalry to Birds Point with directions
to report to you"   Copies, DLC–USG, V, 1, 2, 3, 79; DNA, RG 393, USG
Letters Sent. On Dec. 7, Lt. Col. Edward Prince wrote to Col. Richard J. Oglesby.
"In accordance with your letter of instructions of Date Dec 6th 1861 of the
available force of the 2nd and 7th I. C also of Capt Nolemans Co of Cavalry and
of Four Cavalry Companies from Cairo who reported themselves immediately
before our starting under command of Captain Dollins   Starting—At 7 oclock
P. M. we proceeded by the Rush Ridge Rood   I determined upon the following
course and followed it   One Company was detatched and left at Lucas' place
another about Two miles below and one company at the second open field on this
side of Belmont   Ten men with guides were detatched from each company for the
purpose of reconnoitering some of which were sent through the fields and wood in
all directions   At the last mentioned field in which the company was stationed
three men were sent directly to the river to proceed down the bank of the river to
Belmont   Advance and and rear guards were thrown out and near Belmont the
column moved cautiously   The accidental discharge of a carbine in the hands of
one of the men—was the only shot fired   The head of the column advanced to
the old field immediately in front of the pole fence which constitutes a sort of a
barrier arround Belmont which appeared intirely deserted   The skirmishers sent
over this barrier reported nothing living   Those sent down the river arrived at
this point and reported that there were no cannon or rebels on or near the river
bank   Two steamboats at Columbus were distinctly visible   Bells were rung
and lights were mooving to and fro in considerable abundance   Having found
nothing to fight or capture the head of the Column was put in motion and much
to the mortification of all we returned without having seen a rebel   With no
moon and some clouds the night was intensely dark but I believe none lost the
way   The time of our departure was 7 15 P. M and returned at 7 A. M this day.
The utmost coolness seemed to prevail among Officers and men   I could not
obtain the exact number of troopers but there were about 700   Major Jenkins
1st Cavalry accompanied the expedition and was ready for active service at a
moments ~~service~~ notice   Major Mudd of the 2n Cavalry and Major Rawalt of
the 7th Cavalry accompanied and commanded the Detatchments of their Divisions"   ALS, *ibid.*, District of Southeast Mo., Letters Received.

To Maj. Gen. Henry W. Halleck

By Telegraph from Cairo Dec 8th *1861*

To Maj Gen H W Halleck

St Louis

Have received yesterday Four Thousand *4000* Stand of Arms. Gen. McClernand's Brigade expect Four Thousand *4000* more which will nearly fit us out. One Thousand *1000* more will be Sufficient.

U. S. Grant

Brig. Gen.

Telegram received (punctuation added), DNA, RG 94, Generals' Papers and Books, Telegrams Received by Gen. Halleck; copy, *ibid.*, RG 393, Dept. of the Mo., Telegrams Received. On Dec. 7, 1861, Maj. Gen. Henry W. Halleck had telegraphed to USG. "Have you unarmed troops at Cairo? If so, how many?" Copies, *ibid.*, RG 94, Telegrams Sent by Gen. Halleck; *ibid.*, RG 393, USG Hd. Qrs. Correspondence; *ibid.*, Dept. of the Mo., Telegrams Sent; DLC-USG, V, 4, 5, 7, 8. On Dec. 7, Halleck had also telegraphed to Flag Officer Andrew H. Foote. "I can give you a regiment of unarmed Volunteer recruits, if you require them for the gun-boats." Copy, DNA, RG 94, Generals' Papers and Books, Telegrams Sent by Gen. Halleck. On Dec. 7, Col. James D. Morgan, Mound City, telegraphed to USG. "I have Just been informed that some fine Guns are arriving. Don't forget the 10th Regt." Telegram received (punctuation added), *ibid.*, RG 393, Dept. of the Mo., Telegrams Received. On Dec. 9, Capt. Wilbur F. Brinck wrote to USG. "I have the honor to inform you that in accordance with your orders, I have furnished the following named Regiments with Rifled Muskets (Cal 69) received from New York

8	Ills	Regt	Col Oglesby	384
11	"	"	" Wallace	384
20	"	"	" Marsh	180
22	"	"	" Daugherty	488
28	"	"	" Johnson	432
7	"	"	" Cook	400
48	"	"	" Haynie	384
18	"	"	" Lawler	384
10	Iowa	"	" Purcell (comdg)	360
			Total	3396

Leaving on hand (if the Invoice of 4000 be correct) six hundred and four (604) I find the accoutrements with few exceptions in very good condition, therefor have issued but to Col Cook who furnished me with three hundred and seven sets, that I intend sending to Col Kirkham at Shawneetown Illinois I have informed the different commanders of Regiments if any of their accoutrements were not fit for service to request a board of survey and if they were condemned, new ones would be furnished. I consider it would be bad policy to issue the new ~~ones~~ accoutrements and take back some that are second hand, but still fit for service. Some of these muskets have been altered from Flint, to Precussion Locks, But are good muskets" LS, *ibid.*, District of Southeast Mo., Letters Received.

To Capt. John C. Kelton

———

Head Quarters, Dist. S. E. Mo.
Cairo, Dec. 8t 1861

Capt. J. C. Kelton
A. A. Gen. Dept. of the Mo.
St. Louis Mo.
Capt.

I have just got in a man who spent yesterday in Columbus. He reports the enemy strongly fortified there with fifty-four pieces of heavy ordnance, less than I have understood heretofore thay had. In addition to this they have ten batteries of Light Artillery with Forty-seven regiments of Infantry & Cavalry, (all arms.)[1]

There is not the slightest intention of attacking Cairo but the strongest apprehension exists that Columbus is to be soon attacked.

I believe that I have full means of keeping posted as to what is going on South of this point and will keep you fully informed.

Respectfully
Your Obt. Svt.
U. S. Grant
Brig. Gen Com.

ALS, DNA, RG 393, Dept. of the Mo., Letters Received. *O.R.*, I, vii, 482.

1. C. S. A. returns indicate about 20,000 men available for duty under Maj. Gen. Leonidas Polk at this time. *Ibid.*, pp. 727–28.

To Capt. John C. Kelton

Head Quarters Dist. S. E. Mo
Cairo Dec 8th 1861

ASST. ADJT. GENL.
DEPT. OF THE MISSOURI
ST LOUIS MO
SIR

In compliance with your order, endorsed on communication of Capt. J. P. Hawkins of date Nov 28th 1861, and which, is herewith enclosed, I have the honor to transmit herewith, copies of all orders, relative to the Govts. possession of, and use of the Cairo and Fulton Rail Road, also report of A. H. Waterman Suprt. of same. I have no knowledge or information upon the subject, except such as is furnished by enclosed Orders and report.

I am sir very respectfully
Your Obt. Svt.
U. S. GRANT
Brig. Genl Comdg.

LS, DNA, RG 393, Dept. of the Mo., Letters Received. See letter to A. H. Waterman, Nov. 15, 1861. On Nov. 28, 1861, Capt. John P. Hawkins wrote to Maj. Robert Allen. "About the 1st of August, 61 Major Genl Fremont took charge of for Govment, the Cairo and Fulton Rail Road, running from opposite Cairo to Fulton Mo. An Agent and hands were also employed to take care of the Road and keep it in order. In the opinion of General Grant and myself the road is of no purpose for military use, being very short, connecting no strategic points and of limited quantity of rolling stock, and on the latter account no move could be made by means of it but would have to be made by teams. For these considerations with the approval of General Grant I would respectfully recommend that all the Government employees on it be immediately dismissed and the road be left to the care and expense of those who own it." ALS, DNA, RG 393, Dept. of the Mo., Letters Received. The letter was endorsed by Allen. "Respectfully referred to the Commanding General of the Department, with a recommendation that an order issue to discharge the employees as recommended by Captain Hawkins" AES, *ibid*. The letter was also endorsed by Brig. Gen. Schuyler Hamilton. "Genl. Grant will please report if he has any knowledge of the existence of any contract on this subject—If he has not he will please call upon the agent for such as he may possess—If he has a contract Genl. G. will forward a copy of it and all the information he can obtain on the subject for the information of the Commdg Genl—" AES, *ibid*.

In an undated letter (probably early Dec.) Waterman wrote to USG. "Enclosed you will find the papers you requested me to send. I hope you will keep the Originals, the first time I come over I will call for them. I see that Hawkins is something of a meddler with others business. I have no doubt but he has been meddling with mine. he was very much dissatisfied about your allowing me to draw Commissary Stores, in bulk, as Genl. Fremont desired me to do. I could not have done anything without some such means of keeping the men while at work. We worked four months without receiving one dollar from the Govt. The whole Expense on the road, from the commencement, does not amount to $5,000, and we have rebuilt nearly one half mile of Bridgeing, and several Culverts, beside this the Road was very much out of order Generally, I have put in some 1500 new Ties have reballesed a great portion of the old bed of the Road. There was no Water Tanks nor Wells. I have dug two wells and built two large Water Tanks, and have built 900 ft. of new track. The caving in of the river bank to such an extent, destroyed all the shops and Water priveliges that was connected with this end of the road. I have also repaired two Engines, which was very much out of order, and several cars. I have received in all from the Commissary, between five and six hundred Dollars, and it has been charged to the workman, and will be deducted from the money drawn from Major Hatch to pay these Bills. I do not see when I have abused the priveleges given me so much, as that man Hawkins, would like to make out. beware of him he is treachorous" Copy, *ibid*. Waterman enclosed a letter of Aug. 3 from Lt. Col. Chester Harding to Col. William H. L. Wallace. "You will afford A. H. Waterman Esq every facility in your power to enable him to repair and take charge of and keep in running order the rolling stock of Cairo and Fulton Railroad" Copy, *ibid*. Also enclosed was Special Orders No. 4 issued by Harding. "The Quartermaster and Commissary of the 1st. Brigade Ills Vols will furnish to A. H. Waterman upon his requisition, any supplies in thier respective departments, which he may require for himself & his parties of workmen in repairing and keeping in running order the rolling Stock of the Cairo and Fulton Rail-Road" Copy, *ibid*. Also enclosed was Special Orders No. 5 issued by Harding. "A. H. Waterman Esq is hereby authorized to use any of the artificers or laborers, enlisted in the U. S. Army, and stationed at Cairo or Birds Point, which he may find nescessary to repair, and place, and keep, in running order, the rolling stock of the Cairo & Fulton Rail Road He is also authorized to hire such other artificers & laborers, as may be required for that purpose" Copy, *ibid*. See letter to Col. Richard J. Oglesby, Dec. 18, 1861.

To Capt. John C. Kelton

———

Head Quarters Dis. S. E. Mo
Cairo Dec 8th 1861

Capt. J. C. Kelton
Asst. Adjt. Genl.
Dept. of the Missouri
St Louis Mo
Sir

In compliance with your Circular of Nov. 28th 1861, I have the honor to report to you the following list of Officers as available for Court Martial, Duty, also one capable to act as Judge Advocate

Brig. Genl. J. A. McClernand—President	
Col. W. H. L. Wallace	11th Ill Vols
Col. James Reardon	29th ” ”
Lieut Col. Wm Erwin	20th ” ”
” ” H. E. Hart	22nd ” ”
” ” F. A. Harrington	27th ” ”
” ” L. H. Waters	28th ” ”
” ” Thos. H. Smith	48th ” ”
Major R Rowett	7th ” ”
” J. P. Post	8th ” ”
” J. C Bennett	10th Iowa ”
” D. B. Bush	2nd Ill Cavalry
Capt. C. T. Hotchkiss	11th Ill Vols. to act as Judge Advocate

I am sir very respectfully
Your Obt. Svt.
U. S. Grant
Brig. Genl Comdg.

Copies, DLC-USG, V, 4, 5, 7, 8, 78; DNA, RG 393, USG Hd. Qrs. Correspondence. On Nov. 28, 1861, Capt. John C. Kelton wrote to USG. "You will please furnish a list of officers at your post available for Court martial Duty, and select some one capable of performing the duties of Judge Advocate. The Court is for the trial of Col Lawler, & other officers." LS, *ibid.*, District of Southeast Mo., Letters Received.

On Nov. 2, Brig. Gen. John A. McClernand wrote to USG. "In compliance with your verbal request, I have the honor to inclose to you, herewith Copies of the correspondence between Col. M. K. Lawler Commanding the 18th Regiment Illinois volunteers and myself touching the execution of Joseph Dickman." ADf and copy, McClernand Papers, IHi. On the same day, Col. Michael K. Lawler wrote to McClernand. "I hasten to answer your communication of yesterday. Many of the particulars for which you enquire, are given in my report to you of 30th September, of which the following is a Copy

'Head Quarters 18th Regt I V
Mound City Sept 30th 1861

Genl.

An aggravated case of murder occured this morning at two O'clock, A. M. *Robert Dickman*, of Company "G" shot *Wm. Evans* and killed him instantly. *Evans* formerly belonged to the same company, and was transferred to the Artillery, Lieut Morgan commanding. I thought, at first, to turn the culprit over to the civil authorities; but on reflection, I recollected a of a similar case that occured in Texas, some years since; and, if I recollect rightly, the murderer was tried by a court martial. I think the case occured some five or more years ago, where a private Shot a sergeant, and was tried by a C. M. and executed. Perhaps you have some knowledge of the case. I wait your orders in this case.

very respectfully,
Your Obt. Servt.
M K Lawler, Col Comdg
W B Fondey Adjt.'

In answer to this note, I received a communication from you of the same date, which, after stating what you deemed to be the rule of law in such cases, You add: —'The case, therefore, goes properly, to the civil authorities of Pulaski County' In compliance with this suggestion, I immediately offered to deliver the prisoner, to the civil authorities of Pulaski county, for trial, but they refused to receive him, stating that a court of competent jurisdiction to try him, would not sit in that County for some months—by which time, the witnesses to the homicide, being Soldiers, would probably be beyond the reach of process; and that, to *receive* him, under the circumstances, would be, in effect, to *release* him. The apprehensions awakened by this answer, caused great excitement and commotion in the regiment, not only lest the prisoner might escape, but that another of its members might become the victim of his fury. This apprehension was justified by the fact, that he had, a short time before, threatened to kill others of his comrades, and had charged his gun, as he alleged, for the purpose of Shooting *Joseph Campbell*, sergeant of the same Company, and was only prevented from doing so, by being knocked down. In deference to the just indignation of the regiment, and for the purpose of preserving proper order and descipline in it, I delivered the prisoner into the hands of his Company, until I should hear of their determination. On the next day, the Captain of his company summoned twelve men from its number, who, after being empannelled and sworn, as a Jury, to try the prisoner, accordingly did so, and found him guilty of murder. The Captain passed sentence upon him, and the next day, he was hung. The Jury who rendered the verdict, was composed of his own neighbors, and therefore may be supposed to have been uninfluenced by improper feelings towards him. Left, as I had been, from the beginning up to the period of your assuming command of this Post, isolated, and having been injustly assailed, by the Press, upon various groundless pretexts connected with the discipline of my command, I thought proper for these, and other reasons, to permit the sentence which had been passed, to be carried into effect. In doing so, I only yielded to what I conceived to be a Military necessity, involving the good order, the proper discipline, and the indevidual safety of my Command. If, in what I did, or rather *permitted* to be done, I have committed an error, it was an honest one, devoid of all feelings or purpose of disrespect to any one, and only from an earnest desire to preserve the efficiency of my regiment; that they might, in the most efficient manner, serve their country." Copy, DNA, RG 153, Michael K. Lawler. On Nov. 3, USG endorsed Lawler's letter. "Respectfully refered to Head Quarters, Western Department." AES, *ibid*. Although the execution of Private Robert Dickerman was the chief charge in Lawler's court-martial, other factors were involved. See William A. Pitkin, "Michael K. Lawler's Ordeal with the Eighteenth Illinois," *Journal of the Illinois State Historical Society*, LVIII, 4 (Winter, 1965), 357–77. See letter to Col. Michael K. Lawler, Jan. 2, 1862.

To Capt. John C. Kelton

Head Quarters Dist. S. E. Mo
Cairo Dec 8th 1861

CAPT J. C. KELTON
ASST. ADJT. GENL
DEPT. OF THE MISSOURI
ST LOUIS MO
SIR

In compliance with your orders, I have the honor to report to you the following list of Officers available for a Military Commission, also one to act as Judge Advocate.

Col. I. N. Haynie	48th Ills Inftry.
Lieut. Col. A. J. Babcock	7th ″ ″
Major Jonas Rawalt	7th ″ Cavalry
″ A. J Kuykendall	31st ″ Inftry
Capt. J. M. Hanna	8th ″ ″
″ Warren Stewart	of the Cavalry
″ J. J. Dollins	″ ″ ″
″ Smith Atkins	11th Ill. Inftry. to act as Judge Advocate

The prisoners to be tried are charged as being spies. The particular charges and specifications of offense, I will cause to be made out and presented

> I am sir very respectfully
> Your Obt. Svt.
> U. S. GRANT
> Brig. Genl. Comdg.

Copies, DLC-USG, V, 4, 5, 7, 8, 78; DNA, RG 393, USG Hd. Qrs. Correspondence. See letter to Capt. John C. Kelton, Nov. 29, 1861.

To Brig. Gen. John A. McClernand

> Head Quarters Dist. S. E Mo
> Cairo Dec 8th 1861

GENL.

I am instructed by Brig. Genl. U. S. Grant to say, owing the the inability of the Gun Boats to cooperate the proposed expidition to New Madrid is postponed

> I am sir very respectfully
> Your Obt. Servt.
> JNO A RAWLINS
> Asst. Adjt. Genl

To Brig Genl. J. A. McClernand
Comdg. Post
Cairo Ill

Copies, DLC-USG, V, 1, 2, 3, 79; DNA, RG 393, USG Letters Sent. *O.R.*, I, viii, 416. A copy of this message was sent to Col. William H. L. Wallace.

To Capt. John C. Kelton

————

Head Quarters Dist. S. E. Mo
Cairo Dec 9th 1861

Capt. J. C Kelton
Asst. Adjt. Genl.
Dept. of the Missouri
St Louis Mo
Sir

I have the honor to transmit herewith, my Trimonthly Report, the last for the Month of November. Monthly Returns will be forwarded as soon as Sub Returns are received from which to compile them

U. S. Grant
Brig. Genl Comdg.

Copies, DLC-USG, V, 4, 5, 7, 8, 78; DNA, RG 393, USG Hd. Qrs. Correspondence.

To Col. Leonard F. Ross

————

Head Quarters Dist. S. E Mo
Cairo Dec 9th 1861

Col L. F. Ross

Points above Cape Girardeau, I do not regard as strictly within my jurisdiction. You will therefore respect authority from the Collector of Customs and others in authority above that point, and what they authorize to land you will respect

Mr Harris from your say is a good Union Man, and should have all the benefit arising from this yielding of a point

U. S. Grant
Brig Genl Com.

Copies, DLC-USG, V, 1, 2, 3, 79; DNA, RG 393, USG Letters Sent.

To Julia Dent Grant

Head Quarters, Dist. S. E. Mo.
Cairo, Dec. 9th 1861.

MY DEAR WIFE,

Capt. Lagow goes after you. I want you to call in town and say to Mrs. Pope that her letter was received and will be answered. Her letter to her husband went through.

Give my love to all at your fathers house and say that I will write him a long letter soon.

I have just received a letter from Casey.—Emma has a big boy and regrets they were not twins. In that case she would name one after me. Being but one she must name him Fred. after her father.[1] He will have namesakes enough after awhile.

Knowing that I will see you in a few days and having orders written all round me, which I have to dictate, and sign, I write no more.

DODE

ALS, DLC-USG. This letter was probably delivered to Julia Dent Grant just as she was ready to leave Cairo after visiting USG. On the reverse she wrote to "Dear Dode   Come up & sit with me a while wont you? I am so lonesome   bring up St Louis Papers too & be sure & send or bring this back to your Juje"   Mrs. Grant soon returned from St. Louis and remained at Cairo until the departure of the Tennessee River expedition in Feb., 1862. See letter to Mary Grant, Dec. 18, 1861.

1. Frederick Dent Casey was born at Caseyville, Ky., Dec. 2, 1861.

To Capt. John C. Kelton

Head Quarters Dist. S. E. Mo
Cairo Dec 10th 1861

CAPT. J. C KELTON
ASST. ADJT. GENL
DEPT. OF THE MISSOURI
ST LOUIS MO
SIR

In reply to your Order of Dec 3rd. directing me to order Sergt. Major Abraham Bocker of the 53rd Regt. Ill Vols. to report for duty to Dept. Hd. Qrs., I have the honor to inform you he is not within my command.

I am sir very respectfully
Your Obt. Servt.
U. S. GRANT
Brig. Genl. Comdg.

Copies, DLC-USG, V, 4, 5, 7, 8, 78; DNA, RG 393, USG Hd. Qrs. Correspondence. On Dec. 3, 1861, Capt. John C. Kelton wrote to USG. "You will please order Abraham Bocker, Sergeant Major of the 53rd Regiment Illinois Volunteers, now under your command to report for duty at these Headquarters." Copy, *ibid.*, Dept. of the Mo., Letters Sent. The 53rd Ill. was not then in USG's command and it had no officer named Abraham Bocker.

To Col. Leonard F. Ross

Head Quarters Dist. S. E Mo
Cairo Dec 10th 1861

COMDG. OFFICER
CAPE GIRARDEAU

You will cause the Steamer *Henry Fitz Hugh*, now on her way up the Mississippi river, to be stopped, and sent back to this place. Capt. Dollins with his command will go on board of the

Steamer, and return with it, and prevent any landing being made on the return.

U. S. Grant
Brig. Genl Comdg.

Copies, DLC-USG, V, 1, 2, 3, 79; DNA, RG 393, USG Letters Sent. On Dec. 11, 1861, Capt. John A. Rawlins wrote to Capt. James J. Dollins. "You will release the Steamer Henry Fitz Hugh" Copies, DLC-USG, V, 1, 2, 3, 77; DNA, RG 393, USG Letters Sent. On Dec. 13, Dollins wrote to USG. "I have the honor to submit the following Report. On the reception of your special order directed to me on the 10th of this Inst, ordering me to take my command and put them in marching order and proceed to Cape Girardeau on the Mississippi River for the purpose of intercepting and taking possession of the steamer 'Henry Fitz Hugh' enroute for St Louis Mo, and having on board contraband goods. Your order was received at 2.o.clock P. M. on the date aforesaid, and I instantly put my command in marching order and proceeded direct by land to Cape Girardeau, I myself and three others of my company constituting the advance *couriers*, bearing dispatches to Col Ross, in command of U S forces, at the Cape. My 1st Lieut Montreville Fitts, being in charge and bringing up my company or the portion of it going on the expedition No. 51 in number. I with the advance went with all possible dispatch, knowing that I would have to do so to overtake the Boat. we arrived at the River Bank opposite the Cape at 7.o.clock P. M. of that day, amid the storm of wind and rain that was at that time raging, but found no communication ready whatever to take my command across the River, I immediately got a gentleman living this side of the River to take a skiff and row me across the River to the Town, which was rather perilous on account of the high wind and dashing waves. on landing on the Missouri shore I found the Steamer 'Henry Fitzhugh' lying to, with steam up and just ready to start on her trip up the River. I immediately proceeded to the Head Quarters of Col Ross, and deliverd him your written dispatch, and on reception of and reading the same, he forthwith ordered a Guard to take possession of the Boat which they did just in time before she would have started, he then gave orders for the Ferry Boat 'Luellen' to cross the River and bring my command over and place them on the 'Illinois' which was comeing down to Cairo next morning. I then taken took thirty of my company and went aboard the steamer 'Henry Fitzhugh' leaving the remainder of my command in charge of our Horses on the 'Illinois' It being impossible to get them aboard of the steamer 'Henry Fitzhugh' as you directed she being so heavily laden with Freight and in no way suited for the transportation of Horses, I then relieved the Guards placed on the steamer 'Henry Fitzhugh' by Col Ross, and showed the officers of the Boat my authority for taking possession of her, who received me in a verry kind and gentlemanly manner I then agreeably to your order, directed them to get ready and proceed to Cairo Ills, and in a few minutes we were under way we arrived at Cairo, at 5.o.clock A. M. the 11th of this Inst, and delivered the Boat into your possession. I have also to state to you with much reluctance that Jonathan T. Winn a Private in my company killed his Horse who died on arriving at the Cape from exhaustion and overheat, and privates Virgil A. Hendrix, and David W. Vinson so disabled there Horses by the fatigues of the trip as to render them completely unfit for the service. I therefore ask that a board of survey and inspection be appointed to value and condemn the two above disabled Horses and that they be turned over to your Quarter Master and that you pass an order directing your Quarter Master to substitute three serviceable Horses to the above named three Privates in my company, in lieu of the one that was killed and the two disabled ones, and of like value to them before they were injured. I take this opportunity to return my sincere thanks to the officers and crew of the above named Boat for the manifest kindness they showed to me and my men. I also congratulate my first Lt. M Fitts, and every officer and private that was under my command for their noble endurance—energy, and promptness, throughout the entire expedition." ALS, *ibid.*, District of Southeast Mo., Letters Received.

To George W. Graham

———

Head Quarters Dist. S. E Mo
Cairo Dec 10th 1861

G. W. GRAHAM
COMDG. TRANSPORTS

You will on tomorrow the 10th inst. at 7 o'clock, A. M. with a detail of 45 men, (which has been ordered to report to you) and such Transport Steamers and Barges, as can be procured, proceed up the Mississippi river, to where the Gun Boat, Benton is aground, and there use such means as you may deem proper, to put afloat and get her off the Bar. All persons connected with the military authority, will obey your orders, until the object of the expedition is accomplished.

Subject to the approval of Flag Officer A. H. Foote Comdg. Gun Boat Flotilla

By order
Brig Genl Grant
JNO A RAWLINS
A. A. Genl

Copies, DLC-USG, V, 1, 2, 3, 77; DNA, RG 393, USG Letters Sent. On Dec. 10, 1861, Flag Officer Andrew H. Foote reported to Secretary of the Navy Gideon Welles that the *Benton* was aground about seventy-five miles up the Mississippi River. *O.R.* (Navy), I, xxii, 459.

To Capt. John C. Kelton

By Telegraph from Cairo [*Dec.*] 11 *1861*
To Capt. J. C. Kelton
A. A. G.

our Scouts had a skirmish with the enemy to day in which we took sixteen (16) prisoners and lost one man and one horse killed

U. S. Grant
Brig. Gen

Telegram received, DNA, RG 94, Generals' Papers and Books, Telegrams Received by Gen. Halleck; copy, *ibid.*, RG 393, Dept. of the Mo., Telegrams Received. On Dec. 12, 1861, Maj. John J. Mudd, 2nd Ill. Cav., wrote to Col. Richard J. Oglesby. "I have the honor to report. That in obedience to your special Order No   dated 3 O.clock A. M. Dec 11th I marched with my entire force & Capt Nolemans Cavalry Company to Charleston arriving there at 8 O clock & finding the town occupied by the troops under Lieut Col Rhoads   after resting & consulting with Col Rhoads I proceeded to Bertrand where we had the misfortune to loose one of our most gallant soldiers Josiah Clark of Co B from Logan Co. Ill. Lieut Stone was ordered with a squad of men to examine a distillery near the town —owing to some question or doubt about the road Clark & two others seperated from the command & seeing two men on horseback fleeing—pursued them into a swamp, when the fugitives suddenly wheeled and fired killing Clark and the horse of Corp. Wm Miller of Co E. instantly and made good their escape   The rebels were dressed in citizens clothes and Clark lost his life while calling on them to surrender under the mistaken apprehension that they were Citizens. In him we have lost a brave and gallant soldier ever vigilant in doing his duty and only too bold for safety—else he would not have pursued the flying assassins into their home—*the Swamp.* I have to-day sent his remains to his family at home—We returned without farther loss arriving in Camp at dusk with fifteen prisoners six horses two mules five Guns & one pistol. several of the prisoners belong to Jeff Thompsons army some of them I brought for testimony & others on representations of the officers of my command not having time to give them a personal examination. Four of them were found secreted under a house   I trust they may have a speedy examination and such of them as are peaceable citizens, discharged and their property (if we have any of theirs) returned to them. I found in Bertrand, Morgan Rhodes & T. J. McKane, two sick soldiers of Jeff Thompsons army whom (not being in condition to be moved) I left on parole or oath not again to serve against the United States—one of Capt. Noneman's men was wounded in the foot by the accidental discharge of his pistol—In addition to the horse killed we lost one disabled & rendered worthless by a fall, also one Sabre drawn by contact with limbs during the pursuit of the fugitives who killed Clark—The property taken is of little value except one horse & I felt justified in allowing my two dismounted men to mount two of the captured horses & trust my action in the premises will be approved   Some of the property probably belongs to persons who will be released on examination & such will be returned to them & the remainder turned over to the a Quarter Mast. I ask that an order be made that a sabre be furnished to replace the one lost—To Capt Noleman and his men I am indebted for valuable information respecting the people roads &c also for doing their whole duty all the time"   ALS, *ibid.*, RG 393, District of Southeast Mo., Letters Received.

To Capt. John C. Kelton

Head Quarters Dist. S. E. Mo
Cairo Dec. 11th 1861

CAPT. J. C. KELTON
ASST. ADJT. GENL.
DEPT. OF THE Mo
ST LOUIS Mo
CAPT.

I would respectfully request a number of blank, Muster & Pay Rolls, attached, for the use of this command.

There are none of these blanks on hand in this Dist. and without them it makes a great amount of extra labor for the Paymaster.

Respectfully
Your Obt. Servt.
U. S. GRANT
Brig. Genl Comdg.

Copies, DLC-USG, V, 4, 5, 7, 8, 78; DNA, RG 393, USG Hd. Qrs. Correspondence.

To Brig. Gen. John A. McClernand

Head Quarters, Dist. S. E. Mo
Cairo, Dec. 11th 1861.

This dispatch being directed on the envelope to the under-signed was opened.

Capt. Hoskins tendered his resignation and it was accepted some days since.

U. S. GRANT
Brig. Gen Com

AES, McClernand Papers, IHi. Written on a telegram of Dec. 11, 1861, from Ill. AG Allen C. Fuller to Brig. Gen. John A. McClernand. "I cannot find capt Hoskins of Eighteenth regt" Telegram received, *ibid.* Capt. John A. Hoskins resigned on Dec. 2. See letter to Capt. George H. Walser, Sept. 19, 1861.

To Brig. Gen. John A. McClernand

Head Quarters, Dist. S. E. Mo.
Cairo, Dec. 11th 1861.

All prisoners of War may be sent to St. Louis, under escort, with a statement showing when they were taken, names &c.

U. S. GRANT
Brig. Gen. Com.

AES, McClernand Papers, IHi. Written on a letter of Dec. 11, 1861, from Brig. Gen. John A. McClernand to USG. "The following prisoners of war have been confined in the guard house, more than 30 days. W. J. Wilkins   W. J. Guthrie J. Martin   Walter Duolan   I advise you of this fact for special direction, if you should think proper to give any." LS, *ibid.*

To Maj. Gen. Henry W. Halleck

Head Quarters, Dist. S. E. Mo.
Cairo, Dec. 12th 1861.

Maj. Gen. H. W. Hallack,
Comd.g Dept. of the Mo.
St. Louis Mo.
Gen.

The bearer of this, Mrs. Johnson, is just up from Mimphis. She has given me valuable information which she will also give to you in person. For this information I have granted a free pass and required in concideration that she shall call on you in person.

A copy of this will be sent by mail.

I am Gen. very respectfully
Your Obt. svt.
U. S. Grant
Brig. Gen. Com.

ALS, DNA, RG 393, Dept. of the Tenn., Miscellaneous Letters Received. "Mrs Johnsons statements" are attached. "She has been living in Memphis about 2 years & is now looking for her son. Fort Pillow is about 80 miles above Memphis and at this point a chain has been thrown across the river forming a boom to prevent boats passing—This boom has cannon at each end, on land, to fire upon such boats as may be stopped by said boom. 12 Marine batteries gone to Columbus. They were made in New Orleans, by a Frenchman   One floating battery has been towed from Memphis to Columbus, carrying 20 guns according to report and said to be 'impregnable.' It is asserted that there are 6 of of said boats. There are neither fortifications nor cannon in Memphis. The streets are all blockaded excepting one which is left open so that if union troops enter at all they will most likely move along this street which is mined & can be blown up. People are [c]onstantly passing north & south through New Madrid—Cairo to be attacked soon—so says report"

To Maj. Gen. Leonidas Polk

Head Quarters Dist S. E. Mo
Cairo Dec 13, 1861

GENERAL

Mr H. B. Belt[1] of St Louis is here with the releases for Camp Jackson prisoners at Columbus which I promised you should be procured and forwarded—

The Department commander at St Louis does not construe the agreement between Generals Fremont & Price as making provision for the transportation and delivery of "side arms and equipments of officers & personal property of privates" to paroled prisoners who had previously gone beyond our lines & into the enemies service, and therefore will permit nothing to be sent except the releases—

I send Capt Hillyer my aid de Camp accompanied by Mr Belt under a flag of truce to deliver to you the releases

Very Respectfully
Your obt svt
U. S. GRANT
Brig Gen U. S. A
By W. S. HILLYER
A. D. C.

To Maj Gen Polk
Com'g Columbus Ky.

Copy, DNA, RG 109, Documents Printed in *O.R. O.R.*, II, i, 120.

1. Henry B. Belt, former sheriff of St. Louis, was a partner in a real estate firm.

To Capt. John C. Kelton

Head Quarters, Dist. S. E. Mo.
Cairo, Dec. 13th 1861.

CAPT. J. C. KELTON,
A. A. GEN. DEPT. OF THE MO.
ST. LOUIS, MO.
SIR:

From information received this afternoon from Columbus some movement is taking place from that point. I am inclined to believe that it will be made on Birds Point, possibly at an early hour in the morning. I am fully prepared for the best defence our means will allow let it occur where it may.

Every possible disposition has been made to detect the intention of the enemy. All the troops at Birds Point, Fort Holt and Cairo are sleeping upon their arms, with Cartridge boxes filled. Steamers are in readiness to move the Cairo troops to any point at the shortest notice.

I inclose herewith a report from Col. Ross, commanding at Cape Girardeau which may contain some information of interest to the Department.[1]

Respectfully &c.
U. S. GRANT
Brig. Gen. Com.

ALS, DNA, RG 393, Dept. of the Mo., Letters Received. *O.R.*, I, viii, 432. See following letter.

1. On Dec. 12, 1861, Col. Leonard F. Ross, Cape Girardeau, wrote to USG. "I have just recd information from New Madrid—from a reliable source—My informant arrived there on monday last—Gov Jackson was addressing the troops there on his arrival—A Col from Tenn and Jeff Thompson followed—all urging those whose term of enlistment has about expired to re-enlist—stating that they had money to pay off ~~there~~ all the troops—My informant further states that there were two Regiments there from below and ten more expected—that all were well fed & clothed—that there are eight 32 pounders mounted within the fortifications —The speakers stating to the soldiers there that Missouri having been recently recd into the Southern Confederacy would be assisted by the 'United South' in her efforts to 'free herself'—Richard Watkins one of the sons of the General has

come in and taken the oath of allegiance—I rather think the General will be in soon—From two to five of Thompsons daily are coming in and renewing their allegiance & going to their homes—"   ALS, DNA, RG 393, Dept. of the Mo., Letters Received. *O.R.*, I, viii, 432.

To Flag Officer Andrew H. Foote

————

Head Quarters, Dist. S. E. Mo.
Cairo, Dec. 13th 1861.

COMMODORE A. H. FOOTE U. S. N.
COMD.G G. B. FLEED &c.
CAIRO, ILL.
DEAR COMMODORE,

Information that I have received indicates the probability of an attack being made upon either Fort Holt or Birds Point to-night or to-morrow.

I have given instruction to the Commanding officers at these two points; have given directions also to have all the transports fully ready in case a move on the water should be necessary.

I would respectfully ask, your coopperation with the Gun-boats.

Respectfully
Your Obt. Svt.
U. S. GRANT
Brig. Gen. Com.

ALS, DNA, RG 45, Area 5. *O.R.*, I, viii, 430–31; *O.R.* (Navy), I, xxii, 461–62.

To Brig. Gen. John A. McClernand

————

Head Quarters, Dist. S. E. Mo.
Cairo, Dec. 13th 1861.

GEN. J. A. MCCLERNAND
COMD.G POST
CAIRO ILLINOIS.
GEN.

Information just received, in connection with that obtained
a few days ago, leads me to believe an attack upon Birds Point
or Fort Holt, to-night or to-morrow quite iminant.—I have
given the necessary orders to the commanders there;[1] also
orders to secure prompt movements with our transports.[2] Commodore Foote has also been notified of our danger and requested
to coopperate.[3]

It will be advisable to have all the troops at this post notified
that they are to keep within their Camps. Ammunition should be
issued so as to give Cartridge boxes full, and the Command sleep
under arms.

Respectfully
Your Obt. Svt.
U. S. GRANT
Brig. Gen. Com.

ALS, McClernand Papers, IHi. *O.R.*, I, viii, 433. On Dec. 13, 1861, Maj. Mason
Brayman wrote to USG. "Genl M'Clernand instructs me to advise you that your
request of this evening is complied with, and all the forces at this Post placed under
orders for immediate action." ADfS, McClernand Papers, IHi.

1. On Dec. 13, Capt. John A. Rawlins wrote to Col. John Cook at Fort Holt.
"Be on the *qui vive* tonight and tomorrow, strengthen your pickets and tell them
to keep a vigilant lookout. Let every man be at his post and have ~~them~~ your men
sleep on their arms." Copies, DLC-USG, V, 1, 2, 3, 79; DNA, RG 393, USG
Letters Sent. *O.R.*, I, viii, 433. See letter to Col. Richard J. Oglesby, Dec. 13,
1861.
2. On Dec. 13, Capt. William S. Hillyer wrote to George W. Graham. "Let
no boats go out from here tonight. Keep them all fired up, and ready to start at a
moments warning. Report how many transports, and their names, you have now

in port." Copies, DLC-USG, V, 1, 2, 3, 79; DNA, RG 393, USG Letters Sent.
O.R., I, viii, 430.

    3. See preceding letter.

To Brig. Gen. John A. McClernand

———

Head Quarters, Dist. S. E. Mo.
Cairo, Dec. 13th 1861

GEN.

For security and expedition in case of an attack you will
please quarter on the Steamers now in port four regiment.

The following boats can be used Alex Scott, Memphis,
White Cloud & J. Wilson.

Yours &c.
U. S. GRANT
Brig. Gen. Com.

To Gen. J. A. McClernand
Comd.g Post
Cairo Ill.

ALS, McClernand Papers, IHi. *O.R.*, I, viii, 433.

To Col. Richard J. Oglesby

———

Head Quarters Dist. S. E Mo
Cairo Dec. 13th 1861

COL R J OGLESBY
COMDG. U. S. FORCES
BIRDS POINT MO
COL

Indications are that an attack upon Birds Point or Fort Holt,
may be made tonight, or tomorrow

You will therefore instruct your Out Guards to be extra
vigilant, send scouting parties out by the different approaches,

and see that the entire command are kept, at their posts, men sleeping under arms, with their Cartridge Boxes filled.

Information will be given the GunBoats, to the end that they may be able to give all the assistance in there power

> Respectfully
> Your Obt. Servt
> U. S. GRANT
> Brig. Genl Comg.

Copies, DLC-USG, V, 1, 2, 3, 79; DNA, RG 393, USG Letters Sent. *O.R.*, I, viii, 430.

To Brig. Gen. John A. McClernand

———

> Head Quarters, Dist. S. E. Mo.
> Cairo, Dec. 14th 1861

GEN.

On your report to me of the great number of troops that are passing from Birds Point & Fort Holt, I sent over orders to the commanders there to arrest all officers who had granted passes to-day when their commands were, by order, under Arms.[1]

I also called their attention to the fact that a wrong construction was put by them on Sec. 1 of Order No 20.[2] In future passes to cross the lines was to be obtained as prescribed in Orders No 16.[3]

This I think will avoid further difficulties.

> Yours Unofficially
> U. S. GRANT
> Brig. Gen

ALS, McClernand Papers, IHi. On Dec. 11, 1861, Brig. Gen. John A. McClernand wrote to USG. "Permit me to call your attention to the fact that large numbers of men still daily pass between Fort Holt, Birds Point, and this Post, in violation of your General Order No. 16. seriously interfering with my efforts to preserve order, and secure proper discipline at this post. I refer also, to the large number of sailors and marines on shore, at all hours of the day and night, in defiance of known regulations, whereby the peace of the Post is disturbed, and disorders multiplied" Copy, *ibid*.

1. See following letter.
2. On Dec. 6, Capt. John A. Rawlins for USG issued General Orders No. 20. "Sec 1 Commissioned officers of companies will not pass the lines without written permission of their District, Brigade, or Regimental, commanders, and on official business, or for other urgent and satisfactory reasons, to be given in the letter of permission. Sec 2. Non-commissioned officers, and soldiers, are prohibited from passing outside the lines at any time, except when detailed, or ordered by competent, authority. Sec '3' Persons not in the military service of the United States, are not to pass the lines, without permission from the District or Brigade Commander. Sec 4 All persons approaching guard lines, will before attempting to pass, satisfy the officer or guard, of their right to do so. On refusing they will be turned back or arrested, as the case may require. Sec 5 Orders relative to the admission of persons of persons to the guard house, and relating to the custody of prisoners will be rigidly enforced. Officers of regiments and companies and officers of the day, and police, are enjoined to use the utmost diligence, in making known and enforcing all orders nescessary, for the safety of the command." Copies, DLC-USG, V, 12, 13, 14, 80; DNA, RG 393, USG General Orders; (printed), McClernand Papers, IHi.
3. On Nov. 20, Rawlins for USG issued General Orders No. 16. "For the purpose of preventing the confusion consequent upon the continued intercommunication of the troops at Fort Holt, Birds' Point, and Cairo and Mound City, and to secure the advantage of order and soldierly diligence, in the respective Camps at said places, It is ordered, that no Company Officer, or Soldier, shall be allowed to pass from one of said places to another, except by a written permit, to be approved by the Colonel of the Regiment, and the Commanding Officer, of the Post, Camp or Brigade. It is further ordered, That all Officers and men violating the above Order shall be personally arrested—commissioned Officers to be confined, and Non-commissioned Officers and soldiers made to labor on the public works until otherwise ordered." Copies, *ibid*.; (misdated Nov. 23, 1861) DNA, RG 393, USG General Orders. On the same day, USG issued special orders. "Hereafter no citizen will be permitted to pass from the Kentucky or Missouri shore unless furnished with a pass from these Headquarters, except persons of known loyalty; or when they do not expect to return again South. All suspicious persons found in or around Camp will be at once arrested, and sent before the Provost Marshal at Cairo." Copies, DLC-USG, V, 15, 16, 77, 82; DNA, RG 393, USG Special Orders; (printed), McClernand Papers, IHi. On Nov. 27, Maj. Mason Brayman wrote to USG. "The Officer of the Day, complains that large numbers of Soldier's still visit Cairo daily, bringing their *canteens* with them. P. S. Sutlers, selling cider at Birds Point." LS, *ibid*. On Nov. 28, Rawlins endorsed the letter. "I am instructed by Brig Genl Grant to say you will in pursuance of Genl Order No 16 of this District, direct the officer of the day to arrest and place in confinement any person found violating the same." ES, *ibid*.

To Col. John Cook

Head Quarters Dist. S. E. Mo
Cairo Dec. 14th 1861

Col. J. Cook
Comdg. U. S. Forces
Fort Holt Ky
Col

You will at once arrest all officers of your command who have granted passes today whilst the troops were to be under arms.

There seems to be a false construction put upon Sec 1 of Order No 20.

The rule in regard to passes for crossing the river, were not intended to be changed.

Yours &C.
U. S. Grant
Brig. Genl Comdg.

Copies, DLC-USG, V, 1, 2, 3, 77; DNA, RG 393, USG Letters Sent. An identical letter was sent to Col. Richard J. Oglesby. Copies, *ibid*. On Dec. 15, Capt. John A. Rawlins wrote to Oglesby. "You will release all Officers you may have arrested, under my order of yesterday." Copies, *ibid*. See preceding letter.

To J. C. Borland

Head Quarters Dist. S. E. Mo
Cairo Dec 14th 1861

J. C Borland Esq
Special Agt.
Sir

You will proceed to St Louis by Steamer   taking such freight as may offer at all points except between Birds Point and Commerce on the Mo Shore

The usual charges shall be collected and the amounts collected be passed to the credit of ~~the~~ Government

U. S. GRANT

Brig. Genl Comdg

Copies, DLC-USG, V, 1, 2, 3, 77; DNA, RG 393, USG Letters Sent. On Dec. 7, 1861, Brig. Gen. Samuel R. Curtis wrote to USG. "The bearer J C Borland Esq goes as an agent to begin the   I have been directed to institute on the Steamboat commerce of the river. I have given him a pass book which he will use on the S Boat he goes down on and will make the same use of as he returns on any boat you may direct him to come back on. Arrangements are not yet fully consumated, but I hope to get the matter systematised in a few days, so we may check the rascality that has been perpetrated in this channel of trade. Any kindness you may show to Mr Borland will oblige." Copy, Curtis Papers, IaHA. On Dec. 7, Curtis wrote to J. C. Borland. "You will proceed on the Steamboat J W Cheeseman to require all the officers crew and passengers to take and subscribe the oath I have designated for persons traveling and trading on the Mississippi river. You will also require the same from persons shipping goods as far as you may deem it expedient and commence to carry out my orders in relation to the commerce on the Mississippi. You will report to Commanding officer at Cape Girardeau and at other military posts where the boat stops, and get such information and orders as they may deem necessary and proper. At Cairo you will report for orders and return as the Commanding Officer at that place may direct." Kenneth E. Colton, ed., "With Fremont in Missouri in 1861 : Letters of Samuel Ryan Curtis," *Annals of Iowa*, 3rd Series, 24 (1942), 166–67.

Special Orders

Head Quarters, Dist. S. E. Mo.

Cairo, Dec. 15th 1861.

SPECIAL ORDER. No

The excessive amount of fatigue duty to perform at Cairo consequent upon the discharging of Quarter Master & Commissary stores for the general benefit of this District, and the details for this duty having fallen entirely heretofore upon the troops stationed in Cairo, has rendered a division of this labor necessary.

The following orders will be observed in future until otherwise directed.

Fort Holt will furnish daily 20 men under one Commissione[d] and two non commissioned Officers.

Birds Point will furnish fifty men under one Capt. one Lieut & three Non Com. Officers.

These details will form on the Wharfboats in Cairo daily at 9 O'Clock a. m. and will be specially under the direction of the Post Quarter Master & Post Commissary as fatigue parties for the day.

These parties will not be allowed to come onto the Levee except in the performance of their appropriate duties on any account whatsoever.

For the strict observance of this order the officers in charge will be held accountable.

All other details required will be furnished from the Troops at this Post on demand.

U. S. GRANT
Brig. Gen. Com

ADS, McClernand Papers, IHi. On Dec. 14, 1861, Brig. Gen. John A. McClernand wrote to USG. "Pardon me for recalling your attention to a source of increasing disquietude among the officers and men of my command. The relations of Cairo to the camps at Paducah, Caledonia, Mound City, Fort Holt, Fort Lyon, Cape Girardeau and Big Muddy Bridge, make it the centre and base of operations for all of those places, particularly in the Quarter Master's, Commissary's and Ordnance Departments. Hence the fatigue duty for the accomodation of those places, including Cairo, is for the most part performed by the men here. In addition, they have been obliged to handle large quantities of stores for the fleet being fitted out here   The requisitions made upon me from day to day for these purposes are almost incredible, and the continual details made in answer to them are painful to me, while they are rapidly wasting the strength and spirits of my men. Indeed to this cause, may be attributed in large part, the sickness, and in no inconsiderable degree the deaths occuring in my command. Knowing that you sympathize with me in this regard, I venture to appeal to you to remedy or lessen this evil. Perhaps: it might be mitigated by establishing branch depots at a number of the places named, for Commissary's, Quarter Master's, and Ordnance Stores, and requiring Commanders at those places to detail men from their respective commands to handle them. And should not the Commander of the fleet be left to do the same? I would respectfully but urgently recommend this reform as one required by the letter and spirit of paragraph 910 p 128 of Rev. Army Regulations and by justice itself. As an illustration of these representations, I may add in conclusion, that out of an average force of 5800 men for 15 days past, the details for fatigue and guard duty have averaged daily over 1000 men." Copy, *ibid*.

To Capt. John C. Kelton

Head Quarters, Dist. S. E. Mo.
Cairo, Dec. 15th 1861.

Capt. J. C. Kelton,
A. A. Gen. Dept. of the Mo.
St. Louis, Mo.
Capt.

Having seen an article in the "Chicago Tribune" charging corruption upon the Quartermaster of this Post, or his Agt. in having false vouchers made out for lumber purchased there,[1] I have sent an officer of my Staff,[2] Capt. Hatch accompanying, to investigate the matter.[3]

I have used my utmost efforts to have the duties of each department faithfully and economically administered and if corruption exists I want to have the guilty party exposed.

I hope my course in this matter will meet with the approval of the Gen. Comd.g.

I enclose herewith a report of Col. Oglesby, Comd.g at Birds Point, of the result of a reconnoisance ~~if any movement~~ made to ascertain if any movement was being made threatning that point.[4]

That active preparations are being made at Columbus there is no doubt.

I would report to the Gen. Comd.g the case of the Steamer Montgomery now laying sunk and hopelessly destroyed at what is called "Devil's Island" in the Mississippi river. The boat was in Government employment at the time, and if the loss is to be sustained by Government I would recommend that immediate steps be taken to save all of the steamer that can be of value.

Being hard pressed for storage room here some seven weeks since I authorized the hiring of this steamer,[5] then laying here idle and not under charter, as a store ship, for one month, at $600 00   She has since been used as a transport but under what agreement I do not know although I have made frequent enquiries.[6]

Yesterday I directed a report to be submitted to me of the conditions upon which said steamer was employed, to be made in time for the Mail which is now about closing.

The report, ~~in~~ when in, will be forwarded.[7]

Respectfully
U. S. GRANT
Brig. Gen. Com.

ALS, DNA, RG 393, Dept. of the Mo., Letters Received.

1. On Dec. 12, 1861, the *Chicago Tribune* reported that lumber dealers in Chicago stated that a q.m. or his agent had been purchasing lumber for Cairo at one price, then instructing the seller to prepare an invoice at a higher price. "They ask the *Tribune* to ventilate these transactions in order that the higher authorities may know what has been done. . . ."

2. Capt. William S. Hillyer.

3. See letter to Capt. John C. Kelton, Dec. 22, 1861.

4. On Dec. 14, Col. Richard J. Oglesby wrote to Capt. John A. Rawlins. "I have to report that my Scouts are in from all directions. One company went within five miles of Belmont and from near Belmont across the country to within five miles of Charleston—all report the most perfect quiet and no indications of a movement by the enemy upon this point. I will not send them out to-morrow unless directed to do so by the General. I am satisfied no attack is contemplated at this time on this Point. Such being the case men will not lie under arms to-night." ALS, DNA, RG 393, Dept. of the Mo., Letters Received.

5. See letter to Capt. Chauncey McKeever, Oct. 17, 1861, note 2.

6. See letter to Capt. Reuben B. Hatch, Jan. 4, 1862.

7. The report has not been found. See letter to Brig. Gen. Montgomery C. Meigs, Jan. 20, 1862.

To Capt. John C. Kelton

Head Quarters Dist S. E. Mo
Cairo Dec 15th 1861

CAPT J. C. KELTON
ASST ADJT GENL
DEPT OF THE MO
SIR

I have the honor to send you a list of Officers available for Court Martial duty at Cape Girardeau, with one designated as

a capable person for Judge Advocate, also charges and specifications in three cases. There will be other ~~cases~~ to be before the
same court.

The Col Commanding at Cape Girardeau requests that the
Court be convened

> I am sir Very Respectfully
> Your obt Servt
> U. S. GRANT
> Brig Genl Comdg

Copies, DLC–USG, V, 4, 5, 7, 8, 78; DNA, RG 393, USG Hd. Qrs. Correspondence. See letter to Capt. John C. Kelton, Dec. 2, 1861, note 1.

To Capt. John C. Kelton

> Head Quarters Dist S. E. Mo
> Cairo Dec 15th 1861

CAPT J. C. KELTON
ASST ADJ'T GENL
DEPT OF THE MO
SIR

I have the honor to acknowledge the receipt of your communication of date Dec 13th 1861, directing that the returns of
the troops under my command be made out on the blank "Division Returns" furnished from Head Quarters Dept of the Mo.
I have theretofore used blank "Post Returns" no "Division
Returns" having been furnished me. You will please send me a
supply of the "Division Returns" mentioned in your communication and the same shall be used in future.

> I have the honor to remain
> Very Respectfully
> Your obt Servt
> U. S. GRANT
> Brig Genl Comd.g.

Copies, DLC-USG, V, 4, 5, 7, 8, 78; DNA, RG 393, USG Hd. Qrs. Correspondence. The letter to which USG refers was apparently a circular, for it is copied in the letterbooks as addressed to "Commanding Officer 3d Division Rolla, Mo." "The Commanding General directs that the returns of the troops under your command be made out on the blank 'division returns' furnished from this office." Copies, DLC-USG, V, 7, 8, 9; DNA, RG 393, USG Hd. Qrs. Correspondence.

To John Riggin, Jr.

Head Quarters Dist. S. E. Mo
Cairo Dec 15th 1861

SIR

You will proceed by first conveyance to Goose Island, in the Mississippi river below Commerce, and examine some goods said to have been landed there by the Steamer Neptune, on her downward trip, and which with the alleged are said to be now detained.

If there is evidence that these goods are intended to be conveyed to other points than represented, in the invoices or are other than marked, you will ~~forward them~~ take possession of them and forward them to the Provost Marshall St Louis Mo. with a full report of all the facts elicited

Should they have been invoiced for any other point than Goose Island you will report that, as militating against the Steamer that conveyed them.

U. S. GRANT
Brig Genl Comg

To Maj J Riggin Junr.
Vol. Aid de Camp

Copies, DLC-USG, V, 1, 2, 3, 79; DNA, RG 393, USG Letters Sent. John Riggin, Jr., of Mo. served as vol. aide-de-camp to USG until confirmed as col. to rank from May 3, 1862. Although referred to as maj. in this letter and in General Orders No. 22, Dec. 23, 1861, Riggin's rank appears to be honorary.

Circular

———

Head Quarters Dist. S. E. Mo
Cairo Dec 16th 1861

The practice of sending to these Head Quarters for passes for the bodies of deceased Soldiers, and a comrade or two two to accompany them, having become so prevalent and it being so painful to the General Commanding to be oliged to refuse all such applications as he necessarily must do, the attention of this command is called to the fact that the right does not exist to give them passes.

Full provisions are made for the registration of each deceased Soldier in such manner that no difficulty will exist hereafter in friends recovering their remains.

This is a humane provision, and it is hoped no more applications for such passes will be made to these Head Quarters.

U. S. GRANT
Brig Genl Comd.g

Copies, DLC-USG, V, 12, 13, 14, 80; DNA, RG 393, USG General Orders.

To Capt. John C. Kelton

———

Head Quarters, Dist. S. E. Mo.
Cairo, Dec. 16th 1861.

CAPT. J. C. KELTON
A. A. GEN. DEPT. OF THE MISSOURI
ST. LOUIS Mo.
CAPT.

A Gentleman of Charleston Mo., one of the very few Union men there, come up from Columbus last night and reports that four Infantry regiments and three Gun boats left there Saturday night, for New Orleans, where a battle was being fought and the city severely threatened by Federal troops.

This I think reliable so far as the leaving of troops and Gunboats is concerned.

> Respectfully &c.
> U. S. GRANT
> Brig. Gen. Com.

ALS, DNA, RG 393, Dept. of the Mo., Letters Received. All the information was wrong.

To Capt. Thomas J. Larison

———

> Head Quarters Dist. S. E. Mo
> Cairo Dec 16th 1861

CAPT. T. J. LARISON

SIR

Having released one Capt. and one Lieut. from Gen M Jeff Thompsons Army, to secure the release of Lieut Tenney[1] and yourself and having received a letter from Gen. Thompson fully indicating that you would be released on a proper exchange, further being fully assured by Lieut. Col. Chappell, Aid de Camp and Chief of Staff to Gen. Thompson that you might consider yourselves fully released therefore I declare that you are fully absolved from further obligation by your Parole of Honor

> U. S. GRANT
> Brig. Genl. Comdg

Copies, DLC–USG, V, 1, 2, 3, 79; DNA, RG 393, USG Letters Sent. *O.R.*, II, i, 530. See letter to Brig. Gen. M. Jeff Thompson, Dec. 4, 1861.

1. 2nd Lt. Jerome B. Tenney of Atlanta, Ill., 2nd Ill. Cav.

To T. J. Rice

Head Quarters Dist. S. E. Mo
Cairo Dec 16th 1861

T. J. RICE ESQ
SPECIAL AGT.
SIR

You will [*go*] to St Louis by first Government Steamer avoiding all landings on Mo. Shore, between here and Cape Girardeau. At other points you may take such freight, as offers, and such passengers as may come within your instructions, charging usual tariff and passing same to the credit of the United States

U. S. GRANT
Brig. Genl Comdg

Copies, DLC-USG, V, 1, 2, 3, 79; DNA, RG 393, USG Letters Sent.

To Capt. John C. Kelton

Head Quarters, Dist. S. E. Mo.
Cairo, Dec. 17th 1861.

CAPT. J. C. KELTON
A. A. GEN. DEPT. OF THE MO.
ST. LOUIS, MO
CAPT.

On the strength of telegraphic despatch, received from St. Louis, that the prisoners ariving here yesterday were imposters I have ordered them back to St. Louis.[1]

Eight of these prisoners did not claim to have been taken at Camp Jackson, and had with them regular certificates of exchange. As I am anxious to make as few shipments of these men as possible, and as there was nothing in my telegraphic instructions to prevent it, I returned these also.

I would report that I received a despatch a few days ago that
Quinine was being shipped from St. Louis via the Ohio & Mississippi and Ill. C. R. R. to ~~Pulaski~~ Du Quoin, where it was received by special Agt. and transported across land to the Mississippi river, thence through Missouri South. I sent up a Detec-
tive who captured 100 oz. together with evidence that it was
destined for Memphis, and that the Agt. was to receive $500 00
for his trouble if he succeeded in geting it through.[2]

Shall I turn this over to the Marshall of the District,[3] with
the evidence?

I have heretofore reported the fact that the Quartermasters
Department has been carried on at this place, almost without
funds, from the earlyest assembling of troops. There is therefore
necessarily a large indebtedness accrued against Government.
The vouchers issued in payment of these claims are constantly
coming before me for approval, (the Quartermaster declining to
settle anything without) and necessarily occupy much of my
time. As many of these accounts should not be allowed, and
others should be reduced I would respectfully urge the necessity
of sending here an experienced Agt. of the Dept.

Aside from the necessity of an experienced Agt. to settle the
old claims I think the good of the service would be subserved by
having an old officer of the Quarter Master's Dept. here.

> Respectfully
> U. S. GRANT
> Brig. Gen. Com.

ALS, DNA, RG 393, Dept. of the Mo., Letters Received. *O.R.*, I, viii, 440; *ibid.*,
II, i, 120.

1. See letter to Maj. Gen. Henry W. Halleck, Dec. 20, 1861.
2. On Dec. 8, 1861, G. T. Wall, Du Quoin, Ill., telegraphed to USG. "Do
not Send to Pulaski Seized here all right" Telegram received, DNA, RG
393, Dept. of the Mo., Telegrams Received.
3. David L. Phillips, U.S. marshal for the southern district of Ill.

To Brig. Gen. John A. McClernand

———

Head Quarters, Dist. S. E. Mo.
Cairo, Dec. 17th 1861

GEN. J. A. McCLERNAND
COMDG POST
CAIRO, ILLINOIS
GEN.

My attention has just been called again to the insufficiency of the present Guard house.

I would direct that a suitable Guard house be built for the accommodation of prisoners of War and political prisoners, keeping the two separate, retaining the present establishment for soldiers exclusively.

Respectfully &c.
U. S. GRANT
Brig. Gen. Com.

ALS, McClernand Papers, IHi.

To Commanding Officer, 22nd Ill.

———

Head Quarters Dist. S. E. Mo
Cairo Dec 17th 1861

COMDG. OFFICER
22ND ILL VOLS
BIRDS POINT MO
SIR

You will order Capt. J Seaton[1] of your command and seven men that are with him, to return to duty with their Co. and Regiment, within twenty four hours, failing in so doing you will report them as deserters

U. S. GRANT
Brig. Gen Comdg

Copies, DLC-USG, V, 1, 2, 3, 77; DNA, RG 393, USG Letters Sent. Col. Henry Dougherty, 22nd Ill., was still recovering from wounds received at Belmont.

1. Capt. John Seaton of Alton, Ill., 22nd Ill., resigned on June 13, 1862. On Nov. 25, 1861, Seaton wrote to Col. Richard J. Oglesby from Cave in Rock, Ill., where he was in command of 140 men, to report the capture of considerable ammunition intended for the C. S. A. ALS, *ibid.*, District of Southeast Mo., Letters Received. On Dec. 13, Seaton telegraphed to USG from Alton. "The men are out in the country. I will hunt them up & bring them down. Will you send Passes for recruits?" Telegram received (punctuation added), *ibid.*, Dept. of the Mo., Telegrams Received. On Dec. 30, Capt. John A. Rawlins issued special orders for Seaton. "Captain John Seaton of the 22d Regiment Illinois Volunteers, is hereby released from arrest, and restored to duty with his company. The General commanding is induced to overlook the great breach of good order and military discipline of which Captain Seaton was guilty, from the high testimonial of good character and general military conduct given him by his Commanding Officer, and for the conspicuous part he took in the battle of Belmont. It is hoped that Captain Seaton, will not again subject himself to charges of so serious a nature." Copies, DLC-USG, V, 15, 16, 82; DNA, RG 393, USG Special Orders. The nature of Seaton's offense is unknown.

To Maj. Joseph D. Webster

Head Quarters Dist. S. E. Mo
Cairo Dec 17th 1861

Col. Webster
Chief of Engineers
Cairo Ill

You are hereby authorized to employ a foreman and a suitable number of laborers for the purpose of quarrieing Rock on the banks of the Ohio river, near Golconda[1] when the services of the laborers are secured you will releive the two companies now there and return them to their command

U. S. Grant
Brig Genl Comdg.

Copies, DLC-USG, V, 1, 2, 3, 77; DNA, RG 393, USG Letters Sent.

1. Golconda, Ill., on the Ohio River about forty-five miles northeast of Cairo (about seventy-five miles via the river).

To Capt. Thomas J. Haines

Head Quarters Dist S. E. Mo
Cairo Dec 17th 1861.

Capt Haynes
Chief Comdg Dept of the Mo
St Louis Mo
Sir

Enclosed I send you "copy" of complaints made against the bread furnished by the former contractor of this place.

These complaints are new to me but being responsibly made must receive consideration.

Mr Lazare[1] also makes charges of corruption against the new contractor which immediately elicited from me an order suspending the new contract until the question can be decided. He charges that the man who is to bake the bread is to receive but 2¼ cts pr pound.

On the whole I am not at all pleased with the anxiety shown by Capt Leland to change from one contractor to another, nor the disposition of Mr Lazare to extort a price which he now seems willing to fall much below.

I have not the time nor the inclination to watch these matters and would like to have Agts of the Government who I could rely on without the necessity of interferance on my part.

I would recommend that this whole matter be allowed to stand until Capt Du Barry,[2] who is ordered here, arrives

Yours &c
U. S. Grant
Brig Genl Comdg

Copies, DLC-USG, V, 1, 2, 3, 79; DNA, RG 393, USG Letters Sent. See letter to Capt. Thomas J. Haines, Nov. 29, 1861.

1. See *Personal Memoirs of John H. Brinton* (New York, 1914), p. 111.
2. Capt. Beekman Du Barry of N.J., USMA 1849, had recently been assigned as chief of commissariat, forces in the field, west Ky.

To Capt. William W. Leland

Head Quarters Dist. S. E. Mo
Cairo Dec 17th 1861

Capt. W. W. Leland
A. C. S.
Sir

You are directed to notify the parties to whom you gave a contract for baking bread for this command to suspend operations as the work done may be lost to them.

I certainly cannot allow the contract approved by me to go on under the present alleged state of facts, and wish to give timely notice that as little sacrifice be made as possible.

Your &c.
U. S. Grant
Brig. Genl Comdg

Copies, DLC-USG, V, 1, 2, 3, 77; DNA, RG 393, USG Letters Sent. See letter to Capt. William W. Leland, Jan. 1, 1862. Capt. William W. Leland of N.Y. had been appointed commissary of subsistence of vols. on Nov. 16, 1861 at the request of Act. Brig. Gen. Thomas F. Meagher of the Irish Brigade. Lincoln, *Works*, V, 25. For his assignment to the District of Southeast Mo., see letter to Brig. Gen. Lorenzo Thomas, Oct. 20, 1861.

To Capt. William W. Leland

Head Quarters Dist. S. E. Mo
Cairo Dec 17th 1861

Capt. W. W. Leland
Com. of Sub.
Cairo Ill

You will furnish Jno Knight and two others of the 7th Iowa Vols. with two days prepared rations each, being wounded and returning to their Regt.

U. S. Grant
Brig. Genl Comdg

Copies, DLC-USG, V, 1, 2, 3, 77; DNA, RG 393, USG Letters Sent.

To Capt. Livingstone

———

Head Quarters Dist S. E. Mo
Cairo Dec 17th 1861

CAPT LIVINGSTONE
SPECIAL AGENT
SIR

The man sent you has just reported himself to me as a Camp Jackson Prisoner with the accompanying release.

You will return him with the other prisoners in your charge, to the Provost Martial in St Louis and report his case.

U. S. GRANT
Brig Genl Comd.g

Copies, DLC-USG, V, 1, 2, 3, 77; DNA, RG 393, USG Letters Sent. On Dec. 17, 1861, 1st Lt. Clark B. Lagow wrote to Capt. Livingstone. "You will proceed to St Louis with the prisoners in your charge, on board the Steamer D. G. Taylor" Copies, *ibid.* See letters to Capt. John C. Kelton, Dec. 17, 1861, and to Maj. Gen. Henry W. Halleck, Dec. 20, 1861.

To Abraham Lincoln

———

Head Quarters Dist S. E. Mo
Cairo Dec 18th 1861

TO HIS EXCELLENCY
THE PRESIDENT OF THE UNITED STATES
WASHINGTON D. C.

We the undersigned join in recommending Father Hugh Quigley, Catholic Priest for the position of Chaplain of the Army at large.

The great mass of our Volunteer Army being Protestant in belief, we do not feel justified in recommending a Catholic for any particular Hospital, Regiment or small command, but the Army containing many members of the latter persuasion, who from their prejudices cannot receive consolation from others than of their own faith, and as defenders of their country, being equally entitled to moral advice with all others, we urgently recommend the appointment asked for above.

> U. S. Grant
> Brig. Gen. Com. Dist. S. E. Mo.
> John A. Mc Clernand
> Brig. Genl. Comg. Post.

DS, OFH. On April 7, 1862, Father Hugh Quigley wrote to both Secretary of State William H. Seward and Secretary of War Edwin M. Stanton stating that he had served as chaplain for USG's army for five months without receiving a commission or pay, and that no Catholic chaplain was currently with that army. ALS (2), DNA, RG 107, Letters Received. Quigley enclosed in his letter to Seward a letter from Brig. Gen. John A. McClernand, March 25. "I have not yet heard from the President in answer to the application of Genl. Grant and myself —or to my subsequent letter." ALS, *ibid*. By "subsequent letter," McClernand may refer to the postscript of his letter of Jan. 28 to President Abraham Lincoln. ALS, DLC-Robert T. Lincoln.

This correspondence resulted in no known action, and the position of chaplain at large was apparently nonexistent. U.S. Army regulations provided a chaplain for each regt. and no more than thirty assigned to posts. *Revised Regulations for the Army of the United States* (Philadelphia, 1861), pp. 36–37. Chaplains for each vol. regt. were authorized by AGO General Orders No. 15, May 4, 1861, but no additional chaplains were appointed until AGO General Orders No. 55, May 24, 1862, authorized a chaplain for each permanent hospital. Catholic chaplains were fairly uncommon before the Civil War, and none served in the U.S. Army during the Civil War as other than regt. or hospital chaplains. Dom Aidan Henry Germain, *Catholic Military and Naval Chaplains, 1776–1917* (Washington, 1929).

At the court-martial of Col. Michael K. Lawler, 18th Ill., then in progress, one of the charges was that Lawler, himself a Catholic, had appointed a priest, Father Louis A. Lambert, as chaplain of his regt., instead of a Protestant minister favored by the officers. William A. Pitkin, "Michael K. Lawler's Ordeal with the Eighteenth Illinois," *Journal of the Illinois State Historical Society*, LVIII, 4 (Winter, 1965), 366. On Dec. 9, thirty-one officers of the 18th Ill. sent USG a petition. "We the undersigned commissioned officers of the 18th Regiment Illinois Volunteers feeling ever mindful that we are daily making history which will be either creditable or discreditable to ourselves our children and posterity are greatly impressed with the necessity of having the moral faculties of the men composing our command well cultivated and instructed in all those divine principles calculated to make men honest upright and humane having a reverential respect for the rule of right instead of wrong and believing this can be more easily attained by having proper religious discourses delivered by authorized persons ordained by the rules and regulations of the various Protestant denominations extant in our country Most respectfully ask that we be permitted to set forth unto your honor the grievances which are weighing us and our command down almost

beyond endurance   1st On or about the first days of July last our Colonel M K
Lawler appointed Father Louis Lambert a roman catholic to the office of Chaplain
of this regiment who has been regularly mustered and paid as such from the day
of his appointment until this time although he is seldom amongst us he has never
on a single occasion held any kind of religious services in this regiment, he has
never visited our sick either in quarters or in hospital nor has he made a single
quarterly report showing the moral and religious condition of the regiment as
required by the Army regulations but has wholly neglected to perform any of the
duties of chaplain   2d Said Chaplain and Col M K Lawler are the only officers
in the regiment of the roman catholic persuasion nine tenths of the men of the
regiment are protestants holding strong prejudices against all catholic priests
who would not attend his ministration without compulsion were he disposed to
hold any   3d The commissioned offices of this regiment supposing that their
wishes and desires would be consulted by said colonel in the appointment of a
chaplain most respectfully petitioned Col Lawler to appoint a Protestant minister
of acknowledged ability and extensive usefulness to the chaplaincy of this regiment which petition was in writing and signed by ten captains and twelve or
fifteen Lieutenants of said regiment in fact and truth all officers to which it was
shown signed it except the Major which petition was personally ~~delivered~~
presented to Col Lawler by Captain Brush many days previous to the appointment
of said Lambert   Yet in despite of these respectful representations of our desires
Col Lawler appointed said chaplain upon the sole ground that he was a roman
catholic   4th We further show that a majority of the members of this regiment
are members of and belong to churches of the protestant persuasion and are very
conscientious in their devotions and maintain a fair reputation for religious deportment and rectitude   5th From some cause or law unknown to your petitioners
Col Lawler required that the morning reports at several different times and for
many days at a time should show that the chaplain was present when in fact and
in truth he well knew he was not   this act still increased the indignity and aroused
a new the prejudices existing against said chaplain thus destroying all the good he
possibly might otherwise have been able to accomplish   6th And we further
show that the whole number of catholics in the regiment is but ninety whilst the
number of Protestants is eight hundred and thirty   7th And we further show
that on various occasions when catholic service has been held in Cairo those of that
persuasion have been indiscriminately permitted by Col Lawler to pass the guard
lines for the purpose of attending church and that instead of attending the same
or after attending the same before their return to their quarters became intoxicated
thereby giving great trouble and annoyance to the offices of the regiment thus
bringing disgrace upon the entire command from the effects of which we are in a
measure remidiless   8th We further show that a large majority of the men of
this regiment are free holders and pay large amount of taxes at home and are
honored members of the communit~~y~~ies in which they live being by occupation
Farmers Physicians Lawyers [sc]hool teachers preachers and Mechanics   their
time property and lives they are willing to sacrifice for their country but their fair
reputation they hold most sacred and will not shrink from maintaining it in tact
9th We further show that other catholic priest in this immediate vicinity who are
personally acquainted with Father Lambert and his general deportment have
expressed themselves to the effect that he was not at all qualified to fill the position
which he now occupies and speak of him in a very desultory manner clearly showing that he is not held in fair esteem by his peers   These a few only of the many

grievances which we might present in regard to this matter are sufficient we doubt not for a moment ~~will~~ to enlist your co operation and approval to such an extent that you will readily give us such relief as may be in your power   We do not prefer charges for a court martial but ask and claim that he be withdrawn from the service by those possessing the power and in duty bound we will ever pray" DS, DNA, RG 94, Carded Records, Vol. Organizations, Civil War, Louis A. Lambert. Muster rolls show that Lambert was not on active service with the 18th Ill. after 1861, though he was at Pittsburg, Tenn., when he resigned. On April 2, 1862, Lambert submitted his resignation. "My reason for doing so is that, by having greater liberty I can enlarge the sphere of my usefulness, to those of the Army who desire my services." LS, *ibid*. On April 11, USG endorsed Lambert's letter. "Approved and Respectfully forwarded to Department of the Mississippi." ES, *ibid*. The resignation was accepted as of April 17.

To Capt. John C. Kelton

Head Quarters, Dist. S. E. Mo.
Cairo, Dec. 18th 1861.

CAPT. J. C. KELTON
A. A. GEN. DEPT. OF THE MISSOURI
ST. LOUIS, MO.
CAPT.

A man sent by me to Columbus Ky. and who spent several days there, and also a man who deserted this morning from the Steamer Grampus,[1] have been in, one this afternoon, the other this evening.

They both confirm the report that three of the Gunboats have left for the South and that a great many of the troops are gone. Three regiments however have gone but eight miles, to Camp Burnett, on the Clinton[2] road. Three more have gone to reinforce Bowen at Feliciana.[3]

One reports that he heard that the Federals had taken Fort Jackson.[4] I am not aware that any of our Naval expeditions have been out long enough to make this story probable, but give it for what it is worth. It confirms news reported by me a few days since.

The army is reported to be composed of boys, badly disciplined and drilled, and badly off for shoes. Clothing is coming in from the country, particularly from Arkansas.

Many articles of a soldiers rations are becoming scarce, but Cornmeal & beef are yet abundent. If salt can be kept out however they will have some difficulty in saving their bacon.

There are seven companies of the 45th Regt. Ill. Vols. at Camp Douglas,[5] with improved arms for 1000 men, and clothing for the same, who are anxious to come here. If they could consistently be sent before being mustered into the service of the United States I would be much pleased.

This application is made because the the desire to come has been expressed by the senior officers of this Regt.[6]

> I Am Capt.
> Respectfully
> Your Obt. Svt.
> U. S. GRANT
> Brig. Gen. Com.

ALS, DNA, RG 393, Dept. of the Mo., Letters Received. *O.R.*, I, vii, 507. See letter to Capt. John C. Kelton, Dec. 16, 1861.

1. The *Grampus*, converted to a gunboat, was later used in the defense of Island No. 10 and sunk by the C. S. A. when the island fell. *O.R.* (Navy), I, xxii, 725.

2. Clinton, Ky., was not much more than eight miles southeast of Columbus.

3. Feliciana, Ky., about twenty miles southeast of Columbus.

4. Fort Jackson, La., at the mouth of the Mississippi River, remained under C. S. A. control until the capture of New Orleans in April, 1862.

5. Camp Douglas, Chicago.

6. The 45th Ill., also known as the Washburne Lead Mine Regt., was recruited in Jo Daviess and surrounding counties. Col. John E. Smith of Galena was a prewar friend of USG, and this probably explains the request for assignment at Cairo. Despite USG's request, the regt. was mustered in at Chicago on Dec. 25, 1861, before leaving for Cairo on Jan. 12, 1862.

To Capt. John C. Kelton

Head Quarters Dist S. E. Mo.
Cairo Dec 18th 1861.

CAPT J. C. KELTON
A. A. GENL DEPT OF THE MO
ST LOUIS, MO
CAPT

The bearer hereof represents that he recd a pass from the Genl Comdg the Dept, to this place to rejoin his Regiment, (3d Ills Cavalry) which not being here, I have given him a pass to return to St Louis, there to ascertain the whereabouts of his Regiment, so that he may rejoin the same.

I am Sir Very Respectfully
Your obt Servt
U. S. GRANT
Brig Genl Comd.g

LS, DNA, RG 393, Dept. of the Mo., Letters Received. The circumstances surrounding this letter are unknown. The 3rd Ill. Cav. was then at Rolla, Mo.

To Col. Richard J. Oglesby

Head Quarters Dist S. E. Mo
Cairo Dec 18th 1861

SPECIAL ORDER

Col R. J. Oglesby, Comdg U. S. Forces, at Birds Point, Mo, will appoint a suitable person from his command to receive and receipt for, the rolling stock, fixtures &c of the Cairo & Fulton R. R.

Col A. H. Waterman will turn over all such property to the person so appointed.

By Order
U. S. GRANT
Brig Genl Comdg

Copies, DLC–USG, V, 15, 16, 77, 82; DNA, RG 393, USG Special Orders. See letter to Capt. John C. Kelton, Dec. 8, 1861.

To Capt. Reuben B. Hatch

———

Head Quarters Dist. S. E. Mo
Cairo Dec 18th 1861

SPECIAL ORDER

The Dist Quarter Master Capt Hatch, will report to these Head Quarters with as little delay as ~~possible~~ practicable the amount of money received by the Ferries, Transports and all River craft in the employ of Government, in his charge, up to this date, for passage, rent of Bars, and other priveledges, and how the same have been Applied.

Hereafter a report will be made each Saturday to the same effect.

By Order
U. S. GRANT
Brig Genl Comdg

Copies, DLC–USG, V, 15, 16, 77, 82; DNA, RG 393, USG Special Orders.

To Mary Grant

———

Cairo, Dec. 18th 1861

DEAR SISTER:

I have been wanting to write to you for some time and am not so indifferent as you would make out. I wish you could be here for a day or two to see what I have to go through from breakfast until 12 O Clock at night, seven days in the week. I have now just got through with my mail for to-night, and as it is not yet 12 and the mail does not close until that time, I will devote the remainder of the time in pening you a few lines. I have no war news to communicate however.

Julia and the children have returned from St. Louis. They will not make you the promised visit whilst I remain here.

Capt. Foley[1] arrived to-day and I showed him all the attention I could but I regret to say it was not much. He will excuse it however. I am sorry you did not come with him. I believe I would let the children go back with you.

I have learned through private sources that an attack has been made upon Fort Jackson Louisiana and the place has been taken.[2] That is to say such is the report in Columbus but I do not know whether to credit the report. Something has taken place to call off many of their troops. They still have a much larger force than I have.

Whilst I am writing several Galena gentlemen are in talking. They will remain until the office closes so you must excuse a disconnected letter.

I do not now see that the probabilities are so strong that I will likely be removed. A full disposition seems to have been made of all my seniors.

Father seems to be very much inclined to criticise all our Generals. It may have been a little inexcusable in Gen. Buell not to allow troops to stop for a few hours when near their homes. But he should recollect that Gen. Buell was not on the spot to see the circumstances fully, and he does not know what necessity may have existed to have got the troops through by a certain time.

At your request I send a small batch from my cranium. I doubt whether it is long enough for the purpose you want it.

If you will come out here you might spend a few weeks pleasantly and I hope you will not loose such an opportunity as has just occured.

I will close this. My love to all at home.

Your Brother
ULYS.

ALS, James S. Schoff, New York, N.Y.

1. See letter to Jesse Root Grant, Aug. 27, 1861.
2. See letter to Capt. John C. Kelton, Dec. 18, 1861.

To Capt. John C. Kelton

Head Quarters Dist. S. E. Mo
Cairo Dec 19th 1861

CAPT. J. C. KELTON
ASST. ADJT. GENL.
DEPT. OF THE MO
ST LOUIS MO
SIR

In compliance with Circular from Head Quarters Dept. of the Mo St Louis Dec 11th 1861, I send you the following names of Officers from which to constitute a Board for the examination &c. of Volunteers Officers "Viz"

1	Col. James D. Morgan	10th Ill Vols	
2	” W. H. L. Wallace	11th ” ”	
3	Lieut Col. H. E. Hart	22nd ” ”	
4	” ” L. H. Waters	28th ” ”	
5	” ” John H White	31 ” ”	
6	” ” Edwd Prince	7 ” Cavalry	
7	Major R. Rawalt	7 ” Vols	
8	Capt. Ezra Taylor	Taylors Battery	

I am sir very respectfully
Your Obt. Svt.
U S GRANT
Brig Genl Comdg

Copies, DLC-USG, V, 4, 5, 7, 8, 78; DNA, RG 393, USG Hd. Qrs. Correspondence. On Dec. 26, 1861, Capt. John A. Rawlins issued a circular. "A Board of Officers having been appointed by Special Order No 83 from Head Quarters Department of the Missouri to convene at this place, all commanders of Posts Brigades Regiments or Detatchments are directed to send in the names of such officers of their respective commands as they believe to be disqualified from any cause to to fill the position assigned them by their Commissions. The names of such persons as can testify to character capacity &c will also be sent. Commanders at

Cape Girardeau Paducah and Shawneetown will furnish the names of all officers
they may desire to bring before this commission as early as possible   The names
of all persons recommended to fill vacancies of commissioned Officers, (to be
taken from Companies where vacancies exist) will also be sent before this Board"
Copies, DLC-USG, V, 12, 13, 14, 80; DNA, RG 393, USG General Orders.

To Brig. Gen. John A. McClernand

Head Quarters, Dist. S. E. Mo.
Cairo, Dec. 19th 1861

GEN. J. A. McCLERNAND
COMD.G CAIRO ILL.
GEN.

Being required to make a report, to leave by to-nights mail,
of the probable cost of improvements made within my command,
the cost of the same, the number of troops ~~accom~~ quarters have
been built for, the style of stables built and for how many horses,
I would be obliged if you would furnish me the data from your
command.

The exact cost is not demanded but the probable amount
when the buildings are completed.

Respectfully &c.
U. S. GRANT
Brig. Gen. Com

ALS, McClernand Papers, IHi. On Dec. 19, 1861, Maj. Mason Brayman wrote
to USG. "I am instructed by Genl. M'Clernand to transmit, in compliance with
your request of this day, the Report of Capt. Jas. Dunlap, asst. Qr. Master U. S. A,
of Expenditures for buildings &c" ADf, *ibid*. See letter to Brig. Gen. Samuel
D. Sturgis, Dec. 19, 1861.
In addition to the required information, McClernand also supplied a lengthy
letter addressed to Maj. Gen. Henry W. Halleck, dated Dec. 17, in which he
reviewed the history of his brigade and listed its deficiencies in equipment. LS,
DNA, RG 393, Dept. of the Mo., Letters Received. On Dec. 24, Capt. John C.
Kelton wrote to USG. "The General Commanding has received and examined the
very full, and satisfactory, report of Brig. Genl. McClernand on the condition of
his command. He regrets that at present he has no arms to furnish him, not having
half enough to supply the troops which are here waiting to take the field. All other
supplies will be furnished him as soon as possible on regular requisitions on the
proper departments. It is hoped that arms may soon be received" LS, *ibid.*,
Letters Sent (Press).

To Brig. Gen. John A. McClernand

Head Qrs. Dist. S. E. Mo.
Cairo, Dec. 19th 1861.

The fact of a soldier being an Alien is no ground whatever upon which to predicate a discharge.

U. S. Grant
Brig. Gen. Com.

AES, McClernand Papers, IHi. Written on a letter of Dec. 19, 1861, from Brig. Gen. John A. McClernand to USG. "Having received a letter from I. Edward Wilkens, B. C. at St Louis, referring, among other things, to a man by the name of 'Groom,' a soldier in the service of the U. S. who is represented to be a British subject; I refer the same to you. If I understood Dr Turner aright Mr. Wilkens desires that Groom should be discharged. The passage in Mr. Wilkens letter referred to is as follows. Viz:—'I am also anxious to ask your favorable consideration of the case of a man named Groom the particulars of which I have mentioned to Dr Turner. The uncle of Groom is, or was, well known to my friends in England, as an official assignee of the court of Bankruptcy.' " LS, *ibid.* Private Edwin P. Groom of Champaign, Ill., served in Co. A, 20th Ill., until discharged for disability on March 15, 1863. McClernand wrote to USG again about Groom in a letter dated only "Dec. 1861" but enclosing a letter from Groom dated Dec. 20. "I have the honor to enclose you the following communication's concerning the discharge of Edwin P Groom a private of Company "A" 20th Regt Ill Vols who claims and is represented to be a British subject, for your consideration." Copy, *ibid.*

To Brig. Gen. John A. McClernand

Head Quarters Dist. S. E. Mo.
Cairo, Dec. 19th 1861

Gen. J. A. McClernand
Comd.g Cairo, Ill.
Gen.

Col. Totten[1] Chief of Artillery is here to inspect the Artillery. He desires that Capt. Dresser's[2] Battery be got in readiness for

inspection this forenoon and Capt. Schwartz's by 3 O'Clock
P. M.

Will you please give the notice.

Yours Truly

U. S. GRANT

P. S. Col. Totten wish to see all the men, cooks, sick in quarters
and all that can be on the ground. He also wishes a prepared list
of all the members of the company ready.

GRANT

ALS, McClernand Papers, IHi. On Dec. 19, 1861, Maj. Mason Brayman wrote
to USG. "Your order for the Inspection of Capt. Dressers Battery this forenoon
and Capt Schwartz at three, is received at *one*. They are ordered for *two* and three.
Will that be satisfactory?" ADfS, *ibid*.

1. Lt. Col. James Totten of Pa., USMA 1841, was serving as chief of art.,
Dept. of the Mo. His inspection of art. in USG's command was ordered in Special
Orders No. 68, Dept. of the Mo., Dec. 17, 1861. Copy, DNA, RG 393, Dept. of
the Mo., Special Orders.
2. Capt. Jasper M. Dresser commanded Battery D, 2nd Ill. Light Art.

To Brig. Gen. Samuel D. Sturgis

———

Cairo, Dec. 19th 1861

DEAR STURGIS;

Hereto appended I send you about the cost of improvements
made in the way of Winter Quarters, stabling, store houses &c.
at Birds Point & Fort Holt.[1]

As requested by you I called upon the Qr. Masters for these
reports but have not yet received them for this post. We have
built here for four regiments of Infantry and some four odd companies with stabling for two or three hundred horses. As building material for this post had all to be purchased the cost of
improvements in Cairo will probably cost more that at both the

other points. If I get in the report to-morrow I will mail it at once.

The buildings at Cairo will be of service for storehouses, or other purposes for a long time to come if required, if not the material should sell for about one half the original cost.

Taking into view the fact that most ~~the~~ of the tents furnished the Army have been of poor material, and to have staid in Camp during the Winter new ones would have to been supplied, the cost of Quarters has been low.

They were built by order of Maj. Gen. Frémont, on my recommendation.

Yours

U. S. GRANT

P. S. I have also expenditures for Cairo and transmit herewith. Cost less than I supposed.

U. S. G.

ALS, DNA, RG 393, Dept. of the Mo., Letters Received. Brig. Gen. Samuel D. Sturgis of Pa., USMA 1846, served as chief of staff to Maj. Gen. David Hunter during his brief command of the Western Dept., then was sent by Maj. Gen. Henry W. Halleck on a tour of inspection of posts on the Ohio and Mississippi rivers in Dec., 1861. See letter to Brig. Gen. John A. McClernand, Dec. 19, 1861.

1. On Dec. 19, Capt. John A. Rawlins wrote to Capt. Reuben B. Hatch. "You will send to these Head Quarter immediately a Report of the Am.t and cost of Building material used at Birds Point & Ft. Holt for building Barracks and making improvements of different kinds." Copies, DLC-USG, V, 1, 2, 3, 77; DNA, RG 393, USG Letters Sent.

To Col. Amory K. Johnson

———

Head Quarters Dist S. E. Mo
Cairo Dec 19th 1861

Col Johnson
Comd.g Ft Holt Ky
Col.

Col Totten, Chief of Artillery will be at Fort Holt Ky at 10
o.clock A. M. tomorrow to inspect the Battery of Capt McAllister.

He wishes to have all the entire company paraded, Cooks,
sick in quarters and all, also wants a list of the company prepared
ready for him.

Yours &c
U. S. Grant
Brig Genl Comd.g

Copies, DLC-USG, V, 1, 2, 3, 77; DNA, RG 393, USG Letters Sent. Col.
Amory K. Johnson of Petersburg, Ill., commanded the 28th Ill. See letter to Brig.
Gen. John A. McClernand, Dec. 19, 1861.

To Col. Michael K. Lawler

———

Head Quarters Dist. S. E. Mo
Cairo Dec 19th 1861

Col. M. K. Lawler
Comdg. 18th Regt. Ill Vols.
Col

You are directed to cause to be returned to Capt. Brinck
Ordnance officer, the accoutrements obtained by your Regiment
without requisitions duly signed.

Yours &c
U. S. Grant
Brig. Genl. Comdg

Copies, DLC-USG, V, 1, 2, 3, 77; DNA, RG 393, USG Letters Sent. On Dec. 20, 1861, Maj. Mason Brayman wrote to USG. "Genl. McClernand directs the transmission to you of the ~~endorsed~~ enclosed copy of report of Military Comn. in the matter of examination &c of accouterments for 18th Regiment." Copy, McClernand Papers, IHi.

To Col. Leonard F. Ross

Cairo, December 19th 1861

Col. Ross.

Has the Steamer "Memphis" left yet? She has not arrived here yet.

U. S. Grant.

Telegram, copy, DNA, RG 393, Post of Cape Girardeau, Telegrams. On Dec. 18, 1861, Col. Leonard F. Ross had telegraphed to USG. "Memphis arrived safely this morning. Review at one P. M. Please notify Head Quarters at St Louis of Sucess of Telegraph operations at this post. Accept best wishes of myself and command at this post." Copy, *ibid*. On Dec. 18, USG had telegraphed to Ross. "Dispatch Received." Copy, *ibid*. On Dec. 19, Ross telegraphed to USG. "Memphis left here for St Louis at twelve O'clock last night." Copy, *ibid*.

To Commanding Officer, Military Prison, Columbus, Ohio

Head Quarters Dist S. E. Mo
Cairo Dec 19th 1861

To The Officer in command of Military Prison
Columbus Ohio
Sir.

Enclosed you will find copy of an order this day received from Hd Qrs Dept of the Mo.

By forwarding the said Prisoner John Groves at once, a speedy exchange can be effected.

> Very Respectfully
> Yours &c
> U. S. GRANT
> Brig Genl Comd.g

Copies, DLC-USG, V, 1, 2, 3, 79; DNA, RG 393, USG Letters Sent. *O.R.*, II, i, 531. See letters to Capt. John C. Kelton, Nov. 29, 1861, and to Maj. Gen. Leonidas Polk, Jan. 23, 1862. Command of the military prison at Camp Chase, Columbus, Ohio, rotated among commanders of regts. stationed there. Phillip R. Shriver and Donald J. Breen, *Ohio's Military Prisons in the Civil War* (Columbus, Ohio, 1964), p. 11.

To Maj. Gen. Henry W. Halleck

> Head Quarters, Dist. S. E. Mo.
> Cairo, Dec. 20th 1861.

MAJ. GEN. H. W. HALLACK U. S. A.
COMD.G DEPT. OF THE MO.
ST. LOUIS, MO.
GEN.

Your second despatch saying "it is most extraordinary that you (I) should have obeyed a telegram sent by an unknown person & not even purporting to have been given by authority," is received.

In justice to myself I must reply to this telegram. In the first place I never thought of doubting the authority of a telegram received from St. Louis, supposing that, in Military matters, the telegraph was under such surveilance that no military order could be passed over the wires that was not by authority; Second, the signature to the telegram was made with so many flourishes that I could not make it out atal, and to send a copy to your Head Quarters was obliged to send to the office here for a duplicate; Third, before this telegram was received Capt. Livingston,[1] who come in charge of these prisoners, reported to me that several ~~that~~ who were to come had proven to be imposters, and that he had reason to believe that two of those still with him were under assumed names; Fourth, directions sufficient to detain prisoners (Camp Jackson exchanged prisoners) might come from the Provost Martial's office, from Gen. Curtis' or from Head Quarters, and I do not know the employees of the former, nor the Staff of the latter.

The fact is I never dreamed of so serious a telegraphic hoax eminating through a large and responsible office like that in St. Louis. Enclosed I send you copy of the despatch received.

> I am Gen. Very respectfully
> Your Obt. Svt.
> U. S. GRANT
> Brig. Gen. Com

ALS, DNA, RG 393, Dept. of the Mo., Letters Received. *O.R.*, II, i, 121. On Dec. 15, 1861, USG received a telegram with a signature which looks like "W. J. Bud Col." "The D. G. Taylor left here at one p m today   Stop her & send back all the Camp Jackson men   They all have assumed names"   Telegram received, DNA, RG 393, Dept. of the Mo., Letters Received. The signature is given as "W. H. Buel" in *O.R.*, II, i, 121. USG considered this a valid order. See letter to Capt. John C. Kelton, Dec. 17, 1861.

On Dec. 19, Maj. Gen. Henry W. Halleck telegraphed to USG. "By what authority did you send back exchanged prisoners? They are not under assumed names: all were identified here before exchanged." Copies, DNA, RG 94, Generals' Papers and Books, Telegrams Sent in Cipher by Gen. Halleck; *ibid.*, RG 393, Dept. of the Mo., Telegrams Sent; *ibid.*, USG Hd. Qrs. Correspondence; DLC-USG, V, 4, 5, 7, 8. *O.R.*, II, i, 121. On Dec. 19, USG telegraphed to Halleck. "The following telegraph was rec'd here:—'The D. G. Taylor left here at one P. M. today. Stop her and send back all the Camp Jackson men   They all have assumed names.' Signed W. H. Buel Co[l]"   Copies, DNA, RG 94, Generals' Papers and Books, Telegrams Received by Gen. Halleck; *ibid.*, RG 393, Dept. of the Mo., Telegrams Received. On Dec. 19, Halleck again telegraphed to USG. "No such man as W. H. Buel, Col, known at these Headquarters. It is most extraordinary that you should have obeyed a telegram sent by an unknown person, and not even purporting to have been given by authority. The prisoners will be immediately returned to Cairo." Copies, *ibid.*, RG 94, Telegrams Sent in Cipher by Gen. Halleck; *ibid.*, RG 393, Dept. of the Mo., Telegrams Sent; *ibid.*, USG Hd. Qrs. Correspondence; DLC-USG, V, 4, 5, 7, 8. *O.R.*, II, i, 121. On Dec. 20, Halleck telegraphed and wrote to USG. "The person who sent the Telegram about the prisoners, has been discovered & placed in confinement. He has no authority whatever. You will hereafter be more careful about obeying telegrams from private persons, countermanding orders from these Head Quarters." LS, DNA, RG 393, USG Letters Received. *O.R.*, II, i, 122.

    1. See letter to Capt. Livingstone, Dec. 17, 1861.

To Capt. John C. Kelton

———

BY TELEGRAPH FROM Cairo Dec 21 *1861*
TO CAPT J. C. KELTON
A. A. G.

    Capt Atkins,[1] Recorder of the Military Commission convened here being sick, may I appoint J. M Hannah[2] of the Commission in his place

U. S. GRANT
Brig Genl.

Telegram received, DNA, RG 393, Dept. of the Mo., Letters Received. See letter to Capt. John C. Kelton, Dec. 8, 1861. Capt. John C. Kelton drafted his reply at the foot of USG's telegram. On Dec. 22, 1861, Capt. John A. Rawlins issued special orders. "Captain Smith Atkins, appointed Judge Advocate for Military Commission, by virtue of the following order by telegraph from Hd Qrs Dept. of the Mo, is hereby releived and Captain J. M Hanna appointed in his stead. . . . 'Capt. Atkins is relieved & Capt. Hannah appointed in his stead' " Copies, DLC-USG, V, 15, 16, 77, 82; DNA, RG 393, USG Special Orders.

    1. Capt. Smith D. Atkins of Freeport, Ill., 11th Ill.
    2. Capt. Joseph M. Hannah of Pekin, Ill., 8th Ill.

To Flag Officer Andrew H. Foote

———

Head Quarters, Dist. S. E. Mo.
Cairo, Dec. 21st 1861

Commodore Foote U. S. N.
Comd.g Flotilla
Cairo Ill.
Commodore;

I have just seen Capt. Hatch, in person, and he assures me that the Wharf boat having the hay aboard shall be removed at once, or the hay taken out.

Yours Truly
U. S. Grant
Brig. Gen. Com.

ALS, Charles Roberts Collection, Haverford College, Haverford, Pa. On Dec. 21, 1861, Flag Officer Andrew H. Foote wrote to USG. "Notwithstanding your order to have the hay & combustible materials removed from the Wharf Boat lying astern of the Graham Wharf Boat occupied with all the stores of the Flotilla, nothing has yet been done; although the Quarter Masters Clerk assured me yesterday, that it was unnecessary to trouble you with the matter, as he would have the hay removed. I therefore respectfully request that this hay, which is endangering all the stores of the Naval Flotill[a] by its exposure to fire, *may this day be removed*. So great have I deemed the exposure of our stores from the combustible material in the boat astern of us, that I have not been free from the greatest anxiety day and night, lest the whole Flotilla should be rendered useless by a fire, to which it has been greatly exposed for several days." Copy, DNA, RG 45, Letters Sent by A. H. Foote.

To Col. Richard J. Oglesby

———

Head Quarters Dist S. E. Mo
Cairo Dec 21st 1861

Col. R. J Oglesby
Comdg. Birds Point Mo
Col

Understanding that a heavy trade is being carried on between points North of Birds Point and Charleston Mo, and

South by means of teams, I am desirous of breaking it up.

To this end, you will send tomorrow or, Monday a sufficient force, say two squadrons of Cavalry, under Lt. Col. Prince,[1] to the neighborhood of Belmont with directions, to proceed back on the main traveled road, towards Charleston, taking possession of all teams, loaded with produce, or goods, destined for the south, and send them back to Birds Point.

The object of this expedition it is hardly nescessary for me to inform you should be kept, entirely secret.

> Yours &c
> U. S. Grant
> Brig. Gen Comg

Copies, DLC-USG, V, 1, 2, 3, 79; DNA, RG 393, USG Letters Sent. *O.R.*, I, viii, 453–54.

1. Lt. Col. Edward Prince of Quincy, Ill., 7th Ill. Cav., was promoted to col., June 1, 1862.

To Capt. William J. Kountz

> Head Quarters Dist. S. E Mo
> Cairo Dec 21st 1861

Capt. Kountz,
A. A. Q. M.
Sir

I understand that you are here, making inquiries into matters pertaining to this command.

You will desist from further inquiriesvestigation, until you have reported to me, and shown your authority.

If duly authorized, every facility will be given you, to carry out your instructions, if not, I will be compelled to express to you my decided disapprobation of your course.

To say the least you have acted in a manner displaying great

ignorance of Military usage in not reporting to the Commanding Officer the object, and authority of your visit

I have no official knowledge of your holding any position
under the Government.

Yours &c.

U. S. GRANT

Brig Genl Comdg

Copies, DLC-USG, V, 1, 2, 3, 79; DNA, RG 393, USG Letters Sent. William
J. Kountz of Allegheny, Pa., owner of a steamboat fleet, was appointed superintendent of river transportation in May, 1861, by Maj. Gen. George B. Mc-
Clellan. On Nov. 16, Kountz was appointed asst. q.m. of vols. with the rank of
capt. and ordered to St. Louis. About Dec. 19, he arrived at Cairo, to "examine
into all River Transportation." His reputation for quarrelsomeness, obstinacy,
and meddling counteracted his expert knowledge of steamboating. Theodore R.
Parker, "William J. Kountz, Superintendent of River Transportation Under
McClellan, 1861–62," *Western Pennsylvania Historical Magazine*, 21, 4 (Dec.,
1938), 237–54.

On Dec. 23, Brig. Gen. John A. McClernand wrote to USG. "Capt W. J.
Kountz, Asst Qr. Master U. S having called on me, as Commandant of this Post,
a few days since, and advised me that he was charged with the duty of inquiring
into the expense attending the transport service, here, and the condition of the
same, I promptly welcomed his mission and offered him every facility in my
power in that regard. The result of his labors as reported to me, will be found
briefly but clearly set forth in the accompanying tabular statement, which I have
the honor of submitting to you as coming from him. Capt Kountz thinks that a
great reduction might be made in the expense of the transport service, here, and
at the same time its efficiency increased, and doubtless, as an officer of extensive
experience, in such service, his opinions are entitled to much consideration. He
recommends a reorganization of this whole branch of the public service upon a
more economical and solid basis. He recommends that the practice of Chartering
transport steamers, by private contract, be discontinued and that such transports
be chartered in pursuance of public advertizement inviting competition among
those who might desire to contract to furnish them. He also recommends that all
such contracts should contain stipulations binding the furnishers of the transports, to furnish crews of proper numbers and upon just and reasonable terms to
run them; likewise that contracts should be made for the boarding of the crews,
rather than having Government directly, to do it. These recommendations appear
to me judicious and if carried into effect, by substituting individual vigilance and
economy for governmental action in matters of practical detail, would promote
the ends of economy in the public service. I respectfully recommend them together
with the whole reform proposed by Capt Kountz to your favorable consideration."
Copy, McClernand Papers, IHi. Kountz's report on current transport arrangements and his recommendation for changes is a DS, *ibid*. On Dec. 23, McClernand
again wrote to USG. "May I ask ~~you~~ the favor that you will call at my office on
matters of importance, that should be brought to your notice at once." Copy,
ibid. There is a notation at the foot of this letter. "Genl. G called at 8 o'c. P M and

met Capt Kountz & Messrs McClusky & Boyd in reference to frauds in coal contracts—"

On Dec. 6, Capt. John A. Rawlins issued special orders. "Louisville Canal Company Will Pass Tow Boat and Barges, belonging to John McClusky, loaded with Coal, purchased by the Government for the use of the Army at this place. On acct. of Quarter Masters Department" Copies, DLC-USG, V, 1, 15, 16, 77, 82; DNA, RG 393, USG Special Orders. In testimony taken by the Commission on War Claims at St. Louis (Davis-Holt-Campbell Commission), John A. Mc-Closkey stated that he was the major supplier of coal to the U.S. at Cairo, that he was paid ten cents per bushel, but that he believed some of the coal he delivered was credited to a coal contract held by V. B. Horton of Cairo. Capt. William J. Kountz told the commission that soon after his arrival at Cairo he learned that the U.S. was paying twelve cents per bushel for this coal. *Ibid.*, RG 217.

On Dec. 28, McClernand wrote to Kountz. "Capt W J Kountz, Assistant Quarter Master of the United States army having been assigned by Major Robert Allen, Quarter Master U. S. A. of the Department of the Missouri, at St Louis to take charge of the River business of the Government, and such other business as may be assigned to him, has reported to me as commanding officer of the Post of Cairo, for duty, in pursuance of orders from Major General H W Halleck commanding the Department of the Missouri In pursuance of such authority, I do therefore, hereby, authorize and require Capt W J Kountz, to take immediate charge of all river transports, boats and craft, together with the property, money, accounts, and every thing pertaining to the same, including the financial affairs of the same, which are attached to this Post. He will settle and adjust all claims against the Government, accruing on account thereof, in a fair and reasonable manner. He will collect and receive all monies due the Government, or remaining in the hands of any officer, employee, or other person, on account of, or connected with the transport service. He will take such measures, and make and enforce such orders as will secure these ends and the usefulness and efficiency of the service of his department All officers now in charge of transports are hereby releived from further duty, and will make full returns to him. He will report to these Head Quarters from time to time, what he shall have done by virtue hereof, and the condition of the service under his control." LS and ADf, McClernand Papers, IHi.

To Maj. Gen. Leonidas Polk

———

Head Quarters Dist. S. E. Mo
Cairo Dec 22nd 1861

GENERAL

I send you under a flag of truce, some seventeen of the Camp Jackson prisoners, who are released under the Fremont Price agreement.

These prisoners were brought here on Tuesday last, and would have been immediately forwarded to Columbus, but that, a dispatch, was sent to me purporting to be official, stating that they were imposters, and were not the men they assumed to be.[1]

In consequence of this dispatch, I arrested the parties, here and put them at labor for a few hours, and then sent them back to St Louis

It turned out however that the dispatch was a wicked hoax perpetrated by an individual in St Louis who has been arrested, and will be properly punished. No one regrets the occurrance more than I do.

Col Webster has charge of the expedition, and will receive any communication you may desire to send me

> I am sir very respectfully
> Your Obt Srvt
> U S Grant
> Brig Genl Comg

Copies, DLC-USG, V, 1, 2, 3, 79; DNA, RG 393, USG Letters Sent. *O.R.*, II, i, 122. On Dec. 22, 1861, Maj. Gen. Leonidas Polk replied to USG. "I have the honor to acknowledge the receipt of your communication of this date, and of the list of Camp Jackson prisoners. I perceive there are at Columbus Ohio, a number of Confederate prisoners, which I now make overtures to exchange, grade for grade and man for man, for the Federal prisoners now in my possession, say Ninety; officers to be exchanged for men at rates to be agreed upon. I am also informed there are Eight or Ten prisoners at Paducah, which I would prefer to have included in the list to be returned to me." LS, DNA, RG 94, War Records Office, Dept. of the Mo. *O.R.*, II, i, 531. On the same day, USG sent this letter to St. Louis. "Respectfully refered to Head Quarters Dept. of the Missouri." AES, DNA, RG 94, War Records Office, Dept. of the Mo. On Dec. 25, Capt. John C. Kelton endorsed the letter, presumably to USG. "The Com'd'g Genl directs me to say that the whole matter in regard to the exchange of prisoners has been referred to Washington, and that he cannot act until an answer is received—" ES, *ibid.*

1. See letter to Maj. Gen. Henry W. Halleck, Dec. 20, 1861.

To Capt. John C. Kelton

Head Quarters Dist. of Cairo
Cairo Dec 22nd 1861

CAPT. J. C KELTON
A. A. GEN. DEPT. OF THE MISSOURI
ST LOUIS MO
SIR

On the 15th inst I reported that I had directed Capt. Hillyer, Aid de Camp, to proceed to Chicago, and investigate charges of fraud made by the Chicago Tribune against the Quartermaster, or his Agt. in the purchase of lumber for this command.

Herewith you will find all the evidence adduced together with Capt. Hillyers report.

It proves a state of facts that in my opinion, should lead to a full investigation of all the disbursements made at this place, from its first establishment as a Military post. As there has been but little actual cash paid, upon purchases & contracts made here, all overcharges against the Government, might be yet corrected and dishonest agts disappointed in their expected profits.

I have not arrested Mr Wilcox as was my first inclination upon seeing the evidence against him, because I have no place to keep him except the Guardhouse.

A deserter from the Confederate Army has been in this evening. He reports that the Militia from Tenessee Mississippi & Lousiana, are flowing into Columbus by every boat & every train. They are armed with Muskets Shot Guns & Ordinary Rifles. He also reports the sinking of Submarine batteries, shortness of provisions, in Columbus and discontent among the troops.

It has been reported to me that a trade is being carried on with the South by the way of Jonesboro, in this State, thence to the Mississippi river and through Missouri. Also that an armed body of desperadoes, infest the Illinois shore, where these goods are crossed crossed. I have ordered a Company of Cavalry, raised in the neighborhood of Jonesboro, to the scene of these infractions of law, with the hope of breaking up this traffic, and this body of men   The Cavalry will leave tomorrow taking with them ten rations[1]

> Respectfully
> Your Obt. Svt.
> U. S. GRANT
> Brigr Gen Comdg

Copies, DLC-USG, V, 4, 5, 7, 8, 9, 78; DNA, RG 393, USG Hd. Qrs. Correspondence. The two final paragraphs are printed in *O.R.*, I, vii, 510–11, with the explanation: "Some personal matter omitted." See letter to Capt. John C. Kelton, Dec. 15, 1861.

On Dec. 22, 1861, Capt. William S. Hillyer wrote to USG. "In pursuance of your instructions I proceeded to Chicago on Monday last arriving there that night for the purpose of investigating the truth of the charges made in the 'Chicago Tribune' of fraudulent lumber contracts—I called on Tuesday at the Chicago Tribune office and stated to Mr Bross one of its proprietors the purpose for which I was sent to Chicago and asked him if he was prepared to furnish me the evidence to substantiate his charges. He replied to me that his partner Mr Medill had written the article, that Mr M. was not there and would not be that day. That if I would call the next morning Mr Medill would furnish me the names of witnesses to substantiate the charges. I called on Wednesday morning saw Mr Medill and he gave me such information as enabled me to proceed in taking the testimony which accompanies and is made part of this report. It may be proper to state that Capt R. B. Hatch at his own request and with your consent accompanied me to Chicago. On arriving at Chicago about 10 o'clock at night Capt Hatch and I went together to the Tremont House and were given a room together. The room assigned us was No 4 on the office floor, a large accessible room—I mention this because the meeting of lumbermen alluded to in the depositions was in room No 6 a private room of the same size on the same floor. On Tuesday morning I breakfasted with Capt Hatch and at the table he told me that he would ascertain the whereabouts of all the parties who had sold lumber and furnish me the information to facilitate my investigation and I could commence that afternoon   I did not see Capt Hatch after that until dinner time when I met him at the Tremont House in company with Mr Robert Foss to whom he introduced me and we all dined together, but I was not informed and did not know that he was one of the lumbermen—This was the afternoon at which the testimony shews the lumbermen met at the Tremont House and were paid off. I think we dined at about ½ past one o'clock. Capt Hatch said nothing to me of the proposed meeting nor did I know anything about it until the testimony developed the fact, although I must have been in the Hotel at the time, as the testimony shews the meeting occurred about 2 o'clock—Why this meeting was not held in our room No 4, an equally large, convenient and accessible room—Why I was not asked to be present or at least informed that the parties would be there—Why I was not subsequently informed by Capt Hatch of the meeting having been [he]ld—are matters I leave for your consideration—About supper time I met Capt Hatch and told him that I had seen Mr Bross of the Tribune and I was to be furnished next morning with the names of witnesses—He told me he also had seen Mr Bross and shewed him a certificate which satisfied him—At the same time ~~he asked~~ he handed me a certificate which he said he supposed would satisfy me. The paper was signed by Marsh & Foss and stated substantially that they had received pay for 500,000 feet of lumber at $10—per thousand and that neither Capt Hatch nor his only authorized agent Mr Wilcox had been paid any portion of it nor was there any agreement or understanding by which they or either of them were to receive any portion of it. I told Capt Hatch that this did not satisfy me that I must have the sworn statement of all parties concerned—He then told me that he had disavowed the Thomas & Wilcox arrangement and paid the parties the fair value of their lumber without any commissions added. That Wilcox had done very wrong and he should discharge him as soon as he (Hatch) returned to Cairo and asked me when I would be ready to return—I told him I could not tell but that I certainly should not return till I had obeyed your instructions to the letter—That you had instructed me to remain until I had the whole matter thoroughly investigated. I would state that I went to Chicago with a conviction that Capt Hatch was innocent —that the fraud if any had been perpetrated was done by his agents without his knowledge or connivance and supposing that he was anxious for a full investigation of the facts—I regret to add that my investigation was not facilitated by Capt Hatch—I would state further that the first testimony I took was that of Thomas. At that time I had no information that there had been previous purchases of lumber in November. That after ascertaining this fact I had a conversation with Thomas in which I asked him if the November contracts were made under similar arrangements with the December contracts   He said they were. I then charged upon him that he had divided profits on the November contracts with Wilcox—He did not deny it, but said he did'nt know what my information on that subject might be, but said he had no prior agreement to do so and that he considered that if a man had thrown buisiness in his way he had a right to make him a present afterward. Another incident which may have some bearing on the case is this. Mr Mears when I first saw him requested me to call next day and he would then give me his testimony. He afterwards told me that when I left he went immediately to see Mr Foss—that he said to Foss 'you have got us all into a scrape. There is a fellow with brass buttons and shoulder straps that has been to see me about the lumber contract and says he is going to shew up the whole thing'   To which Foss replied 'is it Capt Hillyer ?' on being answered affirmatively Foss replied, 'Oh you need'nt be afraid of him, he rooms with Hatch & eats with Hatch, and Hatch will fix it all right with him.' The witness Thomas gave his testimony with great hesitation. He consulted counsel before he gave it at all—He would not consent to be sworn ~~until~~ before he gave his testimony, insisting on having it written out that he might read it before he swore to it—The evidence clearly establishes these facts—The lumber purchased in December was purchased at $9 25 and $9 50 per thousand feet and invoiced to Capt Hatch at $10— and $10 50. The November purchases were similarly bought and invoiced—The purchases and the false invoices were made with the knowledge and consent of Henry Wilcox confidential clerk of Capt Hatch, through the agency of Thomas a brother in law of Wilcox. Capt Hatch with a full knowledge of the facts paid the parties for the December purchases an excess above what they had sold and deliverd the lumber for, to some fifty cents per thousand to others seventy five cents per thousand. I would simply add that I recovered from the parties $225—(and $50—more will be forwarded to you), which has been paid to you—All of which with the accompanying testimony is respectfully submitted—" ALS, DNA, RG 92, Consolidated Correspondence, Frauds. Between Dec. 18 and Dec. 20, Hillyer assembled a file of affidavits substantiating his report. DS, *ibid.*, RG 393, District of Cairo, Letters Received. On Dec. 19, Baldwin & Co. of Chicago wrote to USG. "Enclosed we send you fifty-dollars, for the benefit of the U. S. Government; to whom it rightly belongs. Capt. Hillyer will explain the matter to you." ALS, *ibid.*, District of Southeast Mo., Letters Received.

On Dec. 30, Capt. Reuben B. Hatch wrote to USG. "The morning I left Cairo I chanced to see the article in the Chicago *Tribune*, which I allude to in the enclosed letter to my brother. Had I seen it before I left Cairo I should have remained until you returned, even had I known that my family would have suffered. I know no reason (but one which I will explain to you when I see you) why I should be so persecuted. I have tried to do my duty—I may and probably have come short in many respects. My letter to my brother explains every point in the article except one, I think, and that is the one referring to my having in my possession ninety or more mules over what I had recepted for, and that I had boasted of it. Now I am not in the habit of boasting, and if I ever mentioned having mules over, it was with the expectation of tracing up receipts given and not having regular transfers, which I discovered to be the fact with a lot sent by Maj. McKinstry, before Maj. Allen took his place. There may be and probably is more lots the same way, and I am only afraid I may come short, as many of my mules, before I had yards made, broke loose, and it is uncertain that they were all returned. I have been compelled to trust much of my business to clerks, and naturally having confidence in mankind, there may have been dishonest ones among them. It would be strange if all the men I have been compelled to use in my various Departments should all be honest men. I hope and expect to have my returns ready to be forwarded in a very few days after the 1st of January, 1862, at which time, unless I am relieved by having the claims at Cairo paid off in some way, I wish to take some other position in the army. Any would be preferable to being dodged from morning until night for money. I understand an objection is raised at Washington against sending money to me at Cairo; that the amount is much larger than anticipated. They don't consider that I have run the Department since the twenty-fifth day of last April, and the Department owes less than seven hundred thousand dollars, taking from my estimate for funds up to the first of January what has been paid. It has been my great desire since, under your command to consult you much oftener than I have, having the fullest confidence in your judgment in matters pertaing to my department, but you have been so encubered with cares and business, I have been compelled to act upon my own judgment oftener." *Illinois State Journal*, Jan. 16, 1862. Included also was a Dec. 30 letter from Hatch to his brother, Ill. Secretary of State Ozias M. Hatch. "In your communication with me, you refer to an article in the Chicago *Tribune*, copied from the Alton *Telegraph* of the 24th inst., which reflects upon me and my family. I have the following explanations to make to you. Those who know but little of such matters would, on reading the article referred to, think my business was connected with the gunboats, which is not true. My only connection with them has been to supply them with such things I had, and they required. I have never received a commission on lumber, or anything else, directly or indirectly. I never had piles of lumber over in Cairo, but, on the other hand, have, since cold weather, been harrassed from morning till night for 'more lumber.' As to buying or contracting for wagons from parties hostile to our Government, I can only answer, that charge probably refers to Messrs. Sanger & Casey. I never purchased or contracted with them for any wagons or anything else. The wagons I received from them were contracted for to St. Louis, to be delivered to me at Cairo— these wagons receipted for, the receipt being filled up by Major Allen, Quartermaster in St. Louis, ready for my signature. If Messrs. Sanger & Casey are secessionists, and opposed to the Union, they alone are answerable for it, not me. The first team I had in Cario was taken from my little farm and used in Government service, without charge, until I was ordered by the commanding officer to purchase teams for the use of the post, when I returned the team to my farm. The stock sent to my farm was not mules, as stated, but was old mares and poor colts, taken at the Charleston fight. These I was directed to dispose of to the best advantage for and on account of the Government. My wagon master tried to sell them for some time, repeatedly assuring me that they were not worth keeping for a single day, and advised me to have them killed. I directed him to have them appraised, and I would send them to my farm. With regard to the soldiers expecting to be cheated, let me say I never have heard or known of a Quartermaster coming out ahead of the soldiers, and my opinion is, that as to dissatisfaction existing to any extent, it is a barefaced falsehood. No man ever lived who has tried to make the soldier comfortable more than myself, and I have especially devoted time and put myself to much trouble to oblige the representatives of the press, and strangers generally." *Ibid.* Hatch also supplied three documents relating to his lumber contracts.

Testimony concerning lumber contracts, taken March 14, 1862, is in *HRC,* 37-2-2, part 2, 1090–1137. At that time it was brought out that Hatch had sent his issuing clerk, Henry M. Wilcox, to Chicago to purchase lumber and that Wilcox had turned the matter over to his brother-in-law, Benjamin W. Thomas, who had arranged the deceptive invoices. Thomas had sent a share of the profits to Hatch. When the business was uncovered, Hatch sent Wilcox to the farm of his brother, Sylvanus Hatch, of Griggsville, Ill., to wait for the matter to blow over. *Ibid.*, pp. 1096, 1125–33.

1. See following letter.

To Brig. Gen. John A. McClernand

———

Head Quarters, Dist. S. E. Mo.
Cairo, Dec. 22d 1861.

Gen. J. A. McClernand
Comd.g Cairo Ill.
Gen.

A trade being carried on between Jonesboro and the Mississippi river, thence with the Southern Army, by the way of

Nealey's Landing,[1] I want Capt. Steward's[2] company to go to the neighborhood of the Mouth of Big Muddy and, if practicable, break up the trafic.

There is also a number of armed desperadoes in that vicinity that I am in hopes may be broken up.

The Company will go on the Steamer Memphis taking with them ten days rations. Forage for their horses can be procured where they encamp giving proper vouchers to be settled by the Quartermaster at this place.

I would like the company to go to-day, if practicable, if not early to-morrow. I will see Capt. Steward before he starts and give him all the information in my possession on this subject.

> Respectfully
> Your Obt. Svt.
> U. S. GRANT
> Brig. Gen. Com

ALS, McClernand Papers, IHi. See preceding letter.

1. Neely's Creek flows into the Mississippi River from Mo. about sixty-five miles upriver from Cairo.
2. Capt. Warren Stewart.

To Capt. Hugh Fullerton

Head Quarters Dist of Cairo
Dec 22d 1861

CAPT H. FULLERTON
COMD.G CALEDONIA, ILLS
SIR

In all cases where citizens purchase arms or clothing from a soldier, as in the case of Healy, take from them the articles purchased without restitution of the amount paid, and notify them that for the second offence they will be expelled from the neighborhood or prosecuted before the civil authorities.

A soldiers clothing arms and rations are [*not*] his own except
for legitamate purposes and where he trades them off he likewise
subjects himself to such punishment as may be inflicted by sentence of a Court Martial. I refer you to acts of Congress March
16th 1861.

> Yours &c.
>
> U. S. GRANT
>
> Brig Genl Comd.g

Copies, DLC-USG, V, 1, 2, 3, 79; DNA, RG 393, USG Letters Sent.

General Orders No. 22

———

Head Quarters Dist of Cairo
Cairo Dec 23d 1861

GENL ORDER NO 22

In pursuance of Special Orders No 78 from Head Quarters
Department of the Missouri, the name of this Military District
will be known as the "District of Cairo," and will include all the
Southern part of Illinois, that part of Kentucky west of the Cum-
berland River, and the southern counties of Missouri south of
Cape Girardeau.[1]

The force at Shawnetown will be under the immediate command of Col T. H. Cavanaugh 6th Illinois Cavalry, who will
consolidate the reports of his command weekly, and forward to
these Head Quarters.

All Troops that are or may be stationed along the bank of the
Ohio, on both sides of the River, east of Caledonia and to the
mouth of the Cumberland, will be included in the command having Head Quarters at Paducah, Ky.

Brigadier General E. A. Paine[2] is assigned to the command
of the forces at Birds Point Missouri.

All supplies of Ordnance, Quartermaster and Commissary
Stores, will be obtained through the Chiefs of each of these

Departments at District Head Quarters, when not otherwise provided for.

For the information of that portion of this command, newly attached, the following list of Staff Officers is published.

Capt John A. Rawlins Asst Adjt Genl
    ”   Clark B. Lagow   Aid-de-Camp
    ”   Wm. S. Hillyer   ”   ”   ”
Major John Riggin Jr Vol ”   ”   ”
Capt R. B. Hatch Asst Quarter Master U. S. Vols Chief Q.M.
    ”   W. W. Leland A. C. S. U. S. Vols. Chief Comsy
    ”   W. F. Brinck, Ordnance Officer.
Surgeon James Simons U. S. A. Medical Director.
Asst ” J. P. Taggart U. S. A. Medical Purveyor
Major I. N. Cook, Pay Master.[3]
Colonel J. D. Webster Chief of Staff and Chief of Engineers.

By order

U. S. GRANT

Brig Genl Comd.g

Copies, DLC-USG, V, 12, 13, 14, 80; DNA, RG 94, 9th Ill., Letterbook; *ibid.*, 48th Ill., Letterbook; *ibid.*, RG 393, USG General Orders; (Printed) McClernand Papers, IHi. *O.R.*, I, vii, 515. The change from District of Southeast Mo. to District of Cairo clarified two previously ambiguous points: the forces at Paducah were definitely placed under USG's command and those at Ironton were removed. See letter to Maj. Gen. John C. Frémont, Sept. 17, 1861. These orders also revised Special Orders No. 70, Dept. of the Mo., Dec. 17, 1861, through which Maj. Gen. Henry W. Halleck had placed Col. William P. Carlin in command of the District of Southeastern Mo., which included all Mo. south and east of the Meramec River, excluding Bird's Point. *O.R.*, I, liii, 511. On Dec. 21, Capt. John A. Rawlins wrote to Col. Leonard F. Ross. "I am instructed by Brig. Genl. U. S. Grant to say, the enclosed Special Order No 75, was received at these Head Quarters, but as the companies therein named, are at Cape Girardeau, which is not now in his command, he transmits it to you, for its enforcement, also for same reasons, Furlough and app. for Leave of absence, are returned to you, Cape Girardeau, being now within the command of Col. Carlin, as per Special Order, No 70, a copy of which was sent you yesterday. The Certificates of Disability have been forwarded to Hd. Qrs Dept. of the Mo." Copies, DLC-USG, V, 1, 2, 3, 79; DNA, RG 393, USG Letters Sent. The nature of USG's command was further clarified by Special Orders No. 90, Dept. of the Mo., Dec. 24. "Brigr. Genl. U. S. Grant will hereby assume command of Cape Girardeau as constituting a part of the Military District assigned to his command—The commanding officer of Cape Girardeau will report to General Grant & also to these Head quarters.—" DS, *ibid.*, RG 94, Orders and Circulars, Dept. of the Mo. *O.R.*, I, lii, part 1, 201. See letter to Capt. John C. Kelton, Dec. 25, 1861.

1. "Brigr. Genl. U. S. Grant is hereby placed in command of the District of Cairo including the Southern part of Illinois, that part of Kentucky west of the Cumberland, & the Southeastern counties of Mo. South of Cape Girardeau—" Copies, DNA, RG 94, Orders and Circulars, Dept. of the Mo.; *ibid.*, RG 393, Dept. of the Mo., Special Orders.

2. Special Orders No. 78, Dept. of the Mo., Dec. 20, also transferred Brig. Gen. Eleazer A. Paine from Paducah to Cairo. Copies, *ibid.* This transfer may be explained by the anger of Brig. Gen. Charles F. Smith concerning Paine's disobedience of orders during the battle of Belmont. *O.R.*, I, iii, 300, 303–4. Smith also believed that Paine was conspiring to remove him from command. Bruce Catton, *Grant Moves South* (Boston and Toronto, 1960), pp. 88–89. On Dec. 24, Smith wrote to Rawlins. "I have rec.d S. O. No. 78 from the Hd. Qrs. of the Dept. of the Misso. dated on the 20th. inst.; pursuant to which I have relieved Genl. *Paine* from duty here and ordered him to report to the commander of the District (See copy of my order enclosed), inferring from Genl. *Grant's* telegram I was to do so." ALS, DNA, RG 393, District of Cairo, Letters Received. On Dec. 23, Smith had telegraphed the substance of this letter to USG. Telegram received, *ibid.*, Dept. of the Mo., Telegrams Received.

3. On Dec. 23, Rawlins issued special orders. "Maj. I. N. Cooke Paymaster U. S. A. will without delay make requisition for funds and Pay the troops now stationed at Paducah and Smithland Ky" Copies, DLC-USG, V, 15, 16, 77, 82; DNA, RG 393, USG Special Orders.

To Capt. John C. Kelton

————

Head Quarters Dist of Cairo
Cairo Dec 23d 1861

Capt J. C. Kelton
A. A. Genl. Dept of the Mo
St Louis, Mo
Sir

Some time before orders were given for the erection of Winter Quarters ~~were given~~, I recommended to the commander of the Department of the West the use of *Coal Barges* for this purpose[1] Now that the Pontoon Bridge, across the Ohio is broken up,[2] I would respectfully renew the recommendation, suggesting the use of these Boats for that purpose, or such portion of them as cannot be profitably employed otherwise. By making these Boats with double decks, each Boat would comfortably quarter two companies, and as transports would accommodate double the number. One Steamer, of small burthen, could transport, several regiments, and a portion of the troops would always have quarters, so long as the line of travel was upon the river.

A few days ago I requested that the 45th Regiment of Ill. Vols. then not completed might be ordered here[3]   I was mistaken in saying that it had not been mustered into the service of the United States

This Regiment has since been filled up, and as you will see by the enclosed telegram, received today from the Adjt. Genl. of the State disirous of being placed on duty[4]

Respectfully
Your Obt. Svt.
U. S. GRANT
Brig. Genl. Comg

Copies, DLC-USG, V, 4, 5, 7, 8, 9, 79; DNA, RG 393, USG Hd. Qrs. Correspondence.

1. See letter to Capt. Chauncey McKeever, Oct. 9, 1861.
2. See telegram to Maj. Gen. John C. Frémont, Sept. 20, 1861. The bridge had been broken by ice floating down the river.
3. See letter to Capt. John C. Kelton, Dec. 18, 1861.
4. On Dec. 26, 1861, Maj. Gen. Henry W. Halleck telegraphed to USG. "You are authorised to request the forty fifth Illinois Volunteers to be sent to Cairo if you can quarter them. Hereafter, all requisitions on States for troops will be sent through these Head Quarters." Copy, DNA, RG 94, Generals' Papers and Books, Telegrams Sent in Cipher by Gen. Halleck; *ibid.*, RG 393, Dept. of the Mo., Telegrams Sent; *ibid.*, USG Hd. Qrs. Correspondence; DLC-USG, V, 4, 5, 7, 8. On Dec. 27, Ill. AG Allen C. Fuller telegraphed to USG. "Your dispatch about the forty-fifth Regiment, Col. Smith, is recd. & will be responded to as soon as possible. You may expect the Regiment next week." Telegram received (punctuation added), DNA, RG 393, Dept. of the Mo., Telegrams Received.

To Capt. John C. Kelton

————

Head Quarters, Dist. of Cairo
Cairo, Dec. 23d 1861.

Capt. J. C. Kelton,
A. A. Gen. Dept. of the Mo.
St. Louis, Mo.
Sir:

I would respectfully request a book of blank passes to be used in passing persons, on duty for the Government, over the different routes of travel. I would also request a map of the state of Ky. and if they can consistantly be supplied, of Tennessee & Arkansas also.

Respectfully &c.
U. S. Grant
Brig. Gen. Com.

ALS, DNA, RG 393, Dept. of the Mo., Letters Received. On Dec. 27, 1861, Brig. Gen. George W. Cullum replied to USG. "I am directed by General Halleck to say that no transportation passes can be issued except from these Head Quarters. We have no supplies of Maps here, you will therefore make requisitions upon the quartermaster, for such as are indispensable to you, the authorization for which, if necessary, will be given by the Comdg General" LS, *ibid.*, District of Cairo, Letters Received.

To Col. John Cook

————

Head Quarters, Dist. of Cairo
Cairo, Dec. 23d 1861

Col. J. Cook
Comd.g. Fort Holt, Ky.
Col.

There is no objection to people passing from the South to the North, provided they desire to remain North.

The lady brought in by Mr. Bodkins has a letter from her

husband which has been suffered to pass here requesting her to come up.

[As you suggest proper caution] should be used to see that improper persons are not admitted within our lines, but at the same time we should reflect that there are thousands of persons in the South who would like to get North & who we should welcom. On the old principle that it is better that ninety-nine guilty persons should escape than that one inocent person should suffer, we may be deceived some times.

Yours Truly
U. S. GRANT
Brig. Gen. Com.

ALS, IHi.

To Col. Leonard F. Ross

Cairo December 23d 61

COL. ROSS.

Mr. Childs under arrest at the Cape had better be kept.

U. S. GRANT,
Brig. Genl. Com'dg.

Telegram, copy, DNA, RG 393, Post of Cape Girardeau, Telegrams. On Dec. 24, 1861, Col. Leonard F. Ross wrote to USG. "We have not found in Capt Childs sufficient evidence to convict him—though I am satisfied, from his conduct, that he is guilty—I return him to you in charge of a Lieut and file of men—to report to you" Copy, *ibid.*, Letters Sent. On Dec. 26, Ross again wrote to USG. "The evidence against 'Capt Childs'—is purely circumstantial— He first called on me last Saturday night (22nd)—for permission to cross the river from the *Ill. Shore* to *Commerce* for the purpose of buying wheat as he said —After some conversation—I suspected his loyalty—Allowed him to return to Steam Boat—then arrested him, and took possession of his effects—After a pretty thorough examination—discharged him—and supposed he had returned to Cairo —But ont the 24th Inst. learning that he was still in town—and receiving your note of the 23d concluded it best to have him returned—The only evidence against him is, his very singular conduct—" Copy, *ibid.* On Jan. 1, 1862, William A. Jones, Zanesville, Ohio, wrote to USG "in relation to a man by the name of Childs attempting to pass the Federal lines." DLC-USG, V, 10; DNA, RG 393, USG Register of Letters Received. On Jan. 6, William H. Childs wrote to USG "in reference to his arrest, and asking an immediate trial." *Ibid.* The arrest of William H. Childs, described as an official of the Mobile and Ohio Railroad, is discussed in a letter of "L. C.," Dec. 24, 1861, in *Cincinnati Commercial*, Dec. 27, 1861.

To Capt. Reuben B. Hatch

———

Head Quarters Dist. of Cairo
Cairo Dec 23rd 1861

Capt. R. B. Hatch
Dist. Q. M. Cairo Ill
Sir

You will give such orders, as will secure Mr O. H. Ross Special Mail A'gt. between Cairo and Paducah a salary of fifty Dollars per Month from the 12th of September 1861. The period when he commenced the duties, to be paid so long as he continues out of the proceeds for passengers &c on boat carrying Mail

By order
U. S. Grant
Brig. Genl. Comdg.

Copies, DLC-USG, V, 1, 2, 3, 77; DNA, RG 393, USG Letters Sent. See letter to John A. Kasson, Sept. 13, 1861.

To O. K. Brooks

Cairo, Dec. 23d 1861

MASTER O. K. BROOKS,
CLEVELAND OHIO;
MY DEAR YOUNG SIR:

Your letter of the 16th inst. asking for my signature to place among many others you are collecting is received.

I am pleased to furnish it.

> Yours Truly
> U. S. GRANT
> Brig. Gen. U. S. V.

ALS, IHi. This represents the earliest surviving request for USG's autograph.

To Capt. John C. Kelton

Head Quarters Dist S. E. Mo
Cairo Dec 24th, 1861

CAPTAIN

I can purchase single Bedsteads here for two dollars apiece which will last for years. This I think is cheaper than cots, and they are in every respect more desrable. I would respectfully recomend that permission be given to purchase them for the General Hospital at Mound City.

> Respectfully
> U. S. GRANT
> Brig Genl U. S. A

To Capt J. C. Kelton
Asst Adjt Genl
St Louis Mo

Copies, DLC-USG, V, 4, 5, 7, 8, 78; DNA, RG 393, USG Hd. Qrs. Correspondence. See letter to Capt. John C. Kelton, Dec. 1, 1861. On Jan. 5, 1862, Surgeon

Edward C. Franklin, Mound City, wrote to Maj. James Simons. "I have the honor, in reply to your communication of yesterday, to state, that the buildings known as the General Hospital, were occupied by authority of Brig. General U. S. Grant about the first of October last. The Hospital is composed of 12 Store houses, forming a half-block, is three stories high, built of brick and rudely finished for business purposes. To render the building comfortable, and adapted to the requirements of a General Hospital, it has been necessary to expend a sum of money not exceeding $2500—which sum will, I think, cover all the indebtedness necessary to complete the building for the reception of 1000 patients   The buildings have been condemned by a Board of Survey, appointed by Brig. Genl Grant, for the purposes of a General Hospital, which board fixed the sum of $1500 per year, rent—The furniture in Hospital is exceedingly limited, poor, and in many instances unfit for for use, the larger proportion of which was sent here at the breaking up of the Brigade Hospital at Cairo, and the most of which was *broken, mutilated* and *unfit for use.* There is at present in Hospital

Bedsteads	no 140	(new)
Sofa Lounges	" 65	(Second hand)
Camp Cots	" 242	(unfit for Hospital)
" " (broken)	62	(can't be used)

making in all 447 beds, including the camp cots, which are unfit for Hospital use especially during the winter months, as they are too short, exceedingly liable to break down, & are constantly requiring repairs to keep them in a condition even fit to lie upon. Thirty one of these are used by the attendants of the Hospital which leaves only 416 beds for the sick. To accommodate 1000 patients, there are required 584 more bedsteads, including the cots now in use, and 790 excluding them. There are 352 chairs in Hospital, and not one medicine stand, a proportionate number of which would be very desirable. Of course to fill up the Hospital equal to its capacity, an equal, or rather proportionate number of bed sacs, sheets, pillows, blankets, & such like furniture will be required to make patients comfortable. As soon as the required furniture can be obtained the building will be ready to receive as high as 1000 patients"   ALS, *ibid.,* Dept. of the Mo., Letters Received. On Jan. 11, Capt. John C. Kelton endorsed the letter to USG. "Brig Genl Grant is authorized to purchase (500) five hundred bedsteads at $2." AES, *ibid.*

To Capt. John C. Kelton

Head Quarters Dist of Cairo
Cairo Dec 24th 1861

Capt J. C. Kelton
A. A. Genl, Dept of the Mo
St Louis, Mo
Sir

Enclosed herewith, I send charges prefered against the Lieut. Col. & Maj. of the 18th regiment of Ill Vols. There is a court now in session before which these cases might be tried, but I refer the matter to the Genl Comdg. the Dept. because the charges have been prefered by Col. Lawler of same regiment, who is now undergoing trial before the Court.

I believe there is such a feeling existing in this regiment, especially among the officers, as to seriously effect its efficiency unless corrected, but I doubt, the propriety of accepting charges prefered by an officer, whilst himself undergoing trial.

The question is respectfully refered

Respectfully
U. S. GRANT
Brig. Gen. Comdg.

Copies, DLC-USG, V, 4, 5, 7, 8, 78; DNA, RG 393, USG Hd. Qrs. Correspondence. The enclosure has not been found. Lt. Col. Thomas H. Burgess resigned on Sept. 3, 1862, and Maj. Samuel Eaton resigned on April 1, 1862. See letter to Brig. Gen. John A. McClernand, Dec. 24, 1861.

To Flag Officer Andrew H. Foote

Head Quarters, Dist. of Cairo
Cairo, Dec. 24th 1861.

COMMODORE FOOTE
COMD.G CAIRO FLOTILLA.
COMMODORE:

Will you be kind enough to permit my friend from Galena, Mr. Hicks, to visit one of the Gun boats.

Yours Truly
U. S. GRANT
Brig. Gen. Com

ALS, USG 3. George Hicks is listed in the 1858 *Galena City Directory* as a law student.

To Brig. Gen. Don Carlos Buell

By Telegraph from Cairo [*Dec.*] 24 *186*[*1*]

To Gen D C Buell

Notify Louisville bankers against purchasing vouchers for coal delivered in Cairo

U S Grant
Brig Gen Comdg

Telegram received, DNA, RG 393, Dept. of the Ohio, Telegrams. On Dec. 27, 1861, N. W. Casey, Louisville, Ky., telegraphed to USG. "You warn the Bankers here not to purchase vouchers for Coal supplied the Govt. at Cairo. Please say whether or not it applies to me for Coal furnished Quarter master at Smithland & Paducah." Telegram received (punctuation added), *ibid.*, Dept. of the Mo., Telegrams Received. See letter to Capt. William J. Kountz, Dec. 21, 1861.

To Brig. Gen. John A. McClernand

Head Quarters, Dist. of Cairo
Cairo, Dec. 24th 1861

Gen. J. A. McClernand
Comd.g, Cairo Ill.
Gen.

I have just received a pass signed by Col. Lawler as Comd.g his regiment.

The articles of War clearly require an officer undergoing trial to be placed under arrest and deprived of his Command, until the promulgation of sentence by the proper reviewing officer.

You will please therefore have Col. Lawler at once placed in arrest.

Respectfully
Your Obt. Svt.
U. S. Grant
Brig. Gen. Com.

ALS, McClernand Papers, IHi. On Dec. 24, 1861, Maj. Mason Brayman wrote to Capt. John A. Rawlins. "Genl. M'Clernand instructs me to acknowledge the receipt of Genl. Grants letter of this morning, concerning pass issued by Col. Lawler. Genl. M'Clernand had last evening called Col. Lawler's attention to the Articles of War applicable to his case. Early this morning he tendered his sword, & reported himself under arrest. Lt. Col. Burgess and Major Saml. Eaton of the same regiment being similarly situated, an order was issued placing the three officers named under arrest, until the finding of the court &c. The same order placed Senior Capt D. H. Brush of Comp. "K" in command of the regiment in the interim. By this you will see that Genl. Grants wishes are ~~carried into~~ complied with." ADfS, *ibid*. See letter to Capt. John C. Kelton, Dec. 24, 1861.

To Capt. John C. Kelton

Head Quarters Dist of Cairo
Cairo Dec. 25th 1861

CAPT. J. C. KELTON
A. A. GENL. DEPT. OF THE MO.
ST LOUIS MO
SIR

Enclosed I send you copy of Gen Order No. 22[1] from these Hd. Qrs. also Circular of the 23rd inst.[2]

I would respectfully ask authority to place Maj. I. N. Cook Paymaster U. S. A who is stationed here, on duty, as Chief Paymaster for this District, also to retain Col. J. D. Webster, now appointed or to be appointed Col. of the 1st regiment of Ill Light Artillery, as Chief Engineer of the Dist. & Chief of Staff as published in the enclosed order

Respectfully
U. S. GRANT
Brig. Genl Comdg.

Copies, DLC-USG, V, 4, 5, 7, 8, 78; DNA, RG 393, USG Hd. Qrs. Correspondence. On Dec. 27, 1861, Capt. John C. Kelton endorsed this letter to USG. "The Comdg. Genl. directs me to say, that Paymasters are assigned to duty by the Paymaster General, and do not belong to any particular district. He also directs me to say, that he is not aware of any authority for the Staff organization of Genl. Grant, given in 'Genl Orders' No. 22, and therefore cannot approve it." Copy, *ibid*., Western Dept., Endorsements.

1. See General Orders No. 22, Dec. 23, 1861.

2. On Dec. 23, USG issued a circular. "Commanders of Regiments or Detachments, who have Officers or enlisted men on recruiting, service without the authority of Major General Halleck, will notify them to return immediately to their respective commands. It is expected that all such absentees will be present for duty on the 31st inst. In pursuance of General Order No 22 from Head Quarters Department of the Missouri, Commanders of Regiments and companies, will immediately report all vacancies of commissioned officers, in their respective commands, and make recommendations for promotions to fill such vacancies." Copies, DLC-USG, V, 12, 13, 14, 80; DNA, RG 94, 9th Ill., Letterbook; *ibid.*, 48th Ill., Letterbook; *ibid.*, RG 393, USG General Orders.

To Col. John Cook

Head Quarters Dist of Cairo
Cairo Dec 25th 1861

Col. J Cook
Comdg. Fort Holt Ky.
Sir

Your communication in relation to Mr Mercer, is received. I will see that he does not trouble your Camp in future, so frequently as formerly. I am satisfied however from other evidence than his own of his loyalty, and regret that he should have come so much under your suspicion

Whilst we wish to keep every thing from the enemy, it is our duty to alleviate, the hardships, consequent upon a state of war, of our Union friends in the border states as far as practicable.

I gave permission for a man to go into your Camp for the purpose of recovering his fugitive slaves. If Gen Order No. 3 from Head Quarters Dept. of the Mo.[1] had been complied with this would not have been nescessary. Mr Mercer now reports to me that these negroes were found concealed in one of the Huts at Fort Holt, and that the owner was forcibly prevented from recovering his property.

If true this is treating law, the orders of the Comd.r of the Dept. and my orders with contempt. Mr Mercer does not charge that this was by your order, but after your attention was called to the fact that fugitive slaves were in your Camp as the pass over my signature informed you, was probably the fact, an investigation should have been had, and the negroes driven out—I do not want the Army used as negro cat[c]hers, but still less do I want to see it used as a cloak to cover their escape. No matter what our private views may be on this subject there are in this Department positive orders on the subject, and these orders must be obeyed

I direct therefore that you have a search made, and if you find, these or any other fugitive slaves in Camp at Fort Holt you have them expelled from Camp, and if hereafter you find any have been concealed or detained you bring the party so detaining them to punishment

Yours truly

U. S. GRANT

Brig Genl Comg

Copies, DLC-USG, V, 1, 2, 3, 79; DNA, RG 393, USG Letters Sent. *O.R.*, II, i, 794. On Dec. 25, 1861, Col. John Cook wrote to Capt. John A. Rawlins. "The communication containing special order from the Gen'l. Comd'g. bearing even date herewith in relation to Mr Mercer and Fugitives from labor has been duly received; and am compelled to acknowledge that it has taken me entirely by surprise. If any act of mine has induced the belief at any time, that I desired to oppress Loyal citizens in any manner, no one could regret it more than I do, and none more willing to make the amende honorable. The Comd'g Gen'l. gave permission to a man to enter my Camp in search of his negroes, and being confined to my bed without stopping to issue my own order, for the search and delivery of the Fugitives, and that the officers at this Post might feel the greater weight of the signature of the Comd'g. Genl, I gave it my hearty approval, instructing the Adjutant to make authority for search good for one day only, for the following reason, that I had been informed that citizens of Kentucky had stayed over night in my camp on board the Young Mr Mercer's boat without my knowledge. This, permit me, through you, to assure the Comd'g Genl, was intended for neither disrespect to him or disregard to his order. As soon, after the issue of Gen'l. Order No. 3. Hd Qrs Dept of the Mo. as I discovered the existence of Fugitives within my lines I had all that could be found sent beyond the lines and the guard are regularly instructed not to allow *any one* to pass unless provided with a pass signed by the Comd'g Genl. The Gen'l. will doubtless remember the vast length of line, the limited number of troops at this Post have to guard, and will doubtless readily perceive with what little difficulty our lines may be passed either day or night by negroes, since almost if not all, the Officers employ as servants free negroes from Illinois. Mr Mercer reported to the Genl.

that the Fugitives sought 'were found concealed in one of the huts, and the owner forcibly prevented from recovering his property.' After Mr Mercer obtained the authority to make search no obstacle whatever was thrown in his way to success-fully execute it. Mr Utterback reported to the Adjutant, (not to me) that he had been prevented looking under one of the beds in Cavalry quarters, and the Adjt informed me that he returned with Mr U. in person and remained until a satis-factory search was made, and no complaint what ever has been made to me by Mr. U. or any one else of any threatened violence to any one, and especially to parties in the discharge of duty. The Pass, over the Comd'g Gen'ls signature to which he alludes, received at my hands the earliest attention possible. The delay in its execution was occasioned solely by the lateness of the hour Mr Mercer arrived here from Blandville, he having gone there the night before. The pass was dated the 23d inst and was not presented until the 24th. Please find below copy of Order issued in accordance with the Gen'l's Command.

> Head Quarters 4th Brig
> Fort Holt Ky.
> Dec 25, 1861.

'General Order No 22

    In pursuance to Special Orders Dist. of Cairo. Brig Genl. U. S. Grant Comd'g, Commanding Officers of Regiments and Detachments at Fort Holt Ky are required to search or cause to be searched the quarters of their respective commands for fugitive slaves and have all such fugitives forthwith expelled the lines of Camp.

    If hereafter any such fugitives are concealed or detained in or about the Camp, the party or parties so detaining will be brought to punish-ment.

> By Order Col John Cook.
> Comd'g 4th Brig.
> L R Waller A A A Genl.'

No officer more gladly receives or executes, to the best of his ability, more cheer-fully, orders emanating from Head Quarters Dist of Cairo, than does Your Obt Servt." LS, DNA, RG 393, District of Cairo, Letters Received. *O.R.*, II, i, 794–95. On Dec. 27, Rawlins wrote to Cook. "I have the honor to acknowledge the receipt of your communication of the 26th inst. relating to the alleged con-cealment of 'Fugitive Slaves' at Fort Holt, and am instructed by Brig Genl U. S. Grant Comd.g to say, Your explanation of the matter is highly satisfactory, but no more so than from all his previous official intercourse with you he had reason to expect." Copies, DLC-USG, V, 1, 2, 3, 79; DNA, RG 393, USG Letters Sent. *O.R.*, II, i, 797.

    On Nov. 23, Cook had written to USG. "Yours of the 14th inst by the hands of Mr Mercer is just received to day, Mr M. having in my absence refused to place the same for me in the hands of the A A A Gen'l. of this Post. Due regard has ever been paid to your orders previously issued in regard to slave property and am most certain that no portion of the command has either aided or assisted in any manner the enticing or holding of any slave, owing service under the laws of any slave state in or 'out of the Union,' and when such have asked protection, they have only temporaily obtained it, and I still hold as under previous orders from you any such when in my Command in readiness to be instantly turned over either to the lawful owner or any identified agent of said owner. There may be negroes at the 'Fort' who have never been liberated, but if there are I have never been notified of their presence except in one instance and I have issued a special order this day to require him under escort to be sent without the lines. Capt Delano has just informed me that Old Man Mercer has during the fore part of the day given him no little trouble in regard to one man in his camp, whom the Capt informs me is not only the property of a secessionist but has been used in aid ~~of~~ of treason by his master. This however I am not officially apprised of and cannot of course act as I would under other circumstances. Enclosed please find copy of Gen'l order issued in relation to such characters and oblige Your Most Obt Servt" ALS, DNA, RG 393, District of Cairo, Letters Received. *O.R.*, II, i, 778–79. Cook enclosed his General Orders No. 17, Nov. 23. "No Officer or soldier shall be allowed to arrest, secrete or harbor or in any way interfere with persons held to service (Negroes) property of citizens of slave holding States." ADS, DNA, RG 393, District of Cairo, Letters Received. *O.R.*, II, i, 779.

1. General Orders No. 3, Dept. of the Mo., were issued on Nov. 20, 1861. "1. It has been represented that important information respecting the numbers and condition of our forces is conveyed to the enemy by means of fugitive slaves who are admitted within our lines. In order to remedy this evil it is directed that no such person be hereafter permitted to enter the lines of any camp or of any forces on the march and that any now within such lines be immediately excluded therefrom. 2. The general commanding wishes to impress upon all officers in command of posts and troops in the field the importance of preventing un-authorized persons of every description from entering and leaving our lines and of observing the greatest precaution in the employment of agents and clerks in confidential positions." *Ibid.*, p. 778.

To Brig. Gen. Don Carlos Buell

Head Quarters Dist of Cairo
Cairo Dec 26th 1861

GEN. D. C. BUELL
COMDG. DEPT. OF THE OHIO
LOUISVILLE KY
GEN

I enclose you herewith an order defining the limits of my command. The object is that you may know its extent, and to express to you a desire to cooperate with you as far as practicable, especially in suppressing the smuggling that is now being carried on along the Ohio, to some extent, with the enemy.

I would respectfully request a Copy of such orders as you may have published on this subject.

> Respectfully
> Your Obt. Servt.
> U. S. GRANT
> Brig. Genl Comdg.

Copies, DLC-USG, V, 1, 2, 3, 79; DNA, RG 393, USG Letters Sent. *O.R.*, I, vii, 516–17. See General Orders No. 22, Dec. 23, 1861.

To [Col. Richard J. Oglesby]

> Head Quarters Dist of Cairo
> Cairo Dec 26th 1861

COMD.G OFFICER
8TH ILLS VOLS
SIR

You are directed to break up immediately the Regl Hospital of your Regiment in Cairo

But one Regimental Hospital can be allowed, such patients as cannot be taken to the Hospital at Birds Point will be sent to Genl Hospital either here or at Mound City

> U. S. GRANT
> Brig Genl Comd.g

Copies, DLC-USG, V, 1, 2, 3, 77; DNA, RG 393, USG Letters Sent.

To Allen C. Fuller

Head Quarters Dist of Cairo
Cairo Dec 26th 1861

COLONEL A. C. FULLER
ADJ GEN STATE OF ILLINOIS
SPRINGFIELD ILLS.
DEAR SIR.

The Colonel of the 12th Illinois[1] is in command of a Brigade at Paducah. The regiment is divided one detachment being at Smithland in command of the Lieut Colonel[2] the other detachment being at Paducah under command of the Major.[3]

I would be most happy to accommodate you in any way I could, but the request you make is not only impracticable as you perceive from the condition of the regiment, but if it were practicable I would not have the right to grant your request. That is the right alone of Gen Halleck commanding the Department—

I am truly sorry that I cannot accommodate you—

U. S. Grant
Brig Gen Com'g
By W. S. HILLYER
A. D. C.

ALS (facsimile), IHi. Allen C. Fuller was appointed Ill. AG on Nov. 11, 1861. On Dec. 25, Fuller telegraphed to USG. "You are requested to permit Maj. A. C. Ducat, twelfth (12th) Ills. Regt., to take temporary Command of the fifty-sixth Regt. Mechanics Fusiliers, Chicago, by order of Commander-in-Chief." Telegram received (punctuation added), DNA, RG 393, Dept. of the Mo., Telegrams Received. On Dec. 30, Fuller wrote to USG. "I have the honor to acknowledge the receipt of your favor of the 26th inst, and beg leave to say, that while I very much regret your inability to accomodate Major Ducat and this Department as requested, yet the reasons assigned for declining are entirely satisfactory. I beg leave to call your attention to another subject, in which we are all greatly interested; to wit: Arms for our troops. In the early part of the present month, an Agent of the State was dispatchd to Cairo & vicinity to distribute Arms to certain Illinois Regiments, with instructions to receive, and return, old or imperfect Arms that the same might be repair'd at our State Arsenal & made servicable for further use. These instructions to exchange Arms were given in conformity with instructions to Govr Yates while in Washington. This Agent reports, that he was unable to obtain the unserviceable arms as directed, and he has been directed to return to Cairo, & complete his commission if practicable, and in case he is not able to effect the exchange, to bring back with him the new Arms not already deliv'd. I would thank you to render him such facilites as in your judement he is entitled to. I beg leave to return you my thanks, for the cordial maner in which you receive'd, and treated, an Agent of this Dept, collecting statistical information concerning Illinois troops. P. S. The 45th Reg. Col Smith will be sent forw'd as soon as they receive their pay on the first proximo." LS, *ibid.*, District of Cairo, Letters Received.

    1. Col. John McArthur.
    2. Lt. Col. Augustus L. Chetlain.
    3. Maj. Arthur C. Ducat.

General Orders No. 25

Head Quarters Dist of Cairo
Cairo Dec 28th 1861

GENERAL ORDER NO 25

Major A. J. Kuykendall of the 31st Regiment Ill. Vols is hereby appointed District Provost Marshall.

All local Provost Marshalls within this District, will be subject to, and obey his orders and through him make all reports, (required to be made) to the Provost Marshal General of the Department of the Missouri

All assistants, that may be required in the Offices of Provost Marshall, will be detailed from the Military Serving where the office is situated.

Great caution is enjoined upon persons holding this office, to see that improper persons, are not permitted to pass, and repass our lines, and to arrest, and collect the proofs against all suspected spies, smugglers and persons affording in any way aid and comfort to the enemy

By order of
Brig. Genl. U. S. Grant
JNO A RAWLINS
Asst. Adjt. Genl

Copies, DLC-USG, V, 12, 13, 14, 80; DNA, RG 94, 9th Ill., Letterbook; *ibid.*, RG 393, USG General Orders. Andrew J. Kuykendall, a lawyer of Vienna, Ill., served nineteen years in the Ill. House of Representatives before his appointment as maj., 31st Ill.

General Orders No. 26

Head Quarters Dist. of Cairo
Cairo Dec 28th 1861

GENERAL ORDER No 26

Whereas, there are now at Cape Girardeau, Paducah & Smithland & Cave in Rock, places within this Military District, many persons, who have been driven from their homes, and depived of the means of subsistence, by the acts of disloyal citizens of Kentucky and Missouri, and their substance taken, for the support of a rebellion against this Government, humanity dictates that these people should be comfortably supported, and justice demands that the class of persons who have caused their sufferings should bear the expense of the same.

It is ordered therefore, that at the places named, suitable quarters, shall be provided and contributions collected for their support and accounted for, in the manner prescribed in General Order No 24[1] from Head Quarters Dept. of the Missouri, with this addition.

Persons of Northern birth and education who are liable to assessment, under this order, will be taxed fifty per cent more than Southern men of their class of guilt and means.

The refugees at Cave in Rock will be invited, and means of transportation provided to Smithland or Paducah.

These contributions will be collected as far out, as the Military Arm can securely extend, and at these distant points will be assessed and collected, without the intervening of time between assessment and collection.

Commanding Officers at Paducah Ky. and Cape Girardeau
Mo. are particularly charged with the execution of this order

By order of
Brig. Genl U. S. Grant
Jno A Rawlins
A. A. Genl

Copies, DLC-USG, V, 12, 13, 14, 80; DNA, RG 94, 9th Ill., Letterbook; *ibid.*,
RG 393, USG General Orders. *O.R.*, I, vii, 518–19; *ibid.*, II, i, 531–32.

1. General Orders No. 24, Dept. of the Mo., Dec. 12, 1861, provided for the
relief of Union refugees from southwest Mo. by assessments upon persons in St.
Louis "known to be hostile to the Union." *Ibid.*, I, viii, 431–32; *ibid.*, II, i, 150–
51. See W. Wayne Smith, "An Experiment in Counterinsurgency: The Assessment of Confederate Sympathizers in Missouri," *Journal of Southern History*,
XXXV, 3 (Aug., 1969), 361–80.

To Brig. Gen. John A. McClernand

Head Quarters Dist of Cairo
Cairo Dec 28th 1861

Special Order No

All the 2nd Ill Cavalry, now at Cairo, will proceed, without
delay to Paducah Ky. and report for duty to Brig. Genl. Smith

Two companies of the Cavalry force now at Paducah, will be
sent to Smithland Ky. as soon as practicable after the arrival of
the 2nd Cavalry

The Post Quarter master will furnish the nescessary transportation.

By order
U. S. Grant
Brig. Gen. Com.

For Brig. Genl J A McClernand
Comdg. U. S. Forces
Cairo Ill

DS, McClernand Papers, IHi. See letter to Capt. John C. Kelton, Dec. 29, 1861.

To Brig. Gen. Montgomery C. Meigs

Head Quarters Dist of Cairo
Cairo Dec. 29th 1861

Gen M. C. Meigs
Qr. Mr. Gen. U. S. Army
Washington D. C.
General

Yours of the 21st. inst enclosing copy of an article from the Chicago Tribune, charging corruption upon the Qr. Master's of this command or his Agts, was received, during my absence from here, inspecting some of the posts ~~of~~within ~~my command~~, this Dist.

In reply, I can state that two weeks ago, as soon as my attention was called to the article in question, I ordered one of my Aid de Camps to Chicago, to make a full investigation He returned one week ago, and made a full report, which was forwarded to Maj. Gen. Halleck

I regret to say the investigation fully sustains the charges made by the Tribune.

I will forward you by next mail a copy of the report.[1]

I at once made application to have a competent officer, sent here to settle up the affairs of the Department, stating that as little money has ever been sent here Government might yet be protected against any frauds, that have been intended.

I have ordered an Asst. Qr. Mr. from Paducah, who will at once be put in charge here[2]

I am Gen Very Respectfully
Your Obt. Svt.
U. S. Grant
Brig Gen Comdg.

Copies, DLC-USG, V, 4, 5, 7, 8, 79; DNA, RG 393, USG Letters Sent. Brig. Gen. Montgomery C. Meigs of Pa., USMA 1836, was appointed q.m. gen. on May 15, 1861. On Dec. 21, Meigs wrote to USG. "The enclosed Copy of an article from the Chicago Tribune is respectfully submitted for your information

with a request that you will investigate the charges therein made." Copy, *ibid.*,
RG 92, Letters Sent. On Jan. 4, 1862, Meigs wrote to USG. "I have the honor
to acknowledge the receipt of your letter of the 29th ult. The thanks of this Department are tendered to you for your promptness in the investigation of the
affairs of the Qr.Mr's Dept at Cairo, to which your attention had been called. All
the debts of the Quarter Master at that post, are by order, to go before the Commission, on debts of the Western Department, Sitting at St Louis. The report to
which you refer in your letter, is not yet received, and the name of the guilty
person is unknown to this office as yet." LS, *ibid.*, RG 393, District of Cairo,
Letters Received. See letter to Brig. Gen. Montgomery C. Meigs, Jan. 13, 1862.

1. For the report of Capt. William S. Hillyer, see letter to Capt. John C.
Kelton, Dec. 22, 1861.
2. Capt. Algernon S. Baxter. See letter to Capt. John C. Kelton, Jan. 1, 1862.

To Capt. John C. Kelton

————

Head Quarters, Dist. of Cairo
Cairo, Dec. 29th 1861.

Capt. J. C. Kelton,
A. A. Gen. Dept. of the Mo.
St. Louis, Mo.
Sir:

On Thursday night[1] I left here to visit Shawneetown and all
other points occupied by troops, within this Military District,
on the Ohio river. At Shawneetown I found a regiment of
Cavalry, with but few arms, and five companies of the regiment
that have not yet been Mustered into the service of the United
States; also a regiment of Infantry, claiming to number over 800
men, still in the state service, with about four hundred Muskets
that I had previously sent them from arms that had been turned
in by troops here, to receive better ones.

These troops have a large Steamer at their service for which
they seem to have no other use than to send up the river after
hay for the Cavalry horses. This Steamer appears to have been
chartered by state authority. As a claim will likely come against
the Government for all money paid in this way I would recom-

mend that the Governor of the State be requested to send a
Mustering officer to Muster these troops into the service of the
United States and I can then supply their wants without keeping
a large Steamer expressly for that purpose.

At Cave-in-Rock there are many refugees who have been
driven from their homes in Kentucky and are now living in the
Cave in a very distitute circumstances.

The country on the Kentucky side has been nearly stripped of
all supplies, the Secessionests receiving pay and the Unionests
driven from their homes.

This portion of Ky. is within the Department of the Ohio but
is remote from any of the troops of that Dept.

The citizens are very clamerous for Federal protection.

There is an encampment of rebels at Hopkinsville, said to
number about 3000 men, poorly armed & equipped, who if
driven out would save this portion of the state much annoyance.

Camp Beaurigard (Feliciana) has been entirely evacuated,
the troops going to Bowling-green. This gives reinforcements
to that point of about 7000 men.[2]

Finding Cavalry much needed both at Paducah & Smithland
I have ordered up five companies from here. Also ordered two
companies to Cape Girardeau to replace those ordered to Carondelet.[3]

There is evidently great dissatisfaction among the troops of
Gen. Jeff. Thompson. There has been recently between three
and four hundred of his men come into Cape Girardeau and
voluntarily applied to take the oath of allegiance to the Government. They express themselvs as anxious to retire to their
homes and live in quiet.[4]

I have had a man in Columbus the last week who has succeeded in completing a map of the enemies works which I have
every reason to believe to be as accurate as it is possible to get
it before it falls into our possession. The floating battery has
been removed to New Madrid. Many of the best disciplined
troops have been removed and their places supplied by Militia.
This informant says that he heard a planter remark that many of

the troops were now distributed in squads of twenty, and over, upon the plantations in the South to repress insurrection. Being able to speak the German language he learned that there are about 1200 of that nationality who, with some 600 Irish, intend to turn upon the Garrison as soon as they feel there is any security in doing so when an attack is made. I am well aware however that it will not do to rely upon this sort of support.

Respectfully

U. S. GRANT

Brig. Gen. Com.

ALS, DNA, RG 393, Dept. of the Mo., Letters Received. *O.R.*, I, vii, 523–24.

1. Dec. 26, 1861.
2. On Dec. 24, Maj. Gen. Leonidas Polk decided to send about 5,000 troops commanded by Col. John S. Bowen from Camp Beauregard to Bowling Green. *Ibid.*, p. 790. On Dec. 27, Brig. Gen. Charles F. Smith learned of the movement. *Ibid.*, p. 517. On Dec. 28, Smith sent troops under Brig. Gen. Lewis Wallace to verify the information. *Ibid.*, pp. 66–68, 527. In order to prevent further transfers of C.S.A. troops from western Ky. to central Ky., Maj. Gen. George B. McClellan ordered demonstrations in western Ky. *Ibid.*, pp. 527–28.
3. See special orders for Brig. Gen. John A. McClernand, Dec. 28, 1861. On Dec. 28, Col. Leonard F. Ross wrote to USG. "Reliable information has reached me that on Monday & Wednesday next at a point near Moses Haines about twenty miles below Bloomfield one hundred and fifty or two Hundred waggons will be sold for the purpose of raising funds to pay off Jeff Thompsons troops. By special order of Genl Halleck directed to these Head Quarters Capt Langan & Capt Pfaffs companies of 'Benton Hussars' are ordered to Carrondolet, Mo. This leaves this post entirely destitute of Cavalry. They constitute a very essential Branch of operations—and I desire to ask that as much as can be furnished this post without manifest prejudice to the interest of the service at other points be sent as soon as practicable. I have cause to congratulate myself upon being placed within your jurisdiction again, thereby relieving me from an unpleasant duty. I trust no change of the same character will be made soon again. Deserters still come in daily with an earnest intention of being loyal" ALS, DNA, RG 393, District of Cairo, Letters Received. On the same day, Capt. John A. Rawlins issued special orders. "Major Jenkins with the two companies of the 1st Illinois Cavalry, will proceed from Birds Point, with as little delay as practicable, to Cape Girardeau, Mo., and report to Colonel L. F. Ross, for duty. Transportation will be provided by the Post Quartermaster." Copies, DLC-USG, V, 15, 16, 82; DNA, RG 393, USG Special Orders. On Dec. 30, Rawlins wrote to Brig. Gen. Eleazer A. Paine. "I am instructed by Gen Grant to say that two companies of 1st Ills cavalry at Birds Point, under orders to proceed to Cape Girardeau, will remain at Birds Point. You will direct Lt Col Prince to designate from his command (7th Ills Cav) two companies under command of a Major, to proceed to Cape Girardeau and there report for duty to Col. L. F. Ross, commanding post.

Transportation will be sent from Cape Girardeau. They must be in readiness to embark upon arrival of steamer." Copies, DLC-USG, V, 1, 2, 3; DNA, RG 393, USG Letters Sent.

4. During the last weeks of 1861, while Brig. Gen. M. Jeff Thompson was constructing a fort at New Madrid, Mo., his force dwindled due to the expiration of enlistments until he had about 600–700 left on Dec. 21. *O.R.*, I, viii, 717. On Dec. 27, Ross wrote to USG. "I have the satisfaction of reporting daily desertions from the Colum of Jeff Thompson   Many young men are coming into these Head Quarters from New Madrid Mo—taking the oath and pledging themselves to go home and remain peaceble & quiet. Between three and Four Hundred have so surrendered themselves. They uniformily report great dissatisfaction, much suffering and distress, and a general desire of their Comrades to get Home—out of the service. In this connexion I desire to ask instructions in reference to the mails, and also trade into the interior   A careful consultation with many of the citizens of Scott, Bollinger—Stoddard & surrounding Counties convince me that there are many Union men in those localities, who are deprived of the actual necessaries of life because of the refusal of the Authorites to permit intercourse. If some means for relieving them would be devised by the Department—it would result in much good to the cause. In addition—a more thorough understanding of the objects of the Federal Government could be disseminated—causing as I am convinced a great revulsion in sentiment of those several localities   I beg then that you will consider the matter of sufficent importance to authorize instructions upon this subject to this Command—I am credibly informed that Thompsons Command is being very much reduced by desertions—& refusals to Reenlist" LS, DNA, RG 393, District of Cairo, Letters Received.

On Dec. 29, with only twenty-seven men, Thompson captured Commerce, Mo., and shelled the steamboat *City of Alton*. *O.R.*, I, viii, 45. On the same day, Ross telegraphed to USG. "Jeff. Thompson with 50. men attacked the 'City of Alton' at 3 O'clock this P. M. at Commerce. He was up after Mules and clothing —left Commerce at 4 ½ O'clock—All pretty drunk—will stay tonight at Crows or Hunters below Benton. Cant you catch them?—"   Copy, DNA, RG 393, Post of Cape Girardeau, Telegrams. On Dec. 30, Ross again telegraphed to USG. "Mr Hawkins who was taken prisoner at Commerce last night by Thompson escaped eight miles below Benton & is now here"   Telegram received, *ibid.*, Dept. of the Mo., Telegrams Received; copy, *ibid.*, Post of Cape Girardeau, Telegrams.

To Maj. Gen. Henry W. Halleck

By Telegraph from Cairo [*Dec.*] 30 *1861*
To Maj Gen Halleck

I have no unarmed troops except Cavalry that are mustered into the Service of the United States

U. S. Grant

Telegram received, DNA, RG 94, Generals' Papers and Books, Telegrams Received by Gen. Halleck; copy, *ibid.*, RG 393, Dept. of the Mo., Telegrams Received. On Dec. 29, 1861, Maj. Gen. Henry W. Halleck telegraphed to USG. "Detail any unarmed troops you may have for service under Flag Officer Foote, & report them to him for duty." Copies, *ibid.*, RG 94, Telegrams Sent in Cipher by Gen. Halleck; *ibid.*, RG 393, Dept. of the Mo., Telegrams Sent; *ibid.*, USG Hd. Qrs. Correspondence; DLC-USG, V, 4, 5, 7, 8. On Dec. 17, Halleck had detailed 1,100 to 1,200 men from Benton Barracks, St. Louis, for service on the gunboats. *O.R.*, I, viii, 441; *O.R.* (Navy), I, xxii, 464–65, 468. He apparently changed his mind later, and sought to furnish part of the total from unarmed troops at Cairo.

To Capt. John C. Kelton

By Telegraph from Cairo Dec 30th *1861*

To Capt J C Kelton

Have Quarters for one more Regiment   all other Troops will have to go in Ten[ts]

U S Grant

Telegram received, DNA, RG 94, Generals' Papers and Books, Telegrams Received by Gen. Halleck; copy, *ibid.*, RG 393, Dept. of the Mo., Telegrams Received. On Dec. 28, 1861, Maj. Gen. Henry W. Halleck telegraphed to USG. "For how many more troops can quarters be supplied in Cairo?" Copies, *ibid.*, RG 94, Telegrams Sent in Cipher by Gen. Halleck; *ibid.*, Dept. of the Mo., Telegrams Sent; *ibid.*, USG Hd. Qrs. Correspondence; DLC-USG, V, 4, 5, 7, 8.

To Brig. Gen. Charles F. Smith

Head Quarters, Dist. of Cairo
Cairo, Decr. 31st 1861.

Gen. C. F. Smith
Comd'g U. S. Forces
Paducah, Ky
Genl.

Genl. Paine reports to me that there is a large amount of lumber at Paducah which was captured from the Rebels.

If you have any not absolutely necessary for the comfort of your command it can be ~~properly~~ profitably used here.

Please inform me, and if practicable have it loaded on one or more of the Bridge Boats to be brought down.

> Respectfully
> Your Obt. Svt.
> U. S. Grant
> Brig. Genl. Com'g

Copies, DLC-USG, V, 1, 2, 3, 79; DNA, RG 393, USG Letters Sent.

To Capt. John C. Kelton

> Head Quarters Dist of Cairo
> Cairo Jany 1st 1862

Capt. J. C. Kelton
A. A. Genl. Dept. of the Mo
St Louis Mo
Sir

I have ordered Capt. A. S. Baxter[1] A. Q. M., from Paducah Ky., with the intention of placing him in the position now occupied by Capt. R. B. Hatch. As the latter is senior, in rank to Capt. Baxter, I feel a delicacy, in placing him in a subordinate position.

I would respectfully ask how the difficulty can be obviated.

As there has been, but little money for the use of the Quarter Masters Dept here, from the time, the place, was first occupied, by troops, ~~pertaining to the Quarter Masters Department~~, and as there are large outstanding claims, I would respectfully suggest that Capt. Hatch be retained to assist in the adjustment of these accounts

> Respectfully
> Your Obt Svt.
> U. S. Grant
> Brig. Genl. Comdg.

Copies, DLC-USG, V, 4, 5, 7, 8, 9, 88; DNA, RG 393, USG Hd. Qrs. Correspondence.

1. On Jan. 2, 1862, Capt. John A. Rawlins issued Special Orders No. 4. "Capt. A. S. Baxter, Asst. Qr. Master, U. S. Vols. having reported for duty ~~in his Department~~, is assigned as purchasing and receiving Quarter Master. All purchases will be made by him, and he will transfers ~~made~~ to Brigade Quartermaster, on proper requisitions and receipts. Immediate steps, will be taken to secure a supply of forage for the public animals within this District." Copies, DLC-USG, V, 15, 16, 82, 87, 89; DNA, RG 393, USG Special Orders. Capt. Algernon S. Baxter of Vt. served as asst. q.m. of vols. from Nov. 23, 1861, to April 27, 1862.

To Flag Officer Andrew H. Foote

————

Head Quarters, Dist. of Cairo,
Cairo, Jan.y 1st 1862.

COMMODORE FOOTE
COMD.G FLOTILLA,
CAIRO, ILL.
COMMODORE;

Will you be good enough to authorize the use of one of the little Tenders to run between here and Mound City, for a few days, to transport the sick to Hospital and return the convalesents.

I would like to have it make a trip this afternoon and hereafter start at 10 O'Clock A. M. returning as soon as released by the Surgeon in charge of Hospital, making one trip per day.

I will have a boat on the line in a few days.

Very respectfully
Your Obt. Svt.
U. S. GRANT
Brig. Gen. Com.

ALS, DNA, RG 45, Area 5.

To Capt. William W. Leland

———

Head Quarters, Department of Cairo.
Cairo, Jan. 1st, 1862.

Capt. W. W. Leland, A. C. S.,
Cairo, Illinois:
Sir:

In reply to your statements of this morning relative to an attack made in the Alton *Telegraph*, reflecting upon the honesty and integrity of the Commissary of this place, particularly in the letting of a bread contract, I feel it but justice to you, and take great pleasure in making a full statement of facts.

The same charges were made to me that are now repeated in the *Telegraph*. I felt it my duty to have the matter investigated, which investigation entirely exonerates you of the charge made, and convicts the author, which traced back, proves to be Lazare or his wife, without a statement from any one to support it, of base calumny. This man Lazare, when he supposed that no one but himself could furnish bread, told me that at 2½ cents, he was losing money every day—that 3 cents was as little as he could furnish it at.

Knowing that such a price would be regarded as exorbitant, and feeling, as Mr. Lazare did, that no one but himself could furnish it, I tried to prevail upon him to take the contract at 2¾ cents. His reply was that his expense was great. Water had to be hauled from the river, flour from the wharf-boat, freights were high, and he was always required to be prepared for the contingency of an increase of the number of troops.

As an inducement, then, I told Mr. Lazare that if he would continue to furnish bread at 2¾ cents, I would require the public teams to do all his hauling at this place, and possibly the authorities at St. Louis would allow Government boats, when they were coming here without a full cargo, to put some flour on for him, free.

Upon these terms he agreed to continue. About this time

you made a contract at 2⅝ cents, the contractor to do all his hauling, freighting, and everything, free of expense or labor. Of this contract I was not advised until it was completed. This was probably the worst feature in the whole transaction.

Since this matter was stirred up, complaints have come to me from all quarters where bread has been furnished by Mr. Lazare, stating that the bread has been bad continuously, and sometimes short in weight.

Samples have been sent to my office which were totally unfit for issue, and if fair samples, as they were represented to be, I have no hesitation in saying that the bread furnished has been a fruitful source of sickness in this command.

These complaints were never officially made to me; but I now learn were made to local commanders frequently, and that the grievance has been of long standing.

The investigation I have caused entirely exonerates you from the charges, and, as before stated, traces the authorship back to Lazare (or his wife) a man who represented to me that at 2½ cents per pound he was losing money every day, and that at 2¾ cents he must have other benefits worth, to him, several dollars per day.

Yours, &c.,

U. S. GRANT,
Brigadier General Commanding.

Chicago Tribune, Jan. 5, 1862. The USG letter was appended to a letter of Jan. 1, 1862, from Capt. William W. Leland to the editors of the *Chicago Tribune*. "Enclosed I send you a copy of a letter addressed to the editor of the Alton *Telegraph*, together with letters from Generals Grant and McClernand, which I would respectfully ask you to publish as an answer to certain injurious imputations cast upon my character and official action, in a communication by an anonymous correspondent of the *Telegraph*, and copied into your paper of the 31st ult., under the head of 'More of the Cairo Frauds.' The statement of the miller who furnished a portion of the flour used by Lazare, which is also furnished, is important, as showing the quality of the bread furnished by him. In order to furnish good bread to the soldiers, I found it necessary to make a new contract, and thus displace a Jew *who claims that he owes no allegiance to the United States*; and I believe that I have thus not only ministered to the health and well-being of the soldiers, but also have saved to the Government some fifty dollars daily. I cannot doubt that you will do me the justice to publish all these documents, and thus enable the public to judge whether I have been justly assailed or not." *Ibid.* In addition to the USG letter, Leland added to his communication a copy of his letter of Jan. 1 addressed to the editor of the *Alton Telegraph* protesting the original complaint; a copy of a letter of Dec. 23, 1861, from Chas. Galegher & Co. to Leland itemizing the quality of flour furnished to the baker Lazare; and an undated statement of Brig. Gen. John A. McClernand. "Having carefully read the foregoing letter, and being called upon to make a statement upon the subject to which it relates, I have no hesitation to say, that the concurrent testimony of all, or many of the officers in my command, condemns not only the quality of the bread furnished by Lazare for some months past as impure and vicious, but himself unconscionable and dishonest. More than once did I bring grave complaints upon the subject to the attention of the late Commissary here, but without any advantage to the Government or the suffering men in my command. I would have long before dismissed Lazare if I had felt myself authorized to do so, and now fully justify Captain Leland in having done it. The act was required by common humanity, and if he had omitted it, he would have become a guilty accomplice. The bread supplied by the new contractar is good, and approved both by officers and men, and costs the Government considerably less than the base article furnished by his dissatisfied predecessor." *Ibid.* See letters to Capt. Thomas J. Haines and to Capt. William W. Leland, Dec. 17, 1861. See also letter to Brig. Gen. Lorenzo Thomas, July 25, 1862.

To Brig. Gen. Montgomery C. Meigs

> Head Quarters, Dist. of Cairo,
> Cairo, Jan.y 2d 1861. [*1862*]

Brig. Gen. M. C. Meigs
Quartermaster Gen. U. S. Army,
Washington D. C.
Gen.

Herewith Capt. Baxter A. Q. M. who relieves Capt. Hatch in the disbursments of his Department, encloses estimate for funds for the month of Jan.y.

By having funds here the credit of Government can be restored and, as suggested by Capt. Baxter, this made one of the cheapest points in the Country for supplying the Army.

Contracts have been lett here for the supply of forage, but as it was done without my knowledge or approval, and at prices full 20 per cent above what it can be purchased for, I have taken the liberty of annuling them and refered the matter to Head Quarter of the Department.[1]

Hoping that the funds asked for will be furnished I remain
Respectfully
Your Obt. Svt.
U. S. GRANT
Brig. Gen. Com.

ALS, Mrs. Walter Love, Flint, Mich. The estimate, marked "Approved" by USG, called for $100,500. DS, *ibid.* See letters to Capt. John C. Kelton and to Capt. Reuben B. Hatch, Jan. 2, 1862.

1. On Jan. 8, 1862, Capt. William S. Hillyer wrote to A. H. Covert, Chicago. "Your communication of the 6th has received the consideration of the Commanding General. Gen. Grants instructs me to inform you that he has already annulled the forage contract made by Capt. Hatch for the reason that they were, as he was informed, given to the highest instead of the lowest bidder. Your letter has been forwarded to Gen. Halleck, and the whole matter will be investigated. Capt. A. S. Baxter, A. Q. M. is alone authorized to make contracts for forage for this District until further orders." Copies, DLC-USG, V, 1, 2, 3, 85; DNA, RG 393, USG Letters Sent.

To Brig. Gen. Montgomery C. Meigs

———

Head Quarters, Dist. of Cairo.
Cairo, January 2nd 1862.

GEN. M. C. MEIGS
QR. MASTER GEN.
WASHINGTON D. C.
SIR—

I have the honor to transmit herewith to you, my quarterly accounts, for the quarter ending Dec 31st 1861, of all moneys received, and amounts expended for Secret Service.

Very Respectfully,
Your Obt Servant
U. S. GRANT
Brig Genl Commdg.

Copies, DLC-USG, V, 7, 85; DNA, RG 393, USG Hd. Qrs. Correspondence.

To Capt. John C. Kelton

Head Quarters Dist of Cairo
Cairo Jany 2nd 1862

Capt. J. C. Kelton
A. A. Genl. Dept. of the Mo
St Louis Mo
Sir

I find that the Quarter masters here, and ~~also~~ at Paducah Ky. have advertised for bids, to furnish forage at the two places, and have closed the contracts.

This was done without my knowledge, and ~~the contracts~~ I do not look upon the contracts as favorable for the Government. I have therefore taken the liberty of annuling the contracts made here, and directed the Quartermaster, Capt Baxter to purchase for the present.

From the statement of Capt. Baxter, about 20 per cent can be saved, below the contract prices, on hay, and about 15 per cent on ~~the~~ grain.

I would respectfully ask ~~if~~ whether I have not the power, and ~~if~~ whether it is not my duty, to examine, all contracts made within this District, and if ~~desired~~ satisfactory to me, require that they ~~should~~ be sent to Maj. Allen Chief Quartermaster of the Department for approval, before becoming binding upon Government.

I would suggest that the plan of letting large contracts, that can only be taken by men of large capital, must nescessarily be expensive.

To avoid this I would require the Quartermaster, to purchase all the forage offered, at Market price, until public notice was given that no more would be required, or if contracts, must be made receive all bids, for whatever amount of any one or more articles the bidder might propose to furnish.

This would enable the farmer to make a bid, for his crop, without having it pass through the hands of a speculator.

This is intended more in the way of asking for instructions than making suggestions.

> Respectfully
> Your Obt. Servt
> U. S. GRANT
> Brig. Genl. Comdg.

Copies, DLC-USG, V, 4, *5*, 7, 8, 9, 88; DNA, RG 393, USG Hd. Qrs. Correspondence. On Jan. 1, 1862, Capt. John A. Rawlins issued Special Orders No. 3. "Captain A. S. Baxter A. Q. M. U. S. A. is hereby appointed to inspect, the Forage, received by the Post, Quarter Master of this place to day, and see that the quality, and weight is in accordance, with the contracts under which it is furnished." Copies, DLC-USG, V, 15, 16, 82, 87, 89; DNA, RG 393, USG Special Orders.

On Jan. 2, Maj. Robert Allen wrote to USG. "I had approved a contract made by the Qr Master at Paduca for corn before I received your dispatch. I was assured that it was the lowest bid although it appeared to be high, 42 cts per bushel. Will you enquire whether all is right in regard to this transaction, and let me know at your earliest convenience" ALS, DNA, RG 393, District of Southeast Mo., Letters Received. See letter to Elihu B. Washburne, Nov. 7, 1862.

To Flag Officer Andrew H. Foote

> Head Quarters Dist of Cairo
> Cairo Jany 2d 1861. [*1862*]

COMMODORE FOOTE
COM.G CAIRO FLOTILLA
COMMODORE:

Will you please direct a gunboat to drop down the river this morning, as far as the head of the first Island, to protect a steamer I am sending down to bring up produce for some loyal citizens of Ky.

> Respectfully
> Your Obt. St.
> U S GRANT
> Brig. Gen. Com

Copy, DNA, RG 45, Correspondence of Henry Walke. *O.R.* (Navy), I, xxii, 482. Flag Officer Andrew H. Foote transmitted a copy of this letter to Commander Henry Walke with his endorsement. "Comr Walke will proceed in execution of this request." AES, DNA, RG 45, Correspondence of Henry Walke. *O.R.* (Navy), I, xxii, 482. Walke's brief report is *ibid.*, pp. 482–83.

To Col. Michael K. Lawler

Head Quarters, Dist. of Cairo,
Cairo, Jany. 2d 1862.

Col. M. K. Lawler
18th Regt. Ill. Vols.
Col.

Your note of this date is received and I take pleasure in replying. My acquaintance with you commenced since the beginning of our present difficulties. Since taking command of this District I have ever found you attentive to your duties, and the result is a well drilled Regt.

Aside from the high testimonial of character given you by Gen. McClernand, who has known you from childhood, my own observation would establish the justice of his statements.

Respectfully
Your Obt. Svt.
U. S. Grant
Brig. Gen.

ALS, DNA, RG 153, Michael K. Lawler. On Jan. 2, 1862, Brig. Gen. John A. McClernand wrote to Col. Michael K. Lawler. "Your note of this date, relating to charges preferred against you as a military officer and inviting such a statement as my long and intimate acquaintance with you justifies, is received. In answer I have to say, that I have known you as boy or man over forty years and throughout with good report of you. Having been strictly temperate, moral and upright in all your actions I could not say anything else. Your opportunities for intellectual improvement, particularly in the acquisition of military knowledge have always been diligently and profitably employed. No man stands higher among your neighbors than you do. As a citizen, your precepts and examples have always went together in behalf of your country and obedience to its laws and authorities. As a soldier and officer you are not unknown. As a Captain of the 3d

Regt of Ill. Vols. you took an active and meritorious part in the seige of Vera Cruz and the battle of Cerro Gordo. After the appointed expiration by your service in that capacity, you returned home to raise another company for the Mexican War, and through my application as your representative in Congress, obtained authority from President Polk to raise a company of Cavalry to serve during the war, and accordingly did so. Interested as I was in your success, I recollect that your company of Cavalry was reported, by the press, to have been honorably mentioned by Genl. Churchill, Inspector General of the United States Army, as one of the best, if not the best drilled company in the service. Of your conduct as an officer, here, in this war, I can say but little more than is generally known. Common report gives you the credit of having constructed the defences of Camp. Lyon, at Birds Point, and of the expedition made early during the past summer, eventuating in the capture of 50 rebels and their arms and horses, which I believe was our first success in South East. Mo. For some month or more past you have been in my command, and it is but just to say that during that time you have been diligent, faithful and efficient in the discharge of your duties. I deem it no injustice to others to say that you have one of the best drilled regiments at this Post, and that my reliance upon you as an officer of experience, courage and conduct would be confident in the hour of trial. With regard to the execution of Dickman for insubordination and mutiny in your camp, which I understand as one of the charges preferred against you, I can only say now what I have before officially communicated to you,—that the act, in my judgement, was irregular. Your explanation of the matter in a very able paper addressed to me, certainly, affords a very strong case of extenuation if not justification. of the act. You put his execution upon the ground of a military necessity, which if true left you no other alternative. Whether such a necessity actually existed you were called on to decide upon your own responsibility, and having done so, as I believe, in good faith and with a view to the public good, I trust your action will be judged in the spirit in which it was dictated. Not having been able to sit as a member of the Court trying you upon this and other charges, in consequence of unceasing and urgent pressing military engagements, I have felt myself at liberty as an old acquaintance and friend to furnish you this answer for such use as you may think proper to make of it." LS, *ibid.* On the same day, Lawler wrote to Capt. John C. Kelton. "I would respectfully submit the enclosed letters to the Major General Commanding—and ask that in the consideration of papers forwarded by Court Martial, he give them such weight as they may be entitled to." ALS, *ibid.*

   These letters coincided with the conclusion of Lawler's court-martial. On Jan. 2, Capt. John A. Rawlins wrote to Col. William H. L. Wallace. "The Court will upon getting through with the trial of Col. M. K. Lawler, or any other case in which it may now be engaged in the trial of, at this time, adjourn, *sine die.*" Copies, DLC-USG, V, 1, 2, 3, 85; DNA, RG 393, USG Letters Sent. Although the court sentenced Lawler to dismissal from the service, the verdict was overturned by Maj. Gen. Henry W. Halleck on Jan. 8 by General Orders No. 12, which restored Lawler to duty. On Jan. 8, Rawlins issued special orders. "1.. Colonel M. K. Lawler, Lieutenant Colonel T. H Burgess, and Major Samuel Eaton, 18th Illinois Volunteers, are hereby temporarily released from arrest and restored to duty with their regiment. These Officers will report for instructions to Brig. Gen. John A. McClernand, Commanding Cairo forces for instructions at Cairo." Copies, DLC-USG, V, 15, 16, 82, 87, 89; DNA, RG 393, USG Special Orders.

To Capt. Reuben B. Hatch

Head Quarters, Dist of Cairo.
Cairo, January 2nd 1862.

CAPT. R. B. HATCH
QUARTER MASTER,
CAIRO, ILLS.
CAPTAIN:

The contract made with Mr. Dill, and all others for the supply of forage, is disapproved. Such forage, as has been delivered will be settled for as a purchase, and parties, notified to furnish no more on the contract

U. S. GRANT
Brig Gen. Commdg

Copies, DLC-USG, V, 1, 2, 3, 85; DNA, RG 393, USG Letters Sent. See letter to Capt. John C. Kelton, Jan. 2, 1862.

To Capt. John C. Kelton

Head Quarters Dist of Cairo
Cairo Jany 3rd 1862

CAPT. J. C. KELTON
A. A. GENL. DEPT. OF THE MO
ST LOUIS MO
SIR

I would respectfully represent, that, there are now at this time 500 Carbines, in the hands of Adams Express Company in Springfield Ill. held for the payment of charges on them, and 500 more previously received, all sent to the 4th Ill Cavalry, now a part of this command.

These arms were sent by Capt. Balch,[1] of the Ordn. Dept.

from Springfield Mass. Why they should have been sent by Express, I dont know, but they were so sent by a Government Officer, and now Capt. Eddy[2] Quartermaster in Springfield, declines paying charges, without orders to do so.

I am opposed to having much Cavalry armed with Carbines, but as the 4th Ill. Cavalry have no Pistols, and are not likely to receive any, these arms, are nescessary to arm them.

I enclose herewith copy of dispatch from Gen. Ripley,[3] Chief of Ordnance, to Capt. Batch, on the subject, wh[i]ch will probably explain ~~this is the only explanation~~, why these arms, were sent by Express.

I would respectfully request that these arms be secured to this Regt.

With the exception of Cavalry Arms, this command is generally well supplied. Requisitions are in, for every thing to ~~complete~~ equip this entire command for taking the field, I think, except, for teams, and Ambulances. Wagons & harness there can be no great deficiency. ~~in but quite a~~ A number of mules, ~~must~~ are still ~~be~~ required.

I will forward requisitions for every thing required as early as possible.

I have not yet got a single tent for Hd. Qrs although requisitions were sent in months ago. Gen Smith at Paducah and I believe Gens. Paine and McClernand are in the same predicament.

> Very Respectfully
> Your Obt. Svt.
> U. S. GRANT
> Brig. Gnl. Comdg.

Copies, DLC-USG, V, 4, 5, 7, 8, 88; DNA, RG 393, USG Hd. Qrs. Correspondence. See telegram to Maj. Gen. Henry W. Halleck, Jan. 13, 1862.

1. Capt. George T. Balch of Ohio, USMA 1851, then on special duty to procure ordnance supplies at Springfield, Mass.
2. Capt. Asher R. Eddy of R. I., USMA 1844, then assigned as chief q.m., states of Ill. and Wis., with hd. qrs. at Springfield.
3. Brig. Gen. James W. Ripley of Conn., USMA 1814, chief of ordnance.

To Brig. Gen. Eleazer A. Paine

———

Head Quarters, Dist of Cairo.
Cairo, January 3rd 1862.

GENL. E. A. PAINE
COMMDG 2ND BRIGADE
BIRD'S POINT, MO.

Your communications, one asking authority for your Post
Qr. Master, to purchase grain, and another appointing a Post
Quarter Master are received.

The appointment of Capt D. D. Forks as Post Qr. Master is
disapproved, there is no authority for appointing a Capt. as Act.
Asst. Q. M. such appointments always being confined to
Subalterns. Even in the Regular Service where a Lieut. appointed
A. Q. M. with the rank of Capt. when he is promoted to the same
rank in the line, he is obliged to vacate one of the appointments.

In regard to the purchase of grain, or other forage, it must
all be done by the Chief Quartermaster at this place. He may
however authorize your Qr. Master to purchase, giving orders
on him for payment, and forwarding Receipt at the same time for
the forage.

This, however, I hope will not be necessary after a few days.
Instructions are already given for the supply of an abundance of
forage to be kept on hand at all times, and for furnishing a Wharf
Boat at Bird's Point to facilitate landing your suppies.[1]

There is no man in Missouri that I am aware of that has been
in my employ as a Scout. I may have been imposed upon in permitting some goods to pass there, for the person you speak of.

There are but two or three persons living near Bird's Point
who are of sufficient loyalty to be entitled to pass our lines.

Col. Oglesby or Wallace can inform you who these are.

Respectfully
Your Obt. Servant
U. S. GRANT
Brig. Genl. Commdg.

Copies, DLC-USG, V, 1, 2, 3, 85; DNA, RG 393, USG Letters Sent. On Jan. 1, 1862, Capt. John A. Rawlins issued Special Orders No. 3. "The whole of the forces at Birds Point, are hereby consolidated into one Brigade, Commanded by Brig. Genl. E. A. Paine, and will be known as the 2nd Brigade. The force at Fort Holt Ky. Commanded by Col. John Cook, will hereafter be known as the 3rd Brigade, and the Command at Cape Girardeau Mo. as the 4th Brigade" Copies, DLC-USG, V, 15, 16, 82, 87, 89; DNA, RG 393, USG Special Orders. *O.R.*, I, viii, 478.

1. On Jan. 1, Rawlins issued special orders. "Capt. W. J. Kountz A. Q. M will receive and receipt for the Steamer Stevenson, and have her fitted up, without delay, for a Wharf and Store Boat to be used at Birds Point, Mo." Copies, DLC-USG, V, 15, 16, 82, 87, 89; DNA, RG 393, USG Special Orders.

To Maj. Robert Allen

Head Quarters, Dist. of Cairo
Cairo January 3d 1862

MAJOR R. ALLEN
CHIEF Q. M. DEPT. OF THE MO.
ST. LOUIS MO.
MAJ.

I telegraphed you this morning to respect no contract made in this District untill you heard from me. I wrote to Genl. Hallack on the subject last night,[1] which letters probably will be laid before you.

Extravagance seems to be the order of the day, and now that I am investigating every Department, and all that is done here I find that contracts are not given to the lowest bidders. There is probably some explanation that can be given, such as bids being put in informally, arising from ignorance more than any other cause

I would recomend that Capt. Baxter, A Q M now the purchasing Quartermaster here, be allowed to purchase in open market until the atmosphere is purified somewhat. This is not applicable to Cairo alone but to Paducah also—I do not know the merits of the contracts given but I do know that near 20 pr. cent can be saved to Government by annuling present contracts, made without my knowledge, and adopting the purchasing system.

If contracts must be given, I would suggest the plan of receiving bids for any amount of corn, oats or hay any bidder might propose furnishing.—This plan would enable the farmers to bid for his crop without having it pass throgh the hands of ~~the~~ speculators.

I would be in favor of a law authorizing the impressment of all fraudulent contractors into the ranks or still better into the Gun Boat service, where they could have no chance of deserting.

Respectfully Your Obt. Svt.
U. S. Grant
Brig. Genl. Comdg.

Copies, DLC-USG, V, 4, 5, 7, 8, 9, 88; DNA, RG 393, USG Hd. Qrs. Correspondence.

1. See letter to Capt. John C. Kelton, Jan. 2, 1862.

To Capt. Reuben B. Hatch

Head Quarters, Dist of Cairo.
Cairo, Ills. Jany 4th 1862.

Capt R. B. Hatch
A. Q. M. Cairo, Ills.
Captain:

I have approved the Voucher for the hire of the Steamer "Montgomery," as a store ship, having authorized her employment in that capacity. You having employed the Steamer should by all means give Vouchers, and not wait for my approval, in advance.

This method of approving Vouchers by a Commanding Officer is entirely a new feature in the Quartermaster's Dept. and one that I am sorry I ever inaugerated, and it was only done in the first instance to give confidence to holders, that they would ultimately get their pay. No money of consequence having ever been expended here by the Dept, and the credit of the Government at this place apparently being at a low ebb, some such course seemed necessary.

Hereafter all transactions will be required to have either the sanction of law, or will be sustained by an order from proper authority, so that my signature will not be necessary to any more Vouchers.

Respectfully
Your Obt Servant
U. S. GRANT
Brig. Genl. Commdg.

Copies, DLC-USG, V, 1, 2, 3, 85; DNA, RG 393, USG Letters Sent. On Jan. 4, 1862, George W. Graham wrote to USG. "Capt Hatch and myself chartered Str. James Montgomery at Six hundred dollars pr month as storage for the Gun boat outfits, and in case she was used afterwards or during the time of said storage, as a Transport Steamer, the charter price to be made Equal to boats of her class, which was decided by several steam boat owners to be fifty dollars pr day—" ALS, *ibid.*, District of Cairo, Letters Received. See letter to Capt. John C. Kelton, Dec. 15, 1861.

To Col. Leonard F. Ross

———

Head Quarters, Dist of Cairo
Cairo, Ills. Jany 5th 1862.

COLONEL:

Your communication of the 30th ult. enclosing a copy of the "Daily Eagle" published at Cape Girardeau is received.

I am instructed by the Genl. Commdg to say, there appears to be nothing in it so objectionable, as much, that is published in Northern Papers, which daily find their way South, and their existence still tolerated by the Government. Until something more objectionable, appears, than any thing contained in the copy sent, it will not be suppressed. Its publication, under the construction of existing laws, cannot be interfered with, because of its being property of one in rebellion against the Government, unless it is used for the purpose of promoting the interests of rebellion, which in his judgment does not sufficiently appear in this case.

> I am Very Respectfully
> Your Obt Servant
> JNO A RAWLINS
> Asst Adjt. Genl.

To Col. L. F. Ross.

Copies, DLC-USG, V, 1, 2, 3, 85; DNA, RG 393, USG Letters Sent. On Dec. 30, 1861, Col. Leonard F. Ross wrote to USG. "I desire to call your attention, to the existence of a paper in this place—the tone of which is clearly inimical to the interests of the Government—That it works an injury—I have no—doubt—in addition to which it is owned by Jeff Thompsons QuarterMaster. I send you a marked copy—With your approbation, if the nusiance continues—I will suppress it" Copy, *ibid.*, Post of Cape Girardeau, Letters Sent.

One account states that the *Cape Girardeau Eagle*, partly owned by a man named Moore, was seized by the 1st Wis. Cav. in April, 1862. Beginning May 10, it was published by the troops for some three months as the *Eagle (Union Series)*, after which the press was destroyed. Felix Eugene Snider and Earl Augustus Collins, *Cape Girardeau: Biography of a City* (Cape Girardeau, 1956), p. 276.

To Col. Leonard F. Ross

> Head Quarters, Dist of Cairo
> Cairo, January 5th 1862.

COL. L. F. ROSS.
COMMDG. U. S. FORCES
CAPE GIRARDEAU, MO.

I am instructed by Gen. Grant to say to you, that he has carefully read your communication with reference to the slave of Dr. Henderson, and fully concurs in your views of the case. While it is not the policy of the Military Arm of the Government, to ignore, or in any manner interfere with the Constitutional rights of loyal citizens, except when a military necessity makes individuals subservient to the public interest, it certainly is not the policy of our Army, to, in any manner aid, those who in any manner aid, the rebellion.

The slave, who is used to support the Master, who supported the rebellion, is not to be *restored* to the Master by Military Authority. If such a master has a civil right to reclaim such property he must resort to the Civil Authorities to enforce that right.

The General Commdg. does not feel it his duty to feed the foe, or in any manner contribute to their comfort.

If Dr. Henderson has given aid and comfort to the enemy neither he, nor his agents have any right to come within our lines, much less to invoke our aid and assistance for any purpose whatever.

Very Respectfully,
Your Obt Servant
WM S. HILLYER
Aid de Camp

Copies, DLC-USG, V, 1, 2, 3, 85; DNA, RG 393, USG Letters Sent. On Dec. 31, 1861, Col. Leonard F. Ross wrote to USG. "I desire to present for your consideration, the following question. Dr Henderson, a Slave holder, and Secessionist —who has Contributed greatly, to aggravate the present condition of affairs, has a black, Boy in the Cape whom he desires to recover. Through his Wife he has made several ineffectual efforts to induce the boy—willingly to go—While he still persists in remaining—Agreeably to Gen'l Halleck's—Order—I have turned *them* from our Camp, Some have returned—The policy I have hitherto adopted has been to offer no obstacle to the recovery of all fugitives—at the same time affording no assistance to those, who come for the avowed purpose of such recovery. In this instance—I feel, that duty as an Officer would dictate, that so far from sending the Black boy—back to support the family—while the natural protector —abandoning them for the purpose of aiding those in arms against us—that I should the rather—retain him in some useful employment for the Government— I am personally free to admit, that in my opinion—the politic course to be pursued is—When the Slaves of known rebels come and remain within our lines—after exhausting the order of Gen'l Halleck—to put them, as before said, in a shape— that they may contribute to the general good of the Government—Still I desire to report, the particular case of Dr Henderson—to you—that I may obtain the well digested advice of the District Commander.—I am satisfied, that if those who escape, are permitted to return for the purpose of family support, Thompson's Command in this Dep't. will hold together—much longer—than if the men—composing the same—could be compelled by the necessities of their families to leave the army for the purpose of their support—" Copy, *ibid.*, Post of Cape Girardeau, Letters Sent. *O.R.*, II, i, 797–98.

To Capt. John C. Kelton

————

Head Quarters, Dist. of Cairo
Cairo, Jan.y 6th 1862.

Capt. J. C. Kelton
A. A. Gen. Department of the Missouri,
St. Louis Mo.
Capt.

From information just received from Columbus, the Garrison there, is now reduced from what it was a few weeks ago, by the withdrawel of the sixty day men, who are supposed, many of them, to have gone to Camp Beaurigard. This leaves a force of probably thirty regiments in Columbus.[1]—Gen. Pillow has resigned and gone to his home in consequence of being ordered to Bowling green.[2]

The rebels have a chain across the river about one mile above Columbus. It is sustained by flats, at intervals, [the] chain passing through steeples placed about the waters edge, the chain passing under the boats. Between each pair of boats a Torpedo is attached to the chain, which, is expected to explode by concussion.

An experiment was made with one of these machines, about ten days ago by directing a Coal boat against it. The experiment resulted satisfactory to the enemy. The position of these being so distinctly marked cannot be regarded as much of an obstical. Others are supposed to be planted in the river above these, not so distinctly located.

From information received through a gentleman up from Memphis, there are about six hundred Torpedoes in the river from Columbus to that City.

There are quite a number of soldiers in the Guard house here for desertion, disorderly conduct &c. I would suggest, in view of the difficulty of getting men for the Gunboat service, that these men be transfered to that service.

Also that authority be given to transfer unruly men herafter.

I have spoken to Commodore Foote on this subject, and I believe it meets with his approval.

If it meets with the approval of the Gen. Comd.g the Department I would be pleased to visit Head Quarters on business connected with this command.

Very respectfully
Your Obt. Svt.
U. S. GRANT
Brig. Gen. Com.

ALS, DNA, RG 393, Dept. of the Mo., Letters Received. *O.R.*, I, vii, 534.

1. Returns of the troops at Columbus for Dec., 1861, and for the week ending Jan. 7, 1862, total the aggregate present and absent at 18,673 and 18,675 respectively. The aggregate present, however, declined from 16,862 to 12,030. *Ibid.*, pp. 824, 826. The return for Dec., 1861, reported 2,577 present at Camp Beauregard, but on Dec. 31, Brig. Gen. James L. Alcorn stated that he commanded "but 1,700 infantry and cavalry combined ready for duty." *Ibid.*, pp. 813, 826.

2. Brig. Gen. Gideon J. Pillow had submitted his resignation about Dec. 27, after quarreling with Maj. Gen. Leonidas Polk. *Ibid.*, iii, 313–16. His resignation was not accepted, and he was later assigned to defend the Tennessee and Cumberland rivers.

To Capt. John C. Kelton

Head Quarters Dist of Cairo
Cairo Jany. 6th 1862

CAPT. J. C. KELTON
A. A. GENL. DEPT. OF THE MO
ST. LOUIS MO.
SIR

Enclose find Charges and Specifications against Lieut. Col. Thos. H. Burges and Maj. Samuel Eaton, 18th Ill. Vols returned to you, to gether with the document marked "A" refered to and made a part of each case. I supposed it had been forwarded before, this was procure from the Officer perferring the charges.

I am Sir very respectfully
Your Obt. Sevt.
U. S. GRANT
Brig. Genl. Comdg.

Copies, DLC-USG, V, 4, 5, 7, 8, 88; DNA, RG 393, USG Hd. Qrs. Correspondence. See letter to Capt. John C. Kelton, Dec. 24, 1861.

To Brig. Gen. Eleazer A. Paine

Head Quarters, Dist of Cairo.
Cairo, Ills. Jany 6th 1862.

Gen. E. A. Paine
Commdg 2nd Brigade.
Bird's Point, Mo.
Gen:

I wish you to send a squadron of Cavalry tomorrow morning towards Belmont, to return same day. Three Gun Boats will leave at 8 O'clock, A. M. to make a reconnoisance and it will not be necessary for these troops to go further down the river than the boats.

Respectfully
Your Obt Servant,
U. S. Grant
Brig. Genl. Commdg.

Copies, DLC-USG, V, 1, 2, 3, 85; DNA, RG 393, USG Letters Sent. Also on Jan. 6, 1862, Capt. John A. Rawlins wrote to Brig. Gen. Eleazer A. Paine. "I am directed by the Genl. Commdg to say to you that you will order the balance of the Battallion of Cavalry, part of which is now at Cape Girardeau Mo. to hold themselves in readiness to move on Wednesday the 8th inst. to the same place with Camp and Garrison Equipage to report to Col. Ross for duty." Copies, *ibid.*
    On Jan. 7, the gunboats *Essex, Lexington,* and *Tyler,* the fleet commanded by Flag Officer Andrew H. Foote, proceeded downriver to within range of the batteries at Columbus to check reports that torpedoes (mines) had been placed in the river. *O.R.* (Navy), I, xxii, 486–87. Although Foote found no more than one torpedo, C.S.A. correspondence indicates plans for an extensive network of torpedoes at Columbus. *Ibid.*, pp. 806–7. See also Milton F. Perry, *Infernal Machines* (Baton Rouge, 1965), pp. 10–11.

Calendar

1861, OCT. 1.   Capt. John A. Rawlins to Brig. Gen. John A. McClernand. "I am directed by Brig. Gen. U. S. Grant, to request, that you order all Skiffs and boats, from Norfolk to Mound City, and on the Mississippi in the vicinity of Cairo and Birds Point be gathered up and delivered to the Quarter Master at Cairo who will receipt for them and take them in his charge."—ALS, McClernand Papers, IHi. The letter is endorsed "Make the necessary orders to Capt. Hatch."

1861, OCT. 1.   Brig. Gen. Charles F. Smith to USG. "An elevating screw for Thirty two pounder not received. Please have it sent. Two thousand men from Columbus Reported at or near Feliciana."—Telegram received (punctuation added), DNA, RG 393, Dept. of the Mo., Telegrams Received. See *Calendar*, Oct. 12, 1861.

1861, OCT. 1.   Maj. John H. Kinzie, additional paymaster of vols., to USG "in reference to the creation of the State of Illinois as a separate pay district."—DLC-USG, V, 10; DNA, RG 393, USG Register of Letters Received.

1861, OCT. 2.   Capt. John A. Rawlins to Capt. Wilbur F. Brinck. "You will recruit at Cincinnatti Ohio all the men you can get for the artillery at Cairo Illinois. When you are ready to return you will call upon Quartermaster at Cincinnatti Ohio, who will provide transportation for yourself and recruits"—Copies, DLC-USG, V, 1, 2, 3, 77; DNA, RG 393, USG Letters Sent.

1861, OCT. 2.   USG special orders assigning Capt. John E. Detrich and Sgt. Henry Smith, 22nd Ill., to recruit at Sparta, Ill.—Copies, DLC-USG, V, 15, 16, 77, 82; DNA, RG 393, USG Special Orders.

1861, OCT. 2.   USG special orders granting leave to 1st Lt. Robert C. Nelson, 31st Ill.—Copies, DLC-USG, V, 15, 16, 77, 82; DNA, RG 393, USG Special Orders.

1861, OCT. 2.   Capt. Chauncey McKeever to USG. "The Major General commanding directs that you send a company from your command to Carondelet, to guard the gunboats building there."—Copies, DNA, RG 393, Western Dept., Letters Sent; DLC-USG, VIA, 2.

1861, OCT. 2. Brig. Gen. John A. McClernand to USG. "Allow me to invite your attention to the accompanying letter as relating to a matter falling within your jurisdiction rather than mine. I suppose some of the old muskets here might be placed in the hands of the Company referred to"—Copy, McClernand Papers, IHi.

1861, OCT. 2. Maj. Mason Brayman for Brig. Gen. John A. McClernand to USG. "The Deputy Prov. Marshal at St Louis requests the return of Angus McKinnon a convict sent down for 60 days &c. Wishes him returned under Guard. Have you means of sending him?" —Copy, McClernand Papers, IHi. See telegram to Maj. Gen. John C. Frémont, Sept. 15, 1861.

1861, OCT. 3. Capt. John A. Rawlins to Brig. Gen. John A. McClernand. "I am directed by Brig Genl U. S. Grant to request that you have Col Lawlers command at Mound City releived and he would like if it meets with your approval to have it releived by the 27th Ill Regt Col Buford commanding"—LS, McClernand Papers, IHi.

1861, OCT. [3]. Capt. Chauncey McKeever to USG. "Brig. Genl McClernand has given a leave of absence to an officer of the 2d Iowa regt: at Birds point for thirty five days. You will Please instruct Genl. McClernand as to the regulations on this point, and order the officer to rejoin his regt. forthwith."—Telegram, copies, DNA, RG 393, Western Dept., Telegrams; DLC-USG, VIA, 1. On Oct. 3, Brig. Gen. John A. McClernand wrote to Maj. Gen. John C. Frémont. "Gen. Grant, commanding District of South East Missouri, has communicated to me the contents of your telegram of this date concerning the leave of absence given by me to an officer of the 2d Iowa Regiment, for thirty five days. When the leave of absence was approved by me it was amid a multitude of pressing engagements, which account for the inadvertance. I regret the mistake, and the like will not, again, occur. I will immediately order the officer to rejoin his Regiment."—LS, DNA, RG 393, Western Dept., Letters Received.

1861, OCT. 4. USG special orders assigning Capt. Warren Stewart to recruit for his cav. co. at Jonesboro, Ill.—Copies, DLC-USG, V, 15, 16, 77, 82; DNA, RG 393, USG Special Orders.

1861, OCT. 4.   USG special orders assigning seven men to duty as hospital attendants.—Copies, DLC-USG, V, 15, 16, 77, 82; DNA, RG 393, USG Special Orders.

1861, OCT. 5.   USG signature on a petition to Secretary of War Simon Cameron asking the appointment of Ezekiel Folsom as hospital chaplain at Cairo.—Copy, DNA, RG 94, Letters Received. Folsom was appointed a hospital chaplain of vols. on June 4, 1862.

1861, OCT. 5.   USG special orders granting leave to 2nd Lt. John C. Tobias, 20th Ill.—Copies, DLC-USG, V, 15, 16, 77, 82; DNA, RG 393, USG Special Orders.

1861, OCT. 5.   Brig. Gen. John A. McClernand to USG. "Capt Lagow gave me the name of a man this evening with instructions from you that I should cause him to be arrested. Although his name was furnished, I can not lay my hand on it at this moment. Please send it by the bearer."—LS and copy, McClernand Papers, IHi. A notation on the LS reads "Called on Gen Grant and ascertained the name to be James Taylor. Oct. 6 1861"

1861, OCT. 6.   USG General Orders No. 10. "Hereafter all requisitions for clothing, Camp, and Garrison Equippage and all supplies furnished by the Quarter Masters Department will be sent to these Head Quarters for approval, and will be furnished through the Post Quartermaster. Ordnance Stores will be furnished through the Ordnance Officer at the Post"—Copies, DLC-USG, V, 12, 13, 14, 80; DNA, RG 393, USG General Orders. On Oct. 5, Capt. Reuben B. Hatch wrote to USG. "I am directed by the Quartermaster at St. Louis that all supplies for this division shall hereafter be issued through my Department at this place as Post Quartermaster. He further directs me to forward at once a requisition for everything needed by the army in your division including Paducah and to facilitate making up my requisition will you direct each Regiment to send me as soon as practicable a statement of their wants."—ALS, *ibid.*, District of Southeast Mo., Letters Received.

1861, OCT. 7.   Capt. John A. Rawlins to Brig. Gen. John A. Mc-
Clernand. "I am directed by Gen Grant to request, that you, have,
detailed eight men under the command of a commissioned officer, to
carry paymasters money chest, on board of boat, & guard the same to
Mound City. They will report immediately to Major Larned U. S. Paymaster at the St. Charles House in this city."—ALS, McClernand
Papers, IHi.

1861, OCT. 7.   Brig. Gen. Charles F. Smith to USG. "Please tele-
graph for me to Major Robt. Allen, qr. mr. at St. Louis as follows:
'Missouri money will not answer here: it is at a large discount.' "—
ALS, MH.

1861, OCT. 7.   Brig. Gen. Charles F. Smith to USG. "In answer to
your suggestion about Shawneetown I have to state that the Conestoga
is now up the river, gone to Henderson, and I have no other gunboat.
The New Era which I expected has not arrived. I can't spare any
troops.—"—ALS, DNA, RG 393, District of Southeast Mo., Letters
Received.

1861, OCT. 9.   USG endorsement. "Refered to Dept. Hd Qrs for
orders without recommendation"—AES, DNA, RG 109, Records of
the U. S. War Dept. Relating to Confederates, Union Provost
Marshal's Citizens File. Written on a sworn statement of Charles
Thrupp and Samuel Wilson of Cairo, asserting that they purchased a
cask of cognac brandy for $63 in Louisville, Ky., on Aug. 29; that it
was shipped from Louisville on Sept. 5; that it was transferred to the
Empress at Paducah on Sept. 8; and that members of five cos. of the
8th Ill. drank it all between Paducah and Cairo. Thrupp and Wilson
advertised as "Dealers in Boat and Bar Stores, Groceries, Provisions,
etc., No. 6, Springfield Block, Cairo."—*Cairo Gazette*, Aug. 15, 1861.

1861, OCT. 9.   USG special orders for Capt. Reuben B. Hatch.
"Hereafter the Post Quartermaster will only issue Hospital tents
Ambulances or other Hospital Stores Camp or Garrison Equipage
upon requisition approved by the Medical Director"—Copies, DLC-
USG, V, 15, 77, 82; DNA, RG 393, USG Special Orders.

1861, OCT. 9.   1st Lt. Donald Campbell, Lockport, Ill., to USG. "Send requisition for transportation. Recruits ready tonight. Send requisition by telegraph, also requisition for passes on Central Road. Answer."—Telegram received (punctuation added), DNA, RG 393, Dept. of the Mo., Telegrams Received.

1861, OCT. 9.   Ill. AG Allen C. Fuller to USG. "Arms & Clothing have been refused Illinois troops in St. Louis. We are without arms, but are daily sending Clothing to our troops in Missouri. Shall have one or two Regiments ready in a few days. The Gov is in Washington."—Telegram received (punctuation added), DNA, RG 393, Dept. of the Mo., Telegrams Received. On Oct. 10, Fuller telegraphed to USG. "We have not such a Company here. Hope to have by next week. The Govr will then be home & aid you if possible."—Telegram received (punctuation added), *ibid.*

1861, OCT. 10.   Capt. John A. Rawlins special orders convening a court-martial for Oct. 14, 1861, for the trial of 1st Lt. Edgar Potter, 18th Ill.—DS and copy, McClernand Papers, IHi. Another copy, DLC-USG, V, 80, bears the notation that "This order was countermanded not being in power of Genl Comdg Dist to issue such order was ordered by Dept Head Quarters Oct 21st 1861 (*with changes*)" On Oct. 11, Brig. Gen. John A. McClernand wrote to USG. "I wish to ascertain whether you have issued notices to the officers composing the Court Martial to be held on the 14th day of October, or whether the notices should be issued from this office"—LS, McClernand Papers, IHi. Potter resigned on Dec. 23, 1861.

1861, OCT. 10.   Capt. Sterling P. Delano, Co. L, 2nd Ill. Cav., to USG "requesting authority to raise another company of Cavalry."—DLC-USG, V, 10; DNA, RG 393, USG Register of Letters Received. In a letter of Oct. 14 to President Abraham Lincoln on the same matter, Senator Orville H. Browning stated that USG had written a letter in Delano's behalf.—ALS, *ibid.*, RG 107, Letters Received, Irregular Series.

1861, OCT. 11.   USG special orders granting leave to Lt. Col. Marcellus M. Crocker, 2nd Iowa.—Copies, DLC-USG, V, 15, 16, 77, 82; DNA, RG 393, USG Special Orders.

1861, OCT. 11.   Capt. John A. Rawlins to Col. William H. L. Wallace. "Capt Littler of 2d Iowa Regt of Vols with his company is temporarily detached for duty in Fort Prentiss. He will Proceed to Fort Prentiss without delay"—Copies, DLC-USG, V, 15, 16, 77, 82; DNA, RG 393, USG Special Orders. On Oct. 11, USG wrote to Wallace. "The order for the detachment of Col Littlers Compy 2d Regt Iowa Vols for duty at fort Prentiss is hereby Countermanded"—Copies, DLC-USG, V, 2, 77; DNA, RG 393, USG Letters Sent.

1861, OCT. 11.   Col. Joseph B. Plummer, Cape Girardeau, to Capt. John A. Rawlins. "I have the honor to enclose herewith certificates of Disability in the cases of Privates A N Thompson and John Blew of the 11th Mo Vols. I beg leave to inquire of the Commanding General of the Destrict if there be any Orders or regulations in regard to discharging soldiers in the Volunteer Service, for disability. Other than those found in the Regulation of 61. The Revised Edition I have not seen, I acted in two or three extreme cases, being informed that the Commander of the Forces here had the right to do so, but finding no order to that effect, I would respectfuly refer the matter to the General Commanding"—Copy, DNA, RG 393, Post of Cape Girardeau, Letters Sent.

1861, OCT. 11.   Maj. John W. Goodwin, 20th Ill., to USG forwarding "statement of officers of his command in relation to depredations committed at Charleston, Mo."—DLC-USG, V, 10; DNA, RG 393, USG Register of Letters Received.

1861, OCT. 11.   Capt. Franklin D. Callender, St. Louis, to USG. "Despatch recd. I cannot get the Shoulder belts made. Every body is Employed making the infantry accoutrements without the shoulder belts indespensibly required."—Telegram received (punctuation added), DNA, RG 393, Dept. of the Mo., Telegrams Received; copies, *ibid.*, USG Hd. Qrs. Correspondence; DLC-USG, V, 7.

1861, OCT. 12.   Capt. Chauncey McKeever to USG. "Send Gunboat Lexington to Paducah & Owensboro pending the repairs of the New Era."—Telegram, copies, DNA, RG 393, Western Dept., Telegrams; (misdated Jan. 12, 1862), *ibid.*, USG Hd. Qrs. Correspondence; DLC-USG, V, 4, 5, 7, 8. McKeever repeated verbatim the instructions telegraphed to him the previous day by Col. Joseph H. Eaton, military secretary to Maj. Gen. John C. Frémont.—Copy, DNA, RG 393, Western Dept., Telegrams.

1861, OCT. 12. Brig. Gen. Charles F. Smith to USG. "I avail myself of your offer of heavy guns (thirty two's I suppose) to request you to send me seven. I want them for the redoubt at the Hospital. If three 24-pdrs. howitzers are sent from St. Louis then I should only require four of the guns from you. If you can spare 7 send them, for I can easily send them back if I get the howitzers. Please send ammunition for the guns & all the fixtures. The two Elevating screws for the 32s. at Smithland have not been recd. Please send them up."—ALS, DNA, RG 393, District of Southeast Mo., Letters Received.

1861, OCT. 13. To Maj. Gen. John C. Frémont. "Refered to Head Qrs. Western Department with the recommendation that the resignation be accepted to take place at once."—AES, Lawler Papers, ICarbS. Written on a letter of Capt. William Hunter, 18th Ill., to Col. Michael K. Lawler. "I hereby respectfully tender my resignation as Captain of Company of the 18th Regiment of Illinois Volunteers, on to take effect on the first day of November next; and assign as cause therefor, that I have been appointed by the Governor of the State of Illinois, as Colonel of a new Regiment of Infantry, now being organized in this State."—ALS, *ibid.* On Oct. 16, Capt. William McMichael endorsed the letter. "Respectfully returned to General Grant.—The attention of Captain Hunter is called to par: 4th Genl. Orders No 57 A. G. office, August 15, 1861."—AES, *ibid.* Hunter resigned on Nov. 26, and was appointed maj., 32nd Ill., on Dec. 31, 1861.

1861, OCT. 13. Private Cyrus L. Edwards to USG "requesting a transfer to 1st Mo. Light Art."—DLC-USG, V, 10; DNA, RG 393, USG Register of Letters Received. On Oct. 14, Capt. John A. Rawlins issued special orders. "Private Cyrus L. Edwards a private belonging to Company 'I,' 7th Regt Illinois Volunteers, is hereby transferred to the 1st Regiment Missouri Light Artillery; transfer to date from 1st instant."—Copies, DLC-USG, V, 15, 16, 77, 82; DNA, RG 393, USG Special Orders.

1861, Oct. 14.   USG special orders granting leave to Col. Michael
K. Lawler.—Copies, DLC-USG, V, 15, 16, 77, 82; DNA, RG 393,
USG Special Orders.

1861, Oct. 14.   Brig. Gen. John A. McClernand to USG. "Capt
Dunlap Assistant Quarter Master &c, attached to my brigade, has
shown me an order from you to Capt Hatch, Assistant Quarter Master
&c. requiring him to take all 'contraband' property at this post into his
possession. I beg to suggest whether it is advisable to turn over to him,
at once, a number of mules taken yesterday as the property of Frank
Rodney; also a number of Cows and Calves taken at the same time, as
there seems to be some doubt whether the particular property referred
to, is liable to *forfeiture*, as the property of rebels, and as that question
is now under investigation by me."—LS, DNA, RG 393, District of
Southeast Mo., Letters Received; copy, McClernand Papers, IHi. On
Oct. 13, Capt. John A. Rawlins wrote to Capt. Reuben B. Hatch. "All
contraband property taken will be turned over at once to the Post
quartermaster who will receipt for same"—Copies, DLC-USG, V, 1,
2, 16, 77, 82; DNA, RG 393, USG Letters Sent.

1861, Oct. 14.   Col. Richard J. Oglesby, Decatur, Ill., to USG.
"Can remain here until Thursday safely & would like to"—Telegram
received, DNA, RG 393, Dept. of the Mo., Telegrams Received.

1861, Oct. 14.   "a Union citizen" of Ballard County, Ky., to USG.
"in Greate haste I drop you this note to inform you of a Plan that is
Laying to cross the River Between Mound city and Caladonia By the
Rebles   they intend By the aide of a citisen of Caladonia to cross fifty
men and capture a new Steamboat Hull that Lays at Caladonia and
Bring it over to this Side for the purpos of ~~crossing~~ conveying ordinance and troops across to the illinoise Side   P. S. for fear of this
being intercepted I will not Subscribe my name as it would place me
in a Dangerous position."—AL, DNA, RG 393, District of Southeast
Mo., Letters Received. On Oct. 15, 1st Lt. Clark B. Lagow wrote to
Commander William D. Porter, U. S. S. *New Era*. "You will imidiati-
ly proceed to Caledonia ~~Ills~~ where you will find a new steam Boat Hull,
which you will take possession of and bring to this place"—Copies,
DLC-USG, V, 1, 2, 3, 77; DNA, RG 393, USG Letters Sent. On the
same day, Lagow wrote to Col. Silas Noble, 2nd Ill. Cav. "I am

directed by Genl Grant to say to you that you will direct your four companies of Cavelry that are at Metropolis to keep a close watch on the citizens and people about Caledonia as he has information that they have some designs upon that place."—Copies, *ibid*. On Oct. 18, Porter directed Commander Henry Walke to tow the hull to Cairo.—*O.R.* (Navy), I, xxii, 372.

1861, OCT. 15. Brig. Gen. Charles F. Smith to USG. "The mail Steamer Chancellor arrived here and departed last night without my knowledge or consent. It was by chance only I learnt of her arrival and when I sent my orderly to the boat with dispatches she had already gone. I beg that Commodore Graham will apply the proper corrective Johnston and Hardee have gone to Bowling Green. I deem this reliable."—ALS, DNA, RG 393, District of Southeast Mo., Letters Received.

1861, OCT. 15. Commander William D. Porter to USG "requesting pass for Mr. Atkinson to Saint Louis and return."—DLC-USG, V, 10; DNA, RG 393, USG Register of Letters Received.

1861, OCT. [15?]. Capt. Parmenas T. Turnley to USG concerning the possibility of obtaining forage, grain, and hay near Cairo.—*HRC*, 37-2-2, part 1, 984–85.

1861, OCT. 16. Capt. Chauncey McKeever to USG. "The contract for Coal made by Capt Hatch is hereby annulled and declared void. Hereafter no contracts or purchases will be made by Capt Hatch unless the approval of the Major Genl. Commanding be first obtained. You will order Capt Hatch to send to Major Robert Allen, Chief quarter master at St Louis copies of all contracts heretofore made by him, together with a complete list of his outstanding debts."—Telegram, copies, DLC-USG, V, 4, 5, 7, 8; DNA, RG 393, USG Hd. Qrs. Correspondence; *ibid*., Western Dept., Telegrams. McKeever drafted his telegram on the reverse of an unrelated telegram of Oct. 16 received from Col. William P. Carlin.—ADfS, *ibid*., RG 107, Telegrams Collected (Unbound). On Oct. 16, Capt. John A. Rawlins wrote to Capt. Reuben B. Hatch, quoting McKeever's telegram in full. "You are therefore hereby ordered to send to Major Robert Allen Chief Quarter Master at Saint Louis copies of all contracts heretofore made by you, together with a complete list of your indebtedness."—Copies, DLC-USG, V, 1, 2, 3, 77; DNA, RG 393, USG Letters Sent. Also on Oct. 16, Hatch telegraphed to McKeever. "I have no contracts for coal or other supplies, all that I have purchased has been by order of the Commanding officer or by the necessity of the case. A complete report of Indebtedness will be forwarded as soon as it can be made out."—Copy, *ibid.*, Western Dept., Telegrams.

1861, OCT. 17.   USG to Capt. Chauncey McKeever. "This is refered to Hd Qrs. Western Department hoping that it will be found practicable to send a Paymaster to Cape Girardeau at an early day."—AES, DNA, RG 393, Western Dept., Letters Received. Written on a letter from Col. Joseph B. Plummer to Capt. John A. Rawlins, Oct. 15. "I hear frequent complaints from men under my command who have been in the service from four to five months, that their families are suffering for the want of food in consequence of their not having been paid I beg leave to call the attention of the Commanding General to the fact, and also that none of the troops at this station have ever been paid."—LS, *ibid.* Further endorsements state that paymasters went to Cape Girardeau on Oct. 19.

1861, OCT. 17.   To Capt. Reuben B. Hatch. "You will as soon as practicable proceed to supply all the necessary materials by purchase or otherwise for furnishing the General Hospital established at Mound City"—Copies, DLC-USG, V, 1, 2, 3, 77; DNA, RG 393, USG Letters Sent.

1861, OCT. 17.   To Capt. Reuben B. Hatch. "You will pay out the Quarter Masters Stores, Clothing Camp and Garrison equippage now in your possession to the proper Officers of the Army upon their receipts   This order does not conflict with the one previously issued regarding the supplies to Hospitals. You will observe both these orders"—Copies, DLC-USG, V, 1, 2, 3, 77; DNA, RG 393, USG Letters Sent.

1861, OCT. 17.   Capt. William S. Hillyer to Col. Silas Noble, 2nd Ill. Cav. "You will detail three of your best armed companies to proceed without delay to Birds Point and report to Col Wallace comdg

3d Brigade   transportation will be provided"—Copies, DLC-USG, V, 1, 2, 3, 77; DNA, RG 393, USG Letters Sent.

1861, OCT. 18.   Brig. Gen. John A. McClernand to USG. "I write to ascertain whether an order has been issued from Head Quarters of the Dept. of the West, prohibiting furloughs and leaves of absence or not? If so please communcate a copy—I hope such an order has been made"—Copy, McClernand Papers, IHi. See letter to Capt. Chauncey McKeever, Oct. 17, 1861.

1861, OCT. 18.   Lt. S. Ledyard Phelps to USG. "I am to leave for the Cumberland river, and the Ohio above, tomorrow morning. I have requested the Captains of the mail boats, and the Post Master at Cairo, to bring and send the mail for this boat without avail. I will be much indebted if you will have our letters, &c, put on board the Steamer Charley Bowen on her next trip to Evansville. I will be on the look out for her along the river."—ALS, DNA, RG 393, District of Southeast Mo., Letters Received.

1861, OCT. 19.   Capt. Reuben B. Hatch to USG. "I am informed by Mr. Abbott the Ill. Cent. R R Agt. that you have the necessary pass books for passing Officers & men over the R R's Numerous orders are sent here to pass such persons and it is necessary that the proper order should be presented to the R. R. Agt. and this Dept has not been supplied. Will you send *one* of the books you have if you can spare it and much oblige"—LS, DNA, RG 393, District of Southeast Mo., Letters Received. On the same day, W. P. Johnson, general passenger agent of the Illinois Central Railroad, wrote to USG from Chicago. "In Compliance with a Circular received from Assist Adjt Genl Mc-Michael, we have made arrangements for the issuing of Tickets at our various Stations upon army orders; I Enclose you Coppies of Circulars of instructions which I have issued to our Agents in Carrying out this plan. I send these for the purpose of Explaining to you the Manner in which we are Conducting this business"—ALS, *ibid.*

1861, OCT. 19.   Capt. Reuben B. Hatch to USG. "The note of Capt: Schwartz referring to the unfinished condition of his stable and the issue of forage was received yesterday. I have the honor to report that the orders from St Louis interdict the purchase of everything. Requisition has been made on the Qr. M. at St Louis for Hay & oats. The oats were received this morning by the Str Memphis but no hay. I have been making arrangements to get a supply of hay and expect it hourly. when it arrives all parties shall be supplied promptly as has been the case in the past."—LS, DNA, RG 393, District of Southeast Mo., Letters Received.

1861, OCT. 20.   Col. Joseph H. Eaton for Maj. Gen. John C. Frémont to USG. "I am instructed by the Major General commanding the Department to inform you, that it was his intention, in ordering Colonel *J. B. Plummer* 11th Regt. Mo. Vols. to Cape Girardeau, that he should have the immediate command of the troops, and control of the public service at that post and vicinity. He desires therefore that Colonel Cook, 7th Ills. Vols. be posted at some other point with his regiment, substituting therefor some other troops under your orders. In reference to the conduct of Lt. Campion he desires your further inquiry & report, with a view to taking action against him."—ALS, DNA, RG 393, Western Dept., Letters Received. Endorsed by Capt. John A. Rawlins. "Referred to Col Marsh so far as regards the case of Lieutenant Champion who will make further inquiry & report to this office—"—AES, *ibid*. See letter to Capt. Chauncey McKeever, Sept. 26, 1861. Col. John Cook had already been transferred to Fort Holt. See letter to Col. Joseph B. Plummer, Oct. 3, 1861.

1861, OCT. 20.   Lt. S. Ledyard Phelps, Paducah, to USG. "Last Evening I entered the Cumberland River and proceeded up to the State line of Tennessee. At Eddyville three men came on board, representing themselves as Union men driven from their homes—near Linton, Ky:—and that they had come down in a Skiff on their way to Smithland. One of them, by the name of Esell, stated that 2½ miles above Canton, Ky:, they had met with two Flats loaded with flour and being hauled up the river into Tennessee. At 1' O'C. Am, 9 miles below the state line of Tennessee, and 4 miles above Canton, I found the flats tied to the bank, the current, from a rapid rise in the river, evidently being too strong for the hands to work the boats up. Near one were fires where the men had camped; but no person could be found. The barrels of flour have no marks to show to whom they belonged, or for whom intended. The town of Linton, 2 miles below the Tennessee line, could not offer a market for such an amount of flour, and it is known that large amounts of this, and other provisions, are hauled there for shipment, on steamers, to Tennessee. Much no doubt reaches the rebel army at Bowling Green. The sparse population between Canton and the Tennessee line could not create a demand for it. The crews of the flats fled and no one was seen or could be found. The boats were therefore abandoned. Convinced that they were on their way to Tennessee I seized them and have brought them to this place, and General Smith has directed that they shall be taken to Cairo to be delivered to the Civil Authority, and directs me to report the circumstances of capture, &c, to you. The barrels of flour are as follows.—130 Bbls., marked M. M. 168 Bbls.—Magnolia Mills, 196 Extra family Flour. Canton, Ky.—P. S. I enclose a copy for the District Attorney.—"— ALS, DNA, RG 393, District of Southeast Mo., Letters Received. On Oct. 20, Phelps reported to Capt. Andrew H. Foote.—ALS, *ibid.*, RG 45, Area 5. *O.R.* (Navy), I, xxii, 374–75. On Oct. 21, Capt. John A. Rawlins wrote to Capt. Reuben C. Rutherford. "You will receive and turn into the Commissary Subsistence Dept for use One Hundred and thirty (130) bbls Flour Marked 'M. M.' and one Hundred and Sixty eight (168) bbls Flour marked Magnolia Mills 196 Extra Family Flour ~~marked~~ Canton Ky seized as Contraband by Lieut S. L. Phelps comdg Gun Boat and sent to this Post."—Copies, DLC-USG, V, 2, 16, 77, 82; DNA, RG 393, USG Letters Sent.

1861, Oct. 22.   James R. Bull, St. Louis, to USG containing "statements in reference to J. H. McDonald arrested at Cairo with despatches upon his person."—DLC-USG, V, 10; DNA, RG 393, USG Register of Letters Received. "J. H. McDonald, from St. Louis, was arrested here last night by Lieut. Carson. He has been here for two or three days, looking about and taking notes, and yesterday he bought a skiff, preparatory to embarking for New Orleans. On his person and in his trunk were found papers written in cypher, and secesh articles clipped from the New Orleans papers. He had a permit for leaving St. Louis, and claims to be a Union man, but circumstances are strong against him."—*Chicago Tribune*, Oct. 18, 1861. "McDonald, arrested by Lieut. Carson charged with being a spy, was to-day sent to St. Louis by order of the military commission."—*Ibid.*, Oct. 22, 1861.

1861, Oct. 25.   1st Lt. Clark B. Lagow to Capt. Reuben B. Hatch. "I am directed by Genl Grant to say to you *'Again,'* that his approval to any paper or Requisition must be honored at once.—without any notes to this office on the subject. If you have not the articles required you must purchase them"—Copies, DLC-USG, V, 2, 77; DNA, RG 393, USG Letters Sent.

1861, Oct. [25?].   Maj. Gen. John Love, Ind. Legion, Evansville, Ind., to USG. "Meigs left this morning by Rail for Cairo"—Telegram received, DNA, RG 393, Dept. of the Mo., Telegrams Received.

1861, Oct. 26.   Capt. William S. Hillyer to Commanding Officer, Cape Girardeau, Mo. "You will exercise special vigilance to guard against any surprise on the part of the Enemy during the absence of Col Plummers command.—Keep scouting parties in constant reconnoisance & ascertain if possible the wherabouts of the enemy—send immediate report here if any danger is threatened or any important movements of the Enemy is discovered. If necessary to communicate in haste, on any matter of special importance, send messenger to Jonesboro and send Telegraphic dispatch to these Head Quarters"—Copies, DLC-USG, V, 1, 2, 3, 77; DNA, RG 393, USG Letters Sent.

1861, [Oct. 29].   USG endorsement, "Approved," on letter of Brig. Gen. John A. McClernand. "Henry Rice, late of Jacksonville, Illinois, is hereby appointed Sutler of my brigade of Illinois Volunteers—designated and ranking by virtue of General Order No. issued by Brigadier General Grant Commanding the South East District of Missouri as the *first* brigade in said district—with all the rights and privileges and subject to all the restrictions, obligations, and duties usually and properly appertaining to said office."—Copy, McClernand Papers, IHi.

1861, Oct. 29.   Col. Joseph B. Plummer to Capt. John A. Rawlins. "I have the honor herewith to Enclose charges and spicifications against First Lieut J. D. Anderson of the Engineer Regt of Mo Volunteers, and to request that a Court Martial may be ordered for his trial. There are many cases here that should be tried by a General Court Martial, but I have as yet been unable to have the charges drawn up in proper form, having no time to do it myself. Should be glad if he would direct, such cases to be brought before it without the delay of refering the charges to his Hd Qrs if it be not in violation of the Law"—Copy, DNA, RG 393, Post of Cape Girardeau, Letters Sent.

1861, OCT. 30. Capt. John A. Rawlins special orders. "Capt J. G. Cormuck 18th Ill Vols is hereby released from Arrest. He will return for duty with his company. The Comdg General is satisfied that Capt Cormuck intended no violations of orders and if he did, the charges preferred against him show an offence so slight that no law or regulation would warrant a court martial."—Copies, DLC-USG, V, 15, 16, 77, 82; DNA, RG 393, USG Special Orders. Capt. Joseph T. Cormick of Centralia, 18th Ill., resigned on Nov. 16, 1861.

1861, OCT. 31. USG General Orders No. 13. "On the recommendation of the Medical Director of the District, all *Drills* taking place before 10 o.clock a. m. will be dispensed with."—Copies, DLC-USG, V, 12, 13, 14, 80; (misdated Oct. 14, 1861) DNA, RG 393, USG General Orders.

1861, OCT. 31. USG General Orders No. 14. "All citizens employed in Regiments, in the Quartermasters, Commissary, and Medical Departments, will be discharged at once, there being no authority in law for their appointment."—Copies, DLC-USG, V, 12, 13, 14, 80; DNA, RG 393, USG General Orders; (Printed) McClernand Papers, IHi.

1861, OCT. 31. Capt. John A. Rawlins to Mrs. Williams. "Unless the Captain of the company in which your son is enlisted, desires he should be discharged, General Grant can not well do any thing toward having him discharged. He is informed your son was enlisted upon your written consent. And furthermore, by express order from the War Department, 'No discharges will be granted to volunteers in the service of the United States on the ground of minority. P. S. If you are desirous he should be discharged you must see a Lawyer & get out a writ Habeas Corpus, that will determine the question [o]f his right to a discharge"—ALS, McClernand Papers, IHi.

1861, OCT. 31. Brig. Gen. Charles F. Smith to USG. "A box of blanks from the Adjutant Genls. Office was placed in charge of Adams

Express Co. Several weeks since directed to me here. It has not arrived. Will you please have it looked for at Cairo & if found sent to me by mail boat."—Telegram received (punctuation added), DNA, RG 393, Dept. of the Mo., Telegrams Received.

1861, OCT. 31. Col. John J. S. Wilson to USG. "Please send her to Mound City today I will be down tonight"—Telegram received, DNA, RG 393, Dept. of the Mo., Telegrams Received.

1861, [OCT. 31]. Maj. Joseph J. B. Wright, medical director, Western Dept., to USG on certificate of disability for Sgt. Charles Stutz, 1st Mo. Light Art., Oct. 20. "The character and extent of the disability is not stated with proper precision in this case. The Co. officer and the Surgeon differ in regard to it, and I incline to the opinion of the Captain."—Copy, DNA, RG 393, Western Dept., Endorsements.

1861, Nov. 1. Maj. Charles J. Sellon, 28th Ill., Fort Holt, Ky., to USG. "Capt. Bowman is here with his scouts. I have no forage for his horses. Can a boat be sent over for him & his men?"—Telegram received (punctuation added), DNA, RG 393, Dept. of the Mo., Telegrams Received.

1861, Nov. 2. USG special orders granting leave to 2nd Lt. John B. Pearson, 28th Ill.—Copies, DLC-USG, V, 15, 16, 77; DNA, RG 393, USG Special Orders.

1861, Nov. 2. Brig. Gen. James W. Ripley, chief of ordnance, to USG. "In answer to your letter of the 26th ult. I have to state that the Edition of the Ordnance Manual of 1850, is exhausted—There is a new & revised edition now in press of Lippincott & Co. of Phila. which will be distributed as soon as they furnish copies. The Ordnance regulations are contained in the volume of regulations for the Army, and have not yet been published separately."—Copy, DNA, RG 156, Miscellaneous Letters Sent.

1861, Nov. 2. Charles D. Arter, surveyor of the port of Cairo, to USG. "Constant Complaint is being made by the Citizens of Kentucky that they are not allowed to Come to Cairo, By the military in Com-

mand at Fort Holt   These People depend upon this place for their
Supplies & if they are denied access to this market they will undoubted-
ly Suffer. Believeing this restriction is without your knowledge
induces me to make the facts known to you. Nothing is permitted to
Kentucky only in small quantities for family use & then only where the
oath of allegiance is taken & that they will not permit any goods to go
to insurrectionists or Disloyal citizens of the U States, which they may
be permitted to pass from this port"—ALS, DNA, RG 393, District
of Southeast Mo., Letters Received.

1861, Nov. 4.   Capt. Franklin D. Callender to USG. "If possible,
send me at once some musket or Rifle powder. Contractor powder not
received. Will be sent by tomorrow."—Telegram received (punctuation added), DNA, RG 393, Dept. of the Mo., Telegrams Received;
copies, *ibid.*, USG Hd. Qrs. Correspondence; DLC-USG, V, 7.

1861, Nov. 6.   USG special orders. "Col C. C. Marsh Capt. E.
Langen & Lieut. J W Kenard are hereby appointed a Board to examine
~~and~~ and and appraise the value of such Horses of Capt. E. Langen Co. of
Cavalry as have not yet been appraised"—Copies, DLC-USG, V, 15,
16, 77, 82; DNA, RG 393, USG Special Orders.

1861, Nov. 6.   USG special orders granting leave to 1st Asst.
Surgeon Daniel Stahl, 10th Ill.—Copies, DLC-USG, V, 15, 16, 77,
82; DNA, RG 393, USG Special Orders.

1861, Nov. 8.   Capt. John A. Rawlins to Brig. Gen. John A. Mc-
Clernand. "I am instructed by the General Comdg. to say to you, that
from information received from Mr William Mercer of Kentucky, he
is satisfied that Mr Asbury who is now detained as a prisoner, is a
Union Man, so much so, that he not allowed by his secession neighbors
to live in Kentucky, and although he does not think his love for the
Union above suspicion, he requests that he be released, with permission to remain in Cairo."—LS, McClernand Papers, IHi.

1861, Nov. 9.   USG special orders granting leave to Capt. James C.
Parrott, 7th Iowa.—Copies, DLC-USG, V, 15, 16, 77, 82; DNA, RG
393, USG Special Orders.

1861, Nov. 9.   Col. Joseph B. Plummer, Cape Girardeau, to USG. "I have the honor to report that after a thorough examination of the buildings in this city, I find none suitable for Quarters for the troops. There is a mill here, which, with two hundred dollars expended upon it, would make very comfortable Quarters for seven or eight companies, but its position upon the banks of the river, and three fourths of a mile distant from any of the field works, render it objectionable, Besides if the Government had to pay rent, its occupation would be of doubtful econemy. It will cost about two thousand Six hundred dollars, to build sheds, or temporary Barracks for each Regiment, and a coresponding amount for each Detachment here, for winter Quarters. I request of the Commanding General of the District instructions in regard to it."—LS, DNA, RG 393, District of Southeast Mo., Letters Received.

1861, Nov. 9.   Col. John J. S. Wilson, St. Louis, to USG. "Can you inform me where Mr. Washburne is? It is important that his whereabouts are ascertained. Answer."—Telegram received (punctuation added), DNA, RG 393, Dept. of the Mo., Telegrams Received.

1861, Nov. 9.   Private D. W. Crosby to USG "in reference to his discharge from service on account of an oath taken not to serve against the rebels."—DLC-USG, V, 10; DNA, RG 393, USG Register of Letters Received.

1861, Nov. 10.   Col. John Cook, Fort Holt, Ky., to USG. "The good of the service and the ncessary care and attention due the sick at this post indicates the ncessity for the immediate surrender of these Head Qrs. (The Jefferson) to the Surgeon to be used exclusively as an Hospital, the same being required for the following reasons. 1st The tents in which the sick are now quartered are so seriously affected by the dampness arising from the lightest rains that invalids donot come up under medical treatment as the[y] would were they more comfortably quartered—2nd That the number already at the Genl Hospital at Mound City require the care and attention of well men entirely who could be here for duty and convallescent men could in hospital here perform the duties required and thereby increase our strength giving us more men for duty. 3rd The absense of material for the construction of a suitable Hospital and the necessary delay attendant upon the procuring of the same I regard as a potent reason also for the speedy providing for the men—Could the ferry boat 'Ivers' raised by my orders at Cape Girardeau now (I think) lying above Cairo be temporarily used at this Post as head quarters or until such time as Hd. Qrs. could be erected great benifit would accrue to the command over which by your orders I have had the honor to be placed."—ALS, DNA, RG 393, District of Southeast Mo., Letters Received.

1861, Nov. 10. Capt. Franklin D. Callender, St. Louis, to USG. "Dispatch Received   I can furnish the harness"—Telegram received, DNA, RG 393, Dept. of the Mo., Telegrams Received; copies, *ibid.*, USG Hd. Qrs. Correspondence; DLC-USG, V, 7.

1861, Nov. 10. Capt. Franklin D. Callender, St. Louis, to USG. "I have shipped to you, on the steamer Perry 250,000 Cartridges. With each bundle of 10 Cartridges is packed 12 percussion Caps, making 300,000, with the Cartridges; to which I have added 25,000 extra, put up in a separate package. Caps are rather scarce, but if this supply is not sufficient I will send more on your informing me to that effect."— LS, DNA, RG 393, District of Cairo, Letters Received.

1861, Nov. [11]. Capt. Wilbur F. Brinck to USG. "I have the honor to report that much of the Field ammunition on hand at this Post is below the U S Standard and very inferior in other respects consequently beg you will have a commission appointed to examine all of the Field Ammunition now on hand   I would add that much of it in my opinion is unfit for issue   Therefore I very respectfully beg you will please order a commission at an early day"—LS, DNA, RG 393, District of Southeast Mo., Letters Received. On Nov. 11, Capt. John A. Rawlins issued special orders. "Capt. Ezra Taylor Capt. A. Schwartz and Captain William Houghtalings are hereby appointed a Board of Survey for the purpose of examining the Field and Siege Ammunition now on hand and to be designated by Capt. W. F. Brinck acting Ordinance Officer, and make report in relation to quality and condition of the same at these Head Quarters. Said Board will meet at the Office of Capt. Brinck on the 12th inst at 2 o.clock P. M."— Copies, DLC-USG, V, 15, 16, 77, 82; DNA, RG 393, USG Special Orders. On Nov. 13, Capts. Ezra Taylor and Charles Houghtaling, and 1st Lt. Conrad Gumbart, commanding Schwartz's Battery, wrote to USG. "We the undersigned commissioners have the honor to enclose the report of our inspection of amunition agreeable to your order of the 11th November 1861."—LS, *ibid.*, RG 94, Letters Received. "A report of commissioners appointed to make some experiments in testing the various qualities and kinds of amunition at Cairo. The undersigned would report that on the 13th day of November 1861 that they have examined the field amunition, and find it damaged and unfit for service (Springfield Amunition in Magazine No 2)"—LS, *ibid.*

1861, Nov. 12.   Lt. Col. Edward Prince, 7th Ill. Cav., Decatur, to USG. "Will arrive at Cairo at nine or ten Am by Rail Road tomorrow with three hundred fifty five Seventh Ills cavalry"—Telegram received, DNA, RG 393, Dept. of the Mo., Telegrams Received. In an undated telegram, probably of Nov. 12, Governor Richard Yates telegraphed to USG. "first & third Squadron of Seventh Regt cavalry Col Kellog three Sixty nine (369) men arrived & three Seventy one (371) horses Leave here this P M by train to Report to you"— Telegram received, *ibid.* On Nov. 13, Capt. John A. Rawlins wrote to Prince. "You will report with your command to Col. Oglesby Comdg. 2nd Brigade Birds Point Mo. Transportation has been provided and now awaits you, to convey you, and your command with your Horses, Equipments &c from Cairo to Birds Point."—Copies, DLC-USG, V, 1, 2, 3, 77; DNA, RG 393, USG Letters Sent. On the same day, Rawlins wrote to Col. Richard J. Oglesby. "Upon Lieut. Col. Prince of the 7th Ill Cavalry reporting to you with his command, you will assign to him grounds for quarters. Also assign to Col. Cook Comdg. at Fort Holt Ky., one company of the Cavalry now in your Brigade, and the remaining companies to Col. Wallace's Brigade, they will report to the respective commands to which they are assigned *immediately* The first and third squadrons of the 7th. Ill Cavalry under command of Lieut. Col. Prince are for the present assigned to your Brigade"— Copies, *ibid.* Also on Nov. 13, Rawlins wrote to Capt. Reuben B. Hatch. "You will provide water transportation for first and third squadrons of 7th Regt. Ill Cavalry, from Cairo to Birds Point— immediately"—Copies, *ibid.*

1861, Nov. 13.   Capt. Franklin D. Callender, St. Louis, to USG. "For how many horses do you want artillery harness   I do not know what two (2) sets of harness means"—Telegram received, DNA, RG 393, Dept. of the Mo., Telegrams Received; copies, *ibid.*, USG Hd. Qrs. Correspondence; DLC-USG, V, 7. On Nov. 14, Callender telegraphed to USG. "Dispatch recd   The Harness will be sent"— Telegram received, DNA, RG 393, Dept. of the Mo., Telegrams Received; copies, *ibid.*, USG Hd. Qrs. Correspondence; DLC-USG, V, 7.

1861, Nov. 14.   USG special orders granting leave to Capt. Orlando Burrell, 1st Ill. Cav.—Copies, DLC-USG, V, 15, 77, 82; DNA, RG 393, USG Special Orders.

1861, Nov. 15.   USG special orders granting leave to 1st Lt. Samuel E. Barrett, Chicago Light Art.—Copies, DLC-USG, V, 15, 16, 77, 82; DNA, RG 393, USG Special Orders.

1861, Nov. 16.   R. J. Howard, St. Louis, to USG. "Pass Steamer Fred Lorenz if you have no charges against her."—Telegram received, DNA, RG 393, Dept. of the Mo., Telegrams Received.

1861, Nov. 17.   To Brig. Gen. John A. McClernand. "Refered to Brig. Gen. J. A. McClernand who directed the expedition."—AES, McClernand Papers, IHi. Written on the back of Oscar Turner to USG, Nov. 10, 1861. "On 23rd day of October last a body of troops, came up the Ohio river on the Memphis landed opposite Caladonia, & proceeded to my plantation—they carried off according to their own account, as I see published in St Louis papers & also in Chcago papers, thirty five mules & five horses—& professed to be acting under orders of your self from Cairo, the stock was carried to Cairo—the pretense was that there were confederate troops quartered on my plantation & that I was Col. in confederate army—Now for the facts which I desire to state to you—There never has been at any time confederate troops on my plantation—nor have I ever been an *officer* in confederate army or *belonged* to it—I am a private citizen, entertaining opinions in common with vast majority of citizens in southern end of Kentucky—which it is unnecessary here to discuss—It required no searching my house to find out those opinions for they have been public for months & I have

no desire to conceal them—I regarded federal constitution as trampled
under foot, & the rights of our citizens outraged & violated by the
present administration—& feared same would be done in Kentucky—
Have I been mistaken? My house was entered forcibly—my private
papers seized—my land papers & papers of no value to any one
except to my self seized after breaking the locks—two watches were
carried off—two fine walking canes, fine mounted) old keep sakes
from my deceased father were taken & numerous small articles of value
such as could be conveniently carried off were taken, also thirty five
head of mules my wifes riding mare—& four other horses—your own
accounts state that no arms were found—yet they carried off my
pruning knives & knives for cutting tobacco—all this was done by the
aforesaid troops professing to act under your orders & the account
published in St. Louis & Chicago papers, they being informed by
letters writen from Cairo—I appeal to you as an officer & gentleman
to know whether these acts are sanctioned *by law* or *the constitution*—
your proclamation had been published at Paducah—which doubtless you
remember—In which you stated no mans property or person should
be disturbed on account of his opinions that you came to deal with
armed men—Now sir I must think in view of your proclamation that the
seizure of my private property was not authorised *by you*—Hence I
have addressed you this communication—I had on my plantation a
number of negro women & children—dependent for their bread upon
my plantation & a small horse mill & yet Sir your troops had the gear
stripped off of the work mules not leaving even mill mules or work
beast   is this philantropy or humanity—they took from me property
to amount of at least eight thousand dollars—I have never heard of
any union mans property being disturbed in my county or in this county
—I hope you will write to me whether the aforesaid acts were *authorised*—or whether my property or papers will be restored to me—
Please address me at Charleston Missouri—P. S. The statements
refered to state, that the expedition consisted of 3 companies of 2nd
Illinois cavalry & one company of infantry seventeenth reg. under
command of Major I. T. Weed—I have written hastily not giving you
half the outrages perpetrated"—ALS, *ibid.* Below USG's endorsement, Maj. Mason Brayman wrote. "Gen. McClernand directs that
the resan for making the expedition on Turner be here written. The
proceeding was on the ground that Oscar Turner was engaged in acts
of treason and rebellion—giving aid & comfort to the enemy and

consequently subject to punishment & confiscation."—AES, *ibid.* See Cairo dispatch, Oct. 23, 1861, in *Chicago Tribune*, Oct. 24, 1861.

1861, Nov. 17. USG special orders granting leave to Surgeon Owen M. Long, 11th Ill.—Copies, DLC-USG, V, 15, 77, 82; DNA, RG 393, USG Special Orders.

1861, Nov. 19. Brig. Gen. Lorenzo Thomas to USG. "No: You cannot accept the two Companies of Home Guards."—Telegram, copies, DNA, RG 94, Letters Sent; *ibid.*, RG 107, Telegrams Collected (Unbound); misdated Sept. 19, 1861, *ibid.*, RG 393, USG Hd. Qrs. Correspondence; DLC-USG, V, 4, 5, 7, 8.

1861, Nov. 19. Capts. Wilbur F. Brinck, Ezra Taylor, and Charles Houghtaling to USG. "We the undersigned commissioners (appointed by special order of Brig General U S Grant commanding S E Missouri District) as a Board of Survey to examine and report the condition of the Harness of the Light Battery of Captain A Swartz. Have this nineteenth day of November A D 1861 examined said Harness and find that the Leather and Rope portions of said Harness to be old rotton and totally unfit for Field Service   And recommend that it be condemed and ~~given~~ turned over to the Ordnance Officer at this Post In witness we set our hand the date above mentioned"—DS, DNA, RG 393, District of Southeast Mo., Letters Received. On Nov. 17, 1st Lt. Clark B. Lagow had issued special orders. "Capt. Brinck Chief of Ordinance Capt Ezra Taylor and Capt. Houghtalings are appointed a Board of Survey to inspect and make report to these Head Quarters of the quality and condition of Harness of Capt A Schwartz Battery, said Board will meet on the 19th inst at 10 oclock A. M."—Copies, DLC-USG, V, 15, 16, 77, 82; DNA, RG 393, USG Special Orders.

1861, Nov. 20. Capt. William S. Hillyer to Brig. Gen. John A. McClernand. "You will please detail one full Company of Infantry to report to Col Webster at the Wharf boat at 8 o'clock to morrow morning to proceed under his direction to Cave in Rock to assist in getting out stone—they will take with them all their camp & garrison equipage baggage and transportation & ten days rations."—ALS, McClernand Papers, IHi. On the same day, Hillyer wrote an identical letter to Col. Richard J. Oglesby.—Copies, DLC-USG, V, 2, 77; DNA, RG 393, USG Letters Sent. Also on Nov. 20, Hillyer wrote to Surgeon John H. Brinton. "You will detail a surgeon to report to Col. Webster Chief of Engineers, tomorrow morning at 8 o.clock to accompany an expedition to Cave in Rock to be absent about ten days."—Copies, *ibid*. On the same day, Hillyer wrote to George W. Graham. "You will detail a boat (suitable for the purpose) to report to Col. Webster tomorrow morning at 8 o clock to proceed under his direction to Cave in Rock, for the purpose of transporting Rock, you will also provide as many scows as the boat can tow to accompany it"—Copies, DLC-USG, V, 1, 2, 3, 77; DNA, RG 393, USG Letters Sent.

1861, Nov. 20. Maj. John J. Mudd, 2nd Ill. Cav., to Brig. Gen. John A. McClernand. "I have the honor to report that in obedience to your Special Order No.   and your verbal instructions, I assumed command of the Cavalry embarked on Steamers *Rob Roy* and *Key Stone* at three O clock P M, on the 19th inst, with Capt Hotaling's Co A 2nd Ill Cav, Capt Dollin's company of Cavalry attached to the 31st Ill vol, and a detachment of Capt Stuart's company, altogether numbering about 160 Rank and file—Deeming it advisable, I detached Capt Hotelungs with his company with directions to follow the road down the Mississippi river to Fort Jefferson on Mayfield Creek and burn a large coal boat, said to be there and which I was led to believe might be used for a bridge, and then proceed up said Mayfield Creek as far as in his Judgment was prudent, all of which he succeeded to my entire satisfaction, reconnoitering the country as far as Elliotts Mills about ten miles from Fort Holt; and only turned homeward when darkness overtook him. With the balance of my command, I followed the Blandville and Columbus road about six miles; thence diverged to the left and examined the house of Col Wickliffe a noted rebel. Finding no rebels there we passed East to the Caladonia, Blandville and Fort Jefferson road—thence to Fort Jefferson, thence to Fort Holt, and home, being on our way joined by Capt Hotaling and command—arriving at Camp at 9 Oclock P. M. We found no rebels, nor could we hear of any bands of armed men being in the neighborhood for several weeks, save our army under Col. Cook—From information derived from citizens, I infer that rebel scouts do *not* extend more than six miles above Columbus, and that there is no extraordinary movements now being made by them, there is another boat on Mayfield Creek, about two miles above Fort Jefferson which with but little labor might be transformed into a bridge suitable to crossing an army, it belongs to a man named ——— reported to be a rebel and I think ought to be burned. Capt Hotelung's orders not so directing, he left it unmolested. I have to report the loss from holster of *one revolving Pistol*, belonging to one of Capt Hotaling's men. Our return being in the night time and the march rapid—will no doubt sufficiently account for the loss and we trust that an order will be made for substitution. I have also to report that being without supply of ammunition, and not being able to procure any from the Ordnance Dept, I purchased of retailers and herewith file account therefor."—Copy, DNA, RG 393, District of Southeast Mo., Letters Received. On Nov. 21, Capt. William S. Hillyer wrote to Mudd. "You will move the cavalry now at Cairo, under your command, together with their Camp, and Garrison Equipage, baggage, & transportation, to Birds Point Mo & report to Col. R. J. Oglesby on duty" —Copies, DLC-USG, V, 1, 2, 3, 77; DNA, RG 393, USG Letters Sent.

1861, Nov. 21. To hd. qrs., Dept. of the Mo., enclosing "a requisition for Blank Books for the approval of the Dept. Comdr."—DNA, RG 393, Dept. of the Mo., Register of Letters Received.

1861, Nov. 21. Capt. John A. Rawlins to Commander Henry Walke. "I am directed by Brig Genl U. S. Grant to request that you report with Gun Boats at this place tomorrow at 9 oclock A. M."— Copies, DLC-USG, V, 1, 2, 3, 77; DNA, RG 393, USG Letters Sent. *O.R.*(Navy), I, xxii, 440. On Nov. 22, Walke wrote to USG. "Agreeable to your instructions of to day, I have made a reconnoissance (in company with the Gun Boat Lexington, Comr Stemble) down the Mississippi, to the lower end of Lucas Bend; and threw five 64 pr shell, on the low land just below Island No 4, and above Iron Banks, without receiving any response from the enemy. I saw no change in the appearance of their camp since the 7th instant. As we were returning however a small steamer, made her appearance under their batteries, as a decoy, and afterwards followed us up Lucas Bend a considerable distance. She fired a shot just as we were turning the point below Norfolk, under which I turned in pursuit of her, but when seen again, she was further off than befor, retreating rapidly."—ALS, DNA, RG 393, District of Southeast Mo., Letters Received.

1861, Nov. 22.   USG special orders granting leave to Capt. Ezra Taylor.—Copies, DLC-USG, V, 15, 77, 82; DNA, RG 393, USG Special Orders.

1861, Nov. 22.   Lt. Col. Thomas E. G. Ransom, 11th Ill., to USG, transmitting "report of board of survey on captured property."— DLC-USG, V, 10; DNA, RG 393, USG Register of Letters Received.

1861, Nov. 23.   USG General Orders No. 17. "Whereas the respective Governors of the States of Illinois, Missouri, and Kentucky, have appointed Thursday the 28th of November, inst., as a day of Thanksgiving and Prayer to Almighty God, the General Commanding this District, cheerfully and earnestly recommends to the Officers and men of his command, a proper observance of the day. All business will be suspended, so far as it may be compatible with the public service, and Chaplains, will hold appropriate religious exercises in their respective regiments"—Copies, DLC-USG, V, 12, 13, 14, 80; DNA, RG 393, USG General Orders. On the same day, Capt. John A. Rawlins issued a circular. "The Commanding General enjoins upon the Officers and men of his command the propriety and importance of a proper observance of the sanctity of the Sabbath day. No business will hereafter be transacted on that day, which is not required by the exigincy of the public service—and a general attendance at Divine service is earnestly recommended"—Copies, *ibid.*

1861, [Nov. 23].   Maj. Charles J. Sellon, 28th Ill., Fort Holt, to USG. "Pay master & Clerk Left here, Paying Late. Want to get back. Can you send a boat? Please send reply."—Telegram received (punctuation added), DNA, RG 393, Dept. of the Mo., Telegrams Received. The date is taken from the docketing.

1861, Nov. 24.   [Maj. Mason Brayman] to USG. "I am instructed by Genl. McClernand to acknowledge The receipt at this Post, of the following to wit
      54 Copies Comp.y morning Report Books.
      28   "   Army Regulations (Revised)

```
28   ”    Hardees Infty Tactics
 5   ”    Inst Field Artillery”
```
—Copy, McClernand Papers, IHi.

1861, Nov. 25. [Maj. Mason Brayman] to USG. "Will you please detail from Co "E" 8th Regiment, Corporal W. L. Caldwell, to report to these Head Qrs for extra duty, temporarially."—Copy, McClernand Papers, IHi.

1861, Nov. 26. USG Circular. "1st. In compliance with General Orders No 6, Head Quarters Depatment of the Missouri, St Louis Mo, November 23d 1861, furloughs to enlisted men will not be granted in any case whatsoever   2nd. The attention of Commanders of Companies, and Surgeons having part in the discharges of Soldiers for disability, is called to the requirements of the Army Regulations and Instructions, and Note 1, Page 325 of the Revised edition of the same. The cause when known, and other facts connected with the disability, and the degree thereof, and when occured, must in all cases, be stated in the certificates fully and particularly   3d. Hereafter when sick are sent to the General Hospital, the commands sending them, must furnish nurses,—one for every ten men sent, and one for every fraction under ten"—Copies, DLC-USG, V, 12, 80; DNA, RG 393, USG General Orders. This circular is misdated Oct. 24, 1861, and labeled General Orders No. 12 in DLC-USG, V, 13, 14.

1861, Nov. 26. USG special orders. "No dispatches giving army intelligence, will hereafter be permitted to be telegraphed from this post, unless the same are approved at these Head-Quarters."—Copies, DLC-USG, V, 15, 16, 77, 82; DNA, RG 393, USG Special Orders.

1861, Nov. 26. USG special orders. "The commanding officer at Caledonia Ill. will in future prevent all crossing of Citizens, and all intercourse between the people of Ky. and the Illinois shore. All persons known to be engaged in unlawful traffic between the two states, will be at once arrested, and sent before the Provost Marshall in Cairo, with such proof as may be at hand   Whenever any property, is known to be for the use of the Southern Army, the commanding Officer may seize it whether on the Illinois or Kentucky side of the

river   Particular caution is enjoined however in making seizures to
see that no hardship is inflicted upon innocent people   The greatest
vigilence will be observed to prevent contraband trade or intercourse
between the two states"—Copies, DLC-USG, V, 15, 16, 77, 82;
DNA, RG 393, USG Special Orders. *O.R.*, I, vii, 449.

1861, Nov. 26.   Capt. William S. Hillyer to John Weldon, U. S.
District Attorney. "I am directed by Brig Genl U. S. Grant Comdg
this District to write to you and suggest the propriety of getting
from the U. S. District Judge an order for the immediate sale of the
Steamboats now in the custody of the Marshall upon libels under the
confiscation act. There Boats are perishable property,—expensive to
be kept, liable to be destroyed by fire, and a petition could be truly
made setting forth all these reasons which are customary in applications
for a sale *Pendente lite*   If you can get an order of sale, the Quartermaster here might purchase them and the Boats become the property
of the Government & the marshall relieved from the responsibility &
exposure of their safe keeping—These boats have always as you are
aware been used to some extent by the Government, but it is certainly
the interest of all parties that there should be a judicial sale—You are
aware whether this can be done—the writer has had considerable
experience in admiralty practice in St Louis, and unless there is a
special exception in the confiscation act (which I have never had
occasion to examine) my own opinion is that there is no legal obstacle
to prevent an immediate order of sale.—It is certainly the interest of all
concerned. Your Early attention to this matter is respectfully requested."—Copies, DLC-USG, V, 1, 2, 3, 79; DNA, RG 393, USG Letters
Sent.

1861, Nov. 27.   Hd. qrs. of Maj. Gen. Henry W. Halleck to USG.
"Disapproved. Number of officers on Recruiting service from the 20th
Regt. not stated by Col. Marsh."—Copy, DNA, RG 393, Western
Dept., Endorsements. On a letter of Col. C. Carroll Marsh, Nov. 25,
1861, to Capt. Daniel Bradley, 20th Ill., ordering him on recruiting
service.

1861, Nov. 28.   USG General Orders No. 18. "Brigade Commanders
will see that General Order No. 7 from Head Quarters Dept. of the

Missouri, is promptly complied with, and the reports forwarded through these Head-Quarters They will also cause to be made, requisitions upon the proper Departments, for Arms, Clothing, Camp and Garrison equipage, Transportation, and every thing they may be in need of, and that should properly be furnished them"—Copies, DLC-USG, V, 12, 13, 14, 80; DNA, RG 393, USG General Orders; DS, McClernand Papers, IHi.

1861, Nov. 28. Capt. Hugh Fullerton, 2nd Ill. Cav., Caledonia, Ill., to USG. "Send me a boat tomorrow morning, if possible. Answer quick."—Telegram received (punctuation added), DNA, RG 393, Dept. of the Mo., Telegrams Received.

1861, Nov. 28. W. B. Crane, Pilot Knob, Mo., to USG "in reference to a voucher for stationery furnished."—DLC-USG, V, 10; DNA, RG 393, USG Register of Letters Received. See letter to Capt. John C. Kelton, Aug. 14, 1861, note 3.

1861, Nov. 28. Mrs. L. D. Grover to USG "requesting certificate to enable her to draw the pay due her husband, Lieut. Col. B. W. Grover, who was killed in action."—DLC-USG, V, 10; DNA, RG 393, USG Register of Letters Received.

1861, Nov. 29. Brig. Gen. Don Carlos Buell to USG. "In what Condition as to Drill & discipline is Col. Buford's Regt. ? Please answer at once."—Telegram received (punctuation added), DNA, RG 393, District of Southeast Mo., Letters Received; copy (dated Nov. 28), *ibid.*, Dept. of the Ohio, Telegrams Sent.

1861, Nov. 30. Capt. John A. Rawlins to Capt. Reuben B. Hatch. "You will provide Head Quarters and Quarters for Genl Grant and Staff—I would suggest the residence of Col. I. N. Haynie, as the same can be procured at reasonable rates"—Copies, DLC-USG, V, 1, 2, 3, 77; DNA, RG 393, USG Letters Sent.

1861, Nov. 30. Maj. John H. Holman to USG "in reference to joining General Grant with his command."—DLC-USG, V, 10; DNA, RG 393, USG Register of Letters Received. See letter to Capt. John C. Kelton, Aug. 26, 1861.

1861, [Nov.–Dec.].   USG signature on petition to President Abraham Lincoln. "We take pleasure in recommending the appointment of John Crow, a citizen of Pike County in this State, to the office of *Pay Master*. He is a prudent careful, capable, honest man, with good business and financial qualifications. His moral character is above reproach." Also signed by Governor Richard Yates, Secretary of State Ozias M. Hatch, State Treasurer William O. Butler, Auditor Jesse K. Dubois, Col. John Cook, and Capt. Reuben B. Hatch. On Dec. 14, John Hay, Lincoln's secretary, endorsed the petition to Secretary of War Simon Cameron. "Respectfully referred by the President to the consideration of the Secretary of War. The names attached are intimate friends of the President and the most worthy citizens of Illinois."— Typescript, Atwood Collection, InU. No record of the appointment of John Crow has been found.

1861, [Dec.?].   USG endorsement on a bill presented to the subsistence dept. by Samuel A. Turner, Steamer *Memphis*, for meals furnished officers "accompanying Flag of Truce with detachment detailed to bury the dead from the Belmont Battle, etc." "The U. S. A. Will pay the above Account." "The above account is totally wrong as far as furnishing Meals to Officers is concerned." As a result of USG's second endorsement, the bill was reduced from $73.26 to $37.60.— *American Book Collector*, XVIII, 5–6 (Jan.–Feb., 1968), 4.

1861, Dec. 2.   USG General Orders No. 19. "To prevent the over issue of rations within this command the following order is published: Commanders of Regiments, or Detachments, must in all instances compare Provision Returns with the morning report of the day, on which the issue is to be made   The number of rations issued, should be the number of men with the company, excluding absentees, sick in Hospitals, and all who do not mess with their companies   When a soldier is sent to Hospital a statement should in all cases, accompany him, showing to what time he has been rationed. Such rations as are due him should be credited to the Hospital   Regimental and other Commanders are strictly accountable for all over issues within their command. All issues of rations to Commissioned Officers are strictly forbidden. Sales to Officers may however be allowed, to be paid for on the first of every month. When sales to officers are made, the officer purchasing, must certify, to the amount of each component part of the ration he will probably require within the month stating the number of Commissioned Officers in the mess, and the number of servants not to exceed the number authorized by regulations"—Copies, DLC-USG, V, 12, 13, 14, 80; DNA, RG 94, 48th Ill., Order Book; *ibid.*, RG 393, USG General Orders.

1861, DEC. 2.   [Maj. Mason Brayman] to USG. "I am instructed by the Commg Genl. to return you the inclosed Discharge papers as it is out of his command (Fort Holt Ky)"—Copy, McClernand Papers, IHi.

1861, DEC. 2.   2nd Lt. John M. Hunter, Battery C, 1st Ill. Light Art., Ashley, Ill., to USG. "Send me order for transportation to Cairo on agent here"—Telegram received, DNA, RG 393, Dept. of the Mo., Telegrams Received.

1861, DEC. 3.   To Capt. Reuben C. Rutherford. "You are directed to turn over to Lieut. J. M. Snyder, R. Q. M. A. A. C. S. 6th Ill. Cavalry, two days rations for 1200 men, and take his receipt for the same"— Copies, DLC-USG, V, 1, 2, 3, 77; DNA, RG 393, USG Letters Sent.

1861, DEC. 4.   Brig. Gen. George W. Cullum, Chief Engineer, Dept. of the Mo., to USG. "Major Webster is authorized to retain until further orders W. L. B. Jenny, and H. C. Freeman, to assist him in the engineering operations at Cairo &c. if their services are indispensable." —Copies, DLC-USG, V, 4, 5, 7, 8, 9; DNA, RG 393, USG Hd. Qrs. Correspondence.

1861, DEC. 4.   Capt. John C. Kelton to USG. "The order of Colonel T. J. Turner, detailing J. W. Allen, Co. "D" 10th Regt. Ill. Vols., as his Aid de Camp is entirely illegal, and is countermanded."—Copy, DNA, RG 393, Dept. of the Mo., Letters Sent.

1861, DEC. 4.   Col. T. Lyle Dickey, 4th Ill. Cav., Vandalia, to USG. "My Regt. is ordered by Government to Vicinity of Villa Ridge. Genl. McClernand promised to cause forage to be provided there. I can't hear from him—Want forage for ~~one th~~ over one thousand horses there Friday morning."—Telegram received (punctuation added), DNA, RG *393*, Dept. of the Mo., Telegrams Received. On Dec. 5, Dickey telegraphed to USG from Pulaski County. "I will Go to Cairo this Evening. Regiment will arrive tomorrow morning under your order. Ten hundred thirty horses, nine hundred forty men."—Telegram received (punctuation added), *ibid.*

1861, DEC. 5. Capt. John A. Rawlins to Capt. Reuben B. Hatch. "You will have Head Quarters built *immediately by 'contract,'* as per Plan of Genl. McClernand, at the figures spoken of this morning"— Copies, DLC-USG, V, 1, 2, 3, 77; DNA, RG *393*, USG Letters Sent.

1861, DEC. 6. Brig. Gen. John A. McClernand to USG. "Col I. N. Haynie 48th Regt. Illinois Volunteers called on me for an order on my quarter master for teams for his Regiment. I answered that if he would make a regular requisition for them, I would bring the subject to your notice. His quarter master called on me again on the same subject last evening. I repeated that if a requisition should be made, I would 'take such action upon it' as I might deem proper. This morning I am in receipt of the accompanying requisition; also of a communication from Col Haynie sent with it, dated yesterday informing me that some steps have been taken upon the same subject between himself and Capt Hatch, but without reaching a definite result. Either he or Capt Hatch can give you further particulars. All I have to say is that any order you may make upon me or my Quarter Master to purchase mules for the 48th will be promptfully and faithfully fulfilled so far as I can secure it. I await your direction in the premises—"—Df, McClernand Papers, IHi.

1861, DEC. 6. Col. Leonard F. Ross, Cape Girardeau, to USG. "Understanding night before last that a force of some three Hundred Rebels were expected in the town of Benton, on yesterday morning I sent from this place six companies of Infy and our force of cavalry to attack them if found. I also directed Lt Col Wood who commanded the expedition to take possession of the personal property of Col James Parrott now in the Rebel Army, and remove it to this place—No enemy was discovered—but the property of Col Parrott, consisting of Hotel furniture and amounting to five or six hundred dollars in value, was taken and is now in possession of the Q. M. As soon as an inventory can be completed I will forward copy. What shall I do with the property? Some chairs tables & desks &c are wanted at head quarters. If not objectionable I will order some in use. For convenience I have moved Head Quarters to Building opposite St Charles. The steam Boat was so open & cold that it could not be used during the winter—then it was quite objectionable for the reason that no business could be transacted there with any degree of privacy. I have now comfortable & convenient Quarters. The suggestions & instructions contained in yours of 4th Inst will be strictly complied with   Two of Thompsons men were in this morning said they had had enough of war, wanted to quit & return to alligiance. I administered the oath oath and discharged them, beleiving them to be honest ~~and~~ in their professions—They report Thompson engaged in Fortifying at New Madrid"—LS, DNA, RG 393, District of Cairo, Letters Received.

1861, Dec. 7.   Maj. Charles J. Sellon, Fort Holt, to USG. "Is the fourteenth Ills regt in Camp cairo"—Telegram received, DNA, RG 393, Dept. of the Mo., Telegrams Received.

1861, Dec. 9.   Capt. John A. Rawlins to Capt. Hugh Fullerton, 2nd Ill. Cav. "Your communication of Dec 7th is received, and I am instructed by Brig. Genl. Grant to say, that if you are satisfied from all facts, the corn mentioned belongs to a party or parties in the Confederate Army, you will seize it for the use of the Government, making out a statement of the number of Bushels, which you will forward to these Head Quarters. You will arrest Thomas Richey at the first opportunity"—Copies, DLC-USG, V, 1, 2, 3, 79; DNA, RG 393, USG Letters Sent.

1861, Dec. 10.   Capt. John A. Rawlins to Col. John Cook. "I am instructed by the Genl. Comdg. to say, Your Note of today is received. On account of the continued absence of the Telegraph Operator at your Post, you will immediately dismiss him from the service."—Copies, DLC-USG, V, 1, 2, 3, 79; DNA, RG 393, USG Letters Sent.

1861, Dec. 10.   Col. Leonard F. Ross, Cape Girardeau, to USG. "Within the last few days—quite a number of the Citizens of Tennesee have been brought in by my Pickets—They were fleeing North East— to avoid being drafted into the service of the 'Southern Confederacy'—

After satisfying myself thoroghly as to the honesty of their intentions
—I have given them permission to go 'North'—They report Thompson at New Madrid with from one thousand to fifteen hundred troops
—many of them sick—and all of them in a distressed Condition—also
that he has had about 800 Slaves from the South—at work on his
fortifications—These have been sent below, and the work is now carried on by slaves pressed into Service from the Surrounding Country
—and also—That but few if any 'Guns' have been mounted in position
within his fortifications—I have several applications on file by
'*Anxious* 'Fathers'—'Mothers' & 'Brothers'—who have relatives in
Thompson's Army—And who are desirous of visiting New-Madrid—
for the purpose of inducing their friends to leave the Army—In two
cases I have granted permission—One of the parties has returned with
two friends, who came in and took 'the Oath' &c   The other party is
still absent—I have some applications from parties owning property
in the Southern portion of the State—who wish to visit that section—
to attend to business matters—Would you allow them to go?"—
Copy, DNA, RG 393, Post of Cape Girardeau, Letters Sent.

1861, Dec. 10.   Capt. Franklin D. Callender to USG. "I transmit,
herewith, some blank Requisitions to enable officers, who may have
occasion to apply for Ordnance Stores, to comply with the requirements of Paragraphs 6 & 7 of General Order No 15 Hd Qrs Department of the Missouri. Be pleased to distribute them where needed, and
I would be much obliged if when you make, or approve requisitions for
Ordn. Stores to issue to troops under your Command, you would
indicate the number of such troops, so as to enable the proper authorities to act upon them understandingly. N. B. I would be much obliged
if you would cause the commanding officers of the regiments under
your command who have recently recieved the French Rifled muskets
cal. 69 to make requisitions for cartridges for them on the blank
requisitions herewith enclosed, to be approved by yourself and cause
the same to be forwarded to me, & when recieved they will recieve
immediate attention."—LS, DNA, RG 393, District of Cairo, Letters
Received.

1861, Dec. 11.   Capt. John A. Rawlins to Maj. Mason Brayman. "I
am instructed by Brig. Genl. Grant, to inquire if you have any particular
reasons for supposing John. D. Weld a Spy, if so please state them."

—LS, McClernand Papers, IHi. On Dec. 11, Brayman replied to Rawlins. "He wanted to go to Ft. Holt—to Bird's Point—to Mound City—Camp Cairo—Camp McClernand—Ft. Prentiss—for the purpose of enlisting in *some* regiment—did not know *what* regiment—did not know any body in our regiments—Came from St Louis where he could have enlisted and was known—had a provost marshals pass—who has not? Did not look nor talk as if loyal Service was his purpose. Never saw him before."—ADfS, *ibid.* On Dec. 13, Brayman wrote to USG. "This man appears to have visited Fort Holt, Birds Point and Ca[m]ps here on passes enclosed. None were given him here. He will be reported to you f by the guard who arrested him."—ALS, *ibid.* The letter was endorsed by Rawlins. "You will Recp't J D Weld under guard until an opportunity occurs to send him *north*, which you will cause to be carried into effect, unless you think the evidence will be sufficient to convict him before a Military Court."—ES, *ibid.*

1861, Dec. 11. Col. Leonard F. Ross, Cape Girardeau, to USG. "Secession Companies are forming at Bloomfield & Dallas. I want armed Cavalry as soon as possible."—Telegram received (punctuation added), DNA, RG 393, Dept. of the Mo., Telegrams Received.

1861, Dec. 11. Capt. Sterling P. Delano, 2nd Ill. Cav., Fort Holt, to USG. "In obedience to your verbal orders given me on the 9th inst. I proceeded this day with a detachment of my command consisting of fifty-four men rank and file, at 9 o'clock A. M. on a scouting excursion towards Columbus. I marched to the ford of Mayfield Creek, at 'Ellett's Mills,' via Fort Jefferson—making a throrough examination of the country as I proceeded. Finding Mayfield Creek very high, and that to swim it (owing to the condition of the bank) would at least prove dangerous, I scoured the woods up the creek towards Blandville, and being unable to find a crossing, intersected the Blandville road about three miles from that village. Thence I marched to a point about Eight miles in the rear of this Fort and made a thorough examination of all the various roads and approaches leading to it, returning to camp about 5 o'clock. I saw no enemy or any indication of his recent presence in any of the localities mentioned. Indeed from all that I could learn, none of his scouts have been on this side of Mayfield Creek for the last month."—LS, DNA, RG 393, District of Southeast Mo., Letters Received.

1861, Dec. 12. Capt. John A. Rawlins to the officer of the day. "I am instructed by the Genl. Comdg. to say, that upon Mat. Burns,— who is now in Guard House—giving Bond to keep the Peace, you will release him from custody"—Copies, DLC-USG, V, 2, 77; DNA, RG 393, USG Letters Sent. On Dec. 24, Rawlins wrote to Maj. Andrew J. Kuykendall. "You will immediately notify Mat. Burns to leave Cairo Ill. and vicinity within twenty four hours, taking with him his family, and if again seen here, will be arrested, and confined in a Military Prison, the Genl. Comd.g being satisfied from reliable information that he is a dangerous, and improper person to remain at large in this place"—Copies, DLC-USG, V, 1, 2, 3, 77; DNA, RG 393, USG Letters Sent.

1861, Dec. 13. Petition of officers of the 18th Ill. to Governor Richard Yates protesting the appointment of Patrick Lawler, son-in-law of Col. Michael K. Lawler, as capt. An unsigned, undated endorsement in USG's hand reads: "Forwarded through Head Quarters, Dist. S. E. M."—Records of 18th Ill., I-ar.

1861, Dec. 13. Capt. John A. Rawlins to Brig. Gen. John A. Mc-Clernand. "I am instructed by the Genl. Comdg. to say, that the remaining eight companies of the 7th Ill. Cavalry have arrived under command of Major Hall, whom I have directed to report to you You will designate a suitable place for their encampment at this place, where they will remain for the present."—LS, McClernand Papers, IHi. See *Calendar*, Dec. 22, 1861.

1861, Dec. 13. Capt. William S. Hillyer to Capt. Parmenas T. Turnley. "I understand that all charters of Steamboats are to be ended and new charters made. I wish to say to you that the Steamer 'Alex Scott' should be rechartered by all means, if she can be had at a fair price, she is a very light draught for a Steamer, of her tonnage. She can transport two regiments with their equipage & transportation, she has been of more service to me than any other boat, and I have got to regard her as indispensable. It is seldom that I make suggestions in regards to matters of this kind, but I have had occasion to test the advantages of this boat, and should be very sorry to lose her"—Copies, DLC-USG, V, 1, 2, 3, 79; DNA, RG 393, USG Letters Sent.

1861, Dec. 13.   Col. Richard J. Oglesby to USG, "in relation to two men taken at Norfolk, Mo."—DLC-USG, V, 10; DNA, RG 393, USG Register of Letters Received.

1861, Dec. 14.   USG General Orders No. 21. "Having received official notice that Brig. Genl. H. Van Rensslaer Inspector Genl. of the Army, will arrive here today, to inspect the troops of this command, the following order is published. The command at Cairo will be paraded, ready for review at 10 o'clock A. M. on the 16th inst   The command at Birds Point at 2 o.clock P. M. same day. The command at Fort Holt will be held in readiness for review after the review at Birds Point, should the latter end in time to hold both the same afternoon. Otherwise it will take place on the following morning at 10 o'clock   The command at Mound City will be held in readiness at any hour the Inspector Genl. may arrive on the 17th inst   The command at Cape Girardeau will be held in readiness to be reviewed by Brig. Genl Sturgis on the 18th inst."—Copies, DLC-USG, V, 12, 13, 14, 80; DNA, RG 393, USG General Orders. On Dec. 12, Col. Henry Van Rensselaer wrote to USG. "I have the honor to inform you that I propose to make an insepection of the troops at Cairo, under instructions from Major General McClellan. I expect to reach Cairo on Saturday evening next."—Copies, DLC-USG, V, 7, 8; DNA, RG 393, USG Hd. Qrs. Correspondence.

1861, Dec. 14.   USG special orders. "The mail between this point and Birds Point is hereby discontinued. All mail matter for troops or loyal citizens receiving the same from the Post Office at Birds Point will be distributed in the Cairo Post Office untill otherwise directed by competent authority."—Copies, DLC-USG, V, 15, 16, 77, 82; DNA, RG 393, USG Special Orders.

1861, Dec. 15.   Brig. Gen. Don Carlos Buell to USG. "Did you give Captain Carpenter a letter to me?"—Telegram, copy, DNA, RG 393, Dept. of the Ohio, Telegrams Sent. On Dec. 16, USG telegraphed to Buell. "Yes"—Telegram received, *ibid.*

1861, Dec. 16.   Capt. John A. Rawlins special orders. "Special Order of Sept. 21st 1861 appointing a Board of Surgeons to inspect applicants for discharge on Surgeons Certificates of Disability is here-

by rescinded. Hereafter the approval of the Brigade Surgeon will be required to all such Certificates, and also that of the Medical Director"
—Copies, DLC-USG, V, 15, 16, 77, 82; DNA, RG 393, USG Special Orders. See letter to Maj. Gen. John C. Frémont, Sept. 24, 1861, note 4.

1861, Dec. 17.   USG special orders granting leave to Asst. Surgeon J. P. Taggart.—Copies, DLC-USG, V, 15, 16, 77, 82; DNA, RG 393, USG Special Orders.

1861, Dec. 17.   Maj. John J. Mudd, 2nd Ill. Cav., to USG. "Report in regard to prisoners taken at Belmont, Mo."—DLC-USG, V, 10; DNA, RG 393, USG Register of Letters Received.

1861, Dec. 18.   USG Pass. "Mr. McNutt has permission to pass all guard lines of this command, & cross the ferries free."—ADS, IaHA.

1861, Dec. 18.   USG special orders granting leave to 2nd Lt. Thomas N. Francis, 7th Ill.—Copies, DLC-USG, V, 15, 77, 82; DNA, RG 393, USG Special Orders.

1861, Dec. 18.   Maj. Mason Brayman to USG. "Enclosed find charges &c. against Wm. Smith, a private, in Co. "H." 18th Regt. Ills. Vols., for reference to court martial."—ADf, McClernand Papers, IHi.

1861, Dec. 18.   Capt. George S. Ruggles, AGO, to USG. "Respectfully referred to the Commanding Officer at Cairo, who will detail an officer to muster these Bands out of service."—ES, DNA, RG 393, District of Cairo, Letters Received. Written on a letter of Dec. 5, 1861, from Maj. Isaac N. Cooke, additional paymaster of vols., to Col. Benjamin F. Larned, paymaster-general. "Permit me to advise you of the condition of the Regimental Bands of the Tenth (10th) and Twenty seventh (27th) Regiments of Illinois Volunteers. The Bands of these two Regiments have but seven men each and a leader. The Band of the tenth Regiment is musterd thus Six (6) First class and one (1) second class   They have refused to take their pay, on any other than the above classification, & I have refused to pay them, in that way"—ALS, *ibid*. On Dec. 10, Larned endorsed the letter to the AGO.

"Respy referred to Adjt Genl. with suggestion that these bands be mustered out. They cannot now be filled up under Order No 91—and in present condition are perfectly useless and a heavy expense—" —ES, *ibid.* On Dec. 31, Capt. John A. Rawlins issued special orders for Capt. William S. Hillyer. "In pursuance of orders from Headquarters of the Army, at Washington, Captain William S. Hillyer is hereby detailed to muster the Regimental Bands of the 10th and 27th Regiments of Illinois Volunteers out of the service of the United States. He will proceed to muster them out of the service at once."—Copies, DLC-USG, V, 15, 16, 82; DNA, RG 393, USG Special Orders.

1861, DEC. [19]. To Brig. Gen. John A. McClernand. "Refered to Brig. Gen. J. A. McClernand"—AES, McClernand Papers, IHi. Written on a letter of Dec. 19 from Capt. Wilbur F. Brinck to USG. "I would very respectfully inform you that soldiers upon being discharged from guard duty in the morning, go to the River edge to discharge their pieces and in many cases reload and discharge several times. Generally thier officers are not present. Such a waste of ammunition I consider very unnecessary and extravegant   I will add that a very large amount of ammunition especially caps is daily consumed. I am admonished by the chief of Ordnance that our expenditures of ammunition is to[o] great"—ALS, *ibid.*

1861, DEC. 20.   Maj. Mason Brayman to USG. "Genl. McClernand having received the enclosed several charges and Specifications against William M. Thompson, 2d Lieut. Co. "F." 18th Regt and Mordecai B. Kelly, 1st Lieut Co. "F" 18th Regt. which are transmitted for action of the court martial now in session, if you deem proper."— DfS, McClernand Papers, IHi. 2nd Lt. William H. Thompson of Mound City, Ill., was mustered out on April 8, 1862; 1st Lt. Mordecai B. Kelly of Villa Ridge, Ill., was promoted to chaplain on Sept. 6, 1862.

1861, DEC. 22.   USG special orders. "The eight companies of the 7th Ill Cavalry now at Cairo, will as soon as practicable move to Birds Point and form a part of the 3d Brigade. The four companies 2d Cavalry at Birds Point will return to Cairo and form a part of the command of Brig Genl McClernands."—Copies, DLC-USG, V, 15, 16, 77, 82; DNA, RG 393, USG Special Orders.

1861, DEC. 22.   Col. John Cook, Fort Holt, to USG. "Am in possession of information of a large body of stock Hogs now near Blandville on the way to Columbus   Will start tomorrow with your consent I will Endeavor to capture them & would like one of the gunboats to approach near Enough to Columbus to prevent any force from that point surprising us"—Telegram received, DNA, RG 393, Dept. of the Mo., Telegrams Received.

1861, DEC. 24.   Col. Leonard F. Ross to USG. "Teams loaded with provisions are crossing the Ohio at Caledonia for Columbus   Reliable"—Telegram received, DNA, RG 393, Dept. of the Mo., Telegrams Received; copy, *ibid.*, Post of Cape Girardeau, Telegrams. On Dec. 24, Capt. Hugh Fullerton, Caledonia, Ill., telegraphed to USG. "No teams of any description either loaded or empty have crossed the Ohio at Caledonia since I have been here. It is ~~the~~ wholly a mistake & no trade allowed."—Telegram received (punctuation added), *ibid.*, Dept. of the Mo., Telegrams Received.

1861, DEC. 25.   USG General Orders No. 24. "In accordance with instructions received from Head Quarters of the Army. All blankets below the regulation weight, which have been issued to the troops, may on being condemned, be turned in to the Quarter Masters Department, and others of the regulation weight issued in their stead. Those returned, may be used for Hospital Department or for horse blankets."—Copies, DLC-USG, V, 12, 13, 14, 80; DNA, RG 393, USG General Orders; *ibid.*, RG 94, 9th Ill., Letterbook; *ibid.*, 48th Ill., Letterbook; (Printed) McClernand Papers, IHi. On Dec. 13, Brig. Gen. Lorenzo Thomas wrote to Brig. Gen. Montgomery C. Meigs. "In accordance with your reccommendation of the 3d inst endorsed on the letter of Brigade Surgeon A. V. Dougherty, the General-in-Chief desires that blankets below the regulation weight which may have been issued to the troops, may on being condemned be turned into the Quartermasters Department and used for hospital purposes or for horse blankets, and others issued in place of them"—Copy, DNA, RG 393, District of Cairo, Letters Received. On Dec. 19, Meigs wrote to Capt. Reuben B. Hatch. "The enclosed copy of a letter from the Adjutant General dated the 13th inst, in relation to Blankets below the regulation weight which may have been issued to the troops is respectfully submitted for your information   Large stock of Regulation Blankets, now in each Depot subject to requisitions"—Copy, *ibid.*

1861, Dec. 25.   Capt. John A. Rawlins special orders. "Capt. G. P. Foote 11th Ill Vols. Lieut Edward M. Wright of Houghtalings Battery, and Lieut W. A. Dickerman Quartermaster, 7th Ill Cavaly are hereby appointed a Board of Survey to examine and report the quality and condition of two Caisson Carriages and Gun Limbers, ten ~~boxes~~ round Tents issued, by the State of Illinois on or about the 16th day of May last, and five boxes of Overcoats, issued by Capt. R. B. Hatch Post Quarter Master on the 20th Inst., all to Light Battery "B" Capt Ezra Taylor Commanding. said Board will convene on the 26th inst. or as soon thereafter as practicable"—Copies, DLC-USG, V, 15, 16, 77, 82; DNA, RG 393, USG Special Orders. On Dec. 27, the three officers reported to USG. "The undersigned, Capt. G L Fort, Lieut. Ed Wright & Lieut. W A Dickerman appointed by special order No dated Dec 25, 1861, to examine and report upon the quality and condition of certain Public property named in said order. Would respectfully report that on the 27th day of Dec 1861, they personally examined said property and find. That the two (2) Caissons and two (2) gun limberes are old, dangerous, out of repair and unfit for service, and would reccommend that they be turned over to the ordinance officer at Cairo to be sent to the arsenal for repair or other disposition   That the ten (10) round tents, were orrigionally manufactured of light material and by use they are now full of holes, rotten and entirely unfit for the service, and recommend that they be condemned as utterly worthless. And that the five (5.) boxes of over coats eached marked and invoiced to contain thirty (30) great coats, making one hundred and fifty (150) in all upon inspection and actual count: three of said boxes contained thirty (30) each, and one Twenty nine (29.) and another Twenty six (26) making only one hundred and forty five (145) in all and would reccommend that Capt Taylor be allowed a credit of five (5) coats."—DS, *ibid.*, District of Cairo, Letters Received.

1861, Dec. 25.   Brig. Gen. Charles F. Smith to USG. "Muster & payrolls greatly needed."—Telegram received, DNA, RG 393, Dept. of the Mo., Telegrams Received.

1861, Dec. 25. Brig. Gen. Charles F. Smith to USG. "Respect forwarded for the information of the commander of the District of Cairo. The irregularities spoken have been ordered to be corrected."—AES, DNA, RG 393, District of Cairo, Letters Received. Written on a letter of Dec. 22 of Capt. John C. Cox, commissary of subsistence, Paducah, to Smith. "In obedience to your orders of the 20th instant I visited the Acting Asst Commissary of Subsistence at Smithland, for the purpose of general inspection, on the morning of the 21st instant and have now the honor to report as follows   I found Captn S R Wetmore A A C S on duty at his post and was by him furnished with every facility necessary to the object of my visit   By inventory of stock of supplies on hand furnished by the A A C S I find he has sufficient to subsist the force at his post for about *Nine days* with the complete ration, and a margin in portions of the ration ranging from one to fifteen days—By report from him I find the number of men to be subsisted at his post is fourteen hundred (1400) exclusive of sick in hospitals which are estimated at thirty (30) men. On this basis I would report a total to be subsisted of fourteen hundred and fifty (1450)   I found the supplies in good order with the exception of—Thirteen (13) Barrells of Pilot Bread, a lot of about One hundred (100) pounds of Ham and a lot of about four hundred (400) pounds of Bacon which were unfit for issue. The supplies are all under good storage and entirely protected from the weather being within a substantial warehouse with good fastenings   I am informed by Captn Wetmore that the monthly accounts of his post which are now due are ready to be forwarded to your Head Quarters and will be sent forthwith, I am also informed that the accounts for November are in a satisfactory state of preparation   I find that the A A C S has been in the habit of issuing supplies to the different companies at his post upon daily returns—this I consider objectionable and reccommended a change substituting five days as the term of issue instead of one. I also reccommended a change in respect to some slight irregularities which I presumed to arise only from inexperience. I directed that a Commissarys Book be kept and left a blank book at the post for that purpose"—ALS, *ibid*.

1861, Dec. 26. 1st Lt. Henry C. Freeman to USG. "In order to get my account adjusted with the Pay Master at St. Louis I need a certificate from you stating time that I was in the Service under your orders before reporting to Col Webster   I reported to you in St Louis by

Order of Gen Fremont, on the 29th August and about the 4th Sept reported to Col. Webster by your order   Will you have the kindness to furnish me with the requisite certificate"—ALS, DNA, RG 393, District of Cairo, Letters Received. See letter to Maj. Gen. John C. Frémont, Sept. 5, 1861.

1861, Dec. 27.   Capt. Franklin B. Moore, 2nd Ill. Cav., to USG. "Deserted from Camp Holt, this day Joshua McCurdy of Comp. D 2nd Illinois Cavalry.—Please permit Serg. James to pursue said deserter." —DS, McClernand Papers, IHi. Endorsed by Capt. John A. Rawlins. "Approved for not exceeding 4 days"—AES, *ibid.*

1861, Dec. 28.   To Maj. Gen. Henry W. Halleck. "Approved and respectfully forwarded to Head Quarters Dept. of the Mo."—AES, McClernand Papers, IHi. Written on a letter of Dec. 23 from 1st Lt. William S. Bosbyshell, 30th Ill., to Capt. John C. Kelton. "Permit me to solicit the favor of an application for a leave of absence for thirty days to enable me to go to Philadelphia Penna. and attend to important private interests there which demand my immediate and personal attention—My Agent in Philada. writes me that since my absence from there some of my tenants have become refractory refusing to pay their rents until my return; and the foreclosing of a Mortgage, I hold against property there, to be decided at this Decr. Term of the Court, makes my presence necessary, not only to collect my just dues, but in some cases to expel dishonorable persons from my property, the expediency of doing which cannot be entrusted to an Agent—It is also the wish of my family to make a change in the location of their residence and they naturally require my advice and assistance upon the subject" —LS, *ibid.* On Dec. 31, the request was disapproved at hd. qrs., Dept. of the Mo.

1861, Dec. 28.   Capt. Richard McAllister to USG. "Having been ordered by Major General Halleck to relieve Captain W. W Leland, Com. Subs at this post, upon inquiry and investigation as to the management of the Com. Dept. here, I have elicited the following facts: That the issues to the forces in this district, although based, as it is said, upon written special instructions from the Com. Subs. at Cincinnati, has been altogether irregular and in direct violation of the regulations established for the subsistence department; viz: Issues have been made in bulk upon requisition only by the various regimental Quarter-Masters of the different forces drawing supplies from this depot; the requisitions only setting forth the amount of provisions wanted in bulk, without stating the number of men or the period of time for which rations are required. These requisitions in most cases were not only not countersigned by the Colonel, but also not even approved by the post or Brigade Commander.—The Regulations as well as Genl. Order No. 27. from Head-Qrs, Dept. of the Missouri, definitely state, how issues must be made. It furthermore appears, that the storage-room for the stores now at this depot is entirely too limited to admit of taking the care necessary for the preservation of the same. The place designated for the immense and valuable stores consigned to this point is a chartered Steamboat, the 'New Uncle Sam,' in the hold of which the provisions are stowed away in such manner, as to exclude that free ventilation of air so necessary for their proper preservation; the deck of the boat is moreover so crowded and the passage so obstructed that it greatly impedes the facility of issue which on account of the frequent and numerous demands should necessarily be accomplished as expeditious as possible.—As my instructions are strictly to comply in all respects with the regulations established for the Subs. Dept., and with a view of accomplishing this purpose, I would most respectfully make to the General Commanding this district the following suggestions; viz: 1st., The immediate appointment of Asst. Commissaries Subs. for the adjoining posts respectively of Fort Holt and Birds Point; duly authorized to receive subsistence stores from this depot, and issue the same on consolidated provision returns. 2nd., A similar appointment of a Commissary for the gunboats and transports in Government service, inasmuch as the navy ration differs from that of the army, requiring a separate and different kind of abstract: —provided the necessary arrangements have not already been made to accomplish this object.—3rd., That an order be issued by the Commanding General of this district, requiring that from and after the first of January 1862, the mode of issueing shall accord with the regulations and General Orders No. 27th from Head Quarters of this Dept., and prescribing the mode of making out the consolidated return. 4th., That the Commissaries of regiments be required to present their consolidated return to the Commissary of their respective post the day before the issue in order to give time for due examination and consolidation. 5th., That the facilities of storage now furnished this department are

not only insufficient, as regards capacity to receive the large amount
of stores which must be collected at this point, but unsuited in kind to
the service required; and that the interest of the service requires that
the wharfboat formerly used by the department be brought into service
again as early as possible."—LS, DNA, RG 393, District of Cairo,
Letters Received.

On the same day, Capt. John A. Rawlins issued special orders directing McAllister to relieve Capt. William W. Leland as post com-
missary at Cairo.—Copies, DLC-USG, V, 15, 16, 82; DNA, RG 393,
USG Special Orders. On Jan. 1, 1862, USG issued General Orders
No. 1. "I . . . Lieut William Brown, Jr., 7th Illinois Volunteers is here-
by appointed Acting Assistant Commissary of Subsistence at Fort Holt,
Ky., Capt. Richard E. Davis, Asst. Commissary of Subsistence, is
assigned to duty at Bird's Point, Mo., and Capt. W. W. Leland, Asst.
Commissary of Subsistence, at Cairo, Ills. II . . . Capt. W. W. Leland,
Asst. Commissary of Subsistence, at Cairo, will issue to river trans-
ports. H. H. C[*andee*] will act as A. A. C. S. for the Gunboat Flotilla."
—Copies, DLC-USG, V, 12, 13, 14; DNA, RG 94, 9th Ill., Order
Book; *ibid.*, 48th Ill., Order Book; *ibid.*, RG 393, USG General
Orders. The remainder of these orders implemented the third and
fourth of McAllister's recommendations.

1861, Dec. 30. Lt. S. Ledyard Phelps, Paducah, to Flag Officer
Andrew H. Foote. "I have the honor to report to you that I returned
last evening from a cruise up the Ohio River, to as far as Cannelton
Inda, stopping at various points, both going up and returning. There
is entirely too much smuggling done between this point and Evansville, and as usual chiefly by Jews. Steamers still stop at all points along
the Kentucky shore, and the mail is delivered there also. I think both
these practices should be discontinued. Steamers should only be permitted to land at fixed points along the North bank of the Ohio, where
the Government has agents or a Military force. Permitting the mails
to be delivered in the towns on the Kentucky shore, between Smithland and Henderson, is affording a constant means of communication
and information to the rebel force at Bowling Green. The rebels
threaten to burn the Steamers along the Ohio if the mails [*are*] stopped.
The advantage to them of these Steamers is so great that they do not
make prizes of them as could be done at any time. Care on the part of
Steamboat Captains, and visits along the river of Gun Boats from time

to time would prevent the rebels from executing their threats of burning. Goods are brought down by wagons from the Central Rail Roads
of both Indiana and Illinois, and carried across the Ohio thence to rebel
camps. General Grant has a force of one Cavalry Regiment and one of
infantry stationed at Shawneetown, which could do much, not only to
stop smuggling, but also, to put an end to the collection and driving
off by the rebels of hogs and other stock from that part of Kentucky
opposite—one of the greatest hog producing Counties in the State. If
active the Shawneetown force could break up all the rebel marauding
parties thence to the Cumberland. It is the opinion of Union people
along the Kentucky side of the Ohio, that they are protected from
violence at the hands of their secession neighbors, and of marauding
troops, only through fear of the Gun Boats. I was informed that the
population of Caseyville was disposed to be violent towards the few
Union men there, and I warned the authorities of the consequence of
any actual violence or molestation the loyal people should suffer at the
hands of any rebels whether citizens of the place or not."—Copy,
DNA, RG 393, District of Cairo, Letters Received. *O.R.* (Navy), I,
xxii, 479–80. On Jan. 1, 1862, Foote wrote to Maj. Gen. Henry W.
Halleck. "I send herewith a copy of a letter received from Lt. Comdg.
Phelps of the Gun Boat 'Conestoga.' I have given a copy of the letter
to Genl Grant also. I propose sending, to morrow, or the next day, the
Gun Boat 'Lexington' in command of Lt Shirk to join the 'Conestoga'
—placing both vessels under the direction of Lt Comdg Phelps—the
Senior Officer, who is rendering good service in that quarter."—ALS,
DNA, RG 393, Dept. of the Mo., Letters Received.

1861, DEC. 31.   Maj. Montague S. Hasie, Bissell's Mo. Engineers,
to USG. "Reports Capt. J. H. Vreeland and Lieut E. L. Jones, Co. A.
as incompetent."—DLC-USG, V, 10; DNA, RG 393, USG Register
of Letters Received. Capt. Jacob H. Vreeland was cashiered on March
11, 1862; 1st Lt. Edwin L. Jones resigned on March 1, 1862.

[1862, JAN.?].   Hd. qrs. of Maj. Gen. Henry W. Halleck to USG.
"Approved and will be paid accordingly"—Copy, DNA, RG 393,
Western Dept., Endorsements. Written on a letter of H. V. Brink,
Dec. 30, 1861, relating to the pay of a private of Capt. James T. Buel's
battery, previously approved by USG.

1862, JAN. 1. To Brig. Gen. John A. McClernand. "Genl. Grant, asks for a Company of Cavalry to be detailed, to proceed to Brook's' point on the mississippi river and arrest certain persons who are represented as carrying on an illicit trade. To report to Genl. Grant for instructions."—Register of Letters Received, McClernand Papers, IHi. In response, McClernand issued Special Orders No. 16. "Ordered that First Lieutenant and 30 men of Co. "B" cavalry attached to 29th Regt Ills Vols to leave here at 10 O clock, Friday next at 10 Oclock the Lieut to report to Genl. Grant, for instructions."—*Ibid.* On Jan. 7, Capt. Eagleton Carmichael, commanding a cav. co. originally attached to the 29th Ill. but later independent, wrote to USG. "On Friday the 3rd Inst I proceeded to Brookes Point as you directed me and went into Camp On Saturday 4th Inst I examined the Illinois shore for boats and found one. I took posession of it and took a few men with me and went over to the Missouri shore and searched for crafts but found none on that day, on Sunday the 5th ult I again went to the Missouri shore for the purpose of examining more closely and succeeded in finding Two small boats of sufficient size to cross about Eight men in each at one time, and also one flat which had been used for a wood boat. all of these boats I destroyed Those boats did not seem to have any particular owners except one, which was in the possession of a German who lives on Buffalo Island. he seemed to be an innocent man. The one I found on the Illinois shore had been used by a Mr Blackburn who does not bear a very good character, but I could not get sufficient evidence against him to warant his arrest. I gave him to understand what he could expect should he give any cause for reports against him. We were very kindly treated by the people of that neighborhood Returned to Cairo the 7th Ult"—ALS, DNA, RG 393, District of Cairo, Letters Received.

1862, JAN. 1. Col. Leonard F. Ross to USG. "Major Raywalt, arrived here yesterday with a detachment of 7th Ills Cavalry. Contrary to my expectations—the Companies are unarmed, except with Sabres —and are 'Dutch.' For the service in this part of the Country—they do not make good troops—Send me if you please two or three additional Companies, *Americans*—and armed—"—Copy, DNA, RG 393, Post of Cape Girardeau, Letters Sent. On Jan. 3, Ross wrote to USG. "I am exceedingly well pleased with Major Rawalt—Commander of the two Companies of Cavalry sent to this Post—If you will now have the other two Companies belonging to his Command (who are Americans)—sent to this place, we will try and get along—but we should like to have Capt Stewart in addition—"—Copy, *ibid.*

1862, JAN. 2. Brig. Gen. M. Jeff Thompson to USG. "I send with this letter Private Ambrose Wallis, of Co. K, 20th Illinois Volunteers, who was captured by my Pickets some ten days ago. I have sworn him not to fight or serve against the Southern Confederacy, until regularly exchanged. I send by him a few letters, which I hope are not contraband, and which if not, you will please have mailed to their destination. I have several other prisoners, and am anxiously awaiting a decision on the proposition I made Genl. Halleck, for a general exchange. I would like to commence 1862, with a new account and see how we will stand next New Years Day."—Copy, DNA, RG 109, Mo. State Guard, 1st Div., Letters Sent. *O.R.*, II, i, 532.

1862, JAN. 2. Henry Planert and twenty-one others to USG. "The undersigned loyal citizens of Commerce Scott County Missouri beg leave to present to you the condition and state of affairs of this county and especially of this town, and beg your generous consideration of the same. We are here totally unprotected, and entirely at the whim and mercy of Jeff. Thompson and his lawless associates. A great number of our Citizens are in a situation that if left unmolested would have aneough to live on during the winter, but have no means, and would be left totally destitute of everything, if forced to leave their homes, and then they would be thrown on the generosity of the citizens of Ills. who have done so much toward the glorious cause of our Union, and we think it presumtous to tax their generosity any further. There is one fact to which we beg leave to call your attention: we are forever harrassed by the presence of Rebels, pretending to be union men, but whose Character is well known to us, though these men have been insulted by us in every posible manner, yet they continue to come and supply Jeff. Thompson with such information as he wants with regard to this town, and we have no means whatever to rid us of their most ~~dett~~ detestable presence. We would therefore pray if consistant with your Command to send some troops to this town, the importance of its posession you are better informed of, than we can be; We have vacant houses aneough here to quarter one Regiment   For further reference we would pray you to take under your Just & kind consideration the statement of our townsman and fellow citizen Mr. John R. Dooms and if convenient that of Mr. James H. Kane in the U. S. Service under Genl. Payne who was here at the time Jeff. Thompson entered our town on Sunday 29th December 1861. Robbed the Stores, and fired at the Steamer City of Alton. With a firm reliance in the justness of our Cause, and a high regard for your Magnanimity we remain"—LS, DNA, RG 393, District of Cairo, Letters Received.

1862, JAN. 3. Brig. Gen. Charles F. Smith to [USG]. "Recd. last night. The information may be of importance. I have sent the same to Cairo"—AES, DNA, RG 393, District of Cairo, Letters Received. Written on an anonymous letter to Smith from Paducah, Jan. 2. "One of our men from Columbus came in to-day. Have just returned from seeing him, and from his statements gather the following information. There are now at Columbus but two gunboats one is the old E. Howard, mounting four rifle sixty four (64) pounder guns, one astern, three at the bow, the boat is called the Genl Polk. The boat is well known here having been formerly a Paducah and N. O Packet and well worn out. The other boat is a lake-boat from N. O. mounts three guns rifled sixty four (64) pounders two at the bow one at the stern. The floating battery mounts seventeen (17) guns, eight (8) of which are rifled sixty four (64) pounder guns and nine (9) thirty two (32) pounder guns also rifled. The battery is constructed so as to fill with water, to within one foot, has no bulwarks for men to stand behind but is one plain surface on top. Obstructions of different kinds have been placed in the river. The anchors that were spoken of last are being used for that purpose, to assist in mooring them. Torpedoes are placed among them also. While our man was there ~~small~~ several flat boats were sent down, one of which was blown up He says they seem to rely very greatly on the torpedoes. On the river side of Columbus there are fifty two guns of which number twenty (20) are on top of the bluff and thirty two (32) under the bluff. But three guns on top are one hundred (120) and twenty pounder rifled guns, the ballance seventeen (17) are rifled sixty four (64) pounders. Under the bluff twenty (20) are sixty four (64) pounder guns balance thirty two (32). On the end of the fortifications towards river there are four (4) thirty two (32) pounder guns and on the rear of the fortifications (the line comd'g the road into Columbus) there are twenty guns four (4) of which are howitzers and the balance thirty two (32) pounder guns. Directly in the rear of Columbus they are ~~entrenched~~ breastworks from the road to the R. Rd some three hundred (300) yards, and ten guns mounted six (6) thirty two (32) ~~two~~ four (4) twenty four (24) pounder guns. After crossing the R. Rd they have another line of breastworks running parallel with the R. Rd to the on which are mounted eight (8) thirty two (32) pounder guns. At the time he left Columbus the report was current and generally believed that Genl *Pillow* has resigned. From a rough diagram furnished me by our man I will make a correct plan of the fortifications &c, and will send it to you to-morrow or the day after. N. B. You will find late papers with this On Saturday last two regiments left for Bowling Green. On Teusday a detachment of Cavalry was sent out to intercept Genl *Wallace* and coöperate with King but failed to arrive in time"—AL, *ibid.*

1862, Jan. 3. Col. Leonard F. Ross to USG. "Is the rule, granting no discretion in the allowance of furlough's still in force ? I have several boys—in my Regiment whose situation would well warrant the granting of a furlough if I am allowed to do so—One particularly, Corporal Raultson—of Comp "H," 17th Regt—was shot through the hand by the accidental Discharge of a Pistol—while on duty at Commerce the other day—The Surgeon says he will not be fit for duty for fifteen days —Such cases I would very much like a little discretion in"—Copy, DNA, RG 393, Post of Cape Girardeau, Letters Sent.

1862, Jan. 3. Col. Leonard F. Ross to USG. "We have under charge of committing rape, a man by name of Collyer.—Private in 8th Mo Regt. We have a letter from the Adjutant of that Regt charging Collyer—to be a deserter and desiring him to be sent to Paducah for trial —Shall I have him tried here on Gen'l Charges against him—or send him to Paducah under guard"—Copy, DNA, RG 393, Post of Cape Girardeau, Letters Sent.

1862, Jan. 4. Brig. Gen. John A. McClernand to USG. "You will find herewith a copy of Capt Eddy's order, which I promised to send to you."—Copy, DNA, RG 393, District of Cairo, Letters Received. Enclosed were several orders defining the functions of military officials at Springfield, Ill.

1862, JAN. 4. Brig. Gen. John A. McClernand to USG "on the subject of professed fishermen, who convey news to the enemy in Kentucky."—Register of Letters Received, McClernand Papers, IHi.

1862, JAN. 4. Brig. Gen. Charles F. Smith to USG. "Your letter of the 3d. inst. by Mr. *Bradley* in relation to the Negro question is recd. As soon as I recd. G. O. No. 3 I gave orders to the outposts not to allow fugitive slaves to enter the camps. I do not doubt however that there are quite a number in town, who either sneak in or their entry is connived at by sentries. I have 10 or 12 fugitives in charge of the Provost Marshal who ran away from rebel masters in in Tennessee. Those I hold for the future. With regard to the slaves of loyal masters or slaves of those of seccession proclivities who are mere waiters upon providence I have never interposed any obstacle to their being recovered tho' I cannot consent to act as the slave catcher myself unless it is made my duty by law. Perhaps we do not differ about this matter."—ALS, DNA, RG 393, District of Cairo, Letters Received.

1862, JAN. 4. Col. Robert Kirkham, Camp Mather, Shawneetown, Ill., to USG. "At your request as soon as possible I sent Lieut Col W R Browne under the guidance of the County Clerk of Crittenden Co Berry S Young to Marion,—with Two Hundred and Fifty men.—Col Cavanaugh refusing to permit any of his force to accompany him. The expedition started on the Steamer Fanny Bullett from this place on the evening of the 30th Dec. last and returned the night of the 1st January A D 1862, after having fully accomplished everything the said Berry S. Young desired.—I feel gratified that I am authorized to report to you that I feel proud of the action of the officers and men of the entire command who, were sent on the expedition in accordance with your request, and I have only to say that should you need our services in future I will *gladly* perform with promptness and energy."—ALS, DNA, RG 393, District of Cairo, Letters Received.

1862, JAN. 6. USG endorsement. "Respectfully refered to Hd Qrs. Dept. of the Mo."—AES, DNA, RG 94, Letters Received. Written on a letter of Jan. 3 from 1st Lt. James Powell, 4th Cav., to Brig. Gen. Lewis Wallace discussing "the loss of clothing of men of Company "I" 4th U. S. Cavalry, on the abandonment of Fort Washita. . . ."—ALS, *ibid.*

1862, JAN. 6.   Col. John Cook to Capt. John A. Rawlins. "Will the Genl. accept an Escort of one Company from the 7th Regt to Paducah tomorrow on the Erie"—Telegram received, DNA, RG 393, Dept. of the Mo., Telegrams Received.

1862, JAN. 6.   Capt. Daniel H. Brush, 18th Ill., to USG. "I have the honor to report, that in obedience to your orders, I have caused to be arrested, and sent before Provost Marshal for examination, Private Thomas. McKee of Co "B." this Regt charged with throwing overboard a pick and sledge hammer reported to you by Major Webster, Chief Engrs. I also sent witnesses to prove the facts"—Copy, DNA, RG 94, 18th Ill., Letterbook.

1862, JAN. 7.   Capt. John A. Rawlins to Brig. Gen. Charles F. Smith. "Your communication of yesterday, in regard to the furnishing of Clothing to the troops, by their respective States, was received and forwarded to Head Quarters, of the Dept of the Mo. Brig. Gen. Grant. instructs me to say, that he coincides with you on this subject, and as soon as his attention was called to the fact, which was some few weeks since, of the State of Illinois, furnishing the troops here, with clothing, he notified the State Agent, that no more would be received from the State in future. An Order will be issued to-day on the subject. See enclosed notice from Asst Qr. Master, issued at Springfield Ills. relative to the same."—Copies, DLC-USG, V, 1, 2, 3, 85; DNA, RG 393, USG Letters Sent. On Jan. 23, Brig. Gen. Montgomery C. Meigs wrote to Secretary of War Edwin M. Stanton enclosing a letter from Smith "in relation to the lavish issue of clothing by State authorities." —LS, *ibid.*, RG 94, Letters Received. Smith's letter is no longer attached.

1862, JAN. 7.   Brig. Gen. Charles F. Smith to USG. "In regard to examination of officers etc."—DLC-USG, V, 10; DNA, RG 393, USG Register of Letters Received. On Jan. 7, Capt. John A. Rawlins wrote to Smith. "The board for examining into the qualifications of Officers will probably be in Paducah on Thursday. The Paymaster will be there about the same time, and will pay to the first of January."—Copies, DLC-USG, V, 1, 2, 3, 85; DNA, RG 393, USG Letters Sent.

1862, Jan. 7.   Lt. S. Ledyard Phelps to Flag Officer Andrew H. Foote. "Yesterday I ascended the Tennessee river to the State line, returning in the night. The water was barely sufficient to float this boat, drawing 5 ft. 4 in and in coming down we draged heavely in places. The Cumberland is also too low above Eddyville. The rebels are industriously perfecting their means of defense both at Dover and Fort Henry. At Fort Donnelson (near Dover) they have placed obstructions in the river, 1½ mile below their battery on the left bank and in the bend where the battery comes in sight. These obstructions consist of trees chained together and sunk across the river with the butts up stream, the heads floating near the surface, and are pointed. Placed as they are reported to be, any attempt to remove them must be made under a severe fire and where there is very little room for covering boats. The bend is a very sharpe one and the river not more than 150 Yds wide—The battery upon the right bank is upon a hill ½ mile back from the river and considerably below the Fort upon the left hand. It can be seen, I am told, but one mile. four weeks since they had 4—32s mounted on the hill, and had a large force of negroes at work—The fire of Gun Boats here would be at a bad angle. On these, narrow Streams, with their usually contracted channels, it would appear to me very necessary to have the assistances of mortars in reducing earth works strong and complete as those on the Tennesse and Cumberland have been made. The forts are placed especially on the Cumberland, where no very great range can be had, and they can only be attacked in one narrow and fixed line. Short can dismount their gunns (all en-barbett) nothing more. our shell must burst at the moment or they will pass harmless, while there is little room to regulate distance nicely. There is no advantage to be gained by moving in circles or otherwise   Some of the disadvantage of narrow streams would be partially removed by a high stage of water—Fort Henry. I have arrive and the work is formable—Fort Donnelson can only be seen from an easy range of its guns. There are a thousand rumors, but I cnclude that the batteries upon both sides, their situation, the character and location of the obstructions may be considered as known—It is now too late to move against the works on either river except with a well appointed and powerful naval force. Capturing Donnelson and passing up to Clarksville would alarm the army at Bowlen Green, and the capture of the fortifications there Clarksville so to leave the way open to Nashville would complete the demoralization—But at this time the there is no water in the river—Lt Col Shirk received you order yesterday morning   I hope it will be in your power to again send the Lexington here   Genl. Smith does not deem it prudent to leave this place without a Gun Boat on acct of the threatened attack by the rebels, near the Tennessee with Gun boats and land forces. I donot think these boats are ready. It would be well besides watching the Cumberland to make trips along the Ohio with time to loiter at such places as Caseyville Uniontown and other points to break up rebel routs of communications and if the Lexington can be spared this place need not be left without a boat"—ALS, DNA, RG 393, District of Cairo, Letters Received. *O.R.* (Navy), I, 485–86.

Index

All letters written by USG of which the text was available for use in this volume are indexed under the names of the recipients. The dates of these letters are included in the index as an indication of the existence of text. Abbreviations used in the index are explained on pp. xvii–xx. Individual regts. are indexed under the names of the states in which they originated.

at, 386; mentioned, 147*n*, 319–20, 402

Charleston and Savannah Railroad, 158

Charley Bowen (steamboat), 391

Chas. Galegher & Co. (Cairo), 361*n*

Chase, David F. (Ill. Vols.), 153*n*

Chase, Salmon P. (U.S. Secretary of the Treasury), 98*n*

Cheatham, Benjamin F. (C.S. Army), 132*n*

Cheat Mountain, W. Va., 233*n*

Chester, Ill., 41 and *n*, 42*n*, 44*n*, 56*n*

Chetlain, Augustus L. (Ill. Vols.), 347, 348*n*

Chicago, Ill.: and Cairo lumber fraud, 290*n*, 324, 325*n*–27*n*, 351 and *n*; site of Camp Douglas, 305*n*; 56th Ill in, 347*n*; mentioned, 53*n*, 391, 401, 402

Chicago Historical Society, Chicago, Ill.: documents in, 117–19, 220*n*–21*n*, 256*n*

Chicago Light Art. (Ill. Vols.), 196*n*. *See also* Taylor, Ezra

Chicago Tribune (newspaper): charges corruption in lumber contracts at Cairo, 289, 290*n*, 324, 325*n*–26*n*, 327*n*, 351, 351*n*–52*n*; documents printed in, 359–60, 360*n*–61*n*; and bread contract at Cairo, 360*n*–61*n*

Childs, William H. (prisoner), 335, 335*n*–36*n*

Churchill, Sylvester (U.S. Army), 366*n*

Cincinnati, Ohio: art. constructed at, 35*n*; USG wants to send muskets to, 69; recruitment at, 381; mentioned, 25*n*, 149*n*, 244*n*, 423

Cincinnati Gazette (newspaper), 138*n*

City of Alton (steamboat), 355*n*, 429

Clandfelter, Jacob (prisoner), 175*n*

Clark, Charles (C.S. Army), 253*n*

Clark, John L. (Mo. State Guard), 176*n*

Clark, Josiah W. (Ill. Vols.), 275*n*

Clarksville, Ky., 433

Clemson, James Y. (of Mound City, Ill.), 189*n*

Clinton, Ky., 185*n*, 304, 305*n*

Coal: Reuben B. Hatch ordered to supply *Conestoga* with, 8; delivered to Cairo by *Champion No. 2*, 9*n*; q. m. dept. indebted for, 95; for steamer to Shawneetown, 223*n*; contracts for, 322*n*, 389–90; purchase of vouchers for, 340 and *n*

Coal barges, 332–33, 375, 404, 405

Cochram, G. W. (contractor), 174*n*

Cole, Jacob (Ill. Vols.), 162*n*

Coler, William N. (Ill. Vols.), 88*n*

Collyer, Private (Mo. Vols.), 430

Colts Revolvers, 154*n*

Columbus, Ky.: C.S.A. reported moving from, 4; C.S.A. reinforces, 10, 11*n*, 192,

234, 235*n*; William J. Hardee expected at, 11; Gideon J. Pillow at, 11, 34*n*, 247*n*; strength of command at, 11*n*, 24, 25*n*, 63, 208, 375, 376*n*; C.S.A. rumored to have crossed river at, 14 and *n*, 18*n*; USG orders reconnaissance toward, 24; William J. Hardee reported at, 25*n*, 57; C.S.A. art. at, 27 and *n*, 194*n*, 278*n*, 429–30; wood seized near, 33; William T. Sherman asks USG to threaten, 42, 43*n*; casemate battery added to fortifications at, 47, 55; USG sends spies to, 54–55, 58; USG wishes he had sufficient force to take, 63–64, 75–76, 78; USG sends prisoners to, 66 and *n*, 70, 85, 85*n*–86*n*; William J. Hardee leaves, 72*n*; reported reduction of C.S.A. force at, 78; Henry Walke on reconnaissance toward, 100*n*; USG asks Charles F. Smith to threaten, 114; Charles F. Smith sends force to threaten, 114*n*–15*n*, 141, 145*n*, 148*n*; and battle of Belmont, 123, 128*n*, 129*n*, 136, 137, 141, 145*n*, 146*n*, 149*n*–51*n*; USG sends flag of truce boat to, 130, 132*n*, 134, 140*n*; army of Sterling Price reported reinforced from, 145*n*, 149*n*, 150*n*; prisoners at, 159, 162*n*, 211*n*, 219*n*, 239, 279, 323; John A. McClernand feels U.S. forces could attack, 206*n*; C.S.A. reported fearing attack on, 208; drawing of fortifications of, 211*n*, 353; strength of threatens Cairo, 214*n*–15*n*; C.S.A. gunboats at, 230, 234, 293–94, 304, 429; Leonidas Polk sends flag of truce boat from, 233; spies carry information to, 234, 235*n*; citizen to visit family at, 259; steamboats at, 261*n*; C.S.A. fortification of, 263; C.S.A. movement reported from, 280, 289; troops reportedly go south from, 293–94, 304; militia from Tenn., Miss., and La. reported coming into, 324; reported discontent at, 324; conditions at reported to USG, 353–54; C.S.A. mines Mississippi River near, 375, 377*n*; troops sent to Camp Beauregard from, 375, 381; scouting expedition toward, 404–5, 415; hogs on way to, 420; goods reported crossing Ohio River for, 420; mentioned, 154*n*, 193*n*, 196*n*, 230, 305*n*, 308, 404

Columbus, Ohio: prisoners at, 233*n*, 234*n*, 315–16, 316*n*, 323*n*

Commerce, Mo.: expedition to St. Francis River lands at, 105*n*, 108, 112*n*, 144*n*; and trade with enemy, 119*n*, 251*n*, 257*n*, 286; troops to go to from Cape Girardeau, 187, 188*n*; captured Negro to be returned to,